THE
AMERICAN EXPRESS
POCKET GUIDE TO
SPAIN

Herbert Bailey Livesey

PRENTICE HALL PRESS
NEW YORK

The Author

Herbert Bailey Livesey is the author of *The American Express Pocket Guide to New York*, and has homes in both New York and Spain. A novelist and travel writer, he contributes regularly to *Travel & Leisure* magazine — especially on the subject of Spain.

Contributors

Jan Read (Spanish wines)
Christine Barnard (Words and phrases)

Acknowledgments

The author and publishers would like to thank the following for their invaluable help and advice: Antonio Alonso, Lucinda Bartellot of the Spanish National Tourist Office in London, Doris Cassar, Christopher Catling, Pamela Fiori, Charles Ocheltree of the Spanish National Tourist Office in New York, Jan Read, Hal Robinson, Ila Stanger.

Few travel books are without errors, and no guidebook can ever be completely up to date, for telephone numbers and opening hours change without warning, and hotels and restaurants come under new management, which can affect standards. While every effort has been made to ensure that all information is accurate at the time of going to press, the publishers will be glad to receive any corrections and suggestions for improvements, which can be incorporated in the next edition, but cannot accept any consequences arising from the use of the book, or from the information contained herein. Price information in this book is accurate at the time of going to press, but prices and currency exchange rates do fluctuate. Dollar amounts relate to exchange rates in effect in mid-1988.

Series Editor   David Townsend Jones
Editor (first edition 1984)   Leonie Hamilton
Editor (this edition)   Elizabeth Newman
Art Editor   Eric Drewery
Designer (this edition)   Christopher Howson
Illustrators   Jeremy Ford (David Lewis Artists), Illustrated Arts, Rodney Paull
Map Editor   David Haslam
Jacket illustration   Pierre Marie Valat
Indexer   Hilary Bird
Production   Stewart Bowling

Edited and designed by
Mitchell Beazley International Limited,
Artists House, 14-15 Manette Street,
London W1V 5LB

© American Express Publishing
Corporation Inc. 1984
New revised edition © American
Express Publishing Corporation
Inc. 1988
Published by Prentice Hall Trade Division
A Division of Simon & Schuster, Inc.
One Gulf & Western Plaza
New York, New York 10023
PRENTICE HALL is a
trademark of Simon & Schuster Inc.

Maps in 4-color by Clyde Surveys Ltd,
Maidenhead, England.
Typeset by Bookworm Typesetting,
Manchester, England.
Printed in Shekou, China by Mandarin Offset

Library of Congress Cataloging-in-Publication Data
Livesey, Herbert B.
      The American Express pocket
guide to Spain.
      Includes index.
      1. Spain—Description and travel—
1981-   —Guide-books.
      I. American Express Company.
      II. Title.
DP14.L58   1988   914.6'0483   88-9918
ISBN 0-13-025131-3

Contents

How to use this book

The *American Express Pocket Guide to Spain* is an encyclopedia of travel information, organized in the sections listed on the previous page. There is also a comprehensive index and gazetteer (pages 225-240), and there are full-color maps at the end of the book.

For easy reference, the Spain *A-Z* and other sections are, as far as possible, arranged alphabetically. For the organization of the book as a whole, see *Contents*. For places that do not have separate entries in the *A-Z* see the *Index*.

Abbreviations

As far as possible only standard abbreviations have been used. These include days of the week, months, points of the compass, Saint (St), C for century, rms for rooms, and measurements.

In addresses, the prefix *Avenida* is abbreviated to *Av.*; the prefix *Calle* (street) is usually omitted and the street known simply by its name. Addresses without numbers often have the abbreviated suffix *s/n* (*sin numero*).

Floors

To conform with European usage, "first floor" is used throughout the book to refer to the floor above the ground floor, "second floor" to the floor above that, and so on.

Cross-references

Whenever a place or section title is printed in *sans serif italics* (for example, *Basic information* or *Sevilla*) in the text, this indicates that you can turn to the appropriate heading in the book for further information. Cross-references in this typeface refer either to sections in the book — *Basic information* or *Planning*, for example — or to individual entries in the *A-Z* section, such as *Sevilla*.

For easy reference, use the running heads printed at the top corner of the page (see, for example, *Basic information* on pages

---

How entries are organized

Marbella

Map 6I4. Málaga. 59km (37miles) sw of Málaga; 79km (50 miles) NE of Algeciras. Population: 72,000 **i** *Av. Miguel Canol* ☎ *(952) 771 442.*

The most fashionable resort of the *Costa del Sol* and the destination of sophisticated travelers, Marbella has some of Spain's best hotels and most stylish stores and discos, restaurants of distinction, luxurious villas, and extensive golf and tennis facilities. Only the old *barrio*, N of the main road, and the Moorish castle above it are of historic interest. Bullfights are held throughout the year.

Puerto Banús, 8km (5 miles) w of the center, has an astonishing collection of yachts, rows of Rolls-Royces and Lamborghinis to shuttle their passengers to and from the nearby casino, and shoulder-to-shoulder bars and bistros. At least 30 charter cruisers take anglers out to fish for shark; the nearby Sierra Blanca provides quail and partridge shooting; there are eight challenging golf courses within easy reach and 28km (17 miles) of nearly uninterrupted beach.

10-18, or *Sevilla* on pages 165-71).

Bold type is used in the text primarily for emphasis, to draw attention to something of special interest or importance. It is also used to pick out places — shops or museums, for example — that do not have separate descriptions of their own.

Map references

Each of the color maps at the end of the book is divided into a grid of squares, identified vertically by letters (A, B, C, D, etc.) and horizontally by numbers (1, 2, 3, 4, etc.). A map reference identifies the page and square in which the town or place of interest can be found — thus *Alarcón* is located in the square identified as Map 8F7.

Price categories

Price categories for hotels and restaurants are denoted by the symbols ☐ ☐ ☐ ☐ and ☐ which signify cheap, inexpensive, moderately priced, expensive and very expensive, respectively. These correspond approximately with the following actual prices, which give a guideline at the time of printing. Although actual prices will inevitably increase, in most cases the relative price category — for example, expensive or cheap — is likely to remain more or less the same.

Price categories	Corresponding to approximate prices	
	for **hotels**	for **restaurants**
	double room with bath	*meal for one*
	(a single room is	*with service,*
	not significantly	*tax and*
	cheaper)	*house wine*
☐ cheap	under $18	under $7
☐ inexpensive	$18-32	$7-13
☐ moderate	$32-41	$13-27
☐ expensive	$41-63	$27-36
☐ very expensive	over $63	over $36

___Bold blue type for entry headings.

___Blue italics for address, practical information and symbols. For list of symbols see page 6 or back flap of jacket.

Black text for description.
San serif italics used for cross-references to other entries or sections.
Bold type used for emphasis.

Entries for hotels, restaurants, etc. follow the same organization, and are sometimes printed across a half column. In hotels, symbols indicating special facilities appear at the end of the entry, in black.

Parador Nacional del Golf
Apartado 324 de Málaga ☎ *(952)*
381 255 ☐ *40 rms* ☐ *40* ☐ ☐
☐ AE ☐ ☐ VISA
Location: 7km (4¹/₂ miles) E of the town, on the Málaga road. As a rule, *paradores* don't have many recreational facilities, apart from the odd swimming pool. This one is an exception, with a vast circular pool on the way to the beach, tennis courts a step from the entrance, and the first green of an 18-hole golf course not far beyond.
☐ ☐ ☐ ☐ ☐ ☐ ☐ ☐ ☐ ☐

Key to symbols

☎	Telephone	▣	Secure garage
⊙	Telex	⊟	Meal obligatory
★	Recommended sight	⌂	Quiet hotel
☆	Worth a detour	⬍	Elevator
i	Tourist information	⬆	Facilities for disabled people
⊷	Parking		
⏛	Building of architectural interest	☐	TV in each room
		☎	Telephone in each room
†	Church or cathedral	⬚	Dogs not allowed
⊡	Free entrance	⬦	Garden
⬛	Entrance fee payable	⪦	Outstanding views
▬	Entrance expensive	⇌	Swimming pool
⌘	Photography forbidden	⪥	Good beach nearby
⫏	Guided tour available	⊘	Tennis court(s)
▬	Cafeteria	✓	Golf
⚹	Special interest for children	⪤	Riding
		⊶	Fishing
⚘	Hotel	⚐	Conference facilities
▬	Simple (hotel)	⊟	Restaurant
⚏	Luxury (hotel)	⊖	Simple (restaurant)
❁	Good value (in its class)	⌂	Luxury (restaurant)
☐	Cheap	▭	A la carte available
▯	Inexpensive	▬	Set (fixed price) menu available
▮	Moderately priced		
▮	Expensive	⊜	Good for wines
▮	Very expensive	⬟	Open-air dining available
▭	Rooms with private bathroom		
		⚑	Bar
▤	Air conditioning	⊙	Disco dancing
⇌	Residential terms available	❀	Casino/gambling
		♫	Live music
AE	American Express		
CB	Carte Blanche		
⊙	Diners Club		
⊜	MasterCard/Eurocard		
VISA	Visa		

An introduction to Spain

"Now you have two homes" — so goes a Spanish farewell to new friends. But in truth, it is a country we know before we first set foot in it. There is a frisson of recognition at every turning, a snippet from a mental scrapbook composed of half-remembered films, travel posters and meals in Spanish restaurants. The images are sharp. White villages spill down tawny hillsides like heaps of sugar cubes. Whiffs of saffron and burning olive wood rise from tiled foyers and iron-grilled windows. Bent crones in eternal mourning lean from doorways and guitars strum in the night shadows.

Beyond familiarity, visitors who break away from the iron circle of hall porters, waiters and tour guides may discover an empathy with the land and the people almost as strong as they have with their own country. Even on a superficial level, there is much more to Spain than can easily be absorbed. There is the Alhambra of Granada, a magical compound of Moorish palaces and gardens that is of equal stature to the Parthenon. But there is also the Arab mosque at Córdoba, a vast forest of columns and arches with a wildly Baroque cathedral dropped in the middle. The Romans left a city in Mérida, an aqueduct in Segovia and a fortress in Tarragona which equal anything outside Italy. King Philip II left his gloomy Xanadu at El Escorial; the dictator Franco, his monument of humbling proportions in the Valley of the Fallen, dedicated to those killed in the Civil War.

From pagan temples compiled of 30-ton rocks, to Roman bridges still in use, to palaces encrusted with gold plundered from the Americas, to the Surrealism in stone of the visionary Antonio Gaudí, Spain is architecturally unsurpassed. Picasso and Miró have their own museums in Barcelona, in buildings almost as attractive as the works they house. Their late 20thC successors are seen to best advantage in the exciting Museo de Arte Abstracto within the hanging houses of Cuenca. And, of course, the Prado in Madrid is a repository for the greatest of pre-20thC Spanish painters.

Most Spaniards regard their cultural heritage with nonchalance, saving their enthusiasm for the numerous local, and often folkloric, music festivals, fairs and fiestas that mark saints' days in every village, town and city. Popular traditions are, perhaps, maintained more strongly in Spain than anywhere else in Europe.

In Barcelona's Plaça de Catalunya you may see children being taught to dance the Catalan *sardanas*; or turn a corner in its Gothic Quarter to find an orchestra and choral group performing Handel against the backdrop of a Roman wall. Go to Santander for the swimming and gambling and chance upon recitals held in churches and public squares on summer nights. Pause in a village in Aragón for a cool drink and encounter the strange Lenten ritual in which every male beats a drum continuously for 24hrs. Elsewhere, livestock auctions give an excuse for running bulls through the streets.

Orientation

Spain's population of more than 40 million is spread over 504,780sq.km (19,880sq. miles) of mountains, plains, both wild and sandy coastlines, and islands that include the Balearics and Canaries. All but two of Spain's 50 provinces bear the same names as their largest cities, and they are gathered into 15 administrative regions, which roughly correspond to the ancient kingdoms of the Moors and early Catholic kings. The capital and largest city is Madrid, at the approximate geographical center, surrounded by a vast arid plateau. Next in size are the industrial seaports of Barcelona in the NE and Valencia halfway down the E coast.

Castilian Spanish is the official language, with its characteristic lisp. Linguists also recognize as distinct tongues (and locals use) the Catalan of the NE and the Basque of the N: the former sounds like a blend of Spanish and French with strong Latin roots; the latter defies classification. Complex dialects persist, as with the Spanish-Portuguese mix spoken in NW Galicia and the Catalan dialects of Mallorca and Valencia. In resort areas, French and German are more often understood than English.

A brief history

Cave paintings and monolithic structures attest to the presence of Paleolithic people as early as 14,000BC. These early inhabitants were replaced by the immigrant Iberians, who were in turn superseded by Celts from Central Europe. The Phoenicians founded trading posts on the perimeters of the peninsula, the largest on the site of the present-day town of Cádiz, W of the Gibraltar Strait. The Greeks and Carthaginians followed, establishing colonies along the Mediterranean coast and on the Balearic Islands.

By the 3rdCBC the Carthaginians controlled much of Iberia, a hegemony soon challenged by the Roman Empire. By 201BC the Romans were in control of the E and S coasts, with beachheads along the Atlantic coast. They took another century to impose suzerainty over all but the Basque region. Thereafter, the natives enthusiastically embraced the laws and customs of their conquerors and were rewarded with citizenship and integration into the Empire.

Vandals and Suevi swept across the Pyrenees in the early 5thCAD, swiftly displacing the weakened Roman rulers. In less than a decade, they in turn were routed by the Visigoths. Although the latter eventually lost their territories in Gaul and were periodically beset by attacks from the Byzantines and Franks, they remained in control of most of the peninsula until the Arab invasion of AD711. A legacy of fervent Catholicism remained to stiffen the Spanish resistance to the alien Muslims, the Moors. As before, the new invaders conquered all but the stubborn Asturians and Basques. Over the next seven centuries, the gradual Christian Reconquest moved S, aided as often by marriage between monarchs of rival kingdoms and local quarrels among competing Moorish dynasties as by armed conflict.

By 1212, only the emirate of Granada and lesser scattered holdings remained in Moorish hands, but stalemate continued until 1492 when Isabella of Castile and Ferdinand of Aragón captured Granada, and expelled the Moors from their last stronghold. To this day prayers are offered in Middle Eastern mosques for the return to Islam of its erstwhile Iberian territories. America was discovered the same year, and thereafter the plundered wealth of the American Indian empires fueled the Golden Age when Spain became one of the greatest powers the world has known.

Charles I succeeded Ferdinand. On the death of his maternal grandfather he also became Holy Roman Emperor, thereby expanding Spain's European territories enormously. But constant warfare dogged his reign and that of his son Philip II, resulting in the secession of many of these territories, the depletion of the national treasury, and the start of progressive decline under Philip

III and IV. When Charles II died in 1700, with no natural heir, he left the throne to the Bourbon Philip of Anjou and, as a result, plunged much of Europe into the War of the Spanish Succession.

By the early 19thC, most of the American colonies had been lost. In Spain, Napoleon's brother, Joseph Bonaparte, was installed on the throne, but his brief reign ended when the French were defeated by the British. The country then collapsed into anarchistic bickering, revolts and successive civil wars. An experiment with democracy in 1873 lasted a year, but the seed was sown and support began to grow for various radical ideologies. The Spanish-American War resulted in the loss of all overseas colonies except Morocco. In Spain itself uprisings on behalf of separatism and trade unionism were brutally suppressed by the army. Neutrality in World War I sealed Spain's isolation from European affairs. The 7yr dictatorship of Primo de Rivera ended with his self-imposed exile in 1930, when the Second Republic was formed. Its policies fluctuated from left to right and back in reaction to challenges from both extremes.

A massive military revolt was launched from Morocco in 1936, causing the tragic Civil War that resulted in over half a million deaths among civilians and soldiers alike. General Franco took command of the rebel forces early on, espousing a form of fascism under the rubric of the Falangist party.

With Franco's victory in 1939, a rightist regime was installed that lasted until his death in 1975. Gradual liberalization in his later years laid the groundwork for the constitutional monarchy that followed. His designated successor, King Juan Carlos, has proved a deft statesman, and his authority has had a moderating influence on the Spanish tendency toward political extremes. Living standards are at their highest ever, the contentious Basques and Catalans now enjoy a measure of autonomy, press censorship hardly exists, all ideologies are tolerated, the stranglehold of the conservative clergy on issues of public morality has been loosened and support for terrorists has shrunk markedly. Nevertheless the ascendancy of the left in national politics may provoke considerable change in the years to come.

The people

First impressions are likely to be of the innate Spanish reserve, too often interpreted as hauteur but usually masking an underlying warmth. Persistent friendly inquiry about the history of a region or its typical cuisine cuts through a sometimes dour demeanor, and you may quickly find yourself sharing a glass of wine and discussing family photographs.

Over 97 percent of Spanish people are Catholic, although women are more diligent in observance than their menfolk. From the perspective of most foreigners, Spain is a homogeneous nation. Apart from regional distinctions apparent primarily to natives, ethnic and racial differences are minute, and the only visible minorities are Gypsies and a growing number of immigrants from sub-Saharan Africa. Spaniards can be a contentious lot, each man and woman holding strong convictions on family life and politics. Conversation is a primary diversion, so much so that it has been given the formal label of *tertulia*. It is only slight hyperbole to suggest that asking any five Spaniards a question is to ensure the receipt of six opinions. But while pridefulness and unshakeable convictions of utter rectitude are among a Spaniard's least endearing qualities, they are balanced by a nearly universal generosity of spirit. That hospitable facet of the Spanish character is one of the features that makes a visit to Spain so worthwhile.

Before you go

Documents required

North Americans, British subjects and citizens of Western European nations need only their passports for stays of up to three months. For longer visits and for residents of other countries, a visa is required and should be applied for well in advance from the Spanish Consulate. Visitors may be asked for evidence that they have the means to return home or that they can support themselves without working while in Spain. Be certain that your passport is valid beyond the end of your planned visit. No vaccinations are required for entry.

An international driver's license, vehicle registration certificate (logbook), national identity sticker and international insurance certificate (green card) are required when entering with a private car.

Travel and medical insurance

Medical care is at least satisfactory and often excellent, especially in private clinics, but it is expensive and medical insurance is strongly recommended. This can be obtained through local tourist offices in Spain or through your own insurance company or travel agent. Policies are also available to protect you against cost incurred by cancellation of your trip.

Money

The peseta (pta) is the basic unit, which is divided into 100 centimos. There are 1, 5, 25, 50, 100, 200 and 500pta coins, and banknotes for 100, 200, 500, 1,000 and 5,000ptas. Any amount of foreign currency can be imported or exported, but only up to 100,000ptas can be brought in, and up to 20,000 taken out of the country.

Travelers cheques issued by American Express, Thomas Cook, Barclays and Citibank are widely recognized. Make sure you read the instructions included with your travelers cheques. It is important also to note separately the serial numbers of your travelers cheques and the telephone number to call in case of loss. Specialty travelers cheque companies such as American Express provide extensive local refund facilities through their own offices or agents.

Readily accepted charge and credit cards are American Express, Diners Club, MasterCard (Eurocard) and Visa. Carte Blanche is less common and tends to be accepted in major cities only.

Customs

All personal effects that you intend to take with you when you leave are duty-free, except tobacco goods, alcoholic drinks and perfume; current duty-free allowances for these goods are listed below. It is advisable to carry dated receipts for more valuable items, or you may be charged duty.

Tobacco   200 cigarettes *or* 100 cigarillos *or* 50 cigars *or* 250g tobacco.

Alcoholic drinks   1 liter spirits (over 22 percent alcohol by volume) *or* 2 liters alcoholic drinks of 22 percent alcohol or less; *plus* 2 liters still wines.

Perfume   50g/60cc/2fl oz.

Other goods   No restrictions.

Note that the penalties for the possession of illegal drugs can be severe. For a more detailed list of restricted goods contact the Spanish Consulate.

Getting there

By air   The majority of flights from outside Western Europe arrive at Barajas airport, even if Madrid is not the intended destination. From the UK and parts of the Continent there are direct flights to a number of other cities, most notably Barcelona, Málaga, Palma de Mallorca, Santiago de Compostela, Sevilla and Valencia.

By train   Principal railroad crossing points from France are at the opposite ends of the Pyrenees, near Perpignan-Figueres in the E and Biarritz-San Sebastián in the W. A direct service is available from Rome, Paris, Nice and intermediate stations. Speed and superior standards characterize the *Puerta del Sol* express between Paris and Madrid and the *Barcelona Talgo* between Paris and Barcelona. Both leave Paris every evening and arrive early the next morning. There are also Motorail services from Boulogne to Biarritz and from Paris to Madrid.

By bus   The London-based company, **Euroways Express Coach Ltd** (☎*(01) 730 8235*), serves many destinations in Spain, including Madrid and Barcelona.

By car   Roads from France cross into Spain at more than a dozen points. Most approaches twist through mountain passes and it is certainly wise to make these trips during daylight, since the borders may be closed at night. Highways (*autopistas*) run from Biarritz to San Sebastián and from Perpignan to Barcelona. The latter continues almost all the way along the Mediterranean coast to Alicante.

By ferry   Car ferries ply several routes on a weekly or more frequent basis; among the routes they take are Plymouth-Santander, Marseille-Alicante, Marseille-Mallorca and Genoa-Barcelona. Cruise ships usually put in at Cádiz, Málaga, Mallorca, Ibiza and Barcelona.

Climate

As a rule May, June, Sept and Oct are the best months. In July and Aug summer blazes throughout the peninsula, especially in Andalucía, which boasts temperatures of 46°C (115°F). Coolest in July and Aug are the provinces bordering the Cantabrian Sea (Bay of Biscay), warmest in Jan and Feb are the southernmost Costa del Sol and the Balearic and Canary Islands. In deepest winter, only the waters of the Canaries are suitable for swimming. Snow falls in the Pyrenees, Picos de Europa, Sierra de Gredos, Sierra de Guadarrama and Sierra Nevada from Oct-Apr.

Clothes

Informality in dress is increasingly the rule. Jeans are everywhere, on people of all ages, and skimpy bathing costumes are now the norm on most beaches. Elsewhere, casual clothing is acceptable but courtesy demands discretion in churches and religious houses. Raincoats are indispensable from Oct-Apr in northern parts of the country, but extra-warm clothes are only necessary in winter in the mountains. Nowadays men are rarely expected to wear ties in restaurants.

General delivery (poste restante)

The majority of post offices throughout Spain will keep mail marked *lista de correos*. You will need your passport when you collect your mail, but no charge is made. Mail can also be sent to American Express and Thomas Cook offices, but to use the service provided by the former, you must have an American Express card or travelers cheques.

Getting around

Flying

Buses connect major airports with the nearest city, departing every 20-30mins or as demand requires, from about 6am-11pm. The fare is usually 150-300ptas, the trip 30-45mins. Most buses stop at only one or two locations in the city, so connections to hotels must be made by taxi or on foot. In Málaga and Barcelona, there is a rail link between the airport and city center, which costs less than the bus and is faster. The average ride from the airport by metered taxi is 800-1,200ptas.

Iberia flights connect major cities. There is a frequent shuttle service between Madrid and Barcelona with flights leaving from early morning to late evening. Aviaco and Spantax cover similar routes and have flights to other destinations too. Their offices in Madrid are:

Aviaco   Maudes 51 ☎(91) 254 3600
Iberia   Velázquez 130 ☎(91) 262 6731
Spantax   Paseo de la Castellana 181 ☎(91) 279 6900

Railroad services

Routes and quality of service have been upgraded in recent years. There are Motorail (*auto-expresos*) services from Madrid to many major cities, and *Talgo*, TER and *Electrotrén* trains are comparable with the best in France and Switzerland; they are fast and, especially in first class, clean and comfortable. Sadly the reverse is true of provincial lines, where second class, often overcrowded, has wooden benches and airless compartments. Large areas of the country have little or no service. Avoid trains designated *Expreso* or *Rápido* unless time is not a factor.

RENFE (*Red Nacional de los Ferrocarriles Españoles*) accepts the North American Eurailpass and the British InterRail pass, and offers a 15 percent discount ticket, *Chequetrén*, which is good for 15,000ptas' worth of travel with Spain, but supplements may be payable on first-class trains. Senior citizens can buy a *tarjeta dorada* (gold card) for 25ptas, entitling the holder to discounts of 50 percent on trips exceeding 100km (62 miles). The main stations in Madrid are: **El Norte** serving the N of Spain, **Atocha** the S and **Chamartín** the rest of the country.

Metro

Madrid and Barcelona have underground systems which are relatively modern, but less extensive than those of either London or New York; average fares are 60ptas. Stations can be recognized by a diamond-shaped sign with the word *Metro* in the center.

Buses

One-way fares for most destinations within cities average between 30 and 60ptas, and tickets are purchased on the bus. In Madrid a *Bonobus* multi-ticket can be obtained at Cibeles or Sol metro stations. Buses in Madrid operate 24hrs a day, but there is only an hourly service between midnight and 6am. Buses in Barcelona operate 4.30am-10.30pm with a reduced service to 1am. Provincial bus routes are comprehensive, even serving the most obscure villages, although schedules tend to reflect local requirements, such as market times.

Taxis

Metered taxis are usually black or white with a horizontal or diagonal colored band. They are found parked in ranks or can be

hailed in the street. During the day, the window sign *libre* indicates
a taxi is available for hire; at night, a green roof light is
illuminated. Fares are moderate; an average ride within the city
will cost 200-300ptas. Supplementary charges can be bewildering,
with extras for luggage, after-midnight journeys, rides to and from
airports and bullrings, and other trips outside city limits. Tip no
more than 10 percent unless a special service is provided. In resorts
and small towns taxis are often unmetered, so the fare must be
negotiated in advance.

Getting around by car

Roads have much improved in recent years, especially between
major cities, but also those leading to previously isolated villages of
interest to tourists. The speed limit in built-up areas is 60kph
(37mph), on country roads 90kph (56mph), on national highways
100kph (62mph) and on highways 120kph (75mph). Major routes
are patrolled by licensed repair trucks, and breakdown assistance
usually arrives quickly. Even in small villages, mechanics tend to
be competent, but parts for foreign vehicles are not always readily
available.

Always indicate when passing and when turning, and yield to
vehicles coming from the right unless road signs dictate otherwise.
Headlights must be adjusted for right-hand-drive cars, and it is
illegal to drive without spare car light bulbs and a warning triangle
in case you break down. Seat belts are compulsory outside city
limits, and it is forbidden to park your car facing oncoming traffic,
in narrow turnings, on forks in the road and in front of public
buildings.

Renting a car

To rent a car you must bring a valid driver's license from home and
passport. Avis, Hertz, Europcar and the national firm ATESA
have branches in all major cities and airports. These networks
permit rent-it-here-leave-it-there schemes, with drop-off facilities
even in other countries. Daily, weekly and unlimited mileage
packages are available. You will find a great number of small
private agencies in every resort. In exchange for lower and
sometimes negotiable fees, the renter usually has to do without the
protection the larger firms offer in case of breakdown or accident,
and must return the car to the original depot. A charge card or
credit card obviates the need for cash deposits, and comprehensive
insurance is strongly advised.

Getting around on foot

In cities, you will find traffic lights often have pedestrian signals as
well. In the country, make sure you walk on the left, facing the
oncoming traffic. Hitchhiking is tolerated, but rides can be hard to
come by.

Ferry services

Trasmediterránea (*Via Laietana 2, Barcelona 3* ☎ *(93) 319 8212*)
operates regular ferry services between the main Spanish ports and
the Balearic and Canary Islands. It also operates services to
Morocco.

Other transportation

ATESA and other car rental firms provide chauffeur-driven cars.
Alternatively, tourist offices in the larger cities have lists of
accredited English-speaking guides, some of whom will drive your
car while showing you the sights.

On-the-spot information

Public holidays

New Year's Day, Jan 1; Epiphany, Jan 6; St Joseph's Day, Mar 19; Good Friday; Ascension Day; Labor Day, May 1; Corpus Christi; Feast of St John, June 24; Feast of Sts Peter and Paul, June 29; Feast of St James, July 25; Assumption, Aug 15; Hispanic (National) Day, Oct 12; All Saints' Day, Nov 1; Feast of the Immaculate Conception, Dec 8; Christmas Day, Dec 25. In addition, local and regional holidays dot the calendar. Stores and post offices are usually closed on national holidays and opening hours are shorter during festivals.

Time zones

Spain is 6hrs ahead of Eastern Standard Time and from 7-9hrs ahead of the other time zones in the USA.

Banks and currency exchange

Customary business hours for banks are 9am-2pm Mon-Fri and 9am-1pm on Sat, although some reopen their currency exchange (*cambio*) windows from 5-7pm. Rates are less favorable at exchange booths in airports and at hotels, but those at main American Express and Thomas Cook offices are competitive with banks.

See *Money* in *Before you go* for further details.

Shopping, eating and entertainment hours

Stores are usually open 9am-1 or 2pm Mon-Sat and 4.30 or 5-7.30 or 8pm Mon-Fri, although a few large department stores stay open during the afternoon *siesta*. Restaurants serve meals from 1.30-4pm and 9pm-midnight, but in hotels and tourist areas concession is often made to foreign eating habits and dinner is served from 8pm. Cafeterias stay open from about 9am-11pm, without a break. Some discos have "afternoon hours," 7-9pm, but most are open from 10.30pm. The first show at a nightclub may not start until midnight. Cinemas and theaters also keep late hours; matinées are at 7pm Mon-Sat, 4.30pm Sun, evening performances at 10 or 11pm. In large Spanish towns and cities there are markets daily, and in smaller places once or twice a week, details of which can be obtained locally.

Rush hours

In cities, avoid the crush of public transport and the madness of the traffic from 8-10am, 1-2pm, 4-5pm and 7.30-8.30pm.

Post and telephone services

Post offices normally follow 9am-1pm and 5-7pm hours, but the main post office in Madrid and some other central branches keep their *lista de correos* windows open until midnight. Post offices can be recognized by the word *correos* above the entrance; post boxes, similarly marked, are yellow. Stamps can be bought from tobacco stores (*estancos*) as well as post offices.

Public telephones (*teléfonos públicos*) are found primarily in bars and restaurants. They are coin-operated; simply drop in the coin and dial. For long-distance calls, a knowledge of Spanish is essential to deal with intermediate operators. Alternatively, use the hotel operator; surcharges can be high, but some hotels subscribe to Teleplan, which limits the extra calling fee to approximately 25 percent.

The ringing signal is a slow repeating tone; busy is fast repeating. All telephone codes within Spain begin with 9 and are followed by the province code number. For calls to Europe, the country code is prefixed by 07. Information for making international calls is in four languages in any telephone kiosk under the word *internacional*.

For telegrams ☎(91) 232 8800 in Madrid and ☎(93) 317 6898 in Barcelona or use the telex and cable facilities that are standard in larger hotels.

Public rest rooms

Facilities in railroad stations and bars are not appealing, so use those in restaurants, hotels or museums. Ask for *los servicios*, *los aseos* or simply *caballeros* or *señoras*, and tip the attendant a few pesetas.

Electric current

Standard current is 220 volt (50 cycles AC), although many hotel rooms have 110 or 120 volt outlets intended for electric shavers. Two-pin round plugs are standard but converters and adapters are unreliable, so battery-powered units are useful.

Laws and regulations

Possession of illicit hard drugs, even in very small quantities, is a severely punishable offense which can lead to years in prison. Leaving the scene of an accident or driving while intoxicated also carries stiff penalties. A bail bond will be included in car rentals arranged in Spain (make sure you have one if you are driving a car rented outside Spain). This guarantees a cash deposit if you are arrested during your trip, in which case the money must be reimbursed. If crossing into Spain by car with an unrelated minor, you must have written permission from his or her parents. A written statement is also required when driving a car owned by another person. Fines for speeding and other moving traffic violations must be paid on the spot.

Customs and etiquette

Relatives and good friends kiss each other on both cheeks on meeting, but Spaniards are more formal in social situations than other Europeans or North Americans. Men and women shake hands in greeting. Only close friends and family use the *tú* form of address, as opposed to the more common *usted*, and Señor, Señora or Señorita is a customary address for strangers.

Tipping

Restaurant bills include a service charge, usually 15 percent, although another 5-10 percent is expected. Especially good service or more elaborate surroundings call for up to 15 percent extra.

Small tips of up to 100ptas should be given to doormen, room maids, cloakroom attendants and ushers. Porters in airports and railroad stations have fixed charges of 50-100ptas per bag, while taxi drivers expect 5-10 percent of the fare.

Disabled travelers

Few allowances are made for the handicapped in hotels away from the coastal resorts. Lowered curbs and ramps for wheelchairs are not frequently encountered. Guide dogs are permitted everywhere, however, and certain travel agents are familiar with tours specifically designed for disabled people. Madrid and Barcelona city guides for the disabled are obtainable from Cruz Roja Española (*Dr Santero 18, Madrid*) and ECOM (*Balmes 311, Barcelona*). For further details contact SEREM (*María de Guzmán*

52, *Madrid*), the official government department for the disabled, or obtain *Access to the World: A Travel Guide for the Handicapped* (Chatham Square Press, Inc., 401 Broadway, New York, NY 10013) or ask for the leaflet provided by the Spanish National Tourist Office.

Local and foreign publications

Foreign language newspapers and periodicals are on sale at newsstands and international hotels in all major tourist centers. English-speaking residents publish the *Iberia Daily Sun* and the Costa del Sol magazine, *Lookout*. In Madrid, the weekly *Guidepost Magazine* focuses on events of interest to English speakers. Several cities have versions of the *Guía del Ocio*, which covers current sports and entertainment; although printed in Spanish, the listings are not hard to decipher.

Useful addresses

Tourist information

The Madrid tourist office, **Oficina de Informacíon de Turismo** (*Plaza Mayor 3* ☎(91) 266 4874) is usually open Mon-Sat 9am-1.30pm and 4.30-8pm. There is a tourist office desk at Barajas airport, Madrid (☎(91) 205 8656) and at Barcelona airport (☎(93) 325 5829) to help you on arrival. American Express Travel Service (*Plaza de las Cortes 2, Madrid* ☎(91) 222 1180) is a valuable source of information for any traveler in need of help, advice or emergency services.

Details of tourist offices and American Express Travel Service branches in other major cities are given in *A-Z* listings.

Main post offices
Madrid   Plaza de la Cibeles ☎(91) 221 8195
Barcelona   Plaza Antonio López ☎(93) 318 3831

Telephone services in Madrid
News   ☎(91) 095
Speaking Clock   ☎(91) 093
Alarm Call   ☎(91) 096
Weather   ☎(91) 094

Airlines
Iberia   Velázquez 130, Madrid ☎(91) 261 9100
British Airways   Paseo de Gracia 59, Barcelona ☎(93) 215 2112
and Gran Via 66, Madrid ☎(91) 247 5300
Pan Am   Edificio España, Plaza España, Madrid ☎(91) 241 4200
TWA   Gran Via 68, Madrid ☎(91) 247 4200

Tour operators
The following companies have representatives throughout the country. Their main offices are:
American Express   Plaza de las Cortes 2, Madrid ☎(91) 222 1180
Compañía Internacional de Coches-Camas   (Wagons-Lits Cooks) Marqués de Urquijo 28, Madrid ☎(91) 248 3000
Ultramar Express   Rambla Estudios 109, Barcelona ☎(93) 301 1212
Viajes Marsans   Las Ramblas 134, Barcelona ☎(93) 318 7216
Viajes Melia   Princesa 25, Madrid ☎(91) 247 5500

Automobile club
Autoclub Turístico Español   Marqués de Riscal 11, Madrid ☎(91)
207 0702

Major places of worship in Madrid
Catholic   Plaza Mayor
Church of England   Hermosilla 45
Greek Orthodox   Nicaragua 12
Jewish   Balmes 3

Consulates in Madrid
Australia   Paseo de la Castellana 143 ☎(91) 279 8501
Austria   Paseo de la Castellana 180 ☎(91) 250 9200
Belgium   Paseo de la Castellana 18 ☎(91) 401 9558
Canada   Edificio Goya, Núñez de Balboa 35 ☎(91) 431 4300
Denmark   Claudio Coello 91 ☎(91) 431 8445
Finland   Paseo de la Castellana 15 ☎(91) 419 6172
France   Edificio Uap, Paseo de la Castellana 79 ☎(91) 455 5450
Germany, West   Fortuny 8 ☎(91) 419 9100
Greece   Serrano 110 ☎(91) 411 3345
Ireland   Claudio Coello 73 ☎(91) 276 3500
Italy   Agustín de Bethancourt 3 ☎(91) 233 4212
Japan   Joaquín Costa 29 ☎(91) 262 5546
Netherlands   Paseo de la Castellana 178 ☎(91) 458 2100
Norway   Juan Bravo 3 ☎(91) 401 6262
South Africa   Edificio Lista, Claudio Coello 91 ☎(91) 227 3153
Sweden   Zurbano 27 ☎(91) 419 7550
Switzerland   Edificio Goya, Núñez de Balboa 35 ☎(91) 431 3400
United Kingdom   Fernando el Santo ☎(91) 419 0200
United States   Serrano 75 ☎(91) 276 3400

Conversion tables

Length
- cm: 0 — 5 — 10 — 15 — 20 — 25 — 30
- in: 0 1 2 3 4 5 6 7 8 9 10 11 12
- meters: 0 — 0.5 — 1 — 1.5 — 2
- ft/yd: 0 — 1ft — 2ft — 3ft(1yd) — 2yd

Distance
- km: 0 1 2 3 4 5 6 7 8 9 10 11 12 13 14 15 16
- miles: 0 1 2 3 4 5 6 7 8 9 10

Weight
- grams: 0 (¼kg) 100 200 (½kg) 300 400 500 (¾kg) 600 700 800 900 (1kg) 1,000
- ounces: 0 4 (¼lb) 8 (½lb) 12 (¾lb) 16 (1lb) 20 24 (1½lb) 28 32 (2lb)

Fluid measures
- liters: 0 1 2 3 4 5
- imp.pints: 0 1 2 3 4 5 6 7 8
- US pints: 0 1 2 3 4 5 6 7 8
- liters: 0 5 10 20 30
- imp. gallons: 0 1 2 3 4 5 6
- US gallons: 0 1 2 3 4 5 6 7

Temperature chart
- °C: −15 −10 −5 | 0 5 10 15 20 25 30 35 36.9 40 100
- °F: 0 10 20 30 | 32 40 50 60 70 80 90 | 98.4 105 212

Emergency information

Emergency services (Madrid and Barcelona)
Police ☎091
Ambulance ☎227 2021
Fire *(Cuerpo de bomberos)* ☎232 3232
For emergency services elsewhere, call the operator.

Hospitals and medical emergencies
In Madrid, the **British American Hospital** *(Paseo de Juan XXIII* ☎*(91) 234 6700)* has many English-speaking staff.
Centro Maternal de Urgencia Maternité *(Don Ramón de la Cruz 93* ☎*(91) 256 0200)* is for maternity emergencies;
Enfermedades Cardíacas *(Av. de la Reina Victoria 22* ☎*(91) 234 8866)* is for suspected heart attacks; and **Urgencia Médica** *(Bardo 26* ☎*(91) 222 3030)* is for general emergencies. In Barcelona, contact the **Red Cross** *(Cruz Roja) (Dos de Mayo 301* ☎*(93) 235 9300)*. Elsewhere, call your consulate.

Late-night pharmacies
Pharmacies operate a late-night roster, published daily in the local press under *Farmacias de guardia*. Otherwise check the sign on the door of your nearest pharmacy; it usually gives the location of the store on duty that night.

Automobile accidents
—Summon the police immediately.
—Call the number in your car rental agreement.
—Do not admit liability or incriminate yourself.
—Exchange names, addresses, car details and insurance company details with any other parties involved.
—In serious accidents, notify your nearest consulate.

Car breakdowns
—Use the emergency telephones on highways.
—Attract the attention of a patrolling police car.
—Call the RACE, which has an arrangement with the AAA.

Lost passport
Notify the police and go to your nearest consulate to obtain emergency documents. (See *Consulates*.)

Lost travelers cheques
Notify the local police immediately then follow the instructions provided with your travelers cheques, or contact the nearest office of the issuing company. Contact your consulate or American Express if you are stranded with no money.

Lost property
There are lost property offices *(oficinas de objetos perdidos)* in Madrid *(Santa Engracia 120* ☎*(91) 233 0214)* and Barcelona *(Plaça de Sant Jaume* ☎*(93) 301 3923)*.

Emergency phrases
Help! *¡Socorro!*
There has been an accident. *Ha habido un accidente.*
Where is the nearest telephone/hospital? *¿Donde está el teléfono/hospital más cercano?*
Call a doctor/ambulance! *¡Llame a un doctor/una ambulancia!*
Call the police! *¡Llame a la policía!*

Time chart

Origins and conquests

14,000–10,000BC	Late Paleolithic people left cave paintings at Altamira and many other locations.
13th–6thBC	Original Iberian tribes appeared in Spain, probably having migrated from N Africa.
11thBC	Phoenicians established trading ports.
10th–7thBC	Celts from Central Europe came to Spain across the Pyrenees. Some tribes mixed with resident Iberians to form Celtiberians. The Greeks set up trading settlements in the Balearic Islands and along the SE coast, in competition with the Phoenicians.
6th–3rdBC	N African Carthaginians displaced the Greeks and established Cartagena as capital of their colonial empire. They soon came into conflict with the Romans and were vanquished in the Second Punic War.
2ndBC	Roman control expanded over much of Iberia, but was resisted in the NW and the interior until the fall of the Celtiberian city of Numantia in 133BC.
1stBC–1stAD	Spain was divided into three provinces of the Roman Empire. Despite periodic uprisings, the new citizens prospered and assimilated the language, culture and law of their rulers.
2ndC	Christianity spread throughout Spain despite Roman suppression.
5thC	The Romans, unable to stave off the first Hun invaders, enlisted the aid of the Visigothic kings Ataulf and Eurich, who created a fragile unity throughout most of Iberia.
6thC	Although the Visigoths lost Gaul to the Franks in 507, they kept Spain, with Toledo as their capital. Byzantine trading communities occupied parts of the southern coast. The Visigoths declared Christianity the official religion.
7thC	The Byzantines were expelled from Spain in 624 and the Suevi were defeated in Galicia. The Church gained control over education and also influenced secular affairs.

The Moors

8thC	The Moors — a term that links several ethnic groups — under general Tariq defeated a Visigothic army in 711 near Jerez de la Frontera, then swept across the country and into Gaul. Galicia, Asturias and the Basque territories resisted the invaders. The rearguard of Charlemagne's retreating Frankish army was destroyed by Basques at Roncesvalles in 778.
10th–12thC	The caliphates, centered at Córdoba, permitted a measure of religious freedom and established schools and libraries. Frequent rebellions in the N caused them to seek assistance from the N African Berber Almoravid sect, which was in turn succeeded by the fanatic Almohades. Nevertheless the Christian monarchs of Asturias, León, Barcelona, Aragón and Castile continued to gain strength. By 1214, over half the peninsula had been regained by the Catholics and, by 1242, the Moors controlled only the SE kingdom centering on Granada.
13th–14thC	The Granada Emirate enjoyed over two centuries of 14thC prosperity while the Christians were distracted

by civil wars in the reconquered territories. The Alhambra was begun.

The Catholic Monarchs

15thC The kingdoms of Aragón and Castile were united by the marriage of Ferdinand II and Isabella in 1469. She established the Inquisition in Castile in 1478, which was later extended over the rest of the country and led to the expulsion of Jews and Moslems not prepared to convert to Christianity. The infamous Torquemada was named Grand Inquisitor in 1483. The armies of the Catholic king and queen conquered the last Moorish enclave of Granada in 1492, thus unifying the entire nation. It was the same year that Columbus discovered the New World.

1504 Isabella died and Ferdinand acted as regent of Castile until his death in 1517. He was succeeded by his grandson Charles I. With his installation, the expanding empire now incorporated Naples and the islands of Sicily and Sardinia.

The Golden Age

1519 The Golden Age of Spain began with the capture of Mexico by Cortés. Treasure ships returned with cargoes of gold, silver and precious stones. On the death of his Hapsburg grandfather, Charles I became the Holy Roman Emperor, Charles V. The Netherlands, Austria and the German principalities were thereby added to the Empire, which at this point encompassed most of Europe as well as the Spanish colonies overseas.

1522-56 Castilian noblemen, known as Comuneros, revolted against increasing centralization of authority by Charles, but were defeated. Charles became embroiled in numerous wars over his European territories, causing a serious drain on resources. When he could not suppress the German Reformation launched by Martin Luther, he agreed to allow a measure of religious freedom in the affected states. In 1556 he abdicated in favor of his son Philip II.

1559 Philip launched the Counter-Reformation. The Inquisition revived persecution of Christian Moors and the remaining Jews.

1563 Construction of the Escorial began.

1568 The Protestant Netherlands revolted against Spanish rule.

1571 Spain lost Tunis to the Turks. Retribution came at the battle of Lepanto, when a naval force assembled with the aid of the Venice and Genoa city-states destroyed the Turkish fleet. The victory gave Spain control of the Mediterranean. In the Pacific, the Philippines were taken.

1580 Philip forcibly assumed the title of King of Portugal.

1581-88 Despite these successes the Spanish Empire continued to deteriorate. Spoils from the American colonies diminished, and Spanish treasure ships were harried by English privateers. The Protestants of the Netherlands gained support from Germany and England. The enormously costly Armada set out to invade England but suffered a humiliating defeat through inferior tactics and bad weather.

1598 Philip II died, leaving his son, Philip III, most of his inherited empire, but a depleted treasury.

The decline

1609	Philip III expelled all remaining Moors and Jews. The Netherlands were declared an independent republic.
1618	The start of the Thirty Years' War drained Spain's power further.
1640	Portugal broke away from Spain.
1659	Spain's participation in the Thirty Years' War ended with the Treaty of the Pyrenees.
1668	In the War of Devolution with France, Spain lost land in France and the Low Countries.
1700	Charles II died, bequeathing his throne to Philip Duke of Anjou (grandson of the Bourbon Louis XIV of France), which resulted in the outbreak of the War of the Spanish Succession in 1701.
1713	The Treaty of Utrecht ended the War of the Spanish Succession, leaving Philip V only his American and Pacific colonies; Gibraltar was ceded to Britain.
1759	Charles III ascended the throne, introducing many economic reforms.
1788	Charles IV turned administration over to an adviser, Manuel de Godoy, whose intrigues caused Spain to come under French control.
1805	Nelson defeated the combined Spanish and French fleets at Trafalgar.
1808	Charles IV and his son Ferdinand VII abdicated, and Joseph Bonaparte became their unpopular successor. An uprising in Madrid precipitated the Peninsular War, known in Spain as the War of Independence.
1812	A liberal constitution was created and approved by the Cortes (Parliament) at Cádiz.
1813	Wellington finally drove the French force out of Spain at the decisive Battle of Vitoria. In South America several colonies declared their independence.

Nineteenth Century unrest

1814	Ferdinand VII reclaimed the Spanish throne and rejected the 1812 constitution.
1833	Isabella II was proclaimed queen on the death of her father, Ferdinand VII. The NE provinces supported the claim to the throne of his brother, Don Carlos, in the First Carlist War, but were unsuccessful. The Inquisition was formally terminated.
1845	A new constitution provoked the Second Carlist War.
1868	Isabella II abdicated. The Cortes proclaimed a constitutional monarchy, and in 1870 chose Amadeo of Savoy as king.
1873	Amadeo abdicated. The first Spanish Republic was formed but did not survive, and the Bourbon, Alfonso XII, son of Isabella II, assumed the throne.
1885	Alfonso XII died, leaving María Cristina as regent for his son.
1898	With the end of the Spanish-American War, Spain lost Cuba, Puerto Rico and the Philippines.

The Twentieth Century

1902	16-year-old Alfonso XIII ascended the throne.
1904	A secret pact between Spain and France partitioned Morocco.
1914	Spain remained neutral during World War 1, but suffered popular unrest and internal instability.
1921	In Morocco, resentment of European rule sparked

	off the Rif War.
1923	A right-wing dictatorship was founded by General Primo de Rivera. The Cortes was dismissed. Despite a period of prosperity, opposition to restrictive policies grew among intellectuals and workers.
1930	Primo de Rivera was forced into exile.
1931	Alfonso XIII abdicated amid strong anti-monarchist feeling and the Second Republic was born with the reconstitution of the Cortes.
1933-35	Primo de Rivera's son, José Antonio, formed the Falangist party. Political factionalism increased.
1936	The Popular Front (liberal-left coalition) won the national election. José Antonio was imprisoned and his monarchist ally Calvo Sotelo was murdered. The Civil War began. Franco and his troops crossed the Straits of Gibraltar, joining with rebel forces in Sevilla. The Nationalist movement was supported by fascist Italy, Germany and Portugal. The Loyalist Republicans were aided principally by Russia and the International Brigades.
1936-39	The Civil War was marked by its bitterness. Atrocities committed by both sides left a deep-seated legacy of hate.
1939	Barcelona fell in January. The Western democracies recognized the Falange as the legitimate government of Spain. Valencia, the last Loyalist stronghold, surrendered on Mar 30. Franco established a dictatorship that was to last 36yrs.
1940	Recovery began slowly and, after the devastation, suffering was widespread. Authoritarian government and censorship were imposed.
1941	Spain remained neutral in World War II, although Franco sent the "volunteer" Blue Division to fight for Germany on the Russian front.
1942	Franco re-established the Cortes.
1945-55	An agreement in 1953 to allow the United States to establish air bases in Spain signalled an upturn in international relations and Spain was allowed to join the United Nations in 1955. Recovery continued slowly, with continuing emphasis on national unity despite the growing interest in regional autonomy.
1956	Spanish Morocco was annexed by independent Morocco, but Spain retained Melilla and Ceuta.
1968	Spain closed the border with Gibraltar.
1969	Juan Carlos, grandson of Alfonso XIII, was named by Franco as his successor.
1970	Although political restrictions were loosened, discontent with the regime was manifest in strikes, protests and increasing terrorist activity.
1975	Franco died on Nov 20. Juan Carlos was proclaimed king.
1976	Prime Minister Suárez formed a center-right coalition.
1978	The death penalty was abolished and divorce permitted.
1980	Autonomy within a Republican framework was · granted to Catalunya and the Basque provinces.
1981	A right-wing military coup was attempted, but collapsed after the intercession of Juan Carlos.
1982	The national election brought the Socialists to power under the leadership of Felipe González.

Architecture

Testimony to Spain's architectural heritage is encountered everywhere, if only in the scavenged fragments of old buildings imbedded in newer walls. Conquerors built upon the remains left by their predecessors or altered structures to suit their own purposes. And the common people built according to the dictates of climate and available materials, producing villages that are, in their way, as visually captivating as the palaces of kings.

Prehistory

There are remains of ancient structures made of enormous boulders weighing many tons, which are among the very earliest constructions in Spain. They are described as "Cyclopean" after the mythical giants, because the origins of the people who built them are unknown. The ramparts at Tarragona are laid on a Cyclopean foundation, and the dolmens (temple-tombs) near Antequera bear the same label.

   In Menorca there is evidence of Bronze Age conical structures of piled stone called *talayots*, which may have been piers for houses or the roofs of burial chambers. Cave dwellings, which might have been occupied from the same time, can be seen outside Guadix, near Granada. And some of the settlements — now no more than scattered foundations — of the original Iberians, who probably migrated from N Africa between the 13th and 6thCBC, eventually intermingling with Celts from the N, can be seen in remote parts of Galicia and Aragón.

Pre-Roman and Roman (12th CBC-4thCAD)

The Phoenicians, Greeks and Carthaginians preceded the Romans, but left little beyond caches of household implements and trinkets to mark their occupations. The engineering feats of Imperial Rome were more durable. Still surviving are impressive aqueducts in Segovia and outside Tarragona; vestiges of the cities of Itálica near Sevilla and Numantia near Soria; the theater at Sagunto, the bridge at Alcántara, and both theater and bridge as well as other remains at Mérida.

Visigothic (5th-7thC)

Christianity was already established when the Romans left Spain, and it was sustained, although in an altered form, by the Visigoths. The Visigothic legacy was composed less of stone and mortar than of ideas, as in a code of law that persisted into the Middle Ages. But remains can be found, particularly in the Visigoths' capital, Toledo. Intact buildings are few, reflecting Byzantine rather than Roman influences: slender braided columns, stone medallions and vaguely Oriental etched traceries are typical. Horseshoe-shaped arches are also found.

Early Moorish (8th-11thC)

Horseshoe arches, in russet and sand-colored stripes, can be seen to best advantage in the *mezquita* (mosque) in Córdoba. Many of the supporting columns were scavenged from Roman, Visigothic and Carthaginian sites. But the Moors were neither copyists nor parasites. During nearly three centuries, the bright light of Islamic civilization cast Christendom into deepest shadow. Córdoba was the equal of Baghdad, and Moorish influence blanketed nearly all the peninsula. The 8thC Córdoba mosque follows a characteristic rectangular plan. Above the grove of columns are double arches, one on top of the other and this, despite the darkness, contributes to the sense of structural airiness and fluidity of space characteristic of many Moorish buildings.

Pre-Romanesque (8th-11thC)
In Asturias, on the Cantabrian coast, which escaped all but occasional Arab raids, there developed an architectural style that anticipates the Romanesque. Early churches were stolid, simple, often as wide as they were tall, with largely unadorned rounded arches over the doors and windows. Oviedo has two relatively intact examples in the churches of Santa María and San Miguel de Lillo, rich with hints of their Visigothic antecedents.

Middle Moorish (late 11th-13thC)
The relative tranquillity of the early caliphates was shattered by the arrival of the puritanical Almoravid and Almohad Arabs, who not only expelled the "decadent" Jews and Christians but destroyed most major Moorish buildings. In place of these they built mosques and minarets of brutally austere brickwork, such as the Giralda in Sevilla. Pointed, more distinctly Eastern, arches replaced the horseshoe shape, and wood or plaster ceilings of geometrically ribbed design were gradually introduced.

Mozarabic and Mudejar (11th-15thC)
Mozarabs were Christians living under caliphate rule. When they fled to the N, their architects found favor in the smaller villages of New and Old Castile, such as San Miguel de Escalada, near León. The horseshoe-shaped arch was much in evidence, combining Visigothic and caliphate elements, augmented by pierced stone

Left Built in 24BC after the great theaters in Rome, the **Roman theater at Mérida** is remarkably well preserved and one of the finest monuments of this period in Spain.

Below left The superb early Moorish **Mosque at Córdoba** has a vast interior of double-tiered arches in alternating bands of stone and brick.

Below right **Santa María de Naranco** (842-50), with its flat buttress and lofty porch, is a fine example of Asturian architecture.

screens and capitals and corbels carved in floral and bird motifs.

Conversely, the Mudejars were Moors caught up in the
Christian Reconquest. Their work is characterized by patterned
brick construction set off by bands of ceramic tiles, a style
originally developed under the Almohads. This same style spread
to the NE and is still preserved in Aragón, far from the
administrative center of Sevilla. The *alcázar* of Sevilla was built in
the 14thC by Mudejar artisans for the Catholic King Pedro the
Cruel. Imitative of parts of the Alhambra in Granada, it lacks that
monument's lyric delicacy but is nevertheless a valuable and
accessible lesson in the Moorish heritage. The Alhambra itself is
principally 14thC, late Moorish architecture, and is most
renowned for the superlative design and decoration of its rooms
and courtyards. Some scholars see its arrangements of pillars,
arches and reflecting pools as stylized oases of palm trees and
springs, evocations of the builders' ancestral desert origins. A
palace of dreams, it represents the pinnacle of Muslim architecture
in Spain, and remains a worthy memorial to 700yrs of Moorish
rule.

Romanesque (11th-13thC)
By the mid-11thC, Christianity prevailed throughout Europe, and
the various architectural idioms that it had encountered coalesced
in what is called, loosely, the Romanesque style. As a prototype
already existed in northern Spain, it was here that the new style
was most readily adopted. An unprecedented building boom
ensued, strengthened by the religious fervor that drew millions of
pilgrims across the Pyrenees and w to Santiago de Compostela, a

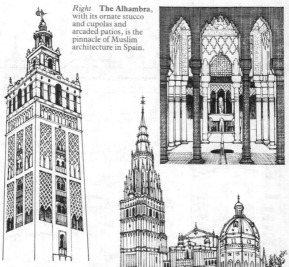

Right **The Alhambra**,
with its ornate stucco
and cupolas and
arcaded patios, is the
pinnacle of Muslim
architecture in Spain.

Above **Giralda tower** is typical
of the 12thC Almohad style, with
an ornate Renaissance belfry.

Right **Toledo cathedral**, begun
in 1226 and modified later, is an
outstanding Gothic monument.

25

city which boasts a superb example of the Romanesque in its cathedral. Inside the superimposed Baroque shell of the cathedral is the Pórtico de la Gloria, which sets the standard against which all similar portals must be measured.

In Romanesque churches, timber ceilings are replaced by rounded barrel or groin vaults, interiors are dimly lit (although some have exceptional rose windows), and the whole conveys the impression of massive solidity, emphasizing the fact that these churches frequently had an additional function as fortresses.

Gothic (13th-16thC)

Unlike the Romanesque, which had partly native roots, the Gothic style, which first appeared in Paris in the 12thC, was alien to Spain and only accepted grudgingly. Considering the innate conservatism and understandable xenophobia of the Spanish, the new French style was an alarming departure. Buttresses, until now merely vertical pillars flat against outside walls, swept far to the sides to contain the thrust of the much higher vaulting. Light entered through expanses of stained glass so great that in some cathedrals, like that at León, the structure of the building was threatened. Stone carving was finer, with more detailing, pierced and scrolled into delicate filigrees. Arches were pointed over doorways and in arcading and ribbed vaulting. The best examples are the cathedrals of Barcelona, Toledo, Sevilla, Tarragona and León.

Renaissance and Baroque (16th-18thC)

With the completion of the Reconquest under Ferdinand and

Above The ornate carving of **Isabeline decoration** is often contained in panels and covers entire facades.

Above **El Escorial**, the famous 16thC monastery-palace built for Philip II, is a massive, austere, rectangular building on five stories with vast corner towers.

Left The flamboyant, undulating facade of **Casa Battló** (1905-7), designed by Gaudí, derives from Art Nouveau, but reflects the architect's highly individual style.

Below **Coca Castle**, a vast 15thC brick fortress, is a magnificent example of Mudejar military architecture.

Isabella, the last spasm of Gothic fancy flared in riots of sculptural detailing which incorporated references to military prowess and secular history as well as theology. The vogue was called Isabeline, and is seen on the facades of churches, municipal buildings and *palacios*, notably in Valladolid, where the college of San Gregorio is an outstanding example. It developed into a decorative style called Plateresque, so called because of the resemblance of its ornamental surface to intricate silverwork. Perhaps most important in this period is Juan de Herrera, who developed the Plateresque into the classical style, and is cited by many as Spain's greatest architect. He is revered for his unfinished Valladolid cathedral and for the Escorial, the monastery-palace he designed for his patron, Philip II.

Madrid's arcaded *plaza mayor* was built during the 17thC and shows a renewed interest in ornamentation, although still drawing upon classical inspiration with its Corinthian capitals, broken pediments and fluted columns. By the 18thC, restraint was cast to the winds in a Baroque excess of voluptuous lines and highly elaborate decorations. At the Rococo extreme was the overblown Churrigueresque style, amusing examples of which can be seen adorning the entrances of the ceramics museum in Valencia and the Museo Municipal in Madrid.

Revivalist *(late 18th-19thC)*
The predictable reaction to the entertaining but shallow immoderation of Baroque was another return to classicism. As there was by this time an abundance of cathedrals and churches, many of which had been shamelessly tampered with during the Baroque era, benefactors and ministers turned to building Greco-Roman fountains and public buildings, particularly in Madrid. This enthusiasm resulted in the intermingling of several styles in a single structure.

Art Nouveau *(late 19th-early 20thC)*
In parallel with the developments of the Impressionists and their followers in painting and sculpture Antonio Gaudí turned the sinuous lines of the revivalist "new art" into a structural form beyond mere surface decoration. In his Casa Milá and Casa Battló in Barcelona, lintels and pediments appear to drip, balconies and towers to melt. Although he was clearly the dominant force in the Catalan architectural movement that came to be known as the "Modernista," there were others nearly as inventive. Among them were Salvador Valeri i Puprull, Josep Puig i Cadafalch and Lluis Doménech i Montaner. Doménech designed the Palau de la Música Catalana, a fantastical structure to rival the work of the visionary Gaudí himself, and one of the most enchanting settings for musical performances in all Europe. The Modernista movement flared brightly but only briefly before submersion beneath the Bauthaus tide, the school of international architecture that insisted that less is more and rejected all traces of non-functional ornamentation. But Barcelona was left with a legacy in stone that is once again attracting the attention of historians and Post-Modernist practitioners.

Post World War II
The devastation of the Civil War, cultural isolation and continued economic recession opposed significant architectural achievement. Building activity concerned itself first with housing the homeless and then with the hordes of tourists that started to arrive in the 1950s. Fake Andalucian villages, modest office towers and largely

27

undistinguished hotels and apartment blocks are the inevitable result. In recent years, however, more adventurous work has been done, pointing to a more optimistic future.

Military architecture

Castles in Spain not only take the traditional medieval form but can also be fortified palaces, monasteries and churches. *Alcazaba*, *alcázar* and *castillo* are the three major types. The *alcazaba*, an integral part of a town's defensive system, was introduced by the Moors, who were also responsible for *alcázares*, fortified palaces such as the Alhambra at Granada. Christian *castillos*, usually constructed on strategic mounds, are among the most characteristic sights of rural Spain, particularly in the landscape of the central plateau, the Meseta. Simple watchtowers and small keeps served as early warning outposts for far larger main fortifications, which had as many protective walls and moats and turrets as the local lord could afford. Many have been maintained and restored, while others have crumbled into heaps and shards. They are seen all over Spain, but are ubiquitous in the heartland, as evidenced in the very name of that region – Castilla.

The arts in Spain

Spain's creativity has flourished in explosions of invention springing from periodically fallow terrain. During the Golden Age of the 16th-17thC, when the nation reached the height of its power, the celebrated painter Velázquez brought the Renaissance to Madrid while the aging El Greco toiled in relative obscurity in Toledo. Cervantes invented his immortal Don Quixote, attaining one of the most esteemed positions in world literature, while the poet and dramatist Lope de Vega succeeded in founding Spanish theater.

From this time until the late 19thC, only the visionary Goya interrupted the slide into artistic and intellectual mediocrity. Around the turn of this century, however, there was a remarkable revival, which produced painters Picasso, Miró and Dalí, composer Manuel de Falla, playwright García Lorca, classical guitarist Andrés Segovia and important figures in other arts. This cultural surge still continues, and is manifest in a lavish program of music festivals and special exhibitions in all parts of Spain throughout each year.

Painting and sculpture

In a sense, Paleolithic artists began the esthetic tradition, with depictions of beasts and hunters painted on the walls of their caves. While those at Altamira are deservedly most famous, examples are found throughout the north and the east. 9,000yrs later Celtiberian sculptors produced astonishingly sophisticated portraits in stone. *La Dama de Elche*, discovered in 1897 and now in the Museo Arqueológico in Madrid, dates back to the 5thCBC. It is a bust of a woman, presumably of royal birth, attired in a robe, heavy necklaces and an unusual head-dress with large decorative discs over the ears. Reminiscent of several Eastern Mediterranean cultures of the period, the grand lady teases with a mysterious grace which surpasses that of better known contemporary Cretan and Grecian sculptures.

Of Spain's successive conquerors, the Romans made the most distinctive mark, especially once they had bestowed citizenship upon their Spanish subjects. Although prolific in their construction of ceremonial buildings, they also left heroic statuary and large, intricate mosaics, examples of which can be seen at Itálica, outside Sevilla, and at Mérida. By the time the Moors arrived in AD711, Christianity was firmly established, and the earliest Christian paintings and sculptures may be assumed to have been commissioned then, although surviving illuminated manuscripts and apse paintings cannot be reliably dated before the late 9thC. In Asturias and the other northern provinces that withstood the Moors, Pre-Romanesque ecclesiastical architecture foreshadowed later developments on the other side of the Pyrenees and gave rise to the carved retables, reliquaries and paintings on wood that are characteristic of this period.

Moorish achievement in the arts was primarily in architecture, although interiors were richly embellished with majolica tiles and reliefs of stylized Arabic script. The true Romanesque period arrived in the 11thC. Detailing on painted altar panels, usually in gilded gesso, employed Arabesque and Byzantine motifs in the depiction of biblical scenes and symbols.

In the wake of the Reconquest and as part of the newly formed international court of Ferdinand and Isabella, French and Italian artistic styles were introduced, and the exuberant Gothic started to replace the more stolid Romanesque. Figures in church polyptychs became more animated, their features and surroundings more finely observed. Works of uncanny similarity to those of the Italian painter Giotto appeared throughout Catalunya and Aragón, anticipating the Renaissance.

In the 16thC, intensive study of anatomy, perspective and painting techniques gave life to scenes of flesh and blood, passion and religious fervor. The debt of Alonso Berruguete (1486-1561) to Michelangelo is clear in the expressive sculptural poses of his tormented figures. Schools of painting developed in Barcelona, Madrid, Valencia and Sevilla, each drawing on French, Flemish and Italian concepts, but each driven by the Spanish love for the dramatic in life and art.

The profound religious fervor, almost demented in its intensity, which provided much of the spiritual impetus for both conquest abroad and the Counter-Reformation in Spain, seems to be reflected in the curiously distorted figures of the later paintings of El Greco (1540-1614). His work was too eccentric for Philip II, and instead of working in the new Escorial he remained in Toledo. The Valencian Jose de Ribera (1591-1652) worked in pronounced chiaroscuro, a style known in Spain as *tenebrismo*, with a restrained palette reminiscent of Caravaggio.

The wealth from the Americas was concentrated in Sevilla and attracted artists from Italy and northern Europe. Juan de las Roelas (1559-1625), emulating Tintoretto and Correggio, laid the groundwork for the far more important Francisco Zurbarán (1598-1664) and Bartolomé Esteban Murillo (1617-82). The supreme master, Diego Velázquez (1599-1660), was court painter to Philip IV. His early compositions show the influence of Caravaggio, and Dutch elements are also apparent. But his later ecclesiastical and court portraits, characterized by their cool and seemingly naturalistic representations of his subjects' attitudes and foibles, were vehicles for his own sophisticated experiments in liquid light and space.

By the end of the 16thC, portraiture, still life and genre subjects were deemed as respectable as the religious themes that had previously been dominant. Support for the arts waned, however, with the decline of Spanish power in the late 17thC. The Bourbon kings favored foreigners, most of them innovators of the romantic classicism engendered by the Baroque. The flaccid landscapes and frolicking wood nymphs of the time are perhaps only memorable as a syrupy counterpoint to the ferocious iconoclasm of Francisco Goya (1746-1828).

Although Goya was Velázquez's equal in technique, he was incapable of that earlier master's detachment. A political liberal by the standards of his day, he was nonetheless a favorite at the court of Charles IV. In his 1800 portrait of the royal family, he mimics Velázquez's *Las Meninas*, showing himself at the easel. The king, queen and their children are depicted as caricatures of inanity, but appear to have been well satisfied by the realism of the painting.

Goya's etchings include biting attacks on corruption and decadence, but neither these nor his outrage over the horrors of the Napoleonic invasions, epitomized in the harrowing scene of the firing squad in *May 3rd, 1808*, harmed his reputation. With increasing despair came his macabre, expressionistic scenes painted on the walls of his house and known as the *Black Paintings*. These are now on display in the Prado Museum and are for many the most compelling examples from the vast body of his work.

During these centuries of ascendancy and decline Spanish sculpture rarely aspired to greatness, concentrating rather on the dramatic polychrome wood sculptures, representing saints and martyrs, which are still central elements of popular religious veneration. Complete with real garments and hair, crystal eyes and glass tears, they stand in shrines and chapels in churches throughout Spain, awaiting the festivals and processions in their honor, during which they are carried through the streets. Otherwise, sculpture was principally associated with architecture, in the form of carved pillars, altars, facades and porticos.

In the early 20thC, following a century of almost continuous warfare, word of a new wave of Impressionism filtered into Catalunya, a region long attuned to French sensibilities. Manet and Cézanne inspired the Cubism of Juan Gris (1887-1927) and Pablo Picasso (1881-1973). Blessed with a voracious inquisitiveness, great energy and a life span that stretched his productivity over eight decades, Picasso was a dominant figure in the international art community until his death. He worked in every conceivable medium: oil, tempera, collage, stone, metal, ceramics, graphics, textiles, pen and ink, often manipulated or applied by unconventional means. He spent his early years in Barcelona, but by 1904 had moved to Paris. After the onset of the Spanish Civil War, he exiled himself permanently in France.

Picasso's younger Catalan contemporaries, Joan Miró (1893-1983) and Salvador Dalí (born 1904) are both described as Surrealists, but the connection is tenuous. Miró's biomorphic forms dancing across two-dimensional planes are more abstract than figurative, while Dalí's wildly dream-like fantasies are executed with superb draftsmanship and coldly meticulous detail.

A number of artists emerged in the wake of the Abstract Expressionism of the post-War New York School. Their early painting was characterized by subdued earthy tones, but their later work has developed into vivid slashes of color and experiments in mixed media. Among the artists of particular note are Antonio Tapies, Luis Feito, Eduardo Chillida, Pablo Palazuelo, Antonio Lorenzo and Antonio Saura. Their works are best displayed in the Museo de Arte Abstracto Español in Cuenca.

Literature

The Spanish literary tradition began with a flourish under the Romans. Seneca the Elder (*c.*60BC-37AD), although a citizen of the

Empire, was born in Córdoba and lived most of his life there. His major surviving works are a history of Rome, collections of orations and simulated legal cases. His son was Seneca the Stoic, who was also born in Córdoba but spent most of his life in Rome, where he accumulated a substantial fortune while engaging in frequent conspiracies and clandestine romances. These activities were at variance with the Stoic philosophy that inspired his numerous essays and plays.

The Moors established centers of scholarship that drew upon the works of Arab scientists and Greek philosophers. Under their relatively tolerant rule, the important Hebrew philosopher Maimonides, born in Córdoba in 1135, was able to produce a vast collection of work which influences Jewish and Christian religious thought to this day.

The exploits of Rodrigo Díaz de Vivar inspired the 12thC epic poem *El Cantar del Mío Cid*, the first significant work in the Castilian language. When Alfonso X ascended the throne in the 13thC, he decreed that Castilian should henceforth be the official tongue, although he himself wrote poetry in Gallego (Galician). Translations of Arabic works, compilations of Spanish history and early efforts at a prose form followed.

With the blossoming of the Golden Age in the 16thC, the stage was set for a true native theater, distinguished by its roots in the life of the Spanish people rather than inspired by the alien cultures of its conquerors. Félix Lope de Vega (1562-1635) is regarded as the father of this school of drama. His astonishingly prolific output included 1,800 plays and numerous epic poems, many of them no doubt inspired by his prodigious appetite for illicit love affairs. His contemporary, Miguel de Cervantes Saavedra (1547-1616), suffered frequent misfortune and was not nearly so prolific. But Cervantes' masterpiece, *Don Quixote de la Mancha*, was alone sufficient to place him in the company of Tolstoy and Dostoyevsky. Humor, pathos, tragedy and triumph illustrate the moving tale of naïve idealism in conflict with corruption and avarice.

Also important during this fruitful period were the richly descriptive poet Luis de Góngora (1561-1627), the satirist, poet and novelist Francisco Quevedo (1580-1645), the dramatists Calderón de la Barca (1600-81) and Tirso de Molina (1584-1648), the latter renowned for his rendering of the story of Don Juan, and the mystics St Teresa of Avila (1515-82) and St John of the Cross (1542-91), significant for their literary skills as well as their expressions of faith.

The important Romantic movement of the 19thC coincided with similar fashions in painting. The poet Gustavo Adolfo Bécquer (1836-70) was a direct descendant of Romanticism, his work contrasting strongly with the gritty realism of the novelists Pedro de Alarcón (1833-91) and Benito Pérez Galdós (1843-1920). The younger novelist Vicente Blasco Ibáñez (1869-1928) bridged the realist-modernist transition and was the first Spanish writer since Cervantes to gain substantial notice outside his country. A prominent anti-monarchist who spent years in prison and in exile, he is best known for *The Four Horsemen of the Apocalypse*.

From the Spanish-American War until the Falangist victory in 1939, prose writers and poets alike were swept along by a wave of political and philosophical awareness, expressions of which took all forms, from the near-Existentialist stance of Miguel de Unamuno (1864-1936) to the matter-of-fact observation of the vagaries of life that almost amounts to nihilism in the work of Pío Baroja y Nessi (1872-1956). Another important voice was that of José Ortega y

Gasset (1883-1955) who, in *The Revolt of the Masses*, argued for an intellectual elite to lead the aggrieved working class.

The poetry and drama of Federico García Lorca (1898-1936) contain echoes of these political and philosophical concerns but are so powerfully individual that they stand alone. Rich metaphors of violence and primitive sensuality, linked with lyrical images of the countryside around his native Granada, often combined with an almost childlike perception of the world, established Lorca as the most remarkable literary figure of this century in Spain.

Although no clear form or new tradition has emerged, the combination of Surrealist and Existentialist influences with the acute sociopolitical perceptions encouraged by Spain's recent history have created a fertile environment for modern Spanish literature. Significant figures include Nobel prize-winner Juan Ramón Jiménez, the dramatist Alejandro Casona and the novelists Camilo José Cela, Carmen Laforet and Juan Goytisolo.

Books about Spain

Spain has consistently inspired non-Spaniards with its sense of mystery and romance, and nowhere is this more obvious than in what has been written about it by foreigners of all statures and stamps. Approaches have varied from the conventional travelogue — of which Richard Ford's *Handbook for Travellers in Spain* (1845, reprinted 1966) is one of the earliest and most acutely observed examples — to much more personal accounts, to treatises on specific aspects of Spanish life or history and, simply, to novels set in Spain. The following offers no more than an introduction to the wide range of reading material available. *Spain*, by Jan Morris, is a descriptive and extremely readable introduction to Spain, both past and present, and is an excellent place to start.

A Visit to Spain, 1862, by Hans Christian Andersen, shows the country a century earlier, when he spent four months there traveling with a companion who was, fortunately for the resulting account, rather more pragmatic and less sentimental than he.

Iberia, by James Michener, offers a third perspective, through his evocative and often sensitive descriptions of the Spain that visitors would like to experience — and that some may actually find.

Death in the Afternoon, by Ernest Hemingway, is for many the classic book on Spain, despite its narrow focus. It remains the definitive account of the ritual and drama of the bullfight.

Homage to Catalonia, by George Orwell, is also too limited to do full justice to the shattering scale and tragedy of the Spanish Civil War. Nevertheless it presents an excellent picture of the war from the side of the Republicans and the International Brigades.

As I Walked Out One Midsummer Morning, by Laurie Lee, is an adventure at the twilight of adolescence, in which the author sets off from England, with only his fiddle for company, on a walk through Western Spain, ending in Andalucía at the outbreak of the Civil War.

A Rose for Winter, also by Laurie Lee, describes his emotional return 15yrs later, giving a rich and often poignant picture of a beloved country in the throes of deep and lasting change.

The Sun also Rises, by Ernest Hemingway, the book that established his reputation, is set partly in the Spain he described in *Death in the Afternoon*.

For Whom the Bell Tolls, also by Hemingway, is a powerful novel of the Civil War inspired by his experience of Spain at that time.

Fandango Rock, by John Masters, is a story of conflicting loyalties, set in a small town near a US Air Force base, in the Spain of the 1950s.

Catalina, by W. Somerset Maugham, approaches Spain in a more reflective vein, telling with delightful satire the story of a young girl whose vision of the Virgin leads to a sequence of remarkable events.

A Companion to Spanish Studies, edited by P. E. Russell, is an indispensable guide to history and culture.

The Defeat of the Spanish Armada, by Garrett Mattingly, is a brilliant exercise in history written for the general reader. Reading like a novel, it affords an illuminating glimpse into the politics and campaigns of Philip II and the Golden Age.

Spain: 1808-1939, by Raymond Carr, is a most authoritative and important book on the period by an acknowledged expert.

The Spanish Civil War, by Hugh Thomas, is certainly the best and most thoroughly researched book on the subject, and is recommended to anyone who wishes to gain more of an insight into modern Spain.

The Catalans, by Jan Read, describes the history of Catalunya and its contributions to culture and the arts from the earliest times to the recent achievement of local autonomy.

Music

The tradition of combined performance of words and music, as a form of courtly entertainment, developed in the 15thC during the reign of Ferdinand and Isabella. By the 17thC the court had moved to Madrid, where musical entertainments were performed in the Zarzuela Palace.

One of the most popular of these entertainments was written by the dramatist Lope de Vega in 1629, and a more specifically musical play, the style of which came to be known as the *zarzuela* (light opera), was popularized by Calderón de la Barca some 20yrs later. Although eclipsed for a time by the more fashionable Italian opera, *zarzuelas* regained popularity in the 19thC, perhaps because of their close resemblance to the operettas much in vogue throughout Europe at that time.

Spain, probably more than any other European country, has retained a strong and lively tradition of popular folk music and dance independent of her more formal musical heritage and often regionally distinct. Characteristic instruments include the oboe of Catalunya, the bagpipes of Galicia and the guitar of Andalucía. Certain traditional forms have acquired widespread popularity, notably flamenco which, in the 19thC, evolved from a Gypsy lament into the now familiar show of snapping fingers, pounding feet and swirling movements.

Some reconciliation between the folkloric and classical heritage occurred in the early 20thC, largely as a result of the efforts of Felipe Pedrell, the Catalan musicologist. Pedrell's interest in the folk tradition inspired composers such as Isaac Albéniz (1860-1909), Manuel de Falla (1876-1946), Enrique Granados (1867-1916) and, a generation later, Joaquín Rodrigo (born 1902) to incorporate essentially Spanish elements — particularly rhythms of dance and guitar music — in compositions of a conventional European classical style.

Falla wrote guitar music especially for Andrés Segovia (born 1893), a musician who did more than anyone to re-establish the guitar as a serious classical instrument. Segovia and his followers have not only commissioned new music for the guitar but have also adapted earlier composers, such as Bach, and resurrected the music of Spanish composers like Fernando Sor (1778-1839) and Francisco Tarrega (1852-1909), both supreme contributors to the repertoire of this essentially Spanish instrument.

Orientation map

National boundaries - - - -
Regional boundaries ········
International airports ✈
Autopistas
Principal roads
Principal railway lines

0   50   100   150   200 km
0   50   100 miles

San Sebastián
Bilbao
PAÍS VASCO
Vitoria
Pamplona
NAVARRA
Logroño
LA RIOJA
Soria
Sigüenza **33**
Guadalajara
ARAGON
Zaragoza
Huesca
Teruel
Cuenca
A MANCHA
Albacete
COMUNIDAD VALENCIANA
Valencia
Castellón de la Plana **5**
REGIÓN DE MURCIA
Murcia **40**
Elche **6**
Alicante
Cartagena
Águilas
ería

FRANCE
ANDORRA
CATALUNYA
Girona **26**   **3**
Lleida
Barcelona **35**
Tarragona **4**
44
41

ISLAS BALEARES
Mallorca **11**   **11**
Palma   **11**
11
Ibiza **10**   **10**
Ibiza
9
Formentera

Mallorca
11
Palma **39**
11   **11**
Menorca **12**
12 Mahón

MEDITERRANEAN SEA

Good beaches
1 Costa Verde
2 Golfo de Vizcaya
3 Costa Brava
4 Costa Dorada
5 Costa del Azahar
6 Costa Blanca
7 Costa del Sol
8 Costa de la Luz
9 Formentera
10 Ibiza
11 Mallorca
12 Menorca
13 Tenerife
14 Gran Canaria
15 Lanzarote

Historic buildings
16 Acueducto Romano
17 Alcázar
18 Alhambra
19 Burgos Cathedral
20 Catedral Nueva
21 Catedral Vieja
22 Coca Castle
23 Colegio de San Gregorio
24 El Escorial
25 Giralda
26 Girona Cathedral
27 León Cathedral
28 Mezquita-Catedral
29 Palacio Real
30 Paseo Arqueológico

31 Santiago de Compostela Cathedral
32 Sevilla Cathedral
33 Sigüenza Cathedral
34 Teatro Romano
35 Templo de la Sagrada Familia
36 Toledo Cathedral
37 Universidad

Natural sights
38 Altamira Caves
39 Artá Caves
40 Huerta del Cura
41 Ordesa National Park
42 Puerto de Pajares
43 Picos de Europa
44 Pyrenees
45 Rías Altas
46 Rías Bajas

35

Calendar of events

Almost every Spanish town has several of its own annual festivals and fairs. These are some of the better known and nationally celebrated events. See also *Public holidays* in *Basic information* and *Events* throughout the *A–Z*.

January
New Year's Day.
  Jan 2. *Granada*. Celebration of the 1492 Christian Reconquest.
  Jan 6. Day of the Kings. Gift-giving and processions.
  Jan 17. Fiesta de San Antonio. Parades, fireworks and ceremonies blessing domestic animals.
February
Feb 5. Commemoration of Santa Agueda.
  Feb 25. Vintage car rally from Barcelona to Sitges.
  Late Feb-early Mar. Carnaval in many cities.
March
Mar 12-19. *Valencia*. Las Fallas. Parades, bonfires and fireworks.
Easter
Holy Week. Extensive and solemn celebrations everywhere.
  Week after Easter. *Murcia*. Spring festival with parades, flower displays and floats.
April
Mid to late Apr. *Sevilla*. Feria de Sevilla, with processions, music and dancing.
  Sun after Apr 25. Pilgrimage from Tafalla to Ujue.
  Late Apr or first week in May. *Jerez de la Frontera*. Feria del Caballo. Flamenco competitions.
May
May 1. Labor Day.
  First Fri. *Jaca*. Celebration recounting the role of the women in repelling an Arab attack in 795.
  May 15-30. *Madrid*. Fiesta de San Isidro, with bullfights and other celebrations.
  Late May. *Sitges*. Festival where flowers cover the streets.
Pontevedra. Round-up of wild horses.
  Late May-early June, Corpus Christi. Devout processions at *Barcelona* and *Toledo*.
June
June 21-29. *Alicante*. Hogueras de San Juan. Parades and bonfires.
  June 23-28. *Barcelona*. Festival in Pueblo Español.
  June 24-29. *Burgos*. Fiesta de San Pedro. *Segovia*. Festivals associated with San Juan and San Pedro.
Sevilla. Folk dancing competitions.

  Late June-early July. *Granada*. Festival of music and dance.
July
July 6-14. *Pamplona*. Feria de San Fermín, with parades, bullfights and the celebrated running of the bulls.
  July 15-31. *Santiago de Compostela*. Feast of St James, with religious processions and fireworks.
  July 17-31. *Valencia*. Festival of St James, with flower battles and bullfights.
August
First week. *Málaga*. Celebrations involving parades and bullfights.
  All month. Cantabrian coast, especially *Bilbao*, *La Coruña* and *San Sebastián*. Festival of Semana Grande, with open-air concerts, plays, bullfights, dancing competitions and films.
  Aug 4-9. *Vitoria*. Fiesta de la Virgen Blanca.
  Aug 10. *El Escorial*. St Lawrence's Day, with bullfights and street celebrations.
  Aug 12-15. *Elche*. Mystery play.
  Aug 15. Assumption.
September
Early Sept. *Jerez de la Frontera*. Fiesta de la Vendimia. Colorful festival to celebrate the grape harvest.
  First week in Sept. *San Sebastián*. Competitions in Basque sports.
  Sept 19. *Oviedo*. Día de las Américas, with dancing, parades and bullfights.
  Sept 19-26. *Logroño*. Celebrations of the Rioja grape harvest.
  Sept 23-24. *Tarragona*. Festival of St Tecla, with folk dancing and human pyramids.
  Sept 24-28. *Barcelona*. Catalan festivities, in honor of the Virgen de la Merced, with dancing and bullfights.
October
Oct 7-15. *Avila*. Feria de Santa Teresa.
  Oct 12. Hispanic Day. Week of Oct 12. *Zaragoza*. Fiesta de la Virgen del Pilar.
November
Nov 1. All Saints' Day.
December
Dec 25. Christmas Day.

When to go

Personal interests dictate vacation choices in Spain just as often as the weather. Skiers find ideal conditions nearly every December-February in the Cantabrian Cordillera, in the Gredos near Madrid and, surprisingly, in the Sierra Nevada to the south. Sometimes skiing is possible as early as October and as late as April. However, those with expectations of a sea warm enough for swimming all year long are usually proved too optimistic. Only a few visitors will want to brave the waters of the east and south Mediterranean coasts from November to February. The season along the northwest Atlantic coast is confined to the period between late June and early September.

Cultural activities follow their own calendar. Formal seasons of opera, concerts and dance usually run from October to May, but there are summer art and music festivals throughout the country. From Holy Week until the harvest festivals of September, only a long streak of bad luck could deny visitors local folkloric fiestas of one kind or another on a two-week tour.

From mid-June to early September, anywhere south of Madrid can resemble a furnace, with temperatures rising beyond 95°F (35°C) for weeks on end. You may well find the stores and restaurants of the inland cities are closed during July and August. Air conditioning is far from universal in hotels, restaurants and public buildings. Taking all these factors into consideration, the best times for a warm-weather visit to Spain are May-June and September-October.

Where to go

Before any other Spanish cities, it is essential to visit Madrid, Barcelona and Sevilla. They harbor the great museums — the vitality, the creativity, the meaning of the nation, and the perspective on the many cultures that have shaped it. Close behind in relevance are the Christian pilgrimage center of Santiago de Compostela, the Moorish enclaves of Granada and Córdoba, and the Roman capitals of Mérida and Tarragona. Among the many smaller towns and cities that deserve attention are Ronda and Baeza in Andalucía, Cuenca and Toledo in the heartland, Santillana del Mar on the Cantabrian coast, Sigüenza northeast of Madrid, and Albarracín in the province of Teruel.

Sun-seekers who hope to have beaches to themselves should consider the largely undeveloped Atlantic Costa de la Luz, or the island of Formentera in the Islas Baleares. Those who prefer elegance with their sunbathing head for Marbella, on the Costa del Sol. For sunshine but moderate temperatures where Spanish tourists still outnumber foreigners, there are the shoreline resorts of Galicia and Asturias.

Gamblers will find casinos either in or within short drives of Alicante, Barcelona, Madrid, Málaga, Palma de Mallorca, San Sebastián, Santiago de Compostela and Valencia. Golfers will find many courses between Estepona and Torremolinos, as well as in or near every major city and on Mallorca. National reserves are set aside for hunters, primarily in the Pyrenees, the Gredos Mountains and the Sierra Nevada. Saltwater anglers head for Marbella and Estepona, trout fishermen for the Basque territories, and sailors for the Islas Baleares.

Area planners and tours

The provinces of Spain are grouped into 15 administrative regions that join districts of similar culture and history, often corresponding to the kingdoms that preceded the unification of Spain under Christian rule in the early 16thC. For the visitor's purpose, the country can be divided into six areas; each can be adequately explored in about a week, whether by driving tours or by day excursions from their principal cities. The areas are described below in approximate order of priority.

Madrid and the central tableland Madrid was imposed upon the outer territories as their capital in the 16thC and, despite past and future royal preferences for Toledo, Valladolid and Burgos, among others, it is still capital of Spain. Philip II decided to transform what was then a minor farming community into the capital of the new Catholic nation simply because it was at the approximate geographical center. As a result, its historic buildings are largely of the 18th and 19thC, with little sense of the earlier civilizations that shaped the country. However, the government ministries and Cortes (Parliament) are located in Madrid — a fact that attracts growing commercial and industrial interest. Long thought a city marked more by provincialism than sophistication, it now complements its numerous museums — including the renowned Prado — with grand boulevards, ultra-chic restaurants of international standing, nightclubs and discos that equal any in the country, and a growing share of multinational corporations in skyscraper districts that were fields only 20yrs ago.

The high plateau on which the city spreads is called the Meseta. Low rolling plains for the most part, it is broken by the granite peaks of the Sierra de Guadarrama and sparsely watered by the river Tajo and its tributaries. Within a 120km (75 mile) radius are several small cities that held proportionally far greater roles than Madrid in Spanish history before 1492. *Toledo*, to the sw, was capital to the Visigoths and Moors, home to the painter El Greco, and has one of Spain's most important cathedrals. To the nw is *El Escorial*, with the vast brooding monastery built by Philip II, *Segovia* and its functioning Roman aqueduct, and *Avila*, surrounded by intact battlemented walls that are little changed from the 11thC. To the s is *Aranjuez*, a favorite royal residence with an 18thC Bourbon palace on the scale of Versailles.

Andalucía Conventional images of Spain, with its white villages, Arab citadels, staccato bursts of flamenco, *matadores* and sun-drenched sands are brought to life in *Andalucía*. It comprises the southern tier of provinces, sweeping from Portugal to the se corner of Spain, and contains *Sevilla*, often called the most Spanish of cities. Cradle of the aristocracy, it is the location of two spring celebrations — one spiritual, one secular, both fervent — that are models to comparable occasions in every community of the land. Three religions meet in *Córdoba*, with one of only a few synagogues left in Iberia and a vast mosque of splendid proportions. *Granada* boasts the magnificent Alhambra hovering above the city, a grand complex of Moorish palaces and gardens. *Málaga* and *Cádiz* are robust seaports. Hill villages such as Ojén (see *Places nearby* in *Marbella*) draw the hedonists from the beach resorts on short outings into another world. The Moorish-Christian city of *Ronda*, high on a plateau split by a deep gorge, is the home of modern bullfighting, with its ancient Plaza de Toros.

Up on the ne border, near the n to s Madrid road, are the unspoiled medieval-Renaissance twin towns of *Ubeda* and Baeza (see *Place nearby* in *Ubeda*). The crowds of Northern Europeans and North Americans that come to Andalucía flock to the *Costa del Sol*. The most popular tourist centers along the coast are *Marbella*, the focus of sophistication, and the brasher resort, *Torremolinos*.

Catalunya and Aragón   These combined regions take up much of the NE quadrant, bounded on the N by the Pyrenees, on the E by the Mediterranean, and fading, in the W and S, into scarred, semi-arid uplands. Cosmopolitan *Barcelona* dominates, and its residents accept without a doubt the conviction that it is superior in every way to the upstart Madrid. As well as its cultural wealth, the seaport has closer bonds with the rest of Europe, commercially and intellectually, than Madrid. People settled in Barcelona in prehistoric times; they were followed by the Phoenicians, Greeks, Romans, Goths and Moors. All left their mark. Like Madrid, the capital of Catalunya serves as a starting point for day-trips to all parts of the region, aided by excellent highways running from the French border S and to the NW coast. Roman *Tarragona* lies to the S along the coastal route, and to the NE is *Girona*, an unjustly neglected city. To the W is *Zaragoza*, Spain's fifth-largest city, and, to the N, the mountain principality of *Andorra*. The craggy shoreline from the French border is called the *Costa Brava*, the first to be developed in the tourist boom that began in the 1950s. South of Barcelona is another string of resorts and beaches, the town of *Sitges* attracting the most attention.

Galicia to the Basque Country   The green Atlantic coast bears little physical resemblance to the countryside to the south. Almost daily rains, often no more than a brief drizzle, ensure a lush verdancy comparable to Ireland's, with which Galicia bears considerable empathy. Celts settled here and, subsequently, on the Emerald Isle, and the wail of the bagpipe (*gaita*) is still heard in the cities of Galicia. A coastal band about 48km (30 miles) wide (in terms of interest to visitors) runs N from the northern Portuguese border, then curls E along the Bay of Biscay, known here as the Mar Cantábrico, all the way to the frontier with France, E of San Sebastián. A dialect known as Gallego, a mixture of Portuguese, Celtic and Spanish, is spoken in the W, and in the E there is a distinct language called Vasco (Basque) that has defied certain identification. *Santiago de Compostela* was the destination of the pilgrims of the Middle Ages who journeyed across this territory from northern Europe to kneel at the shrine of St James. There were hospices and chapels all along the way; many are still open and in use. The important cities are *Bilbao*, *La Coruña*, *Oviedo*, *San Sebastián* and *Santander*.

León and Extremadura   To travel S through this vertical row of provinces is to encounter firsthand the heritage of the country. As the Catholic Spanish pushed back the Moors, they established cathedrals and castles to consolidate their hold on the territory. The northern lip of the region of *León* rises from tableland into mountains. To the S, the red city of *León* harbors a cathedral that overwhelms its setting, with the finest stained-glass windows in Spain. Farther S, *Salamanca* maintains a prominent university, built partly in the Middle Ages and partly in the Renaissance, and an enclosed plaza which has no equal. The two provinces of *Extremadura* contain the towns of the Conquistadors — *Trujillo*, *Cáceres* and *Guadalupe* — that profited from the triumphs of their sons but have attracted only slight attention from tourists. Finally, in *Mérida*, the Roman bridge, aqueduct and circus stand comparison with any site outside Italy.

Valencia and Murcia   The several provinces in these two regions bear the stamp of the Carthaginians and Romans in their irrigation networks and excavated villages. Much of the countryside is mountainous, but wide flat cultivated fields called *huertas* make a greater impression, lined with citrus trees that blossom twice a year and fill the air with fragrances. *Valencia* prospers from shipping, industry and agriculture. The coast to the N is called the *Costa del Azahar*, to the S, the *Costa Blanca*. Scandinavians, Germans and French overwhelm the beaches of both coasts from May to Sept, especially at *Alicante*, *Benidorm*, Javea and Castellón de la Plana.

Most cities and large towns in the areas specified above have railroad services and are linked, together with thousands of villages, by regular bus services. To savor the pulse and subtle distinctions of land and people, however, no method surpasses touring by car. Roads have improved substantially in the last decade, and those that have not simply encourage drivers to slow down and observe the scenery and sights. The terrain changes by the hour, and castles, monasteries and hidden villages continually crop up in regions that appear empty on a standard road map.

Most of the following tour routes are circular; others connect strings of resorts and cities. All can be begun at any convenient point. Most of the places along the way are outlined in the *A-Z*. The tours can be accomplished in a week, some in a day or two, and in total can constitute a fairly complete exploration of the disparate parts of Spain. Lodging of some kind can nearly always be found, even in summer or during fiestas. Leaving your accommodations unplanned allows freedom in itinerary, but if it *is* important to be certain of your hotel, reserve ahead and have written confirmation with you.

Route 1: A spiral around Madrid

The towns around the capital can be seen in easy day-trips, which involve spending each night in Madrid. Another way is to devote 4-7 days to a road trip circling Madrid and returning there to contemplate your experiences.

Head N along Paseo de la Castellana in Madrid toward Burgos, taking care to follow the proper turn where the highway branches just beyond the Chamartín railroad station and connects with the N1, and continue N for 66km (40 miles). About 2km (1¼ miles) beyond the town of Lozoyuela, turn left (W) onto the C604 to Rascafría (25km/15 miles). This road runs to the foothills of the Sierra de Guadarrama, bending SW along the river Lozoya. 2km (1¼ miles) beyond Rascafría is the 14thC Monasterio del Paular, designed by the architect of Toledo cathedral; part of the monastery is now a first-class hotel, and part is occupied by Benedictine monks, who permit visits (*closed Thurs*).

Follow the C604 for a further 27km (16 miles) SW, then turn right (N) onto the N601 over the mountain pass of Puerto de Navacerrada (snow might close the pass in winter months). Descend through evergreen forests, leaving behind the mountains which flatten for 17km (10 miles) to the town of San Ildefonso, also called La Granja. Philip V commissioned a palace and extensive gardens here, reminiscent of Versailles (see *Sights nearby* in *Segovia*). Segovia, with its functioning Roman aqueduct, a *parador* and two good restaurants is 11km (7 miles) farther on.

Take the N603, S out of Segovia, as far as the A6 *autopista* (30km/19 miles). Head N on the A6, leaving at the next exit, onto the N501, and travel W to *Avila* (28km/17 miles). This conspicuous walled town deserves an overnight stay. When you are ready to leave, drive W to the opposite side of town, picking up the

N110 for a short distance before forking to the left on the C502 and continuing through Solosancho, across the Adaja river and then into the Sierra de Gredos. Near the crest, a road branches right (w) toward Parador Nacional de Gredos, built to resemble a hunting lodge with a dining room from which to observe the unspoiled sierra. Afterward, return to the C502, heading s over the Puerto del Pico and descending to *Talavera de la Reina*, known for its flourishing porcelain industry more than for its charm.

If an overnight stop is required, head w, along the NV to Oropesa with its fine *parador* (see *Hotel nearby* in *Talavera de la Reina*) housed in a 14thC castle; otherwise continue 43km (27 miles) E to Maqueda, then bear SE on the N403 to *Toledo*. On the opposite side of the river Tajo, pick up the N400 (E) for *Aranjuez*, 44km (27 miles) away. The Spanish Bourbons had a palace here, damaged by war and fire, but now restored to a semblance of its former grandeur.

It is less than an hour N on the NIV to Madrid. Otherwise, take the unnumbered road E from Aranjuez to Colmenar de Oreja, and turn N for Chinchón (see *Places nearby* in *Madrid*) and one of the newest *paradores* in the chain. From there, it is a short drive back to the NIV.

Route 2: West and north of Madrid

Those already familiar with the inner ring of Segovia, Avila, Toledo and Aranjuez, or who simply wish to get off that beaten track, can choose this triangular tour through Castilla and León. They encounter fewer foreigners and gather insights into the region that sustained the Christian Reconquest before Madrid was designated the capital.

Follow the Gran Via in Madrid w and NW after it becomes Calle Princesa. This soon leads to the NVI and on to the excellent A6

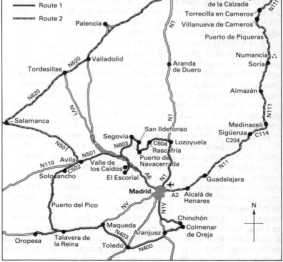

autopista, heading NW. After 21km (13 miles), make a detour to *El Escorial*, 11km (7 miles) to the SW. Here is the vast palace-monastery constructed for Philip II in the 16thC to a design by Juan de Herrera. On the way back to the A6, an access road leads off to the left toward the Valle de los Caídos (see *Sight nearby* in *El Escorial*), where Franco ordered a "basilica" to be dug into the side of the mountain in honor of the Civil War dead.

Once back on the A6 proceed NW. Take the first exit for a detour to Segovia, then continue to the next exit, W towards Avila. From there, it is 100km (62 miles) on the N501 over tawny tableland to *Salamanca*. The ancient medieval university city is a storehouse of Gothic and Renaissance architecture, with adjoining cathedrals and a peerless main square. Allow at least 24hrs to explore the city, perhaps staying at the new *parador* on the N side of the Tormes river. Follow the Valladolid road out of Salamanca, the N620, for 83km (52 miles) to Tordesillas (see *Place nearby* in *Valladolid*), the site of the 1494 signing of the Treaty of Tordesillas, in which Spain and Portugal divided suzerainty over the just-discovered New World. Juana the Mad sequestered herself in the Monasterio de las Claras for 44yrs after her husband died in 1506. There is a new *parador* S of town.

Valladolid is 30km (19 miles) farther on the N620. A frequent residence of noblemen and kings — Isabella and Ferdinand were married here — from its liberation from the Moors in the 12thC until its brief tenure as capital in the 16thC, Valladolid is now an industrial and agricultural center. Examples of important architectural modes of the early Renaissance are scattered throughout the city. The N620 continues NE, bypassing Palencia (as you should) and reaching *Burgos* after 121km (74 miles). This city also functioned intermittently as capital, and profited from that influence, with a cathedral commissioned by Ferdinand III. The old quarter surrounding it encourages strolling, and several traditional restaurants make it a logical stop at lunchtime.

The tour will have taken a leisurely 3-5 days to this point. If it is time to get back to Madrid, the N1 heads due south. The trip of 245km (152 miles) can be accomplished in about 3hrs, with time for lunch in Aranda de Duero. If you have another 3-4 days to spare, continue E on the N120 toward Logroño.

After 67km (42 miles) you will reach *Santo Domingo de la Calzada*, an unprepossessing town along its main street, but of considerable charm along the alleys to the left (N) side, especially around the cathedral. This was a pilgrimage stop on the Way of St James. Visit the church to see the caged chickens. On the same small square, a *parador* has been built in the ruins of a medieval hospice. Continue on the N120 and N232 to *Logroño*, the heart of the famous Rioja wine district. Several fair-to-good restaurants provide venues for testing the principal local product.

Heading S on the N111, the road slowly rises through vegetable fields and orchards along the Iregua river. After 30km (19 miles), an old stone bridge leads right (W) into Torrecilla en Cameros, backed by the peaks of the Sierra de Cameros Nuevo. It is worth looking at the appealing little church. Continue S on the N111, through the charming village of Villanueva de Cameros, onto the twisting road that climbs up to the Piqueras pass, and then down to intersection in Garray. Off a side road to the S is the site of the ancient city of Numancia (see *Sight nearby* in *Soria*), from where in 134BC Iberians held off the Romans for months. Only some foundations remain, as any archeological finds have been removed to museums. Back on the main road, it is 7km (4½ miles) to *Soria*, with its medieval ambience, and a small modern *parador*.

After 35km (22 miles) the N111 leads to Almazán, which retains vestiges of its medieval fortifications and several buildings of the period in which it was a frontier outpost of the kingdom of Aragón. The attractive main square has a Romanesque church and a Renaissance palace. Another 40km (25 miles) farther s, turn into the village of Medinaceli, where a 2ndC Roman arch, several small *palacios* and a 13thC castle still survive. Continuing s, turn right (sw) onto the N11 (not to be confused with the N111, which terminates slightly N). After 12km (7 miles) turn right onto the C114 to *Sigüenza*, a tidily picturesque town with a restored castle that is now an especially appealing *parador*, and a 12th-15thC cathedral next to a sloping arcaded *plaza mayor*.

A secondary road, the C204, leads through increasingly varied countryside to the N11, toward Madrid. The well-surfaced route fortunately bypasses Guadalajara (46km/29 miles). Another 25km (15 miles) farther on is the university town of Alcalá de Henares (see *Places nearby* in *Madrid*). Off to the left (s) is the handsome, bustling Plaza de Cervantes, named after the author, who was born here, and to its s is the Hostería del Estudiante, a former college dining hall, now a restaurant of the *parador* chain. Madrid is only 31km (19 miles) farther west.

Route 3: Andalucía

Leave Sevilla by the Avenida de Kansas City which becomes the NIV to Córdoba. Continue for 33km (21 miles) as far as Carmona (see *Places nearby* in *Sevilla*), with its Roman necropolis and crumbling Moorish walls, within which is a new *parador*. Head N of town on the C432 until it crosses the Guadalquivir, then turn E on the C431.

Up on the right (s), after about 50km (31 miles), stands the perfectly preserved castle of Almodóvar del Río. After another 20km (12 miles), look for the turn left (N) toward Medina Azahara. Once a Moorish palace complex of unimaginable splendor, the site now demands an active imagination to conjure its former dimensions, but there are exposed foundations and some structures to suggest its scope. Most artifacts discovered have been removed to the archeological museum in Córdoba. Return to the C431 and turn left (E) to *Córdoba* where the Mezquita, the second most important Moorish monument in Andalucía, should not be missed.

Córdoba deserves at least one day, and its hotels and restaurants help to fill the gaps between sightseeing. Leave the city by the Paseo de la Rivera, heading E along the N bank of the river, and on to the NIV. Continue as far as Andújar (77km/48 miles), a fortified town of prehistoric origin with a Roman bridge and, in the *plaza mayor*, Gothic and Renaissance buildings and a fountain. At Bailén, 27km (16 miles) farther E, there is Parador Nacional de Bailén, at the intersection with the N to s road NIV. Still heading E, now on the N322, don't pause in Linares, a mining town of little character, but wait until you reach *Úbeda*, one of the first towns in Andalucía to be recaptured from the Moors. Among its monumental center of fine Isabeline and Plateresque structures is a 16thC *parador*. On leaving, find the N321 heading sw. Go through Baeza (see *Place nearby* in *Úbeda*), another Renaissance town of homier proportions, and on toward *Jaén*, where, if it is lunchtime, there is a modern *parador* next to a ruined castle on a cliff high above the city. Otherwise, turn s on the N323 E of Jaén and continue toward Granada, which is 90km (56 miles) to the south. After rising through blunted uplands, the road descends to a fertile plain and runs toward *Granada*, set against the blue-gray backdrop of the Sierra Nevada. The Alhambra of the Moors rears above the city, in which you should plan at least an overnight stay.

The N323 continues s, skirting the w end of the sierra, passing sugar-cane fields and reaching the Mediterranean after 70km (44 miles). Turn right (w) onto the N340 toward Málaga for the first of the popular Costa del Sol resorts, *Nerja*, on a promontory above the sea. Nearby are caves in which prehistoric artifacts have been discovered, and music and dance festivals are held in summer. *Málaga*, the largest city on the Costa del Sol and a major seaport, lies 53km (34 miles) to the east. Its attractions include a ruined Moorish Alcazaba, a Roman amphitheater, and a *parador* on the Gibralfaro hill which is blessed with a dining balcony overlooking the port.

The almost continuous band of Costa del Sol resorts begins 5km (3 miles) sw of Málaga, with *Torremolinos*, Benalmádena and *Fuengirola*. Although diverting for those who choose to spend time on their beaches and in their bars, they have little to delay sightseers. From Fuengirola, a road goes n to *Mijas*, a hill town too close to the coast to avoid commercialization but maintaining a measure of its former charm, an exceptionally pleasant hotel, and several good restaurants.

Back on the coastal N340 road, head w to the stylish resort, *Marbella*, with its luxury hotels and yachts to the w of the center, and a concentration of chic bars and *boîtes* clustered around Puerto Banús. At San Pedro de Alcántara, 10km (6 miles) farther, a right turn n points toward *Ronda* (C339). The once terrifying corniche road has been widened and straightened, and the old hill town can be reached in under an hour. One part of the old town maintains its Moorish character, the other a bullring that may be the oldest in Spain. The present form of bullfighting is said to have been developed here.

Leave Ronda along the C339 heading for Sevilla. After 12km (7 miles) turn left (s) along an unnumbered road for Benaoján and the Pileta Caves (see *Sights nearby* in *Ronda*). Prehistoric wall paintings are the most intriguing remnants of Stone Age inhabitants, but there are ceramics and weapons as well. Return to the C339 and continue to its intersection with the N342. Turn left (w) toward Arcos de la Frontera. From here, the jagged wilderness softens to rounded hills embracing quilted plains. Just as the land threatens to flatten completely, a granite ridge erupts from the valley. The attractive town of *Arcos de la Frontera*, which has a *parador*, crowds the summit.

Leave Arcos by the N342 to *Jerez de la Frontera*, 24km (14 miles) to the w, where guided tours of the sherry *bodegas* are available (see *Spanish wines* in *Special information*). From Jerez, take the A4 *autopista* to Sevilla, 84km (52 miles) to the north.

Route 4: Home of the Conquistadors
Extremadura, in the far w bordering Portugal, is an unfortunately neglected region with majestic plains of rippling grain and shimmering pastures, low, rounded mountains, and cities that illustrate nearly 2,000yrs of national achievement.

For a four-day excursion, follow the NV sw from Madrid for 117km (72 miles) to *Talavera de la Reina*. Turn left (s) along the C503 toward Guadalupe. After 29km (17 miles), at La Nava de Ricomalillo, the road becomes the C401, and the countryside grows more scenic on the approach to the Puerto de San Vicente pass. Within 36km (23 miles) is *Guadalupe*, where a fantastical castle-monastery bristles with turrets and towers against the gray-green folds of the Sierra de Guadalupe. Continue on the C401

sw for 50km (31 miles) to Zorita, and once there head N on the C524 for 28km (17 miles) to *Trujillo*. At the top of this hill town is a shambling irregular square dominated by a Moorish-Spanish castle. From here, take the N521 to *Cáceres*, with its walled medieval quarter which is best explored by moonlight.

Heading s again, the N523 runs for 90km (56 miles) over a range of low hills and past groves of cork trees to Badajoz, close to the Portuguese border. Before reaching Badajoz, take the NV 66km (41 miles) E to the Roman town of *Mérida*. Evidence of its occupation lies in a bridge that is still in use and in an evocative and impressive theater complete with sculptures. Visigoths and Moors have also left their mark, as in the convent, now transformed into a *parador*. Sevilla is only 200km (124 miles) s from here on the N630.

Route 5: Catalunya
Prosperous Catalunya, in the NE corner of the country, is blessed with miles of beaches, fertile valleys, pine-covered uplands, the craggy Pyrenees, and Spain's cosmopolitan second city, *Barcelona*. After at least three days there, set out to the NE along the Gran Via, which quickly becomes the A19 *autopista*. After

about 28km (17 miles), this highway merges with the N11, which hugs the coast through several beach towns of little interest. Just beyond Calella, the N11 bends inland. Turn right toward Blanes (see *Places nearby* in *Sant Feliu de Guíxols*) on the C253 for the beginning of the *Costa Brava*. The corniche twists and curls along the indented shoreline, with repeated viewpoints over rocky coves and crescent beaches. The principal resorts along the way — clogged with buses and tourists from June to Sept — are Lloret de Mar, Tossa de Mar (for both see *Places nearby* in *Sant Feliu de Guíxols*) and *Sant Feliu de Guíxols* itself. From here, find the C250, the inland road for *Girona*. This provincial capital is an unappreciated city, ignored by tourists intent on reaching Barcelona and the southern beaches, and is worth at least a few hours' exploration.

Pick up the N11 N of the city, continuing through Figueres, 27km (16 miles) to the north. From the center of Figueres, take the C252 NE toward Llançà (Llansà). In Llançà, head SE for 17km (10 miles) through rocky hills to Cadaqués. Situated at the rim of a horseshoe bay, it still functions as a fishing port despite its popularity in summer, and retains an attractive *plaza mayor* with a 17thC church.

Return to the road branching toward Roses, another combination of fishermen's village and resort, which began as the Greek colony of Rhoda. Continue W on the C260, passing once again through Figueres and following the signs for Olot (to the W). The C260 soon joins the C150 at the pretty village of Besalú. Continue on this road through pleasant countryside, through Olot to Ripoll, which is the location of a notable medieval Benedictine monastery.

From Ripoll, it is about 100km (62 miles) S on the N152 to Barcelona, perhaps breaking the journey for lunch or for the night at the *parador* outside *Vic*. Otherwise, continue N on the N152. Within 14km (8 miles) at Ribes de Freser, a rack railroad climbs through exciting alpine scenery to the winter resort of Núria. This method of transport (the only way to reach it) takes about 1hr

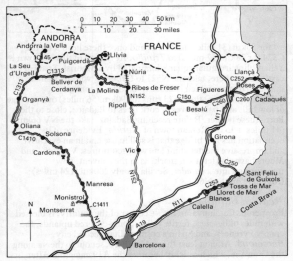

(return) and is worth the fairly expensive fare; schedules vary with the season. Continuing along the winding N152 requires diligent attention by the driver, but passengers are treated to splendid views of the valley below. The road leads past La Molina with its two winter resorts that have drawn international sports competitions, and on to Puigcerdà, on the French border. The geopolitical curiosity, Llívia, a Spanish village entirely within French territory, lies 6km (4 miles) farther N, at the end of a connecting road that is technically neutral. Back in Puigcerdà, take the C1313 SW for 50km (31 miles), past lovely scenery and through the mountain villages of Bellver de Cerdanya and Prulláns, to *La Seu d'Urgell* (where there is a *parador*). From here, the C145 climbs N into *Andorra* and its capital city, Andorra la Vella, which is 20km (12 miles) away.

After a visit, return to La Seu d'Urgell and continue S along the C1313, following the Segre river. Just beyond Organyà, the road skirts the W bank of a man-made lake, then crosses E to the village of Oliana. After 10km (6 miles) turn left (E) and follow the C1410 to Solsona with its 13thC castle and 12thC cathedral. The road descends for 20km (12 miles) to Cardona and its castle, which is now a *parador*. Continue S for 32km (20 miles) to Manresa, with its 14th-16thC cathedral remarkable for its exceptionally wide vaulting. At Monistrol, a further 15km (9 miles) S, either turn right (W) onto a twisting road leading to the monastery of Montserrat (see *Place nearby* in *Barcelona*), or park at the railroad station and take the rack railroad there. From Monistrol, proceed S to the N11, and thence to Barcelona.

Route 6: Palma de Mallorca to Cabo de Formentor

The N shore of the island of *Mallorca* is lined with an unexpectedly high and rugged sierra. A tour along the length of the mountain chain can be accomplished in one long day, but this is arduous driving along corniche roads, so two days should be scheduled, if possible.

Head W from Palma on the C719 shore road toward Palma Nova and Andraitx. With rare exceptions, the resort towns S of this road have spoiled the once glorious beaches there. Continue through the village of Andraitx, heading N on the C710 toward Bañalbufur and Puerto de Sóller. Winding and narrow, the road climbs ever higher up the face of the sierra, with viewpoints (*miradores*) at Ricardo Roca and Las Animas. Terraces, cut into the slopes that fall to the sea, support rows of almond trees, grapevines, vegetables and fruit trees. Continuing up toward the top of the ridge you come to Valldemosa, where George Sand and Chopin spent an apparently miserable winter in 1838. Through this association it has suffered from a certain amount of commercialization, but remains a lovely town of honey-colored houses with green shutters and gardens. The monastery above the town contains the cells in which the writer and composer purportedly stayed. Outside, densely cultivated enclosed gardens afford views down over flourishing green fields.

The C710 continues NE past stone walls and terraced gardens interspersed with glimpses of the sea and through Deyá, home of the writer, Robert Graves; the town appears to cling to the mountainside. After about 12km (7 miles) the road begins to descend to Sóller, which is linked by a picturesque tram to its port, a nearly enclosed bay with several modest hotels and restaurants and a naval base. From Sóller a journey of less than 1hr on the C711 — a road which climbs over the crest of the mountains — takes you back to Palma. Beware of the numerous hairpin bends.

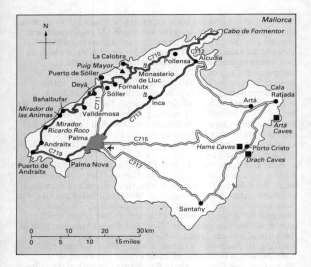

To continue NE, take the C710 up and over the ridge past the village of Fornalutx and Puig Mayor, which is 1,445m (4,740ft) high. For a scenic detour, just past Puig Mayor take a side road to the hamlet of La Calobra. 11km (6½ miles) farther on the C710 is the Monasterio de Lluc, with its museum of artifacts belonging to the earliest settlers on the island. Another 26km (16 miles) of winding road leads to Pollensa and to the hotels and restaurants of its port. For a heartstopping trip with spectacular views, take the corniche road to the tip of Cabo de Formentor. The round trip to Palma via Alcudia and Inca on the C712 and C713 takes about one hour.

Where to stay in Spain

With advance planning, there is no reason to spend more than an emergency night or two in a hotel or inn that does not meet international standards of comfort. On the contrary, the lodging places can be as memorable as their nearby vistas and monuments. However, it must be conceded that the average Spanish hotel is no better than the average hotel in any other nation of the developed world. The tourist boom that started in the 1950s proved irresistible to speculators in pursuit of easy pesetas. Lacking taste, proper financing and management skills, they were and are responsible for the rows of shabby high-rise blocks and overgrown, unfinished structural skeletons that blight many coastal regions. Despite their numbers, these are nearly always avoidable.

Standards
Every single establishment offering beds and/or food to the public is subject to regular inspection and classification by the government. While the standards applied are primarily quantitative, taking into consideration minimal room dimensions and numbers of elevators and rooms with baths, they do give

useful guidance. Signs near the entrance of hotels announce these designations. They are rectangular, with white letters and symbols against a light blue background.

An **H**, underlined by one to five stars (they look more like stylized suns), denotes a hotel with graduated levels of services and facilities. At minimum (one star), hotels have central heating, an elevator in buildings of five floors or more, at least one telephone per floor, shared bathrooms, laundry and ironing service, and a dining room. At the top (five stars), guests are guaranteed air conditioning, elevators, public rooms, a bar, telephones and baths with every bedroom, a hairdresser and, in cities, a garage. An **HR** designation indicates a residential hotel, often distinguished only by the absence of a formal restaurant. There is usually a Spanish-style cafeteria instead, with limited menus and waiter service. **HA** is an apartment hotel, usually without bars and restaurants, but frequently offering kitchen facilities with some of the bedrooms.

Among the generally reliable hotel chains are **Hesperia** (17 hotels, largely in the NE), **HOTASA** (29 hotels in a few larger cities and in several resort areas; usually symbolized by double animal heads), **HUSA** (64 hotels from one to five stars, in most major cities, with 21 in Barcelona alone), **Meliá** (18 hotels in Madrid and the southern cities) and **Sol** (50 hotels, mostly in Mallorca and the Mediterranean resort areas). With few exceptions, these 178 hotels were constructed within the last two decades, in the crisp, comfortable and essentially anonymous "international" style.

Reception and personnel

When you check in at the *recepción* desk you will be asked to leave your passport for registration, but it will be returned within an hour or two. If the hotel has a currency exchange facility it will be located at the reception desk; however, rates of exchange are generally more favorable at a bank.

The old fashioned type of *conserje* (hall porter) is on the decline. That cherished individual once seemed a paragon of fatherly expertise, whether in giving directions, obtaining tickets, arranging transportation, securing guides, or confiding the names of unspoiled clubs and restaurants. All this he conveyed with dazzling multilingual virtuosity. The *conserje* still does these things, in principle, but the position now seems populated by upstarts, who tout dreary "City by Night" bus tours, flashy tourist traps, and costly restaurants and stores, presumably to reap some personal commission. Although there are exceptions, nowadays the *conserje* is best employed posting letters and handing out room keys. With regard to tipping, a small amount based on the length of your stay is appropriate.

The paradores

Nothing so enhances Spain's enviable touristic stature as the *parador nacional* system. Freely translated as a "stopping place," the word *parador* is hardly ever used to describe any other kind of inn or hotel. More than a third of the over 80 *paradores* are former castles, convents, palaces, mansions or royal hunting lodges, and many of the others are new buildings set within ancient fortifications. Old or new, most occupy high ground or seaside locations with pleasant, or even spectacular, vistas. Whatever their age or origins, rooms are usually spacious and decorated with taste and restraint, often including fine antique furniture, suits of armor, tapestries and splendid ceramic tiles, all kept beautifully clean by the diligent staff. Bathrooms are commodious, with deep, long baths and vast towels. Dining rooms serve prodigious portions of regional recipes, with selected local wines to complement them.

The first *parador* opened in Gredos in 1928; the intention of the chain was to provide food and lodging in districts lacking in good hotels. The popularity of the *paradores* is ever increasing, and they still represent good value although they are no longer bargains. Their drawbacks are an occasional whiff of institutional sterility, especially in the modern *paradores*, their shortage of recreational facilities, and the fact that they do not have discos or bars that stay open later than midnight.

Non-residents can eat at *paradores* and, except for Sunday lunch, when local families come to eat there, and days when there are functions, there is rarely a wait to be seated. A la carte and table d'hôte selections are available, and specialties of the house and region, written in red ink on the menu, are translated (with sometimes amusing inexpertise) into French, German and English. The three-course *menú del día* is changed daily and, although it might repeat items from the à la carte section, its price will be lower, but wine, bottled water, coffee and taxes will be extra. A particular delight are *entremeses*, a feature at all *paradores*, often available only at lunchtime. The word means "between tables," a reference to the practice of taking snacks or *tapas* between meals. They arrive on dozens of leaf-shaped dishes, each containing a different treat: *chorizo*, fried squid, meatballs, sardines, potato salad and many other delicacies. Although light by Iberian standards, they constitute an ideal lunch.

Since most *paradores* are small, tour groups are rare. For the same reason, advance reservation is wise; allow three months for high season and at least one for winter. As reserving can be complicated, it is advisable to leave this to a travel agent. (For details of individual *paradores*, see hotels in the *A-Z*.)

Food and drink

One can hardly pretend that Spanish cooking ranks among the world's grand cuisines. Spanish food is the food of the people, and it is sustenance, not elaborate preparation, that is the ruling factor in the kitchen. Spanish notions of hospitality embrace the conviction that to appear parsimonious is dishonor to the host, and so portions of food are typically abundant. At finer restaurants, however, a form of *nouvelle* cooking called *nueva cocina* has taken hold, with the lightness in saucing and content that term implies. (See *Words and phrases* for more common translations.)

Some typical dishes

The best-known dish beyond Spanish borders is *paella*, the only certain ingredients of which are rice flavored with that most costly of spices, saffron; the rest depends on what is available. Usually, this means clams, mussels, chicken, prawns, lobster, squid, sweet red-pepper strips and peas, all simmered in a colorful mixture. When skillfully executed, the ingredients are blended in such a way that each flavor contributes to the others while uncannily retaining its identity. Although Valencian in origin, it is found in every corner of the land.

Next in popularity is the Andalucian cold soup, *gazpacho*, a subtle blend of uncooked tomatoes, bread chunks, garlic, oil, salt, onions and a splash of vinegar. It is served chilled, sometimes in a bowl nestled in ice, and sprinkled with a variety of garnishes. In Málaga, a "white" *gazpacho* made of garlic, ground almonds and grapes may be found. *Zarzuela de mariscos* takes its name from a characteristic light opera and might be translated as "operetta of seafood." Again, any ingredients that come to hand might be used in what is essentially a soup-stew, similar to the Marseille *bouillabaisse*, of lobster, prawns, squid, clams, mussels, eel and salt-water fish. The dish is at its best in Catalunya, but is a staple of all those districts bordering the sea.

The elaborate concoction *cocido madrileño* typically combines joints of chicken, pieces of sausage, veal, ham, beef, pork fat, chick-peas, cabbage, potatoes and carrots, traditionally served as three courses. First is the strained broth, with fine noodles added at the last minute; next are the drained vegetables, and finally the meats. Every region of Spain has its variation of *cocido*, but the classic version is that of the central Meseta. Of the several varieties of the delicious *manchego* cheese from La Mancha, the soft *fresco* is perhaps the most palatable. Other types include one soaked in oil (*en aceite*) and another, which is hard, crumbly, mature and pungent.

Regional dishes

In a country where the separatist instinct runs deep, regional cooking styles are, if anything, more distinct than ever. The opinion, prevalent in France, that Spanish cooking improves in relation to its proximity to the Pyrenees and the glories of the Gallic kitchen, is borne out by the fact that the Basques and Catalans are the most accomplished of Spanish cooks.

Andalucía

Locals claim that they eat only to live, which may account for the fact that a platter of seemingly commonplace fried fish is the favored dish. However, *gazpacho* and *sangría* originated here, and this is the place to discover how that cold tomato soup and red wine punch were meant to taste. Try the almond-based "white *gazpacho*" and *riñones al Jerez* (kidneys sautéed in sherry), and don't neglect *fritura mixta* (a mixture of incomparably delicate and light-fried fish). Andalucía boasts a remarkable variety of seafood: for example, *lubina al sal* (sea-bass baked in a shell of salt which gives a sublime tenderness), and species of prawn and clawless lobster that escape classification. Local table wines are adequate, but sherry is the memorable tipple, drunk before or after meals according to the degree of dryness.

Aragón

Caught between the superior kitchens of the Basques and the Catalans, the cooking of Aragón leaves a pale impression. However, pork and rabbit dishes are surprisingly tender and tasty, and *chilindrón* (a savory blend of tomatoes, garlic and peppers, often with pieces of ham) is a delicious sauce cooked with any meat or poultry. Also try *cochifrito* (fricassée of young lamb) and salted cod *al ajoarriero* (in a hot garlic and tomato sauce). Ordinary table wines may have a metallic aftertaste; the robust wines of the Cariñena district are preferable.

Asturias

Gastronomes who note a family resemblance between Asturian cuisine and regional cuisines in France point to the *cassoulet* type of stew, *fabada*, a hearty concoction of white beans, pork and blood sausage, which may also include ham or pig's feet. Also memorable is *caldereta asturiana* (fish stew reminiscent of Catalan *bullabesa*); one of its ingredients is hot pepper, an unusual touch in a country where fiery seasonings are not common. Finally, try *queso de cabrales*, a piquant cheese that blends the milk of goats, cows and sheep. The local drink is an effervescent cider (*sidra*).

Castilla la Nueva

Castilians make the best of their indigenous ingredients, and the most characteristic recipe is *cocido madrileño* (see *Some typical dishes*, above). *Sopa de ajo* is a simple dish where garlic cloves and chunks of bread are cooked in oil with an egg on the top. *Cochinillo asado* (roast suckling pig) is almost always delicious, but can be off-putting to those unaccustomed to eating meat quite so close to its original state. Thin wild *espárragos* and tiny nugget *fresas* must be tried, as well as *churros* (lengths of fried dough dusted with sugar), which make a tasty alternative to the usual hard roll for breakfast, and *queso manchego* (the mild, semi-soft cheese of La Mancha). Drinkable table wines come from Valdepeñas.

Catalunya

For the uninitiated visitor, *zarzuela* (see *Some typical dishes*, above) might exemplify the Catalan spirit of culinary adventure, as might *bullabesa*, a related fish soup-stew. Hot or pungent spices are more readily used here than in any other region, in recipes such as *romescu* (a tomato, pepper and oil sauce) and *ali-oli* (a strong garlic mayonnaise spread over game or pork). The firm-fleshed *rape* (monkfish) may be unfamiliar to foreigners, but is worth trying however it is cooked. *Jabalí* (wild boar) and *conejo* (rabbit) are often astonishingly tender, and salads combining vegetables and fish make delicious, light summer meals. Finally, try *habas* (white beans with sausage), also called *faves*. For wine, Torres is a reliable and prominent firm, and dessert wines under the Masía Bach label are often exceptional.

Extremadura

Acorn-fed hogs and merino sheep provide the staple meat diet of the Extremaduran kitchen, notably in superior hams, the sausage called *chorizo*, and tender baby lamb. Typical dishes include *caldereta* (lamb stew), *cocido* (boiled chicken, pork and vegetables), *migas* (fried breadcrumbs) and *gazpacho* (see *Some typical dishes*, above). Roast kid and partridge can be very good, as can melons, and the cheeses known as *queso de oveja* and *queso de cabra*. Table wines can be harsh, but the lusty Salvatierra and Mérida red wines are exceptions.

Galicia

There are those who assert that Galician cuisine surpasses those of all other regions, although consensus favors the Basque and Catalan. Certainly there are notable specialties. *Caldo gallego* (meat broth crowded with beans, potatoes and cabbage) has achieved widespread favor. *Empanadas* are flat pies with a variety of meat or fish fillings. Shellfish are plentiful and varied in the region which produces a third of the nation's annual catch. Scallops, clams and prawns are invariably good, while oysters, it must be said, are frequently not. Lobsters of all types are excellent but expensive. Meat and fish roasted over open fires are popular, and tripe, in the form of *callos a la gallega*, is enjoyed by natives if not by visitors. *Pimientas de Padrón* (small triangular green peppers deep-fried and heavily salted) make a popular *tapa*. Local cheeses are soft and mildly flavored. Wines of note include the light white Albariño and the sturdy red Ribeiro.

Valencia

This region is especially conducive to the growing of rice, the basic ingredient of the best Valencian dishes, including of course the famous *paella* (see *Some typical dishes*, above). *Arroz con pollo* (rice with chicken and peas) is the conventional alternative, although it is likely to seem rather pallid after a good *paella*. Local wines are not memorable, tending to be full-bodied and strongly alcoholic, but those produced around Alicante are worth tasting.

Vascongadas y Navarra

In these regions, the sauce is an integral part of most dishes. Ingredients are simmered slowly to help the natural flavors reveal themselves. Cod is a favorite, as in *bacalao al pil-pil* (simmered in garlic, olive oil and possibly hot red peppers). *Trucha a la Navarra* (freshwater trout marinated in wines and spices, poached in the liquid, and stuffed with air-cured ham) and *calamares en su tinta* (tender young squid in a sauce made from their own ink) are also popular. *Angulas* (baby eels), boiled in oil and brought to the table popping and snapping, should be twirled around a wooden fork and eaten whole, an experience not unlike eating "spaghetti with eyes." Cheeses are excellent, but the wines are not. Choose those of adjacent Rioja instead.

Restaurants, tapas and meriendas bars, and cafeterias

As in most Latin countries, the main meal of the day is lunch, which is not eaten until mid-afternoon. Restaurants are open from 1-4pm but most customers do not arrive until 2pm, and then tend to linger over coffee and brandy past closing time. Given that custom, the average Spaniard doesn't even begin to think about dinner until 10pm, and in the cities, people often arrive at restaurants at 11.30pm or midnight. However, as a concession to foreigners, most restaurants are open by 9pm.

In restaurants, service is nearly always attentive and efficient, sometimes to the point of brusqueness. Yet, in the expectation that patrons will linger as long as they wish, waiters tend to bring the bill only after some persuasion. Restaurants are required to produce a fixed-price menu (*menú del día*) consisting of an appetizer, main course, dessert and drink, at a price that is lower than a comparable selection from the à la carte menu. Unfortunately, it tends to include the least exciting dishes, and owners are understandably reluctant even to mention it.

Nearly every bar serves *meriendas* (snacks) from early morning to late evening. In some cases, these are merely sandwiches (slices of meat or cheese between pieces of toasted bread) or *bocadillos* (the same fillings in split hard rolls). But in most cases, set out on the bar or available to order is an array of appetizing delicacies. *Tapas* are served in a small dish that holds no more than two or three nibbles. When served on a larger plate they are called *raciones*. Examples include: wedges of the firm potato and egg omelet called a *tortilla*; *ensaladillas* (tomato, lettuce, onion and tuna salads); *empanadillas* (half-moon turnover pastries with meat filling); chunks of cheese or *chorizo* sausage; mussels; clams; baby eels boiled in oil flavored with pepper and garlic; anchovies in oil; *boquerones fritos* (fried whitebait); several varieties of mushroom, marinated, pickled or fried; *brochetas* (skewers) of pork or fish; thin slices of the wonderful *jamón serrano* (air-cured ham), sometimes served on bread rubbed with tomato pulp and olive oil;

grilled prawns; breaded fried octopus rings; sliced salami; snails in a sauce, or cold and unadorned.

There are also two types of cafeteria which often stay open past midnight. One is *auto-servicio*, where the customer makes a selection from a service counter. The other is strictly table-service, but with a shorter menu and longer hours than a restaurant. Fast food is often featured along with *tapas* and *raciones*.

Drink

Most restaurants and all bars have a cheap house wine, often decanted from cellar kegs and served by the glass or carafe. Local bottlings can be acidic, sharp or merely lifeless, but on the whole, the range is adequate to excellent. The vintages of the Rioja district are superior, often purchased by winemakers of other countries for blending with their own pressings. (For further information, see *Spanish wines* in *Special information*.)

Coffee is very good, but tea is brewed with bags. Hot chocolate is thick and very rich, and *horchata* is a milky, almond-based cool drink that should be tried. The champagne and sorbet drink known as *sorbeta de limón* is refreshingly cool on a hot day. *Heladerías* (ice cream stores) make lemonade. *Café irlandés* (Irish coffee) is popular, its Spanish counterpart being *carajillo con nata* (coffee with coñac topped with whipped cream). *Sangría* is the famous Andalucian iced punch comprising wine, fruit juice, lemonade, soda, brandy and slices of orange and lemon. Among the stiffer drinks is the *sol y sombra*, made of brandy and *anis* and ensuring a good night's sleep. Spanish *coñacs* (brandies) are thick and sweet to smooth and fiery.

Shopping

As a rule, stores open 9.30am-1.30pm and 4-7pm in winter, and 9.30am-1.30pm and 5-8pm in summer. Some department stores, however, stay open throughout the day. Spain is well known for its leather goods, such as handbags and shoes; these can be found in all major towns and cities and especially in the major shopping areas of *Madrid* and *Barcelona*. These two cities are also centers of the Spanish art and antique world, and there are bargains for those with some knowledge of these subjects.

For more lively shopping, try the local open-air markets. These colorful affairs, found in virtually every town, display a wide variety of produce supplied by local farmers. The food here is generally fresher and less expensive than in stores or in supermarkets. Opening days and times vary, so it is advisable to check beforehand at the Spanish Tourist Office or at the town itself. Although prices may be marked, bargaining is acceptable and certainly adds interest.

Regional specialties

Perhaps surprisingly, the Islas Baleares specialize in high-quality, reasonably priced leather goods. Artificial Mallorcan pearls, in soft colors, are made up into attractive jewelry, and local ceramics and glassware are very popular. Folk costumes, flamenco dresses and their associated accessories are readily available in *Sevilla*, which also supports a thriving handicraft industry, including the production of fine lace and embroidered cloth. *Toledo* is renowned for its damascened (inlaid) steel, a craft which has been centered here for many centuries, and is also famous for its embossed leather. See also *Shopping* throughout the *A-Z*.

Clothing sizes

When shops give clothing sizes in inches or centimeters, use the following conversion scale to determine the correct size

12 *in*	16	20	24	28	32	36	40	44	48
30 *cm*	40	50	60	70	80	90	100	110	120

When standardized codes are used, although these may be found to vary considerably, the following provides a useful guide.

Women's clothing sizes

UK/US sizes	8/6	10/8	12/10	14/12	16/14	18/16
Bust *in/cm*	31/80	32/81	34/86	36/91	38/97	40/102
Hips *in/cm*	33/85	34/86	36/91	38/97	40/102	42/107

Men's clothing sizes

European code (suits)	44	46	48	50	52	54	56
Chest *in/cm*	34/86	36/91	38/97	40/102	42/107	44/112	46/117
Collar *in/cm*	13½/34	14/36	14½/37	15/38	15½/39	16/41	16½/42
Waist *in/cm*	28/71	30/76	32/81	34/86	36/91	38/97	40/102
Inside leg *in/cm*	28/71	29/74	30/76	31/79	32/81	33/84	34/86

Men's and women's shoe sizes

UK/US sizes	3/4½	4/5½	5/6½	6/7½	7/8½	8/9½	9/10½	10/11½	11/12½
European	36	37	38	39	40	41	42	43	44

Spain A-Z

The *A-Z* section lists the best-known and most interesting sights and places in Spain. Opening times and entry details are frequently erratic and subject to change. Monday is a standard closing day for museums, but is by no means universal. Cameras are usually permitted, except during church services and sometimes only hand-held and without a flash.

Spanish names are used for *A-Z* entries, with English translations in brackets where relevant. In the region of Catalunya, the local spelling of place names is usually given with the Castilian version in brackets.

Sights and places of interest — a selection

Historic buildings and plazas

Acueducto Romano
  See *Segovia*
Alcázar
  See *Sevilla*
Alhambra
  See *Granada*
Colegio de San Gregorio
  See *Valladolid*
El Escorial
Giralda
  See *Sevilla*
Mezquita-Catedral
  See *Córdoba*
Palacio Real
  See *Madrid*
Paseo Arqueológico
  See *Tarragona*
Plaza mayor
  See *Salamanca*

Teatro Romano
  See *Mérida*
Universidad
  See *Salamanca*

Cathedrals

Burgos
Girona
León
Salamanca
Santiago de compostela
Sevilla
Sigüenza
Templo de la Sagrada Familia
  See *Barcelona*
Toledo

Attractive small towns and villages

Albarracín
  See *Teruel*

Alarcón

Map 8F7. Cuenca. 83km (52 miles) s of Cuenca; 92km (57 miles) n of Albacete. Population: 350.
From the main Madrid-Valencia road, a tiny 15thC castle with a square tower appears to be squatting in the middle of a flat, uncultivated field, the forgotten strategic blunder of an inept feudal lord. On closer inspection, that impression is soon corrected. The Júcar river has slashed a ravine that nearly encircles the craggy spike of rock crested by this hamlet and its protector. The road descends to the river, then spirals up through imposing fortifications that curl over the hillside. Once there, only the bray of a donkey or a barking dog interrupts the stillness.

☞ Parador Nacional Marqués de Villena ♣
Av. Amigos de los Castillos ☎ *(966) 331 350* ▥ *11 rms* ▭ *11* ➡ ⇌
AE ⊕ ⊚ VISA
Location: On the outskirts of the village. Inside the castle is a small paved courtyard, where a large fig tree, an old well and a splendid view of the Júcar gorge draw the eye. Most of the bedrooms are in the massive keep, including one that features a half-canopied bed facing a slotted window so high in the wall that steps are provided to reach it. In the first of the two great halls, leather sofas and chairs are arranged beneath heraldic banners. Suits of armor and racks of lances are spaced along the walls. In winter, firelight dances on rough-cut stone. There is no golf, swimming or room service, but these walls breathe romantic association as no resort hotel can. Don't go alone.
⌂ ≑ ☐ ✿ ⚓ ⅋

Albacete

Map 8G7. Albacete. 247km (154 miles) se of Madrid; 186km (116 miles) sw of Valencia. Population: 107,200 **i** *Av. Rodríguez Acosta 3* ☎ *(967) 223 380.*
Within the boundaries of La Mancha agricultural district, this provincial capital is a center for the distribution of grain, wine and

the most costly of all spices, saffron. Knives with inlaid handles and engraved blades are manufactured here and sold all over the country. The city was badly battered in the Civil War. Reconstruction has emphasized utility over esthetics, and the only significant sights are a Gothic-Renaissance cathedral, containing a Churrigueresque retable, and an archeological museum, featuring prehistoric and Roman antiquities.

Gran Hotel Bristol (*Marqués de Molins 1* ☎(967) 213 787 **III**) doesn't dazzle, but everything is routinely satisfactory; contemporary yet conventional, **Los Llanos** (*Av. España 9* ☎(967) 223 750 **III**) has good facilities and can be a lively place to spend the evening, with a bingo parlor and restrained disco; the quiet **Parador Nacional La Mancha** (*Carretera Madrid-Alicante, km 249* ☎(967) 229 450 **III**), recently built in the style of the region, has more to offer in the way of recreational facilities than most *paradores*.

Gran Hotel Bristol (*address and* ☎*as hotel* **III**) surpass the best restaurants in the immediate area for price and care in preparation. Should a longer stay demand variety, try the **Mesón Las Rejas** (*Dionisio Guardiola 7* ☎(967) 227 242 **III**), where the *gazpacho*, rabbit, pork and partridge recipes are above average; ask for the menu of *cosicas* at the **Nuestro Bar** (*Alcalde Conangia 102* ☎(967) 227 215 *on the Albacete-Murcia road*) and pick from among 20 typical dishes of La Mancha, including cubes of fried cheese, *lomo de orza* and *revuelto de esparragos*.

Place nearby
Chinchilla de Monte Aragón (*11km/6¹/₂ miles SE of Albacete*).
Old houses huddle beneath the ruined 15thC castle on a hill off the Albacete-Valencia road. In the town the principal sights are the 14thC **Santo Domingo** church with a Mozarabic ceiling, an 18thC **Ayuntamiento**, the 15thC church of **Santa María del Salvador**, with a wealth of Plat_resque detailing, and mansions in the several primary architectural styles of the last 500yrs. Local pottery is also of interest.

Alcañiz
*Map **14**E9. Teruel. 103km (64 miles) SE of Zaragoza; 159km (99 miles) w of Tarragona. Population: 12,000.*
The largest city in this isolated NE corner of the province of Teruel, Alcañiz is a convenient place for an overnight stay, perhaps on a Madrid to Barcelona drive. A spike of rock rises high above deeply scarred terrain, surmounted by a complex of buildings begun in the 12thC. Among them, the **fortified convent** was given to the Order of Calatrava by Alfonso II in 1179, and within its keep are Gothic wall paintings of the l4thC. The ground floor is a Gothic chapel, and outside lies a small cloistered garden. The E portion of the castle was converted to a palace for the son of Philip V in the 18thC and is now a *parador*.

The main plaza, which gives access to the hilltop, is bordered in part by an 18thC **collegiate church** with a Baroque facade, a 15thC arcaded **Lonja** and the adjoining Renaissance **Ayuntamiento**.

Parador Nacional La Concordia
Castillo de Calatravos ☎(974) 830 400 **III** to **IIII** 12 rms ⌷ 12 ☰ ⬥
☰ **AE** ⊙ **⊙** **VISA**

Location: On top of the promontory rising from the center of the city. A national monument which preserves elements of the buildings erected on this site between the 12th and 18thC, this *parador* is popular despite its off-the-beaten-track location, so you'd be wise to make your reservation well in advance.
⌂ ‡ ✉ ⚓ ♈

Algeciras

Map 6/4. 121km (75 miles) SE of Cádiz; 138km (86 miles) W of Málaga. Population: 86,000 **i** *Av. de la Marina* ☎*(956) 656 761.*

On the opposite side of the bay formed by the Rock of Gibraltar, Algeciras was founded by the invading Moors in 711. The present name is derived from the Arab "el Gezira," which means "The Island" and refers to the nearby Green Island. The Moors stayed until the 14thC, when they were expelled in the Catholic Reconquest. Population growth accelerated in the early 18thC, after the British took *Gibraltar* and Spanish refugees crossed the bay to settle.

☜ Octavio
San Bernardo 1 ☎*(956) 652 650* **IIII** *80 rms* 🛏 *80* ▦ ➤ AE ⊙ VISA
Location: In the central quarter of the city, near the main road. A contemporary hostelry of no particular distinction, it is handy for the railroad and bus stations as well as the ferry pier. The cocktail bar is lively and sophisticated, as things go in these parts, and the restaurant sets the local standard.
⬍ ❦

☜ Reina Cristina
Paseo de la Conferencia s/n ☎*(956) 602 622* ☎ *78057* **IIII** *to* **IIIII** *135 rms* 🛏 *135* ▦ ➤ AE ⊙ VISA
Location: On a low rise by the bay, S of the business district. The faded charms of this survivor of the Victorian era do not justify its lofty rates. However, there are grand views of the Bay of Algeciras and Gibraltar to compensate, and extensive gardens in which to stroll after lunch on the terrace.
🏨 ➾ ⬍ ❦ ♫ ⛱ ≈ ✠

═ Such delicacies as squid-in-its-ink and grilled fish brochettes dominate the menu at **Marea Baja** (*Trafalgar 2* ☎*(956) 663 654* **IIII**).

Places nearby

Tarifa (*22km/13 miles SW of Algeciras*).   The southernmost point of continental Europe. Medieval walls girdle much of the town with its cobbled streets and whitewashed houses. A Moorish castle (✗ *opening hours are erratic since it is an active army barracks*), named after the Christian general who held it in the late 13thC, Guzmán el Bueno, commands fine views of the Straits of Gibraltar and the African coast.

Alicante

Map 9G8. Alicante. 84km (53 miles) NW of Murcia; 177km (111 miles) S of Valencia. Population: 252,000 **i** *Explanada de España 2* ☎*(965) 212 285.*

Long before it is pointed out, the visitor to Alicante grows aware of the astonishingly clear, mellow light that bathes this section of the coast. In fact, the recorded comments of everyone from the Greeks onward refer to this phenomenon. For example, the Roman name "Lucentum" translates as "City of Light" and, recently, film-makers have flocked to the area to take advantage of this unique atmospheric condition.

   The city itself is remarkable primarily for the fact that it retains its Spanish character despite the tourist hordes who have culturally flattened so much of coastal Spain.
Event   In late June, Hogueras de San Juan. Celebrations include parades and bonfires.

Sights and places of interest

The **Castillo de Santa Bárbara** (*open Oct-Mar 9am-7pm, Apr-May 9am-9pm, June-Sept 9am-10pm*) is Alicante's foremost sight, looming over the last beach before the port district. Its foundations may be Carthaginian, although what survives is primarily 13th-16thC. Take the elevator to the top from the Paseo de Gomis for fine vistas of the harbor and city.

Second in interest might be the **Ayuntamiento**, four streets w of the lower elevator stop. Completed in 1760, it is identified by twin square towers and a Churrigueresque facade. Inside, several of the **Baroque rooms** are open to the public in the morning (*ask the caretaker to let you in*).

Three streets N is **San Nicolás de Bari** (*open 8am-12.30pm, 6-8.30pm, holidays 9am-1.45pm*), a 17thC domed cathedral named after the local patron saint. Apart from the ruined **Castillo de San Fernando**, with its attractive gardens, and the **Museo Arqueológico** (*open 9am-2pm, closed Sun, holidays*), in the Diputación building two streets w of the Plaza de los Luceros, that's about it. Most likely, takeaway memories will be of the **Explanada de España**, the waterfront promenade shaded by regal palms and lined with cafés.

Hotels

Gran Sol
Rambla de Méndez Núñez 3 ☎ (965) 520 3000 ▥ to ▥ *108 rms* ▤ *108* ▦ ▬ ▬ AE ⊕ ⊙ VISA
Location: Two streets from the waterfront esplanade. Straightforward and functional, this hotel seems suited to commercial travelers rather than holidaymakers. The top-floor bar has panoramic views of the port.
‡ ▣ ▧ ⟨⟨ ⟩⟩ Ψ

Leuka
Segura 23 ☎ (965) 520 1744 ☏ 66272 ▯ *108 rms* ▤ *108* ▦ ▬ ▬
AE ⊕ ⊙ VISA
Location: Two streets E of Av. General Marva. This hotel might prove hard to find, for its street changes name frequently. The neighborhood is fairly quiet, and the hotel contemporary in style.
‡ ▣ ❤ ≈ Ψ

Meliá Alicante
Playa del Postiguet s/n ☎ (965) 520 5000 ☏ 66131 ▥ *545 rms* ▤ *545* ▦ ▬ ▭ AE ⊕ ⊙ VISA
Location: In the center of the city, on the waterfront. There is nothing timid about this massive Meliá, which is nearly twice as large as the number of rooms suggest, for another 200 or so apartments are privately owned. It squats on a breakwater overlooking a beach on one side, a marina on the other. With three restaurants, two pools, a nightclub, a bar and several stores, it isn't surprising that many guests never stray more than a few meters from the front door.
‡ ▢ ▢ ❤ ⟨⟨ ≈ ▩ ☺ Ψ ○

Sidi San Juan Sol
Playa de San Juan ☎ (965) 565 1300 ☏ 66263 ▥ to ▥ *176 rms* ▤ *176* ▦ ▬ ▭ AE CB ⊕ ⊙ VISA
Location: On the beach, 8km (5 miles) NE of the city center. Every comfort is present in this sound-proofed beach hotel, only a short drive from the center of Alicante. The indoor pool has a sauna; the outdoor one, on the terrace, gives unobstructed views of beach and sea. The hotel is very popular from late June to Sept and around Christmas and Easter, but advance reservations are probably not necessary at other times.
▣ ‡ ▣ ❤ ≈ ▩ ⟳ ☺ Ψ ○

Restaurants

El Delfín
Explanada de España 12 ☎ (965) 521 4911 ▥ ▭ ▬ ▦ Ψ AE ⊕ ⊙ VISA *Last orders 11.30pm.*
Everyone passes this restaurant three times in his first hour in the city. From the sidewalk tables and indifferent modern interior it might be judged unremarkable, yet the kitchen is imaginative, even daring. Although seafood dishes are prominent on the menu, they are not the clichés of the corner *tasca*, and the chef explores the limits of traditional recipes; they include

lubina con costra mousse langosta, solomillo Wellington (steak in a pastry case) and hoja de col rellena de cigalas. The wine cellar also measures up well.

La Masia
Valdés 1 ☎(965) 520 0975 ⅢⅢ ⏛ ■ ▦ ☒ AE ⊕ ⑩ VISA Last orders 11pm. Closed Sun.
Go for the selection of rice concoctions, all of the famous paella family such as arroz Alicantina (saffron-flavored rice containing peppers, tomatoes, artichoke hearts and boiled fish) or arroz a banda (a rice dish made with seafood and tomatoes, flavored with garlic and spices), or try lubina a la sal (sea bass baked in a hard salt shell which is removed before serving). Rustic trappings characterize the four dining rooms near the Explanada de España.

Quo Vadis ❧
Plaza Santísima Faz 3 ☎(965) 521 6660 ⅢⅢ ⏛ ■ ▬ ♙ ▦ ➤ ☒ AE CB ⊕ ⑩ VISA Last orders midnight.
Eat inside, outside, upstairs, downstairs, at the bar or at a table. They seek to please. The hospitality is so casual and the ambiente so Spanish, with few concessions to foreign tastes, that many visitors don't give it a second look — their mistake. Consider cochinillo, the array of tapas or the cold chest heaped with the catch of the day. The specialties include mejillones marinera (mussels cooked in white wine and herbs), pollo asodo and tortilla. There is also a comprehensive cellar offering 120 different wines. If it's hot outside, choose to eat in the air conditioned dining room at the back.

≈ Despite the name, **Pizzeria Romana** (Finca las Palmeras ☎(965) 526 0602 ⅢⅢ) has an essentially French menu and occupies an attractive garden setting near the Playa Albufereta, 6km (4 miles) from the city center; assorted grilled fish and shellfish are the draw at **La Darsena** (Muelle del Puerto ☎(965) 520 7589 ⅢⅢ), along with immense bowls of a local variation on bullabesa. **Rincón Castellano** (Manero Mollá 12 ☎(965) 521 9002 ⅢⅢ) features Castilian specialties.

Almería
Map 8l6. Almería. 169km (105 miles) SE of Granada; 221km (137 miles) SE of Murcia. Population: 120,000 ℹ Av. Generalísimo 1 ☎(951) 234 705.
Tucked into the SE corner of the peninsula and at some distance from the usual tourist routes, Almería is a pleasant harbor city. The promenade beside the port is lined with date palms and ramparts of the 8thC Moorish citadel rear above the ancient quarter of whitewashed houses. Several resorts stretch along the coast w of the city center.

Phoenicians may have founded a trading post here, and the Carthaginians put down temporary roots. It was called Portus Magnus by the Romans and Al-Mariyat, the basis of its present name, by the Arabs. Pirates controlled the city in the 12thC, prompting Alfonso VII to send a punitive expedition here. After a brief occupation, the Moors retook Almería and held it until 1488.

Sights and places of interest
Alcazaba
▨ Open summer 10am-2pm, 4-8pm; winter 9am-1pm, 3-7pm.
The Moor 'Abd-al-Rahmán III ordered the construction of this fortress in the 10thC. It was later enlarged by his successor, Almansor. Much of it was destroyed by an earthquake in 1522, so there is little to be seen in the interior. Restoration is now under way. Gardens of palms, flowers and cacti are interrupted by splashing brooks, a calm setting for contemplating extensive vistas of city and sea. There is a small **museum** displaying artifacts excavated from the site.
Cathedral ✝
Plaza de la Catedral. Open 8.30am-noon, 5.30-8pm.
This 16thC fortress-cathedral replaced an earlier church, itself a converted mosque, which had been severely damaged by the 1522 earthquake. The

main portals are of classical design, the edifice itself is in Gothic style. Interior appointments include 16thC choirstalls and 18thC retable and pulpits.

☙ **Gran Hotel Almería** (*Av. Reina Regente 4* ☎(*951*) *238 011* **|||** *to* **||||**) enjoyed a vogue with foreign film-makers during the 1960s, and there are still vestiges of that past glory. Paramount among the resort hotels w of the city is **La Parra** (*Carretera Almería-Málaga, km 6, Bahia El Palmer* ☎(*951*) *340 500* **||||**), which has excellent facilities. The numerous other hotels include the placid **Costa Sol** (*Av. de Almería 85* ☎(*951*) *234 011* **|||**), **Indálico** (*Dolores R. Sopeña 4* ☎(*951*) *231 111* **|||**), and **Torreluz** (*Plaza Flores 1* ☎(*951*) *234 799* **|||**).

➡ Sustenance, rather than gastronomical invention, is the priority at Almería's restaurants. **El Rincón de Juan Pedro II** (*Plaza del Carmen 6* ☎(*951*) *235 184* **|||**) is typically phlegmatic with its informality and sturdy regional dishes; the bar has a gratifying quantity of *tapas*, a nightly attraction for locals. **Club del Mar** (*Muelle 1* ☎(*951*) *235 048* **|||**) is directly on the bay and appropriately emphasizes seafood, much of which is unidentifiable but delicious.

Altamira Caves See *Santillana del Mar.*

The Andalucía region
Map 6&7H4&5. The largest and southernmost region in Spain. Airports: Almería, Cádiz, Córdoba, Granada, Málaga, Sevilla.
Andalucía is the Spain of our imaginings, where flamenco was born and little white villages tumble from hilltops, ghostly at dusk, blazing at midday. For much of geological time, Andalucía was part of Africa, and human history has ensured that it remains nearly as Oriental as it is European. The Moors stayed longer here than in any other region, bequeathing a culture that surpassed any in its epoch, as can be seen in the great mosque at *Córdoba* and the complex of palaces and gardens that comprises the Alhambra in *Granada.* The coast and cities swarm with people, yet through miles of forests and parched tablelands of the interior the only signs of previous habitation are piled stone fences and the roads themselves. The mountain ranges of Andalucía provide skiing for six months of the year within a morning's drive of a sea which becomes chilly only in deepest winter.

... in local position, climate, fertility, objects of interest and *facility of access,* [it] must take precedence of all [other provinces] in Spain.

Richard Ford, *Handbook for Travellers in Spain,* 1845

Despite their difficulties — colonization in the past and now high unemployment — the Andalucians are the warmest and most open of Spaniards, naturally gregarious and egalitarian. Although they share the fatalism of their fellow countrymen, it is as an inevitability to be anticipated, not endlessly contemplated.

Andorra
Map 15C10. In the E Pyrenees between Spain and France. Airports: Barcelona, Girona, Carcassonne (in France). Population: 26,500.
The independent principality of Andorra is another of the historical and jurisdictional anomalies that peppered the continent up to the 19thC, and is one of the handful that survives. Disputes in the 13thC between the French lords of Foix and the Spanish bishop of Urgel over control of the enclave led to an agreement of

joint hegemony that persists to this day, although Andorra remains
more Spanish than French.
   The inhabitants are skilled herdsmen, farmers and smugglers —
an occupation that has resulted in many stores in the capital selling
cheap cigarettes, electronic equipment, perfumes, spirits and other
untaxed consumer goods, attracting both locals and tourists.

Andorra la Vella (*Andorra la Vieja*)
*220km (136 miles) NW of Barcelona; 153km (85 miles) NE of Lleida.
Population: 10,800.*
The capital and largest town has a stunning setting to the E of the
Pic d'Enclar at an altitude of 1,029m (3,365ft). The 16thC **Casa de
la Vall** (*open Mon-Fri 9am-1pm, 3.30-7pm, Sat 9am-1pm*) houses
the government council. A modest collection of paintings,
documents dating back to Charlemagne and archeological artifacts
reflecting the history of the principality is on view at the **Museo y
Biblioteca** (*Prada Guillemó s/n, open Sun-Fri 9.30am-1pm, 3.30-
7pm, Sat 9.30am-1pm*).

♨ Three major hotels are centrally located and have modern amenities. The
oldest, **Andorra Park** (*Roureda Guillemó s/n* ☎(9738) 20979 ▥▥) was built in
1958, but is frequently updated; service is efficient and friendly. **Andorra
Center** (*Dr. Nequi 12* ☎(9738) 24999 ▥▥) is the newest, largest and the
closest to being luxurious; **Eden Roc** (*Av. Dr. Mitjavilla 1* ☎(9738) 21000
▥▥) is a comparable alternative. Other possibilities are **Flora** (*Antic Carrer
Major 23* ☎(9738) 21508 ▥▥), **Mercure** (*Av. Meritxell 58* ☎(9738) 20773
▥▥ to ▥▥), and **President** (*Av. Santa Coloma 40* ☎(9738) 22922 ▥▥ to ▥▥).

≕ Andorran cuisine embraces Catalan and French styles of cookery and also
caters to a local preference for Italian food. **Versalles** ✿(*Cap del Carrer 1*
☎(9738) 21331 ▥▥) is a popular bistro which provides French home
cooking. At **Chez Jacques** (*Av. Tarragona, Terra Vella Building* ☎(9738)
20325 ▥▥) the owner-chef prepares classical Gallic recipes, as well as
exploring the cuisines of the former French colonies, and little is likely to
displease; the dining room is small, so reserve ahead. **Ordre d'Eol** (*Carrer de
la Vall 7* ☎(9738) 23433 ▥▥) has a menu that ranges from French to Catalan
to Italian; the essentially Italian **Lou Pizzaiolo** (*Av. Dr. Mitjavilla 36*
☎(9738) 20639 ▥▥) and the Francophile **Charlot** (*Av. Riberaigua s/n*
☎(9738) 21018 ▥▥) are equally good alternatives.

Places nearby
Las Escaldes (*1km/½ mile E of Andorra la Vella*). Cross the river
into this spa, well-known for its mineral baths and waters.

♨ The top hotel is **Roc Blanc** (*Plaça Co-princeps 5* ☎(9738) 21486 ▥▥),
with a gymnasium, pool and sauna.

Sant Julia de Loriá (*7km/4½ miles SW of Andorra la Vella*).   The
first village you encounter after entering Andorra from Spain, it
has a 12thC church with a Romanesque tower.

Antequera
*Map 7H5. Málaga. 48km (30 miles) N of Málaga; 98km (61
miles) W of Granada. Population: 40,000.*
The name of this tidy agricultural-industrial town derives from the
Roman "Anticaria," yet its origins are even earlier. Three
prehistoric dolmens — structures comprised of upright stone slabs
bridged by others nearly as massive — are located nearby. In town,
the principal sights are a 13thC Moorish **castle** and the Plateresque
Iglesia de San Sebastian, as well as the **Iglesia de Santa María la
Mayor** with its marked arabesques, and the **Palacio de Najera**,
which houses a collection of archeological artifacts.

Sight nearby

The dolmens
NE of Antequera, off the Granada road. Open summer 10am-1pm, 4-8pm; winter 10am-1pm, 2-6pm.

Turn left 2km (1 mile) outside the town for the **Cueva de Menga** (✗), the most impressive dolmen, with one stone estimated at 180 tons and engravings dating from at least two millennia BC, and the **Cueva de Viera** (✗), a megalithic temple which is nearly as old. It is less overpowering than the Cueva de Menga, but more finely worked. Farther toward Granada is the less remarkable third dolmen, the **Romeral** (*ask for key at the sugar refinery*).

Parador Nacional de Antequera (☎(952) 840 901 ▥). This once-humble unit of the parador group was recently updated to more representative comforts, including a swimming pool.

The Aragón region
Map 14C8. In the NE, to the w of Catalunya. Airport: Zaragoza.

An ancient kingdom that once reached across the sea to Naples and far into France, Aragón is now only three sparsely inhabited provinces stretching from the mid-Pyrenees south toward *Valencia*. Apart from its northern fringe of snowcapped peaks and green hills, most of the region is scarred brown terrain. The river Ebro flows through the middle of the region from its source in the Cantabrian mountains toward the Mediterranean. The only cities of note are the provincial capitals of *Huesca*, *Zaragoza* and *Teruel*. More appealing, however, is the remote picturesque village of *Albarracín*, s of Teruel. **Ordesa national park** near Biescas is also of interest and is important in the conservation of wildlife and well known for its great natural beauty.

Farmers in Aragón till their patches of land with mule-drawn ploughs as well as with tractors, and the wealthiest man in town is likely to be the storekeeper. Gossip is a favorite Aragonese pastime and secrets are few. Newcomers are objects of an intense yet phlegmatic curiosity, and children — no matter whose — are adored. The Aragonese are generous people, and happy to spend an hour over a small sherry discussing the weather and the last stranger who passed through town.

Aranjuez
Map 12E6. Madrid. 44km (28 miles) NE of Toledo; 46km (29 miles) s of Madrid. Population: 40,000 ℹ Plaza Santiago Ruseñol ☎(91) 899 2694.

Once a popular vacation spot for the Spanish Bourbons, the town has a well-deserved reputation for horticulture. The outlying fields produce strawberries and asparagus that are prized throughout the country. A succession of landscape architects have left a legacy of elaborate gardens, parks and elm-lined walks.

Sights and places of interest

Jardín del Príncipe
▧ Open 10am-6.30pm.

To call this a garden is an understatement; in area it is 150ha (375 acres). Charles IV decreed the planting of many trees, stately elms being interspersed with imported species. Within the park is the early 19thC **Casa del Labrador** (▧ *open 10am-1pm, 3-6pm*). Although the name translates as "House of the Worker," it was intended as a summer residence for members of the nobility. It is a scaled-down version of the Palacio Real, with an interior that is far more appealing. The sculpture gallery of ancient philosophers, Neoclassical furnishings and lavish use of Roman mosaics, gold, silver and frescoes give it a sumptuous elegance.

Also within the park is the **Casa de Marinos** (▧ *open 10am-1pm, 3-6pm*), in which royal boats are on view.

Arcos de la Frontera

Palacio Real
🖼 ✗ *compulsory. Open 10am-1pm, 3-6pm.*

Ferdinand and Isabella lived in a 14thC residence on this site. It was
subsequently enlarged, but suffered two disastrous fires in the 17thC.
Philip V commissioned the present palace which was completed in 1752,
with later additions by Charles III in 1778. Louis XIV's taste in country
cottages was no doubt the inspiration for both exterior and interior. Salon
after echoing salon display extravagant Rococo furnishings, frescoes,
chandeliers, tapestries, paintings, gilt-framed mirrors, and 18thC relief tiles
made in Madrid. There is a modest museum exhibiting costumes of
monarchs and military men as well as antique games, fans and furniture used
by the royal children.

A garden called the **Parterre** lies to the E of the palace. A pair of bridges
lead N over a canalized branch of the Tajo river to the **Jardín de la Isla**
(Garden of the Island), laid out in the 17thC and enhanced by decorative
fountains.

≋ **Casa Pablo** (*Almíbar 20* ☎(91) 891 1451 ▮▮▯) is a tavern where Castilian
specialties, such as roast suckling pig, ham and shellfish, top the menu;
alternatives include **Chirón** (*Real 10* ☎(91) 891 0941 ▮▮ *to* ▮▮▯) and **La
Mina** (*Príncipe 21* ☎(91) 891 1146 ▮▮▯).

Arcos de la Frontera
*Map 6I4. Cádiz. 80km (50 miles) NE of Cádiz; 89km (56 miles)
s of Sevilla. Population: 25,000.*

A granite ridge erupts from a quilted valley of fields, with this
attractive old town crowding its summit. Even though there will
soon appear to be little more than an inch to spare on either side of
your car, continue along the road which climbs the hill to the **Plaza
de España**. The plaza occupies the highest ground, with a
belvedere affording a magnificent view over the Guadalete river.
On the opposite side of the square is the 15thC Plateresque **Iglesia
de Santa María**, and on the other two sides are the fortified palace
of the Dukes of Osuna and the *parador nacional*. In the center is a
space for parking. The steepled church, on a slightly lower level at
the E end of the old quarter, is named after **San Pedro**, and inside
there are several paintings by well-known artists, such as Zurbarán
and Pacheco.

❧ **Parador Nacional Casa del Corregidor**
Plaza Cabildo s/n ☎(965) 700 500. *21 rms* ▭ 21 ▮▮ *to* ▮▮▮▮ ▦ ⊷ ≋
Ⓐⓔ ⓪ ⒹⒸ ⓥⓘⓢⓐ
Location: In the main square. From the terrace outside the spacious lounge
and restaurant, guests can look down at birds gliding on the updrafts around
the cliff towering above the Guadalete river. Some rooms are a trifle cramped
and their furnishings utilitarian, but both the food and views compensate.
⌂ ⬆ ☞ ⬚ ◁ 🍸

The Asturias region (*Principado de Asturias*)
*Map 11B4. On the Cantabrian coast. Airport: S. Esteban de
Pravia (near Oviedo).*

Asturias, which comprises the single province of Oviedo, contains
spectacular snow-dusted mountains, golden beaches, lush emerald
valleys and secluded coves girdled by cliffs. There are many caves,
like those at **Ribadesella** and **Candamo**, which were inhabited by
prehistoric people who left paintings and incised drawings.
Coal-mining is central to the economy and often the source of labor
strife. Fields of maize, orchards and pig farms are the most
prominent agricultural features.

The Kingdom of Asturias can be dated from the Battle of
Covadonga in 772, when the Asturian clans inflicted defeat on the
Moors and started the seven-century reconquest of the peninsula.

It was the first region to be liberated, and evolved socially and culturally in ways that presaged the eventual transformation of the rest of the country. Celtic influences persist, such as the bagpipes, which are integral to local folk music.

In summer the weather is almost ideal, with temperatures of around 21°C (70°F). Winter is often raw and damp, but with abundant snow for skiers. Water-sports, salmon fishing, mountaineering and hunting deer and wild boar are all popular.

Avila

Map 12E5. Avila. 111km (68 miles) NW of Madrid; 64km (40 miles) SW of Segovia. Population: 42,000 i Plaza de la Catedral 4 ☎ (918) 211 387.

The present name derives from the Roman "Avela," although a settlement existed here long before the Romans arrived. For casual visitors, the most impressive feature is its 11thC walls. Astonishingly well preserved, their 88 semi-circular towers and battlements enclose nearly half the present city. The birthplace of the mystic and pragmatic religious, St Teresa, Avila is a place of pilgrimage.

Despite its proximity to the torrid heart of the Meseta, Avila is higher than any provincial capital, ensuring cool summer nights and long cold winters. Heavy snows often block access to the town. Despite its medieval stature, Avila declined after the establishment of the Christian court in *Toledo* and remains something of a cultural backwater today.

Event In Oct, Feria de Santa Teresa.

Sights and places of interest

Basílica de San Vicente † ☆
San Vicente. Open Mon-Sat 11am-1pm, 4-6pm, Sun 12.30-1pm, 4-6pm.

Of transitional Romanesque-Gothic style, the basilica was completed in the 14thC. It stands in a square outside the NE gate in the old wall, on the site where St Vincent is alleged to have been martyred. The W portal is framed in arches composed of engrossing Romanesque statuary.

Casa de los Deanes
Plaza Nalvillos 🖾 Open Mon-Sat 10am-2pm, Sun 11am-1.30pm.

This 16thC residence of the deans of the cathedral is now the provincial museum. The Renaissance architecture is as intriguing as the collections of tiles, tapestries, wood carvings and furniture.

Cathedral ▥ † ☆
Plaza de la Catedral.

Begun in the 12thC, it is essentially Romanesque, with a solidity so pronounced that its E end is incorporated into the town wall. Through the centuries, Gothic and Baroque overlays have been applied both inside and out, with some splendid and some unfortunate results. In the former category is the altarpiece started by Pedro Berruguete, the accomplished Renaissance sculptor whose work resembles that of Michelangelo. Other works by him are on view in the **museum** (🖾 *open summer 10am-1.30pm, 3-7pm; winter 10am-1.30pm, 3-5pm; entrance off the sacristy*), which also boasts an El Greco painting and a 16thC monstrance (receptacle) by Juan de Frías. The main W gate is an 18thC mistake, but the stained glass in the transept and the various Plateresque sculptures are superb.

Convento de San José †
Sáveno s/n 🖾 Open 10am-1pm, 4-7pm.

This church, outside the walls, was the first founded by Teresa (in 1562) after her rise to the upper echelons of the Spanish Catholic church. It is largely Renaissance in design, with a modest **museum** containing relics of the saint.

Convento de Santa Teresa †
Plaza de la Santa. Open 9am-1.30pm, 3.30-8pm.

It is questionable whether St Teresa would have approved of the gaudily Baroque chapel built in her memory on the site of the house in which she was born. The name is misleading, for it is a church rather than a convent.

Monasterio de la Encarnación
Plaza de la Encarnación. Open 10am-1.30pm, 3.30-7pm.
St Teresa commenced her vocation here in 1533 and stayed even after
undertaking the reformation of her order 20yrs later.

Real Monasterio de Santo Tomás
Plaza de Granada
Ferdinand and Isabella supported this late 15thC Gothic monastery, where
they sometimes spent vacations in temperate summers. Their interest caused
it to be a center of the Inquisition, which might seem incompatible with its
additional function as a university. Ferdinand and Isabella buried their only
son here, in the carved marble tomb at the end of the transept. There is a retable
in deep relief by Pedro Berruguete celebrating the life of Thomas Aquinas.
Astonishingly inconspicuous is the grave of the master Inquisitor, Torquemada.
   Entrance to the **cloister** (🖾 *open 10.30am-1pm, 4-7pm*) is to the right of
the monastery.

The walls ★
As remarkable as the fact that they are still intact is that they were erected in
only 3yrs (1088-91). They are over 2,500m (2,725yds) in length, and have
eight gates, the most important of which are those in front of the **Basílica de
San Vicente** and at the Plaza de Santa Teresa. The walls can be mounted at
several points, including the garden of the *parador*, and the walkway is
always open.

🏠 Palacio de Valderrábanos
Plaza de la Catedral 9 ☎ *(918) 211 023* 🔳 *to* 🔳🔳 *73 rms* 🛏 *73* 🍽 🚗
🚗 ⩤ AE CB ⊙ ⊙ VISA
Location: Near the main entrance to the cathedral. Once the elegant home of a
noble 15thC family, that quality is (more or less) maintained by the current
proprietors. Fixtures and details are Old Castilian in spirit, although the
bingo parlor jars. The staff is extremely attentive.
⬆ 🖾 ☀ ⚓

🏠 Parador Nacional Raimundo de Borgoña ✿
Marqués de Canales de Chozas 16 ☎ *(918) 211 340* 🔳🔳 *27 rms* 🛏 *27*
🚗 ⩤ AE ⊙ ⊙ VISA
Location: Near the city center, abutting the walls. Once the palace of Benavides,
built in the late 15thC, this *parador* is essentially a re-creation of that grand
edifice. The gardens are extensive, bordering walkways along the famous
Romanesque walls that afford views of winding streets and the Adaja valley.
⌂ ⬆ 🖾 ⚞ ⚓ 🍽

🚗 Avila is not renowned for its superior restaurants. Apart from the hotel
dining rooms, there are **Copacabana** (*San Millan 9* ☎ *(918) 211 110* 🔳 *to*
🔳🔳), **El Torreón** (*Tostado 1* ☎ *(918) 213 171* 🔳), **Mesón del Rastro** (*Plaza
del Rastro 1* ☎ *(918) 211 218* 🔳 *to* 🔳🔳), and **Mesón el Sol** (*Av. 18 de Julio 25*
☎ *(918) 221 266* 🔳). Expect little more than competent, Castilian dishes.

Badajoz
*Map 6F3. Badajoz. 80km (56 miles) sw of Cáceres; 223km
(138 miles) nw of Sevilla. Population: 103,000* **i** *Pasaje de
San Juan 2* ☎ *(924) 222 763.*
Badajoz does not provide instant gratification. Indeed, the
impossibly narrow Bridge of Palms is almost enough to put anyone
off making a visit. The majority of travelers encounter the ancient
city only as a stop on the Lisbon-Madrid road and pay it little
attention. Yet while the provincial capital is not a major tourist
destination, it is diverting for an overnight stay. Although there
was a settlement here before the Romans, the most significant
buildings date from the Moorish occupation of the 11th-13thC.
The town was recaptured by Alfonso XI in 1229, and it has
suffered the ravages of every war since, including the Civil War.

Sights and places of interest
The 32-arch **Puente de Palmas**, the bridge normally used for entrance to the
city, was completed in the late 16thC, but has been frequently repaired since,

after damage caused by numerous floods and armed conflicts. At its eastern end is the **Puerta de Palmas**, a 16thC gateway flanked by twin circular battlemented towers. The city streets are as narrow as the bridge, so turn left and follow the river NE to the ruins of the Arab **Alcazaba** (*open 9am-1pm, 3-6pm*), in its extensive park-like grounds. There are excellent views from the tower of **Espantaperros**, and next door is an **archeological museum**.

It is best to leave your car here and explore the heart of the city by foot. Using the cathedral tower as a landmark, walk toward the central Plaza de España. The bulk of the Gothic **Catedral de San Juan** (*Plaza de San Juan, open 11am-1pm*) dates from the 13thC, but with additions and alterations made during the Renaissance. A 16thC chancel dominates the nave and there is a Churrigueresque retable. Paintings by Zurbarán and Ribera can be seen, especially in the chapterhouse. There are also paintings by Zurbarán and lesser artists identified with Extremadura at the unassuming **Museo Provincial de Bellas Artes** (*Meléndez Valdés 32* ▧ *open summer 10am-2pm, 5-7pm; winter 10am-2pm, 4-6pm*) not far from the cathedral.

▷ **Gran Hotel Zurbarán** (*Paseo de Castelar 6* ☎(924) 223 741 ▮▯ *to* ▮▮▮▯) compensates for the dearth of good hotels in the region and serves as a starting point for an excursion into Portugal. **Lisboa** (*Av. de Elvas 13* ☎(924) 238 200 ▮▯ *to* ▮▮▯) is a comfortable, contemporary stopover on the way to its namesake city and benefits from being away from the traffic of central Badajoz; meet friends on the terrace or around the pool of the relatively modern and entirely predictable **Residencia Río** (*Av. de Díaz Ambrona s/n* ☎(924) 237 600 ▮▯), located nearby.

▬ **El Sótano** (*Virgen de la Soledad 6* ☎(924) 223 161 ▮▯ *to* ▮▮▯) is a long-term favorite, if only for the busy *tapas* bar at the front; solid regional dishes are on hand in the dining room at the back. **Los Gabrieles** (*Vicente Barrantes 21* ☎ (924) 224 275 ▮▮▯) has roast pork and cod as its specialties.

Balearic Islands   See *Islas Baleares*.

Barcelona
Map 4-5, 15D10. Barcelona. 108km (67 miles) NE of Tarragona; 97km (61 miles) SW of Girona. Population: 1,755,000 **i** *Gran Via de les Corts Catalanes 658* ☎(93) 301 7443.

Barcelona reveals itself slowly, as do many Iberian cities. In the opinion of many Hispanophiles, however, it surpasses all its rivals in sophistication, culture and vigor. To them, it is second to Madrid only in population, and Sevilla alone deserves to be mentioned in the same company.

... wide connecting thoroughfares that once drained the rainwater away from the hillsides and down to the sea and now divide the traffic streams with a succession of shady, decoratively-paved islands where flower- and bird-sellers and boot-blacks ply their trades.

> Elisabeth de Stroumillo,
> *The Tastes of Travel, Northern and Central Spain*, 1980

Capital of the region of Catalunya and Spain's major seaport and manufacturing center, Barcelona prospers in all aspects of commerce, international trade and the arts. Cars, trucks, locomotives, airplanes and electronics are among the major products of the factories that surround the city. Despite some movement to Madrid, most publishing houses are based here. There are numerous art galleries and a munificence of museums and historic monuments. The radical architect Antonio Gaudí left testimony to his genius in luxury flats, a seminary, parks, mansions and the unfinished cathedral, **La Sagrada Familia**, whose towers are emblematic of this city's vitality.

67

The founding of the city is credited to the Carthaginians, and its name is thought to derive from the powerful Barca family. Its influence became substantial as a Roman port and then as a Visigothic capital, falling to the Arabs in the 8thC. Charlemagne wrested it away soon after and incorporated it into the region known as the Spanish March. In the following centuries, the counts of Barcelona expanded the March to take in parts of France, and much of the E coast and Pyrenean fiefdoms. In part this accounts for the similarity between Catalan and the Romance languages of southern France, notably *langue d'oc* and Provençal.

Barcelona has been the center of Catalan separatist activity from the time of the insurrection against Philip V to the Civil War, and recently the names of the Falangists have been replaced by those of Catalan heroes on streets and plazas. The Gran Via de les Corts Catalanes was the Avenida José Antonio Primo de Rivera for 35yrs, but everybody called it "Gran Via," just as they continued to use the name "El Diagonal" which was for the same period called after Generalísimo Franco. The Castilian "calle" is now the Catalan "cerrer" on street signs, "paseo" is "passeig," "avenida" is "avinguda."

Events   In Jan, Fiesta de San Antonio. Celebrations involve parades and fireworks.

In Holy Week and Corpus Christi, devout processions.

In June, fiesta in the Pueblo Español.

In Sept, fiesta in honor of the Virgen de la Merced.

Sights and places of interest
Barrio Gótico (*Gothic Quarter*)
Map 5D5.

Much that is memorable in Barcelona is in the medieval quarter known as the Barrio Gótico (Barri Gótic) or sometimes as the Barrio Romano for its existing walls and excavations of dwellings from the Roman period. Most of it was built between the 12th and 15thC, and it has successfully preserved its medieval character. Constricted lanes pass beneath overhanging balconies and guild signs, and lead to enclosed plazas of palaces and mansions. Behind small-paned windows are antique and book emporia, *tapas* bars, and several of the city's celebrated traditional restaurants. There are also a number of small, inexpensive hotels.

The best way to explore this quarter is on foot. Walk to the far (N) side of the Av. de la Catedral, opposite the main w facade of the cathedral, and on the right are three watch towers of the 4thC town wall; medieval structures fill the spaces between. After a visit to the **cathedral**, leave by the main entrance, turning right (N), then right again. Immediately on the left of the narrow Calle de los Condes de Barcelona is the patio of the **Museo Federico Marés**. Continue to the next corner at the E end of the cathedral and turn left (N) into Baixada Santa Clara which leads to the **Plaça del Rei**. The Renaissance mansion on the right is the **Museo de Historia de la Ciudad** (⊠ *open Mon 3.30-8.30pm, Tues-Sat 9am-2pm, 3.30-8.30pm, Sun and some holidays 9am-2pm; closed some holidays*). With the museum at your back, the **Palacio de los Virreyes** is on the left of the high-walled square, the Gothic chapel of **Santa Agueda** on the right. At the far corner, a staircase of quadricircular steps leads up to the 14thC **Palacio Real Mayor**. Inside, the **Saló de Tinell** was where Isabella and Ferdinand greeted Columbus on his return from the New World.

Retrace your steps into the Plaça del Rei, continuing past the E end of the cathedral, bearing right and then left along the E wall of the cloister. At the next intersection, turn left (E). Directly ahead is the Gothic "bridge of sighs" connecting the **Palcio de la Generalitat** (*open Sun 10am-1pm, closed Mon-Sat*) on the right and the 14thC **Casa de los Canónigos**. Continue on, beneath the bridge, until you come to the bustling Plaça Sant Jaume. Turn right and you will come to the entrance of the Generalitat. The former palace is now the seat of the Catalan government. Inside is a courtyard with a balustraded **staircase**, one of the most photographed sights in the city. Continue into the surprisingly large **Patio de los Naranjos**, where there are a few small orange trees to justify the name, and a 16thC bell tower.

The 19thC **Ayuntamiento** is on the opposite side of the square (*open 9.30am-1.30pm, 4.30-7.30pm, holidays 9.30am-1.30pm; closed mid-Dec to mid-Jan, and Sun*). Wander through the **Salón de Ciento** and the adjoining rooms on the first floor, where you can see combinations of Neo-Gothic and Renaissance detailing.

To the s of Plaça de Sant Jaume is Calle de Ferran. Some distance along this street, an arch to the left leads into the Plaza Real. The facades of the columned, boxy square have been scrubbed clean and there is a new surface on the ground and around the several sentinel palms. The street lamps were designed by Gaudí, and there is a lively coin and stamp market here on Sunday when the weather is good. A café by the w corner of the square serves fresh *churros* (fritters) and hot chocolate, and if you are strong enough to continue exploring, **Las Ramblas** is only steps away (to the s).

Casa Milá ⅏
Map 5C4. Paseo de Gracia 92. Metro Diagonal.

Known locally as La Pedrera, the block of flats created by Antonio Gaudí curls around the NE intersection of Paseo de Gracia and Calle de Mallorca. A biomorphic skin of sculpted limestone undulates over the three-sided facade, with soft-edged rectangular openings for windows and balconies. Diagonally across the *paseo* is a similar but less flamboyant block of flats, **Casa Battló**, by the same architect.

Cathedral † ☆
Map 5D4. Plaça de la Seu s/n. Open 7am-1.30pm, 2-7pm. Metro Jaume I.

Most of the existing structure dates from the 13th and 14thC, a replacement for an 11thC Romanesque cathedral which was also preceded by an earlier church on the same site. Despite some modified Romanesque elements, including the s transept portal that survives from the 11thC, the exterior is Gothic. The main w facade was built only in the late 19thC, but to plans drawn up 400yrs before.

The filigreed, pointed central tower is echoed by smaller versions at the corners; there is no reason to believe they are not far older. At the rear end are two 14thC octagonal towers, marking the ends of the transept. A

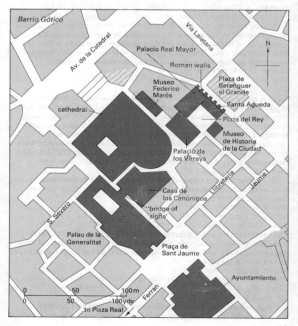

Barcelona

14th-15thC **cloister** is appended to the s wall. It has a shallow pool, where live geese are kept as reminders of the (Christian) Roman occupation.

The interior of the cathedral is divided into three apses. In the middle are a series of adjoining stalls, carved and assembled during the 14th and 15thC. The other aisles are lined with chapels of the 16th-18thC, with interesting decorated grilles (*rejas*).

Energetic visitors may choose to mount over 200 steps in the sw tower for a spectacular view from the top. The **sacristy** and **treasury** (🆒 *open 9am-1pm, closed Mon*), contain a reliquary, illuminated manuscripts, carved altar panels, and crucifixes of precious metals and gems.

Fundación Joan Miró ☆

Map 4F2. Montjuic ☎ *(93) 319 1908* 🆒 💻 *Open Tues-Sat 11am-8pm, Sun and holidays 11am-2.30pm. Closed Mon. Metro Parlamento.*

Devoted to Catalunya's most influential living artist, this modern structure is an effective setting for the prolific lyrical surrealist. His long creative life is depicted in paintings, lithographs, posters, sculpture and weavings. Frequent special exhibitions are staged.

Montjuic

Map 4F2-3. Overlooking harbors s of city center ◁€ *Metro Pueblo Seco.*

The hill seen in gray silhouette to the w of the harbor and city center is Montjuic. At its summit is a **castle** which contains a **military museum** (🆒 💻 ✹ ◁€ *open Tues-Fri 10am-2pm, 4-7pm, Sat, Sun and holidays 10am-7pm, closed Mon*). The castle and grounds afford views of sea, port and mountains. Broad streets lead down to a **public garden** (*open 10am-9pm*) and an amusement park (*open July-Aug noon-9.30pm, closed Sept-July, but opening hours are unpredictable*), with a modest number of rides and snack booths.

There is also a wealth of museums that occupy the middle district of the northerly slope, including the **Fundación Joan Miró**, the **Museo de Arte de Catalunya**, the **Museo Arqueológico** and an **ethnological museum** displaying artifacts from the colonies of the Spanish Empire. Nearby is the **Pueblo Español** and a **Greek theater**, built in 1929 and the scene of summer productions.

Museo Arqueológico ☆

Map 4E2. Lérida ☎ *(93) 233 2149* 🆒 *Open 9.30am-1pm, 4-7pm, holidays 10am-2pm. Closed Mon. Metro Parlamento y España.*

Prehistoric cultures encountered in the *Islas Baleares* and on the mainland are represented by fragments of the Stone and Bronze Ages, as fascinating for the inability of scholars to pinpoint their origins with certainty as for their intrinsic artistic value. They are supplemented by mosaics, sculptures and other stone carvings of the Greek, Carthaginian and Roman epochs.

Museo de Arte de Catalunya ☆

Map 4E2. Parque de Montjuic ☎ *(93) 223 1824* 🆒 *Open 9.30am-2pm. Closed Mon. Metro España.*

Little is understated about the so-called Palacio Nacional de Montjuic, built in ponderous imitation Renaissance-Baroque for the 1929 Exposition. Apart from its great dome, ornate flanking towers and pillared and arched facade, the sound of tiered fountains and waterfalls announce it from a plaza below. Inside is a splendid collection of medieval paintings, sculpture and woodcarvings. Galleries lead from Visigothic and early Christian stonework via reconstructed segments of Romanesque churches to glorious 12th-14thC frescoes and triptychs. There are also canvases by Murillo, Velázquez, Zurbarán, Tintoretto and El Greco.

On the first floor is a separately administered **Museo de Cerámica**, with a fascinating and comprehensive array of pottery and tiles from prehistoric times to the present day.

Museo de Arte Moderno

Map 5D6. Parque de la Ciudadela ☎ *(93) 222 9367* 🆒 *Open 9am-7.30pm. Closed Mon and some holidays. Metro Barceloneta.*

The name is misleading, for this "modern art" is largely 19thC and in the Romantic or Neoclassical style, although there is a Picasso or two and some more recent works, including paintings and sculptures of Catalan artists little known outside the region.

Museo Federico Marés

Map 5D5. Condes de Barcelona 10 ☎ *(93) 310 5800* 🆒 *Open 9am-1.45pm, 4-6.45pm. Closed Mon and some holidays. Metro Jaume I.*

Sculptor and collector Marés gave his extensive collection of medieval sculpture to the city, which housed it in this ancient palace. On display are the ruins of a Roman house discovered on this site, Romanesque, Gothic and Moorish fragments, a host of polychrome religious sculptures from the Middle Ages, and a charming jumble of ordinary objects from the past: dressing gowns, toiletries, jewelry, dolls, matchboxes, women's clothes and accessories.

Museo de Historia de la Ciudad ☆

Map 5D5. Plaza del Rey s/n ☎(93) 221 0144 ▨ but ▣ on Sun. Open Mon 3.30-8.30pm, Tues-Sat 9am-2pm, 3.30-8.30pm. Sun 9am-2pm. Metro Jaume I.

An unexpectedly fascinating repository of art and artifacts concerned with Barcelona's abundant heritage is found in the 16thC Pedellás. The rooms in the basement contain excavated remains of a Roman settlement. The three floors above are crowded with fragments of monumental sculpture, household utensils, weaponry, ceramics, mosaics and paintings. Charts and drawings show the evolution of the city, and there is access to the adjacent 14thC chapel of **Santa Agueda**.

Museo Maritimo

Map 5E4. Puerto de la Paz 1 ☎(93) 318 3245 ▨ Open Tues-Sat 10am-2pm, 5-7pm, Sun and holidays 10am-3pm. Closed Mon. Metro Atarazanas.

At the harbor's edge is the 14thC royal boatyard (**Reales Atarazanas**), now serving as a maritime museum. Beneath its stone-vaulted ceilings are intricate models and actual examples of sailing and steam vessels of the seven centuries since the enclosed dockyard was erected. There is much more too: navigation instruments, drawings, figureheads, and maps, including one by Amerigo Vespucci, the explorer credited with discovering the North American continent.

Museo Picasso ☆

Map 5D5. Montcada 15 ☎(93) 319 6902 ▨ but ▣ on Sun. Open Mon 4-8.30pm, Tues-Sat 9am-2pm, 4-8.30pm, Sun and holidays 9am-2pm. Metro Jaume I.

Housed in the beautiful 15thC Palacio de Aguilar, where a graceful Gothic-Renaissance courtyard rises to the roof and the first floor is arcaded with pointed arches on slender columns, is a collection that concentrates on Picasso's early years in Málaga and Barcelona (*c.*1889-1904). Across the street is the **textile museum**, also housed in a Renaissance mansion (*open 9am-2pm, 4.30-7pm*).

Palacio de Pedralbes

Diagonal 686 ☎(93) 203 7507 ▨ Open Tues-Fri 10am-2pm, 4-7pm, Sat, Sun 10am-2pm. Closed Mon and holidays. Metro Palacio.

This royal residence was built especially for Alfonso XIII, grandfather of the present king. Built between 1919 and 1929, Italianate Neoclassicism might best describe its architecture. Furniture, paintings, tapestries, chandeliers and bibelots are largely Italian and belong to earlier periods.

Palacio de la Virreina

Map 5D4. Rambla de las Flores 99 ☎(93) 222 4289 ▨ Open Thurs, Fri noon-2pm, Sat, Sun and holidays 3-5.45pm. Closed Mon-Wed. Metro Liceo.

The 18thC palace of a Peruvian vice-reine now houses a number of separate and diverse museums. Most important is the **Colección Cambó** on the top floor, named after the benefactor who left his immaculately chosen collection of paintings by artists such as Tintoretto, Rubens, Goya, El Greco, Raphael, Botticelli, Tiepolo and Murillo. On the way down, stop at the **Museo de Artes Decorativas**, with its profusion of 18thC Spanish furnishings, porcelain, carpets and decorative objects. Finally, near the entrance, the **Museo Postal** exhibits samples of the philatelic art, arranged according to country.

Parque de la Ciudadela ☆

Map 5D5-6. Paseo Martinez Anido ▣ Metro Barceloneta.

Barcelona's major park was once the site of a fortress erected during the reign of Philip V, intended to intimidate the rebellious Catalans. The castle was dismantled in the 19thC, but a few buildings remain. One, a former palace, now houses the **Museo de Arte Moderno**. At the NW corner of the park is the **Museo Municipal de Historia Natural** (▨ *open 10am-2pm, closed Mon*). At the NE corner is an extravagantly Neoclassical fountain, an early municipal commission which Gaudí completed in 1882. Angry griffins guard its pool, backed by monumental staircases leading to a pavilion. On weekends there are impromptu performances of *sardanas*. Toward the SW corner of the park is a compact **zoo** and adjoining **aquarium** (▨ *open 10am-7.30pm*).

71

Barcelona

Parque Güell ☆
Calle Larrad s/n 🔲 *Open May-Sept 8am-9pm; Oct-Nov 9am-7pm; Dec-Apr 9am-6pm. Metro Lesseps.*

Gandí's sudden accidental death beneath the wheels of a streetcar ended construction of this project, as well as the **Templo de la Sagrada Familia**. It wasn't to be simply a park, but a housing complex that would inspire a fresh direction in urban planning. The entrance is guarded by roughly circular houses with freeform roof protuberances and a faceted tower surmounted by a four-sided star-cross. Beyond the gate, a double staircase rises to a covered pavilion. Fluted columns in front and angled pillars along side corridors alternately suggest Cretan and troglodyte influences. The scalloped roof is edged with an undulating bench coated with a crazy-quilt mosaic of broken tiles and glass. In one of the two houses actually constructed out of a planned 60 is the **Museo Gaudí**, where there are drawings, models and other memorabilia belonging to the architect.

Pueblo Español ☆
Map 4E1. Av. Marqués de Comillas s/n 🔲 🖴 ✳ *Open June-Sept 9am-8pm; Oct-May 9am-7pm. Closed some holidays. Metro España.*

This "Spanish Village," left behind from the 1929 Exposition, is an amalgamation of native architectural styles, full-size replicas of domestic and municipal buildings from every region of the country. Most are modeled on actual structures. A stroll through the simulated streets and plazas of the complex can emphasize the remarkable diversity of Spanish native architecture. Coin-operated machines that give lectures in any of four languages, in lieu of guides, are dotted about the village.

Las Ramblas
Map 5D-E4.

Tawdry, charming, clangorous, venal, colorful, Las Ramblas is at the thumping heart of Barcelona. A broad, tree-canopied promenade with a one-way street on either side lined with five-to nine-story 19thC buildings, it curves NE near the **Colón monument** by the port to the SW corner of the **Plaça de Catalunya**, a distance of approximately 2km (1¼ miles). It is in fact a single street, although each of its several sections has a different name: "Rambla de los Capuchinos," "Rambla de San José," "Rambla de Estudios."

Along the entire route are all-night book and magazine stands, pavement cafés, pet stores, flower stalls and several second-class hotels. Families mingle with streams of visitors, carousing sailors on leave, beggars, hustlers, transvestites, pimps and watchful policemen. There is nothing quite like this unusual avenue anywhere else in Spain.

The best place to begin a stroll is at the Plaça de Catalunya, the city's main square; and the best time is early evening, although on warm nights this district is still lively at 4am. At this end of Las Ramblas is a drinking fountain: it is said that after a sip of its waters you will never leave Barcelona, but it isn't advisable to test the legend. Nearby, old men gather in voluble groups, discussing politics and soccer, and political activists often put up their banners and pass out literature in this vicinity.

On the right, where the Rambla de Estudios becomes the Rambla de San José (or "de las Flores"), is the 18thC **Palacio de la Virreina**. Immediately beyond, on the same side, is the **Mercado de San José** (*open 8am-1.30pm, 4.30-8pm*). Beneath its high, leaded glass roof are dozens of stalls with luxuriant heaps of sea creatures, loaves of bread, wedges of cheese, marzipan, grapes and artichokes. Above hang rows of *serrano* hams and garlands of garlic.

Back on Las Ramblas, the booths bloom with tubs of cut flowers. At the next intersection, turn left and left again along Calle Cardenal Casañas for a glimpse of the 15thC **Iglesia de Santa María del Pino** and its vivid rose window. Retrace your steps to Las Ramblas; on the right is the **Liceo** theater, entirely devoted to opera and dance, and on the left is the **Barrio Gótico**. Farther on to the right is the **Barrio Chino**, a teeming working-class district of flyspecked bars and doss houses. Next is the **Plaza del Teatro**, dominated by Gaudí's **Palacio Güell**, which has been converted into a theatrical museum (it is not advisable to wander in this area after midnight). At the end of Las Ramblas is the Colón (Columbus) monument, and just beyond is moored a replica of the explorer's *Santa María*. On the right side of the plaza is the restored medieval boatyard which is now used as a **maritime museum**.

For a quieter stroll, there is a continuation of Las Ramblas running from the NW corner of the Plaça de Catalunya to El Diagonal. Its stores are more stylish and its hotels are first-class.

Templo de la Sagrada Familia 🏛 † ★

Map 5B5. Plaza de la Sagrada Familia 🚌 *Open summer 8am-9pm; winter 9am-7pm. Metro Sagrada Familia.*

Although the unfinished church is widely regarded as Antonio Gaudí's masterpiece, or conversely a travesty in stone, it was originally another architect's commission. Francisco del Villar started it in 1882, when Gaudí was still working in a relatively sedate Neoclassical style. He assisted Villar at first and then took control in 1891. The crypt was partially finished, but little else.

Gaudí's style was extraordinary for the time, and is hardly less startling now. His scheme was to erect three main facades, each with four towers, the total representing the Apostles. A dome above the transept crossing was to have four more spires, larger still, a bristling profile piercing the sky. Only the E face was completed, but it is enough to create a picture of what the whole might have been. Peaked canopies above the three doors are carved to suggest molten stone or stalactites, until the eye picks out the groups of sculptured figures illustrating scenes celebrating the Nativity. At the same level, open piers support the perforated towers narrowing at their tips into colorful tile pinnacles ending in vivid starbursts. Work continues on its completion, although the architect died with the details of his concept in his head. At the present pace, the cathedral is unlikely to be finished before the middle of the 21stC.

Tibidabo ☆

🚌 🚃 🎿 *Open 7.30am-9.30pm. Metro Av. Tibidabo.*

On evening walks around the city, you will notice the illuminated church on top of the precipitous hills that rear up to the N and W. To get up there, which is enjoyable in itself, take the Metro to the end of the line at Avinguda Tibidabo and then the tram, a relic as charming as San Francisco's cable cars, that creaks up the steep hill past the curious mansions which belonged to the turn-of-the-century rich. Many are now schools, but they remain bizarre compilations of every architectural style from the Moors to Gaudí, each higher one surpassing the ones below. This trip connects with the funicular (*continuous operation 7.30am-9.30pm*) for the final leg.

It is alleged that *Mallorca* can be seen from the top, but if true this can only be verified on exceptionally clear days, which are rare in Barcelona. Nevertheless, the city sprawls to the sea in a stunning panorama that is perhaps best viewed at dusk. The belvederes are surrounded by a clean, compact, three-tiered and pleasantly dated amusement park. Behind it is a crudely realized church, where a boy's choir sings daily (*6pm*). Above the small church is the granite basilica which can be seen, illuminated, from the city center.

Hotels

Avenida Palace
Map 5C4. Gran Via 605, Barcelona 7 🕿 *(93) 301 9600* ☎ *54734* ▥ *229 rms* ▭ *229* ▤ ▦ ▧ 🅰🅴 ⓞ ⓒⓓ 🆅🆂🅰 *Metro Gran Via.*
Location: Just w of the Paseo de Gracia. The Avenida Palace doesn't qualify for *grande dame* status on the basis of age (it opened only in 1952) but it is as dignified as the **Ritz** if not as luxurious. Beneath its mock towers is a crisply run hotel whose staff is carefully trained and attentive. The location is ideal, equidistant from everything the city offers.
⬍ ▢ ▱ ☙ ♈

Colón
Map 5D4. Av. de la Catedral 7, Barcelona 2 🕿 *(93) 301 1404* ☎ *52654* ▥ *to* ▥ *161 rms* ▭ *161* ▤ ▦ ▧ 🅰🅴 🅲🅱 ⓞ ⓓ 🆅🆂🅰 *Metro Jaume I.*
Location: In the heart of the Gothic Quarter. For those who expect to spend most of their time in the Ramblas-Barrio Gótico district, there isn't a better hotel. The balconied front rooms (the ones on the sixth floor have large terraces) face the 13thC **cathedral**. Public rooms are generously appointed and the bedrooms are comfortable. Recent painting has brightened the once gloomy single rooms at the back, but they are still cramped and viewless. Only breakfast is to be recommended in the dining room.
⬍ ▢ ▱ 〈〈 ☙ ♈

Derby
Map 4C2. Loreto 21, Barcelona 29 🕿 *(93) 322 3515* ▥ *to* ▥ *116 rms* ▭ *116* ▤ ▦ ▧ 🅰🅴 ⓞ ⓒⓓ 🆅🆂🅰 *Metro Hospital Clínico.*
Location: Near Plaza Francescá Maciá, in the NW. Intentionally Anglophile, the Derby strives to emulate a Mayfair club, and the result is a surprisingly successful

evocation of that ambience. Wood trim and ornamentation are polished to a satin finish, fingerprints wiped off as they appear. Lighting is diffused, colors are hushed. In the piano bar, a capable duo whisks up any cocktail you might care to drink. Guinness is on tap in the simulated pub. Two rooms on each floor have large beds, by no means the Spanish norm, and those on the top floor have terraces. The only drawback is the remote location.

⌂ ♯ 🖼 ☻ ⵉ

Gala Placidia ♣

Map 4A3. Via Augusta 112, Barcelona 6 ☎(93) 217 8200 ☎97354 ⅢⅢ to ⅢⅢ 28 rms ▭ 28 ⇌ AE ⊚ ⊚ VISA Metro Plaza Molina.

Location: Next to the fashionable Balmes-Tuset district. Ideal for families or long stays, it has 28 suites, each with a living-dining room, terrace, minimal catering facilities, bath and one or two bedrooms. They sleep three to five people for the price of a standard double in better-known hotels and make a remarkable bargain. The restaurant is justifiably little used, and the suites are not air conditioned — an important consideration in Barcelona's muggy summer.

♯ ☐ 🖼 ⵉ

Majestic ▥

Map 5C4. Paseo de Gracia 70, Barcelona 8 ☎(93) 215 4512 ☎52211 ⅢⅢ 360 rms ▭ 360 ▤ ➹ ⇌ ⇌ AE CB ⊚ ⊚ VISA Metro Aragón.

Location: In the city center, N of Plaça de Catalunya. Despite an air of chilly formality, the Majestic is nearly the perfect hotel, a fact reflected in its prices. It faces the grand Paseo de Gracia, Barcelona's Champs-Elysées, and is within walking distance of virtually every major sightseeing attraction and many of the best stores. For those with fitness mania, there is a gymnasium, sauna, and rooftop pool, still rare facilities in Spanish cities. A happier choice couldn't be made.

⌂ ♯ ☐ 🖼 ⇌ ☻ ⵉ

Princesa Sofía ▥

Plaza de Pío XII, Barcelona 28 ☎(93) 330 7111 ☎51032 ⅢⅢ 514 rms ▭ 514 ▤ ➹ ⇌ ⇌ AE ⊚ ⊚ VISA Metro Palacio.

Location: Near University City. This hotel's only disadvantage is its distance from the city center. Otherwise the picture is positive, if old-fashioned charm is not on your

list of requirements. This hospitable modern hotel is scrupulously engineered to gratify the needs and whims of international travelers. Rooms are well-equipped, and an indoor pool, small gym and sauna help to cure jetlag. Two bars have live music for dancing nightly, and the nightclubs in the Calvo Sotelo district are not far away.

♯ ☐ 🖼 ➹ ⫷ ⇌ ☻ ⵉ 🎵 ♨

Regente

Map 5C4. Rambla de Catalunya 76, Barcelona 8 ☎(93) 215 2570 ☎51939 ⅢⅢ to ⅢⅢ 78 rms ▭ 78 ▤ ➹ ⇌ ⇌ AE ⊚ ⊚ VISA Metro Aragón.

Location: Six streets N of the Plaça de Catalunya. The Regente has so much going for it, from its rooftop pool and its quiet and convenient location to its understated Art Nouveau fittings, that it is surprising how little attention it receives. Rooms are large and decorated in soft colors. The street outside is a quiet, tree-lined extension of **Las Ramblas**.

♯ 🖼 ⇌ ⵉ

Ritz ▥

Map 5C4. Gran Via de les Corts Catalanes 668, Barcelona 10 ☎(93) 318 5200 ☎52739 ⅢⅢ 197 rms ▭ 197 ▤ ⇌ AE ⊚ ⊚ VISA Metro Urquinaona.

Location: Three streets E of Paseo de Gracia. The Ritz was built to accommodate the well-born and well-heeled who toured Europe with steamer trunks and servants, and settled into a hotel for at least three months. They required room to entertain and impress, and the Ritz provided it. Ceilings in both private and public rooms are unusually high. Gold-leaf, damask, brocade and crystal have been used with a lavish hand; skirting boards are marble. After some years of decline, ambitious renovation work was begun. It is now finished, and this grand hotel, where the service is superb, has a traditional, gracious atmosphere, unequaled in the city. The restaurant is among the best in Barcelona, but inevitably prices are high.

♯ ☐ 🖼 ☻ ⵉ

📧 Other recommended hotels include: **Barcelona** (*Caspe 1-13, Barcelona 2* ☎(93) 301 9400 ⅢⅢ); **Euro-Park** (*Aragón 325, Barcelona 9* ☎(93) 257 9205 ⅢⅢ to ⅢⅢ); **Gran Hotel Calderón** (*Rambla de Catalunya 26, Barcelona 7* ☎(93) 301 0000 ⅢⅢ); **Gran Hotel Sarriá** (*Av. de Sarriá 50, Barcelona 29* ☎(93) 239

1109 ▐▐▐▐); **Granvía** (*Gran Via de les Corts Catalanes 642, Barcelona 10* ☎(93) 318 1900 ▐▐); **Manila** (*Ramblas 111, Barcelona 2* ☎(93) 318 6200 ▐▐▐▐); **Nuñez Urgel** (*Urgel 232, Barcelona 36* ☎(93) 322 4153 ▐▐▐▐ to ▐▐▐▐); **Presidente** (*Av. Diagonal 570, Barcelona 21* ☎(93) 200 2111 ▐▐▐▐); **Rallye** (*Travessera de les Corts 150, Barcelona 28* ☎(93) 339 9050 ▐▐); **Regencia Collón** (*Sagristans 13, Barcelona 2* ☎(93) 232 2000 ▐▐ to ▐▐▐▐); **Royal** (*Ramblas 117, Barcelona 2* ☎(93) 318 7329 ▐▐▐▐).

Restaurants

Agut d'Avignon
Map 5E4. Trinidad 3 ☎(93) 302 6034 ▐▐▐▐ to ▐▐▐▐ ⊡ ■■ ▦ AE CB ⊙ VISA *Last orders 11pm. Closed Aug and Sun. Metro Jaume I.*

Merely finding this justly honored restaurant is an adventure (look for the alley off the narrow Calle Avignon). The interior is reminiscent of a hunting lodge, with tiles, stucco, fireplaces, balconies and evocative paintings. *Pollo con gambas, lenguado* and *bacalao* are among the selections from the Basque, Catalan and provincial French cuisines. It is very popular, so reserve ahead.

Casa Isidre
Les Flors 12 ☎(93) 241 1139 ▐▐▐▐ ⊡ ■■ ▦ ⊙ VISA *Last orders 11pm. Closed Sun, holidays, Holy Week, Christmas, and Jul 15-Aug 15.*

The Casa Isidre doesn't need the business these few words might bring it. For nearly 20yrs at the same location (just off Avinguda del Paralel), it has done well as a cherished retreat for titled and artistic Barcelona. For proof, ask to see the guest book, an impressive roster, including such names as Joan Miró. They are drawn by the warmth and informality of a family-run enterprise that features *cocina del mercado* — cooking determined by market availability. Only 41 diners can be seated at one time, and in rather snug quarters at that, so book at least two days ahead. Among possible choices are *surtido de verduritas* and *muslito de pato en civet.*

Eldorado Petit
Dolors Monserdá 57 ☎(93) 204 5506 ▐▐▐▐ ⚬ ⊡ ■■ ⚬ ▾ AE ⊙ *Closed Sun and two weeks in Aug.*

Overpraised by some, underrated by others, this new entry on the scene continues that culinary dual personality. Some of the dishes are traditional recipes in portions filling the plate, others adhere to the *nouvelle* conventions of tiny amounts of food cunningly arranged. Obviously they seek to please all comers, which they may do, although the high prices aren't really justified by the performance and surroundings. Choose the more animated ground floor of the converted mansion, unless the hush upstairs appeals. The restaurant is in the far NW precinct of the city.

Florian
Bertrand i Serra 20 ☎(93) 212 4627 ▐▐▐▐ ⚬ ⊡ ■■ *Last orders 11pm. Closed Sun, Holy Week, two weeks in Aug, Christmas.*

The boldly mustachioed owner exudes confidence as he takes orders and oversees the work of his minions. His attitude is justified, in large measure. Although he adheres to certain conventions of the New Cuisine (such as large, unmatched plates of distinctive design), the food is rarely of the frou-frou cuteness that afflicts too many kitchens of that persuasion. Try the pasta salad with *langostinos,* ravioli filled with mushrooms or monkfish (*rape* or angler fish).

Guría
Map 4C3. Casanova 97 ☎(93) 253 6325 ▐▐▐▐ ⊡ ▦ ▾ AE ⊙ VISA *Last orders 11.30pm. Closed Aug and Holy Week. Metro Hospital Clínico.*

In short, this is a country house with dark paneling and beams, large leather chairs, suitable canvases of the hunt and kitchen, and a collection of ceramic dogs in niches along the staircase leading from the quiet ground-floor bar to the upstairs dining rooms. The effervescent multi-lingual host, the son of the founder, slips easily from colloquial English to voluble Spanish, or from Italian to German, while explaining such interesting Basque dishes, as *alubias rojas* (red kidney beans), *menestra de verduras, gambas al champán, perdiz* and *jabalí,* as well as taking orders.

Neichel
Avenida Pedrables 16 (at the back of) ☎(93) 203 8408 ▐▐▐▐ ⊡ ■■ ▦ ⚬ AE CB ⊙ ⊙ VISA *Last*

orders 11.30pm. Closed Sun,
holidays, Aug, Christmas.
Never mind what is written
elsewhere — *this* is the restaurant
without equal in Barcelona. Alsatian
chef Jean-Louis Neichel is a boon to
travelers weary of *paella*, *gazpacho*
and wan pretenses to *nouvelle* laurels-
of-the-week. He displays a wizardry
that threads a line between picture-
perfect plates and supernal marriages
of flavor and texture. With his
artistry at the stove and his obsession
with every detail of service, only the
absence of foreign-language menus is
a correctable fault. At these prices,
his customers (international business
people and privileged officials) have a
right to know what they are ordering.
But in this case, everything on the
card is truly a specialty, so fear not —
just point.

Reno ⌂
Map *4B3.* Tuset 27 ☎(93) 200
9129 ⅢⅢ ▢ ▬ ▬ ▤ ☞ ❤ AE
CB ◉ ⓒ VISA Last orders 11pm.
Metro Gracia.
Although now forced to share the
pinnacle of *haute cuisine* with younger
competitors, this long-standing
leader hasn't slipped an inch. The
reception is as warm as ever, the
environment formal but
unintimidating, the staff
exceptionally polished, the French-
Catalan menu faultless. Men will feel
most comfortable in a jacket and tie.
The salmon smoked on the premises
is sublime, prawns are revelatory, the
sole is cooked to perfection, and it is
impossible not to be effusive about

the wild strawberries splashed with
sweet wine and sprinkled with sugar.

Siete Puertas
Map *5E5.* Passeig d'Isabel 11
☎(93) 319 3033 ⅢⅢ ▢ ▬ ▤ ♪
AE ◉ ⓒ VISA Last orders 1am.
Metro Correos.
These "seven doors" lead into a
rambling restaurant of several rooms
lit by basket-sized hanging lamps
with peach-colored cloth shades.
Popular prices, attentive waiters, and
the house specialties of *paella*, *arroz
con sardinas*, *bacalao* and *conejo*
contrive to attract the chic and the
bourgeois, the old and the young,
families, couples, and groups of
executives. Everyone is made to feel
comfortable, especially at midday. In
the evenings, dim lights and a piano
player create a romantic mood.

➤ Other restaurants that are worth
trying are: **Bon Vivant** (*Aribau 292*
☎(93) 218 7020 ⅢⅢ); **Casa Costa**
(*Baluarte 124* ☎(93) 319 5028 ⅢⅢ);
Flash-Flash (*La Granada 25* ☎(93)
228 5567 ⅢⅢ); **Los Caracoles**
(*Escudillers 14* ☎(93) 302 3185 ⅢⅢ);
Portofino 2 (*Ganduxer 50* ☎(93) 201
0009 ⅢⅢ); **La Tramuntana** (*Plaza de
San Miguel 2* ☎(93) 302 6175 ⅢⅢ);
La Venta (*Plaza Funicular 2* ☎(93)
212 6455 ⅢⅢ); **Via Veneto** (*Ganduxer
10* ☎(93) 200 7024 ⅢⅢ).
  The best of the many snack,
sandwich and *tapas* bars are: **Alba**
(*Paris 168* Ⅱ); **Casinet del Barri
Gotic** (*Freneria 6* Ⅱ); **Drugstore**
(*Paseo de Gracia 71* ☎(93) 215 3841
▢); **Drugstore David** (*Tuset 17* ▢).

Nightlife
No Spanish city comes alive at night more than Barcelona. The following can
do no more than suggest the plenitude of diversions. As fast as new discos,
clubs, bars and pubs spring up, others close down, and any survey is subject
to change. **Discos** are usually closed Mon, **jazz clubs** Mon-Wed, **bars and
pubs** Sun. Many have no telephone. A copy of *Guia del Ocio* (available from
most newsstands) lists current nightspots, films and concerts. Although it is
in Spanish, it is easily understood.
  Films both popular and obscure have a wide audience. Most are dubbed in
Spanish. Look for the initials "V.O." on posters and in advertisements,
indicating a film in the original language with Spanish subtitles.
  Little is as ephemeral as the status of a **disco**, and a common device to
enhance desirability is to feign a "members only" policy — but few are really
that exclusive. The most *in* place at the very nanosecond of writing, at least
with young Barcelona, is **Otto Zutzz** (*Lincoln 15* ☎(93) 218 0722). Imagine a
two-floored warehouse that once served as a car repair station or small gaol
and that gives a hint of the relentless neo-brutalist decor. Far different is **Up
& Down** (*Numancia 179* ☎(93) 204 8809), a magnet for upscale folk of all
ages. The younger among them head downstairs, the more aged (over 30)
prefer the upper level, with its relatively muted music and restaurant.
Gaining entrance depends upon their need for patrons on a given night, the
appearance of supplicants, and the whims of doorkeepers. **Studio 54** (*Av.
Paral-el 64* ☎(93) 329 5454) provides vast stretches of welcome elbow room
and one of the most imaginative light shows in town.
  There are few good nightclubs in Barcelona, but the following is a

selection of the more agreeable: **Caesar's** (*Av. de Roma 2* ☎ *(93) 325 4872*), **El Duende** (*Ecuador 55* ☎ *(93) 321 8412*), **Scala Barcelona** (*Plaça de San Juan 47* ☎ *(93) 232 6363*), and **El Molino** (*Vila Vila 99* ☎ *(93) 241 6383*). This last is a music hall no doubt modeled on the Moulin Rouge in Paris, complete with a fake windmill on the facade, which has been going almost continuously since 1909. At all the clubs, dinner and show are included in one reasonable price but drinks are extra.

Pubs and bars in the city provide late afternoon and evening entertainment. They vary from simulations of the British "pub" to *coctelerías*, with elaborate menus of alcoholic concoctions and taped or occasionally live jazz or rock music. Passeig del Born is a short street where numerous bars have sprung up in recent years. **17 Bar** (*Passeig del Born 17* ☎ *(93) 319 0048*) is a high-ceilinged room with bamboo and raffia furniture, paintings and "serious" English rock on the stereo. **El Copetín** (*Passeig del Born 19*) serves good Irish coffee on marble-topped tables with bentwood chairs at the end of a long polished entrance bar. Taped blues and jazz constitute the *música ambiental*. Across the street is **El Born** (*Passeig del Born 26*), slightly more ambitious with a claustrophobic dining room upstairs, a carved stone sink converted to a bar, and a compact lounge, warmed by a coal stove in winter.

More fashionable bars can be found in the smarter district just N and s of El Diagonal, between Plaça Francesc Macià and Calle Balmes. **El Dry Martini Bar** (*Aribau 162*) claims to have over 80 brands of gin in stock, and various recipes for the basic brew are on hand. Not far away is the elegant English-style **Ideal Scotch** (*Aribau 89*), with virtually all legitimate brands of the namesake whisky augmented by rum, fruit drinks and canapés. **Maxim's** (*Aribau 250*) is a bar-cafeteria-*coctelería* with satisfying platters of pâtés and cheeses. The snug downstairs bar is for drinking only. **Taberna Inglesa Dirty Dick's** (*Marco Aurelio 2*) is a typical reproduction of the British-style pub with hanging dimpled pint mugs and two or three of Albion's brews on tap.

A recent phenomenon is the establishment of *champanerias*, wherein the principal tipple is just what the name suggests. The emphasis is on Spanish *caves*, generally excellent sparkling wines made by the champagne method. **Xampu Xampany** (*Gran Via 702* ☎ *(93) 232 0716*) is exemplary of the breed, with widely spaced tables in a Post Modernist, Euro-sleek setting. Caviar and smoked salmon canapés are ideal accompaniments. Other possibilities are: **La Xampanyeria** (*Provenza 236* ☎ *(93) 232 0716*) and **La Cava del Palau** (*Verdaguer i Callis 10* ☎ *(93) 310 0938*).

Higher in elevation and pecking order is **Merbeyé** (*Plaza Funicular 2*), halfway up Tibidabo near the base of the funicular. It is currently a haven for the chic of all ages. There is live music between Sept and May, a disc jockey all the time, a terrace for warm evenings, a piano lounge and an upstairs hideaway.

Andalucian folk dance and music has fallen on hard times in Barcelona, as elsewhere. Almost the only **flamenco** club that is certain to remain in operation is also one of the oldest; **Los Tarantos** (*Plaça Real 17* ☎ *(93) 317 8098*) is tucked away in a corner of the Plaça Real. Dark, smoke-filled, with inept murals of Gypsies, and a small stage backed by crimson curtains, it is a typical *tablao*, hinting of tacky sinfulness. Another possibility is **El Patio Anadulz** (*Aribau 242* ☎ *209 3375*). Shows are more or less continuous, from 10pm to 3am or so. Go after midnight, when the performers seem to loosen up.

Gran Teatro del Liceo
Ramblas 61 ☎ *(93) 302 6019* ◼ *Open according to performance schedules.*
Superb acoustics and a grand Neoclassical interior compare favorably with all the great opera houses of Europe. First completed in 1847, assorted vicissitudes both natural and suspect have required repeated renovations. Except when an opening-night crowd eddies around the Ramblas entrance, the gray facade barely attracts the eye. Nevertheless, it is here that the world's most acclaimed singers perform, and concerts and ballets are frequently produced.

Shopping

The acquisitive impulse is abundantly served, or perhaps provoked, in Barcelona, with a vast number of specialty stores along almost every street.

If you're looking for gifts, the logical way to begin is at **El Cote Inglés** (The English Cut) on the E side of the Plaça de Catalunya. One of Spain's major department store chains, its several floors cater to every imaginable need, with boutiques scattered among the larger departments. The relationship between price and quality is good, the selection ample. Its principal rival is **Galerías Preciados** (*Av. del Angel*), just s of El Corte Inglés. At the government-run **Artespaña** (*Rambla de Catalunya 121*), you can buy all kinds of Spanish handicrafts: ceramics, leather goods, silverwork, woodcarvings, clothing, furniture and accessories. Everything is in excellent taste, but there are no bargains.

In the **Barrio Gótico** there are specialty stores around every corner. Dealers in antiquarian books and maps, leather goods, crafts and antiques, confectioners and tobacconists predominate. Try **Calle Freneria**, which runs along the E wall of the cathedral; **Calle Puertaferrisa**, connecting the plaza in front of the cathedral with Las Ramblas; or **Calle Ferrán**, between Plaça Sant Jaume and Las Ramblas.

International chic reigns along the **Paseo de Gracia**, the N to S boulevard between the Plaça de Catalunya and El Diagonal. Although many of the names are familiar from other fashionable capitals, products are often priced lower than might be expected. Spanish firms dealing in shoes and handbags charge substantially less here than in Paris or New York. Serious shoppers can begin by facing N at the SE corner of the Plaça de Catalunya: walk along the right-hand side of the *paseo*, cross W at Calle de Rosellon, and return S along the opposite side. Following that route, you will encounter the men's clothier **E. Furest**, the custom tailor **Pellicer** (for both men and women), and, in the famous Gaudí building, **Casa Milá**, the women's boutique **Parera**. Farther along the *paseo*, **Yanko** deals in superb Spanish shoes, handbags, purses and belts, and **A. Gratacos** in fine fabrics of great variety.

Crossing to the W side of the *paseo*, the pipes, lighters and pen displays of **Gimeno** catch the eye. Head S for **Carlos Torrents**, which focuses on stylish men's clothing of the Armani creed, and down the adjacent Passage de la Concepción you'll find **Pierre Cardin**.

Between Calle de Valencia and Calle de Aragón, an arcade cuts through to Rambla de Catalunya, called **El Bulevard Rosa**, an inviting arrangement of trendy boutiques, quality clothing stores, a bar-restaurant and a courtyard; it is a refreshing change of mood from the sedate aspect of the *paseo*.

Place nearby
Montserrat (*53km/33 miles NW of Barcelona*).   The name refers to both the famous monastery and the mountain range in which it is cradled. Faithful Catholics come here to pay homage to the fabled *Black Madonna*, a wooden statue of the Virgin alleged to have been brought to Barcelona by St Peter and rediscovered in the 9thC (in fact its origins are probably 12thC). Others come for the views or to hear the boys' choir in the basilica. The 19thC **monastery** (✗ *compulsory, inquire at* **i** *in Barcelona*) is a replacement for a 10thC complex of structures destroyed by the French in 1812. The area is now commercial, but still important to Catalans.

Belmonte
Map 8F6. Cuenca. 122km (75 miles) NW of Albacete; 99km (62 miles) SW of Cuenca. Population: 3,000.
Seekers of exemplary castles are obliged to make this short detour off the Madrid-Valencia road. Their expectations will be amply rewarded by the hexagonal ramparts and towers of Belmonte's superb 15thC **fortress**, in such a fine state of preservation that it has been declared a national monument. The owner was the Marqués de Villena, and he installed the remarkable Mudejar interiors. Beautiful 15thC carved wooden choir stalls are the prominent features of the town's second most important sight, the church of **San Bartolomé**.

Benavente
Map 11C4. Zamora. 66km (41 miles) N of Zamora; 70km (44 miles) S of León. Population: 12,000.
Astride an ancient highway that witnessed the passage of armies engaged in the assault of Castile, *Galicia* and *León*, Benavente

was the home of generations of the Pimentel family, who lived in the castle that crowns the hill above the medieval town. The French were the last to bombard this fortress, in the 19thC. Ferdinand II commissioned the 12thC **Iglesia de Santa María**, which is largely Romanesque in aspect but with Gothic and Baroque components within.

🧶 **Parador Nacional Rey Fernando II de León**
Paseo Ramón y Cajal s/n ☎(988) 630 300 **Ⅲ□** *to* **ⅠⅢⅢ** 30 rms 🛏 30 ◂
🚲 ⇌ AE ◑ CD VISA
Location: On a hill above the town. In the 12thC Ferdinand II built the castle that is now a *parador* to fend off assorted Portuguese, Moorish and Castilian enemies. Other forces overran it over the succeeding centuries, and the only part that persisted in relative entirety was the large rectangular keep with cylindrical towers at each corner, an addition made by Count Alonso de Pimentel. Exposed brick and stone are the principal materials, serving as a backdrop to the tapestries that brighten the public rooms.
🏠 🖼 🎿 🜚 ⛷ ♈

🍴 While the **Parador** dining room (*address and* ☎ *as hotel* **Ⅲ□**) is better, **Mesón el Pícaro** (*Las Dominicas 1* ☎(988) 631 793 **□**) is less institutional, and that makes it especially popular for weddings and family celebrations. The food is typically Castilian.

Benidorm

*Map 9G8. Alicante. 143km (89 miles) s of Valencia; 42km (26 miles) NE of Alicante. Population: 29,700 **i** Martinez Alejos 16* ☎(965) 585 3224.
A spit of land contains the remnants of an ancient fishing village, now dwarfed by blocks of flats, reaching ever higher for glimpses of sea. The Manhattanization of the shoreline and the slope rising beyond does not deter tens of thousands of Northern Europeans from swooping down upon the still magnificent beaches that stretch nearly 3km (2 miles) on either side of the original hamlet.

🧶 **Belroy Palace** (*Mediterráneo 13* ☎585 0203 **Ⅲ□**) and **Gran Hotel Delfín** (*Playa de Poniente* ☎(965) 585 3400 **Ⅲ□**) are well located to take advantage of what Benidorm has to offer.

🍴 **I Fratelli** (*Orts Llorca 21* ☎(965) 585 3979 **Ⅲ□**) is pleasant and essentially Italian; **Tiffany's** (*Av. Mediterráneo* ☎(965) 585 4468 **Ⅲ□**) provides piano music, toney surroundings and good fish dishes, but only at night; **Don Luis** (*Orts Llorca s/n* ☎(965) 585 4673 **ⅢⅢ**) proclaims its "kitchen of the market," with meals determined by ingredients available fresh that day, as well as some pasta dishes.

Bilbao (*Bilbo*)

Map 13B7. Vizcaya. 100km (62 miles) w of San Sebastián; 110km (68 miles) E of Santander. Population: 431,000 Alameda Mazarredo s/n ☎(94) 423 6430.
Spain's largest port is at the s end of a long, narrow *ría* formed by the confluence of two rivers. Industrialized since the mid-19thC, Bilbao has prospered continuously despite the severity of military actions from the Carlist period to the Civil War. Iron ore from nearby mines is smelted at furnaces along the E bank of the *ría*. There are also shipbuilding yards, oil refineries and chemical factories.

The combination of war and industry has left the city with few attractions of interest to most vacationers, apart from several fine restaurants, but it serves as a base for excursions along the Cantabrian coast. Its setting also ensures a steady supply of fresh ingredients for the many superb Basque restaurants that constitute a gastronomic vacation in themselves.

Event In Aug, festival with bullfights, theatrical presentations and other spectacles.

Sights and places of interest

Museo de Bellas Artes

Parque de Doña Casilda de Iturriaza s/n ☎*(94) 441 9536* 🅾 *Open Tues-Sat 10am-1.30pm, 4.30-7.30pm, Sun 11am-2pm. Closed Mon.*
An uninviting exterior conceals a surprisingly extensive collection of Spanish and foreign paintings and sculptures from the Romanesque period to the early 20thC. El Greco, Velázquez, Ribera, Ribalta, Zurbarán, Goya and Herrera are represented, in addition to samples of largely unattributed early Gothic and Romanesque religious art. Modernists, from Gauguin to Sorolla, are displayed on the first floor.

Museo Histórico

Cruz 4-6 ☎*(94) 415 5423* 🅾 *Open Tues-Sat 10am-1.30pm, 4-7pm, Sun 10am-1.30pm. Closed Mon.*
A miscellany of Christian artifacts, ceramics, furnishings, replicas of cave paintings and regional art is on view.

🍴 Villa de Bilbao 🏨

Gran Via López de Haro 87, Bilbao 11 ☎*(94) 441 6000* 🕿 *32164* ▥▥▥▥
142 rms ▭ *142* ▦▦ ▬▬ ▭ AE ⊕ ⓒ VISA
Location: Two streets s of the Parque de Casilda Iturriza. Bilbao's newest luxury hotel strives to earn its five stars. It is well designed, has attentive staff and a wide range of facilities, and the bedrooms are larger than in most modern hotels. A helpful hint: the garage is shared with the sister hotel Aránzazu, in the block behind the Villa de Bilbao.
‡ ☐ ⌨ ⛄ ☂ ᠑

🍴 Until the arrival of the **Villa de Bilbao**, **Ercilla** 🏨 (*Ercilla 37, Bilbao 11* ☎*(94) 443 8800* ▥▥▥▥) was Bilbao's most prestigious hotel. Absolutely central and larger than its newest rival, it has high standards and as many facilities. Alternative choices include the above mentioned **Aránzazu** (*Rodríguez Arias 66, Bilbao 13* ☎*(94) 441 3100* ▥▥▥) and the **Carlton** (*Plaza Federico Moyúa 2, Bilbao 9* ☎*(94) 416 2200* ▥▥▥▥).

🍽 Guria ✿

Gran Via López de Haro 66 ☎*(94) 415 0543* ▥▥▥▥ ▭ ▬▬ ▦▦ AE ⊕ ⓒ
VISA *Last orders 11.30pm. Closed Sun.*
This restaurant successfully combines colorful trappings, adroit attendance by skilled waiters, and Basque specialties as they always should be experienced, cooked with exquisite precision from absolutely fresh ingredients. An evening at Guria will probably be a memory of Spain to be treasured years later.

🍽 **Goizeko-Kabi** (*Particular de Estraunza 4 & 6* ☎*(94) 442 1129* ▥▥▥) competes favourably in a city renowned for its excellent cooking. **Bermeo** (*address and* ☎*as Ercilla hotel* ▥▥▥) is an uncommonly good Basque restaurant; reserve ahead at the brisk, straightforward **Colavidas** (*Hurtado de Amézaga 1* ☎*(94) 423 9608* ▥▯ *to* ▥▥), which provides supreme Basque cookery and allows nothing to interfere with the business in hand — eating; there is a classical Basque menu at **Artagan** (*Gran Via López de Haro 87* ☎*(94) 441 6000* ▥▥▥); and a version of "nouvelle Basque" cuisine is available at **Drugstore** (*Telesforo Aranzadi 4* ☎*(94) 443 5017* ▥▯).

Burgos

Map 12C6. Burgos. 156km (97 miles) s of Santander; 121km (74 miles) NE of Valladolid. Population: 152,000 **i** *Plaza Alonso Martinez 7* ☎*(947) 203 125.*
The "Cabeza de Castilla" (Head of Castile) was for a time capital of the kingdom of León and Old Castile. That was a millennium ago, when the legendary El Cid was laying waste to Moorish enemies. His supposed remains are buried in the magnificent cathedral here.

Burgos' founding dates back to the 9thC, when the plain at the edge of the river Arlanzón was chosen as the site for a castle built to oppose the Moors.

Most of the important sights are N of the river, within walking distance of each other. Apart from the castle, largely destroyed by the French in 1813 after a siege by Wellington, the old quarter is fundamentally intact; the city's heritage belongs to the Middle Ages, mixed with late Gothic. The Falangist party officially originated here in 1936.

Event In June, Fiesta de San Pedro.

Sights and places of interest
Cathedral 🏛 ✝ ★
Plaza de Santa Maria 🔲 🗷 ✗ *Open 10am-1.30pm, 4-6.30pm.*

Of all Spain's cathedrals, this must rank with those of *Sevilla* and *Toledo* as the most magnificent in the country. It is a sublime example of the Flamboyant Gothic, with an exterior as visually engaging as the interior. Take a few moments to circle the building, beginning at the far side of the Plaza de Santa Maria before the main W facade. The twin pierced spires bracket a rose window and a profusion of statuary, smaller turrets, scalloped balustrades, inset arches and pillars.

Go up to the steps at this end of the plaza, turn right (E) at the top and you will soon come to the 13thC **Puerta de la Coronería**. At the next corner, steps lead down to the ornate 16thC Plateresque **Puerta de la Pellejería**.

Continue around the perimeter, noticing two box-shaped octagonal towers above the crossing and the **Capilla del Condestable**, and a long wall enclosing the cloister and appended secondary structures. To the W is the main entrance, the 13thC **Puerta del Sarmental**, which is filled with sculptured Biblical figures.

Most of the building was completed in the 13thC, from 1221-77, but exterior and interior decoration continued into the 16thC, with further embellishments and renovation into the 18thC. On the right inside the door is an entrance to the cloister.

Walk straight ahead, along the transept, which passes the **capilla mayor** on the right, with its 16thC retable and the tomb of El Cid and his wife in the crossing floor. Above the crossing is a soaring ribbed lantern supported by four massive piers. At the N end of the transept is an opulent Renaissance double staircase leading to the Puerta de la Coronería, on the higher level already seen from the outside.

Return to the N aisle, walking W past the carved walnut grilles of the choirstall positioned in the center of the nave. On the left is the 15thC **Capilla de Santa Ana**, with a polychrome wood altarpiece, one of the most richly decorated of the 13 pleasingly asymmetrical chapels that bring the cathedral to life. At the end of this aisle, look up at the 16thC clock known as the *Papamoscas* (flycatcher), which performs on the striking of the hour. Turn left (S), then left (E) again, and the chapel on your right, **Santísimo Cristo**, contains a popular image of *Christ* in which leather was used to simulate skin. The figure is thought to be 13thC, but may quite possibly be even older.

Farther along this aisle, cross the transept to the right of the high altar into the ambulatory, where at the center is the 15thC **Capilla del Condestable**, an Isabeline and Plateresque extravagance of grilles, carvings, altars and the tombs of Pedro Hernández de Velasco and his wife. There is a door in the far right corner of this chapel, beyond which is a small room where you can see a painting of *Mary Magdalene* by Leonardo da Vinci.

The door near to the left of the main entrance opens into the **cloister**. Largely of the 14thC, it contains a wealth of sculptures in galleries and in the three chapels along the E wall. The one in the middle also has rare manuscripts and the 11thC marriage contract of El Cid. In the far SE corner is a **chapterhouse** with a Mudejar ceiling containing paintings and tapestries of the 15th and 16thC.

Other sights
Whether approaching Burgos from the E or W visitors will first encounter the **Puente de Santa María**, then the **Arco de Santa María**, a stately vestige of the city's 11thC fortifications. From here it is advisable to drive to the plaza in front of the cathedral, which is the best place to park and begin a walking

tour of Burgos' attractions, most of which are within several streets of one another.

From the cathedral, walk E into the arcaded **Plaza Mayor**. Within sight at the NE corner is the 15thC **Casa del Cordón** (*Av. del Cid Campeador*). Now under extensive renovation, it received its present name from the sculptured cord design employed on the facade. Columbus was received in this palace by the Catholic Monarchs Ferdinand and Isabella after his second voyage to the New World.

Back past the cathedral to the W is the **Iglesia de San Nicolás** (*Fernán González*). Largely of the 15thC, it boasts a grand retable executed by Francisco de Colonia in 1505. Above the church are the battlements that survive from a ruined castle, but a hike up the hill is rewarded only by the view, for nowadays little remains of the fortifications. To the N of the cathedral is the 14thC Gothic **Iglesia de San Estéban** (*San Estéban*).

Finally, check with the tourist office or hotel whether the **Casa de Miranda** is open. This 16thC mansion, which is now a museum housing archeological collections, notable religious artworks and funerary objects dating from the Moors, has been closed temporarily for renovation.

Sights nearby

Cartuja de Miraflores ☆
3km (2 miles) E of Burgos. Open 10.15am-3pm, 4-7pm; holidays 1-3pm; 4-6pm.
The 15thC monastery has as its focus a church containing the tombs of Juan II and Isabel of Portugal, Isabella's parents. The monument to them before the high altar is a remarkable sculptural group.

Monasterio de las Huelgas ☆
1km (½ mile) SW of Burgos 🚌 *X compulsory. Open Mon-Sat 11am-2pm, 4-6pm; Sun and holidays 11am-2pm.*
Only women of impeccable social background were admitted as sisters in this influential outpost of the Cistercian order. Most of the rambling structure is 12th-13thC Gothic, although later additions owe allegiance to Romanesque and Mudejar styles. In the church there are figures of Alfonso VIII and Eleanor of England, the founders and benefactors.

🍴 **Landa Palace** 🏨
Carretera Madrid-Irún, km 236 ☎ *(947) 206 343* IIII *39 rms* 🛏 *39* 🎚
🔳🔳
Location: 2km (1 mile) s of Burgos. An unusual castle keep looms beside the Madrid road. Through the heavy oak door lies a cavernous baronial hall, filled, as is the rest of the de luxe establishment, with Victoriana, real and recent, by turns impressive and amusing. There are indoor and outdoor pools and an attached restaurant, which is considered to be the best in the Burgos area.
🏊‍♂️ ♨ 🖼 ⚓ ≈ 👥 🍸

═ To compensate for the distance from town, the restaurant strives to outperform any of the local contenders, and succeeds.

🍴 It's a long step down from **Landa Palace**, but two centrally located hotels cushion the fall: **Condestable** (*Vitoria 8* ☎ *(947) 205 740* IIII *to* IIII) is a traditional hotel, which is now over 40yrs old; should it be full, the new **Meson del Cid** (*Plaza Santa Maria 8* ☎ *(947) 208 715* IIII) is simple, and situated opposite the cathedral.

═ **Casa Ojeda**
Vitoria 5 ☎ *(947) 209 052* IIII *to* IIII 🍽 ▭ ■ 🎚 🍸 AE ⓐ ⓒ VISA *Last orders 11pm. Closed June-Oct Sun dinner, Oct-June Mon.*
Casa Ojeda leaves little to chance. There is a large bar lined with especially appetizing *tapas*, a store selling regional food products, and a dining room upstairs. The kitchen sends forth traditional Castilian dishes such as *sopa castellana*, *cordero asado* and *alubias con chorizo* (beans with sausage).

═ **Los Chapiteles**
General Santocildes 7 ☎ *(947) 205 998* IIII 🍽 ▭ ■ 🎚 🍸 AE ⓐ ⓒ VISA
Last orders 11pm. Closed Sun.
At this ambitious local restaurant a traditional menu is spiced with "international" specialties. The service is correct, in a smart setting. The

tapas in the bar make excellent appetizers before a meal of *menestra de verduras*, *cordero asado* or *rabo de buey*.

≈ Mesón del Cid
Plaza Santa María 8 ☎ *(947) 208 715* **▥ ▢ ▬ ▼** ⒶⒺ ⊕ ⒸⒹ ⒱ⒾⓈⒶ *Last orders 11.30pm. Closed Feb and Sun night.*
This 15thC house faces the cathedral and remains gratifyingly authentic inside, with a ground-floor bar and four distinct dining rooms on three upper levels. Waitresses in peasant dress dash around the room ensuring that the time from taking the order to settling the account is under one hour. Specialties include *sopas*, *cordero asado* and *truchas variadas*.

Place nearby
Lerma *(37km/23 miles s of Burgos)*. On the road s toward Madrid, fortifications of the medieval town erupt from a mound that rises from the flat surroundings. The old town within the walls is well worth a brief exploration.

Cáceres
Map 6F3. Cáceres. 92km (57 miles) NE of Badajoz; 301km (187 miles) sw of Madrid. Population: 80,000 **i** *Plaza Mayor* ☎ *(927) 246 347.*
Unidentified prehistoric people left traces of their existence here, and were followed by the Celts, Romans and Goths. The Moors gave the city much of its present layout and identity, including the root of its current name — "Qazris." The old town is entirely enclosed by ramparts, erected, destroyed, rebuilt and augmented by the different cultures. Within the walls are mansions and churches of austere dignity, steeples and towers crowned with nesting storks, and hardly a trace of tawdry commercialism. Take an after-dark stroll through the old town, not only to avoid the summer heat, but also to immerse yourself in pools of moonlight and the almost palpable presence of conquistadors.

Sights and places of interest
For a walking tour of the city, begin opposite the arcaded N side of the Plaza del General Mola, and enter the Arco de la Estrella, to its left. Directly ahead is the Plaza Santa María, encircled by noble 16thC houses, including the **Palacio de Mayoralgo**. On the far side is **Iglesia de Santa María**, largely Gothic in design but with Renaissance embellishments at the front portal and in the *capilla mayor*.

Bear right past the facade, to find the **Palacio de los Golfines de Abajo** which was considered suitably grand for visits by Ferdinand and Isabella when they were intent on suppressing the independent instincts of the local nobility. The narrow street rises toward the double staircase leading to the Jesuit **Iglesia de San Francisco Javier** and, to its left, the associated **Colegio de Luisa Carvajal**.

Walk up the street to the right of the church and past the **Casa de las Cigüeñas**, an unobtrusive army headquarters for the last 500yrs. Beyond is the impressive **Casa de las Veletas**, which incorporates parts of a 12thC Moorish palace and an even older cistern, and now functions as a small **archeological museum** *(open 10.30am-3.30pm, 4-7pm)* featuring Celtic and Roman relics and coins.

Looming over the plaza of the same name is the church of **San Mateo**, an essentially Gothic building constructed between the 13th and 16thC. It has an unusually tall nave and a lavishly Baroque main altar. Turn right (N) after the church, and Calle Anacha, on your left, will lead you past several prominent mansions to the State-run **Hostería Nacional** (see below), housed in the 14thC Palace of Torreorgaz. Directly ahead, at the end of the short Calle Condes, is the **Palacio de los Golfines de Arriba**, with its square, 15thC balconied watch tower made of ochre stone.

This walk passes most buildings of importance and along many pleasant streets. Further exploration should include the Gothic **Iglesia de Santiago**, just E of the old town, the **Palacio de Godoy** opposite, and the **Arco de Cristo**, the only remaining Roman arch, in its s rampart.

Cádiz

≈ **El Figon de Eustaquio**
Plaza San Juan Nus 12 ☎ *(927) 248 194* ⅢⒷ ⬛ ▤ ☉ ⓒⓓ 𝑽𝑰𝑺𝑨
Last orders 11pm.
Although a little pricey for the area, this restaurant makes a fitting rest stop after a tramp up and down the fascinating streets of the old town. The food and setting are of predictable yet soothing competence, focusing on dishes of the region. Two of the four rooms are air conditioned.

Cádiz

Map 6l3. Cádiz. 124km (77 miles) sw of Sevilla; 121km (75 miles) nw of Algeciras. Population: 168,000 ℹ *Calderón de la Barca 1* ☎ *(956) 211 313.*
The city spreads over a thumb-shaped peninsula enclosing a long bay, connected to the mainland by a causeway. Within its boundaries are pre-Roman ruins, belvederes overlooking the sea, a good beach, three churches, and a *barrio antiguo* of unassuming charm.

... with an easterly wind filling his sails and fear in the hearts of his crew, some forgotten Columbus of Sidon or of Tyre passed through the Strait, and turning northward, beached his little galley on the peninsula where we stand.

A.F. Calvert, Cook's Handbook for Spain, 1921

The history of Cádiz is long. Phoenician traders settled in the 12thCʙc, followed by the Greeks, Carthaginians, Romans and Moors. It was here that Julius Caesar decided to confer citizenship upon the inhabitants of his Iberian colony. The city faded in importance under the Arabs, then surged back to prominence in the 16thC with the influx of galleons returning from the Americas. Cádiz was a frequent target of the English from the 16th to 19thC. Sir Francis Drake attacked it in 1587, burning ships intended for the Armada, and Nelson bombarded it in 1805.

Sights and places of interest
Catedral Nueva †
Plaza de Pío XII. Open Mon-Fri 5.30-7.30pm, Sat 9.30-10.30am, 5.30-8pm, Sun 11am-1pm.
Over 100yrs were required to complete the "new" cathedral (1720-1838) but since there was no overlapping of styles, it is pure Baroque. The principal attractions are a dome covered in amber tiles and the tomb of the composer Manuel de Falla.
Museo de Cádiz
Plaza del Mina 5 ▨ *Open Mon-Fri 10am-2pm, 5.30-8pm. Closed Sat, Sun and holidays.*
In fact, this building contains two museums. The ground floor is the **Museo Arqueológico**, exhibiting Phoenician and Roman relics. Upstairs, the **Museo de Pinturas** has on display works by Murillo, Zurbarán and Ribera.

≈ Don't judge the *parador* chain by its single oddity, **Atlántico** (*Av. Duque de Nájera 9* ☎ *(956) 212 301* ⅢⒷ), a bland high-rise of little character, bearing no resemblance to most of its fellows. The best of an indifferent selection, it does have views of the sea and the city's largest park; other possibilities include the efficiency **Isecotel** (*Paseo Marítimo s/n* ☎ *(956) 255 401* ⅢⒷ) and the recently built **Regio** (*Ana de Viya 11* ☎ *(956) 279 331* ▣).

≈ **El Anteojo** (*Alameda Apodaca 22* ☎ *(956) 213 639* ⅢⒷ) offers good *tapas* in its ground-floor bar, fine vistas from its upstairs dining room, and large platters of seafood; in the old town, **El Faro** (*San Félix 15* ☎ *(956) 212 501* ⅢⒷ) also specializes in crustaceans and other marine delicacies.

Calatayud
Map 13D7. Zaragoza. 87km (55 miles) sw of Zaragoza; 91km (57 miles) se of Soria. Population: 19,000.
The present name is a direct descendant of the Moorish "Kalat

Ayub," which referred to the ruined 8thC **castle of Ayub** that still
looms above the dun-colored town. Mudejar towers, accented by
bands of ceramic tiles, rise above the peaked roofs. East of town
are the excavated remains of a Roman settlement called **Bilbilis**. In
Calatayud itself, the 13thC collegiate church of **Santa María la
Mayor** incorporates parts of the mosque that originally occupied
this site, and **Santo Sepulcro** was a church of the Knights
Templar, built in the 12thC and renovated in the 17thC.·

≈► **Calatayud** (*Carretera NII km 237* ☎*(976) 881 323* **Ⅲ**) is a comfortable
hotel with an attractive location just E of town on the Zaragoza road.

═ Despite its name, **Lisboa** (*Paseo de Calvo Sotelo 10* ☎*(976) 882 535* **Ⅱ**)
has a typically Aragonese menu.

Cartagena
*Map 9H8. Murcia. 241km (150 miles) NW of Almería; 110km
(68 miles) SW of Alicante. Population: 180,000* **i** *Plaza
Castellini 5* ☎*(968) 507 549.*
The ancient Carthaginian port city is protected from both land and
sea. Its bay is nearly circular, and the narrow opening to the sea is
further constricted by a long quay. Four castles guard the entrance
and heights, and there is an 18thC arsenal and large, active naval
base. Heavy commercial shipping involves the export of mineral
ore, such as lead, iron and zinc, from the nearby sierra and the
import of crude oil for the refinery at Escombreras.

Traces of its occupation by the Romans exist in the remains of a
forum, amphitheater and necropolis.

Sights and places of interest
On top of the promontory to the W of the harbor entrance is the **Castillo de
las Galeras** and on the opposite point the **Castillo de San Juan**. Crowning
the highest hill overlooking the city is the **Castillo de la Concepción**, now
more garden than fort, with fine vistas. The ruined cathedral on the road up
to the castle is the 13thC **Santa María la Vieja**, reduced to its present state
during the Civil War. At the harbor front, near the town hall, is the
submarine invented in 1888 by the local engineer Isaac Peral. In front the
harbor extends, its entrance protected by two breakwaters. The **Torre
Ciega**, just N of the railroad station, is a 1stC Roman monument of uncertain
purpose.

≈► Many visitors prefer to stay at one of the resort hotels along Mar Menor, a
curious, virtually enclosed bay 30km (19 miles) to the NE, partly because of
the paucity of respectable hotels in the city itself. The choice includes
Cartagonova (*Marcos Redondo 3* ☎*(968) 504 200* **Ⅱ** *to* **Ⅲ**) and
Mediterráneo (*Puerto de Murcia 11* ☎*(968) 507 400* **Ⅱ**).

═ The hotel **Mediterráneo** boasts a good restaurant called **Chamonix**
(*address and* ☎*as hotel* **Ⅲ**).

Castellón de la Plana
*Map 9F9. Castellón. 66km (41 miles) NW of Valencia; 121km
(75 miles) SE of Tortosa. Population: 125,000* **i** *Paseo María
Agustina 5* ☎*(964) 227 703.*
Make no needless detour to Castellón. The surrounding
countryside is featureless, the city itself of little interest since the
devastation of the Civil War, its hotels and restaurants routine.
Should circumstances demand an hour or two in the provincial
capital, head for the *plaza mayor*. On the E side is the **Iglesia de
Santa María**, a post-Civil War replacement for the 16thC original.
Nearby is the 16thC **Torre del Reloj** (clock tower), which escaped
destruction. To its W is the 18thC **Ayuntamiento**, and four streets

N along Calle Mayor is the Diputación Provincial, which houses the **Museo Provincial de Bellas Artes**. This museum has several paintings by the Valencians Francisco Ribalta and José Ribera.

Mindoro (*Moyano 4* ☎*(964) 222 300* ⅢＬ *to* ⅢⅢ) is a comfortable modern hotel, whose only fault is dullness; **Myrian** (*Obispo Salinas 1* ☎*(964) 222 100* ⅢＬ) is small, clean and quiet.

Casino Antiguo (*Puente del Sol 1* ☎*(964) 222 864* ⅢＬ *to* ⅢⅢ) is a private club, but the public is permitted into its cool dining room. The *paella de mariscos* is good.

Places nearby
Benicasim (*14km/9 miles N of Castellón*).   Condominiums, restaurants and bustling package-tour hotels skirt the palm-lined beach, with nothing to divert attention from pure pleasure-seeking.

Azor (*Paseo Marítimo s/n* ☎*(964) 300 350* ⅢＬ), **Tres Carabelas** (*Av. Salvador Ferrándiz s/n* ☎*(964) 300 649* ⅢＬ), and **Orange** (*Gran Av. s/n* ☎*(964) 300 600* ⅢＬ), which is the largest and has the most recreational facilities.

El Grao (*4km/2½ miles E of Castellón*).   The capital's port provides anchorage for a sizeable fleet of freighters and trawlers. A 4km (2½ mile) beach known as the **Playa del Pinar** runs N, a magnet for rapid resort development.

Del Golf (☎*(964) 221 950* ⅢＬ) is right on the Playa del Pinar and has good sports facilities.

Seafood is featured at **Rafael** (*Churruca 26* ☎*(964) 222 088* ⅢＬ) and **Arrantzale** (*Av. Buenavista 36* ☎*(964) 230 051* ⅢＬ).

Castilla-La Mancha
Map 8F6&7. In the center of the peninsula. Airport: Madrid.
Although the elevated tableland of the interior is not especially hospitable — short of water and mineral resources, and extreme in climate — geopolitics have dictated that it contains the national capital; first Toledo, then Madrid. During the Middle Ages, kings who wished to impose absolute power failed and were therefore forced to spread their authority. The fiefdoms they awarded resulted in the construction of many castles — the reason for the name Castilla.

The provinces that make up this landlocked region are Albacete, Cuenca, Guadalajara, Ciudad Real, Toledo and Madrid, each named after its principal city. The plateau they occupy is called the Meseta. Castilla la Nueva is divided by the Tajo and Guadiana rivers, its flatness interrupted by several mountain ranges, principally the Gredos W of Madrid, the Guadarrama to the N and the Serranía de Cuenca to the E. Grapes and corn are the primary agricultural products, sheep the dominant livestock, and the wine district of La Mancha, the largest but not the best in Spain, is within its borders.

Castilla y León
Map 12D6. From the Cantabrian coast down to central Spain. Airports: Santander, Valladolid.
Like *Castilla-La Mancha* on its southern perimeters, most of this region is high tableland. The countryside changes dramatically from the range of blue-green mountains backing the Cantabrian

Sea to level, treeless, burnt ochre wasteland. An approximate natural boundary between Castilla y León and Castila-La Mancha is formed by the Sierras de Gredos and Guadarrama. Even with eight provinces — Santander, Burgos, Logroño, Palencia, Soria, Segovia, Valladolid and Avila — the total population does not equal that of *Madrid* alone. However, the capitals are of interest to visitors who want a change from the usual routes.

Given its extreme climate, this region is best avoided from July to Aug and Dec to Feb. The major agricultural and mineral resources are cereals, sheep and mercury.

Catalunya (*Cataluña*)
Map **15***D10. The region in the far* NE *of Spain, bordering France. Airports: Barcelona, Girona, Tarragona.*

Endowed with dramatic mountain ranges cradling fertile valleys, with a scalloped coast sheltering numerous beaches, and with three large rivers providing power for industry and irrigation for farming, the region enjoys sufficient natural resources to maintain an enviable level of prosperity. Grapes, olives and wheat are cultivated in abundance. Motor vehicles, office machines, textiles and heavy equipment are manufactured. International trade and printing are prominent light industries.

The four provinces of Girona, Lleida, Barcelona and Tarragona, each named after its major city as is the Spanish custom, are bound together by a common history dating from Charlemagne, who was asked to expel the Moors and then annexed the region to his empire. With the ascendance of the counts of Barcelona in the 9thC, the Catalans achieved independence and installed a new parliament. Separatist fervor has frequently flared into open rebellion, but a measure of autonomy, wrested from the current democratic regime in Madrid, has muted dissent.

The provinces of Catalunya are also united by their folkloric and artistic heritages as well as a common language, Català (Catalan). The names of certain towns, streets and plazas have been changed from the Castilian to Catalan, and it can be confusing to find your way about.

Ciudad Real
Map **7***F5. Ciudad Real. 192km (119 miles)* N *of Jaén; 116km (72 miles) of Toledo. Population: 46,000* **i** *Toledo 27* ☎*(926) 213 292.*

Perhaps this dusty provincial capital, well off the Madrid-Granada road, was once as grand as Cervantes alleged, but there is little existing evidence to support the contention. Originally a fortified village, the old walls are all but gone, although a 14thC Mudejar gate remains. The Gothic cathedral has a handsome Renaissance retable.

Castillos (*Av. Rey Santos 8* ☎*(926) 213 640* **II◻**) is primarily an executive hotel near the town center; **El Molino** (*Carretera Córdoba-Tarragona km 242* ☎*(926) 223 050* **II◻**) is a small roadside hotel with a decent restaurant.

Miami Park (*Ronda de la Ciruela 48* ☎*(926) 222 043* **II◻**) is both traditional and serviceable.

Place nearby
Almagro (*22km/13 miles* SE *of Ciudad Real*). The 14thC *plaza mayor*, with its stone columns beneath wooden balconies and the 16thC **Corral de Comedias**, encourages visitors to linger. The

latter was and remains the setting for performances of classic Spanish plays. Also in the town is the 16thC **Convento de la Asunción de Calatrava**, now a national monument.

☛The ruins of another convent were reconstructed in 1979 to create **Parador Nacional de Almagro** (*Ronda de San Francisco s/n* ☎*(926) 860 100* **IIII**), which equal the highest standards of the government chain, both in comfort and elegant touches that recall the building's original functions. The beds, however, are of hammock configuration.

Ciudad Rodrigo
Map 10E3. Salamanca. 155km (96 miles) N of Cáceres; 89km (56 miles) SW of Salamanca. Population: 14,000 i Arco Amayuelas ☎(923) 460 561.

This outpost of assorted satraps and lords was fortified against hostile excursions launched by their counterparts in Portugal, the Moorish south and northern Europe. The fortress commanding the heights above the Agueda river achieved its present form in the l2thC, although much older Roman foundations were utilized in its construction. The entire town has now been designated a national monument.

Sights and places of interest
Cathedral †
Casco Viejo. Open 8am-noon, 4-8pm.

The original design was Romanesque, bridging the 12thC and 13thC, but subsequent additions and repairs have given this cathedral a Gothic identity, but with Baroque embellishments as in some of the window treatments. The 14thC **cloister** (entered off the N wall) is attributed to the architect Benito Sánchez. Rodrigo Alemán carved the panels of the choirstalls.

Other sights
Also in the Casco Viejo is the **Casa de las Aguilas** (*closed to the public*), a 16thC Plateresque mansion. In the spritely main square, **Plaza del Caudillo**, there are several more 16thC mansions, including the **Ayuntamiento**, and in a nearby plaza is the **Palacio de los Castros**, in which Wellington is said to have spent a number of nights.

☛ **Parador Nacional Enrique II**
Plaza del Castillo 1 ☎*(923) 460 150* **IIII** *28 rms* ▭ *28* ⬤ ▨ AE ⓪ ⓒⓓ
VISA

Location: Above the river Agueda. The 12thC fortress lay in ruins after the victorious assault by the Duke of Wellington during the Peninsular War. Now, with meticulous restoration of the keep, ramparts and halls, it would admirably satisfy anyone's ambition to sleep in a castle. There is a tranquil courtyard, and the sentry walk of the town walls invites evening strolls. The restaurant is the best in the town.
▨ ▧ ⚓ ♈

☛ When the **Parador** is full, **Conde Rodrigo** (*Plaza de San Salvador 7* ☎*(923) 461 404* **IIII**) is an old, clean building next to the cathedral. ⚌ This hotel also has a respectable dining room.

Córdoba
Map 7H5. Córdoba. 138km (86 miles) NE of Sevilla; 170km (106 miles) NW of Granada. Population: 320,000 i Hermanos González Murga 13 ☎(957) 478 721.

Try to approach Córdoba from the S, across the still-used Roman bridge that ends at the wall of the **Mezquita**, a mosque of singularly graceful proportions that is among the major sights of Spain. Córdoba's history is as long and distinguished as any Spanish city's, although it was eclipsed in importance by Sevilla and Madrid once the Moors were vanquished. The Romans found a thriving Iberian community when they arrived in the 2ndCBC, and eventually made it capital of their province of Baetica. After the arrival of the Visigoths in the 5thC, Córdoba slid into mediocrity.

Under the Arabs it rose once again to a position of influence as the Caliphate that ruled much of Moorish Iberia. The riches of the Islamic Empire poured in, eventually attracting a population of over half a million people, one of the largest in Europe and twice that of the present time. Among its citizens was the great Jewish philosopher and theologian Moses Maimonides.

After 1031, squabbling among Moorish factions provoked a decline. Ferdinand III took the city in 1236, and the monuments and mosques (there were 3,000 at one time) were razed or allowed to disintegrate. Only in the present century has Córdoba begun to regain a measure of its former prosperity, with the introduction of new industry and housing construction.

Sights and places of interest
Alcázar ☆
Amador de los Ríos s/n 🖼 ✗ *Open May-Sept 9.30am-1.30pm, 5-8pm, 10pm-1am; Oct-Apr 9.30am-1.30pm, 5-8pm.*

Behind the palace are terraced gardens (floodlit May-Sept) alive with the music of running water. They face S, across the Guadalquivir. The present buildings were begun in the 13thC and completed for Alfonso XI in 1328, incorporating Moorish courtyards from the citadel that once stood here and which itself employed the even earlier Roman mosaics and 3rdC sarcophagus now on view.

Judería
Low white houses bedecked with flowers spilling from pots and window grilles crowd meandering streets in a quarter that fully satisfies preconceptions of Andalucía. There is a competition each year to pick the prettiest tiled patio, and the winners welcome visitors.

La Sinagoga (*Judío s/n; open 9.30am-1.30pm, 3.30-6.30pm; closed Tues*), is one of only a few synagogues remaining in Spain, although it is a small, plain room with a tiny balcony that betrays little of its original purpose. **Calleja de las Flores** is a lovely cul-de-sac with flowers and greenery trailing from every wall and framing the cathedral tower.

Mezquita-Catedral 🏛 † ★
Torrijos s/n 🖼 ✗ *Open 10.30am-1.30pm, 3.30-6pm.*

Only the Alhambra of *Granada* grants more imposing testimony to the architectural achievements of the caliphs and their subjects, although this mosque, like the Alhambra, was desecrated in part by the ill-advised modifications of the Christians by whom they were expelled. The shrine, one of the largest in Islam, is of a rectangular arrangement enclosed by a buttressed wall. There are several entrances, but for the proper effect choose the **Puerta del Perdón** at the NW corner flanked by a minaret-belfry. It opens on to the **Patio de los Naranjos** (Court of the Orange Trees), with palms and splashing fountains.

Cross the courtyard to the door in the opposite wall. Inside is a dimly lit forest of over 800 pillars supporting striped and scalloped double arches; it is humbling in its six-acre vastness. Most of the columns are of marble or other stone, some are of wood, few precisely alike. Straight along the aisle to the far wall is the *maksourah*, a vestibule for the *mihrab*, a sacred niche. There are three remarkable domes above, exquisitely carved, sheathed in tiles and mosaics, and of a golden tone which dazzles after the shadows of the mosque.

In the center of the mosque the bishops of the Church Triumphant built their 16thC **cathedral**. A grotesque tribute to Gothic-Baroque-Rococo excess, it is routinely deplored by critics offended by the assault on the purity of the Muslim environment. The cathedral is filled with curlicues, friezes, plump cherubim, sculptured saints, coffered ceilings and paintings, stucco, silver, alabaster, marble and jasper.

Museo Arqueológico
Alta de Santa Ana 🖼 *Open 10am-2pm, 4-7pm. Closed Mon.*

The handsome Renaissance **Palacio de Jerónimo Páez** now contains a provincial archeological museum. Carefully mounted displays include artifacts from the prehistoric to the Gothic eras. Roman mosaics, medieval Christian artworks and Moorish relics are all on view.

Plaza de Potro

The small square and fountain with its sculpture of a colt is just N of the Paseo de la Rivera. On the W side is an inn allegedly mentioned in *Don Quixote*. On the opposite, E, side is the **Museo Provincial de Bellas Artes** (**⊠** *open 10am-1.30pm, 5-7pm, closed Mon*), with paintings by Goya, Murillo, Zurbarán, Ribera and more recent artists. Next door (to the N) is a **museum** (*open 10am-1.30pm*) dedicated to the works of the 20thC painter Julio Romero de Torres.

Sight nearby

Medina Azahara

6km (4 miles) NW of Córdoba **⊠** *Open summer 10.30am-noon, 5.30-7pm; winter 10.30am-noon; 3.30-5pm. Closed Tues.*

The excavated foundations and reconstructed wings of a Moorish palace are a tantalizing hint of the vast complex of gardens, armories, stables, pools, mosques, baths, schools, barracks and the support services required for a populace that might have exceeded 20,000. It was razed by a rival Muslim faction in 1013, less than 80yrs after it was begun.

☞ The only serious liability of **Gran Capitán** (*Av. de América 5* **☎**(957) 470 250 **Ⅲ**) is its distance from the Judería and Mezquita, but otherwise it is modern and functional with an attentive staff; **Maimónides** (*Torrijos 4* **☎**(957) 471 500 **Ⅲ** *to* **Ⅲ**) sustains a high level of comfort and is conveniently located for the principal sights; the large, reassuring **Meliá Córdoba** (*Jardines de la Victoria* **☎**(957) 298 066 **Ⅲ**) is anonymous and international, but is only minutes from the Mezquita and has good facilities; **Parador Nacional de la Arruzafa** (*Av. de la Arruzafa s/n* **☎**(957) 275 900 **Ⅲ**) is a bleak, modern *paradore* 4km (2½ miles) N of Córdoba, with large public rooms, a pleasant terrace, a large garden and customary amenities.

═ El Caballo Rojo

Cardenal Herrero 28 **☎**(957) 475 375 **Ⅲ** ⌷ **▄** **▦** **Y** **⊙** **VISA** *Last orders 11.30pm.*

"The red horse" walks away with the local laurels. The present building evolved from an old *mesón* into the present structure, including bars, a terrace and several dining rooms on three levels. The traditional menu has national specialties, such as *rape mozárabe*, *rabos de toro* and *cordero a la miel* (lamb with honey), as well as a few international favorites. The wine list is comprehensive and the service efficient.

═ A street away from the Alcázar there is an old school with a lovely courtyard that has been converted into a restaurant, **Almudaina** (*Plaza de los Santos Mártires 1* **☎**(957) 474 342 **Ⅲ**). Fish in infinite variety is the house specialty and the wine selection excels. The bar is a popular meeting place. **El Churrasco** (*Romero 16* **☎**(957) 290 819 **Ⅲ**) has an advantageous location in the middle of the Judería. The bar has a tantalizing display of *tapas* that constitute a meal in themselves, but there is also a formal dining room that specializes in roast meats.

La Coruña

*Map **10B2**. La Coruña. 65km (40 miles) N of Santiago de Compostela; 325km (200 miles) W of Oviedo. Population: 240,000* **i** *Dársena de la Marina* **☎**(981) 221 822.

This provincial capital sits on a mushroom-shaped peninsula thrusting out into the Atlantic at the extreme NW corner of Iberia. Its natural double harbor inevitably drew the attention of the Romans, who erected a lighthouse in the 2ndC, the **Torre de Hércules**, which is still operational although its exterior was modified in the 18thC. The N edge of the isthmus is a popular crescent-shaped beach, alongside the main commercial district. The S shore borders an active harbor which curves E into the **ciudad vieja** (old city), a quarter easily explored in an hour or two.

La Coruña's most distinctive architectural features are the high, narrow balconies, which are completely glassed over in large panels made up of small panes. The intent is to block the winds and rains that are typical of this region while allowing the sun to enter — a form of passive solar heating. Entire streets appear to be diligently glazed, as modern buildings imitate the device. While these charming *miradores* are seen throughout Galicia, nowhere are they more extensive.

Events   In Aug, festival including concerts, plays, bullfights and dance competitions.

Sights and places of interest

The best way to see the old city is on foot. Begin your tour in **Plaza de María Pita**, an enclosed square named after the woman who raised the alarm against the British attack of 1589. Led by Sir Francis Drake, the invasion was intended in part to consolidate the advantage gained by the defeat of the "Invincible Armada," which sailed forth from this port the year before. On the far N side of the square is the **Palacio Municipal**, an ornate Neoclassical building with three domes which contains a gallery of contemporary art. Immediately W on higher ground are two 18thC churches, **Iglesia de San Jorge** and **Iglesia de San Nicolás**.

Leaving the plaza through the portal at the SE corner, a short climb bearing right brings you to the **Iglesia de Santiago**, completed during the 12th and 13thC and notable for its triple apse and dazzling treasury. Follow the N exterior wall into the **Plaza del General Azcarraga**, which is pleasant despite the presence of an overtly military building on the S side, reinforcing the fact that La Coruña is a major garrison city. Leave the square at the SE corner, cross two streets, turn right into Calle Zapatería, then immediately left into Calle Sinagoga, and you will find the **Iglesia de Santa María del Campo**, built during the 13th-14thC. Proceed E along the Calle de Santa María to the tranquil Plaza Santa Bárbara, bordering the *convento* of the same name, where classical music concerts are held during summer weekends.

Pause for a rest, then continue in the same direction along the Calle de San Francisco to the **Jardin de San Carlos**, where Sir John Moore is buried. Commander of English troops in the Peninsular War, he was killed in 1809 during a retreat before French forces. Beyond the nearby city walls is the **Castillo de San Antón**, which houses a historical and archeological museum.

☞ At the edge of the old city and the harbor, **Finisterre** ♣ (*Paseo del Parrote 20* ☎(981) 205 400 ▯▯▯ *to* ▯▯▯▯) couldn't be better located. It is a superior representative of the inconsistent HUSA chain and has excellent facilities. While **Atlántico** (*Jardines de Méndez Núñez s/n* ☎(981) 226 500 ▯▯▯▯) can't compete with Finisterre in amenities, its location is comparable and the bedrooms are comfortable.

≡**Finisterre** (*address and* ☎ *as hotel* ▯▯) contradicts the prejudice — all too frequently confirmed — that hotel dining rooms are notorious for boring food at high cost. Its kitchen rivals any to be found in the city.

The best of the other restaurants is **El Rápido** (*Estrella 7* ☎(981) 224 221 ▯▯ *to* ▯▯▯▯), which has been in business for over 40yrs, concentrating on grilled shellfish and various seafood, as does its neighbor *Coral* (*Estrella 5* ☎(981) 221 082 ▯▯ *to* ▯▯▯▯); **Duna II** (*Estrella 2* ☎(981) 227 023 ▯▯ *to* ▯▯▯▯) is also nearby, but this one experiments with *nouvelle cuisine*, endeavoring, often successfully, to bring Gallic lightness to Galician recipes; **Casa Pardo** (*Novoa Santos 15* ☎(981) 287 178 ▯▯) is family-run (now in its second generation) and continues to present Galician specialties, which means seafood stews and shellfish in abundant quantity.

Places nearby

The **Rías Altas** to the E and N of the city are not as striking as those along the W coast of Galicia, but they are ideally located for a day-trip from La Coruña. Join the *autopista* in the southern outskirts, following the signs to El Ferrol del Caudillo. At the end of this highway, which is only 23km (14 miles) long, continue to **Betanzos**; with its inviting narrow streets and church, it is a perfect place for a stroll. Then drive N on the Puentedeume road, taking the bridge at Fene across the *ría* into **El Ferrol del Caudillo**, which is not a town likely to detain most travelers, but does boast a *parador nacional* if it's time for lunch.

The C646 road N to **Cedeira** is a scenic upland route which soon brings you to the town, lying by a sheltered bay. Several unpretentious restaurants specialize in local seafood. Leave Cedeira on the same road, traveling NE through Mera to the pretty resort community of **Ortigueira**. Eucalyptus and fir turn the hillsides gray-green along the way to the thriving port of **Vivero**, where the population swells in July and Aug with holidaymakers. At the end of the summer, there is a fiesta here to celebrate the sea's bounty, especially the sardines for which the waters of the estuaries are renowned. There are remnants of 16thC fortifications and an interesting Gothic church, both worth visiting.

A poorly maintained road follows the coast to Foz, after which turn SW towards **Villalba**, where another *parador* has been installed in a restored section of an old castle. Continue 16km (10 miles) and turn right (W) on to the NVI road which, after 46km (29 miles), will bring you back into La Coruña.

Costa del Azahar
Map 14E&F9. Along the central Mediterranean coast, from the mouth of the river Ebro to Sagunto. Airport: Valencia.
Called the "orange blossom coast" due to local cultivation of citrus fruit; the long stretches of sand are interrupted by heavy concentrations of tourist development at Benicarló, *Peñiscola*, Oropesa del Mar, Benicasim and Sagunto.

Costa Blanca
Map 9G9&H8. Along the SE Mediterranean coast, from Denia to Aguilas. Airports: Alicante, Santiago de la Ribera (near Cartagena).
The most striking feature of the "White Coast" is the brilliantly clear light that immerses it. Broad fine-sanded beaches are backed by a coastal plain with low mountains in the distance. The major coastal cities are *Benidorm* and *Alicante*, with dozens of resort villages in between.

Costa Brava
Map 16. Along the NE Mediterranean coast, from the French border to Blanes. Airports: Barcelona, Girona, Perpignan (in France).
The sharply indented and craggy shoreline shelters many small beaches as well as rocky coves. Cliffs bristle with hotels and resort developments; many show signs of aging and of rapid construction. Nevertheless, the region is ruggedly attractive from many vantage points. The hottest and busiest months are July and August.

Costa Dorada
Map 15E10. From Blanes to the mouth of the river Ebro. Airports: Barcelona, Tarragona.
The "Gold Coast" is a haven for the motor trailers of German visitors and the tents of enthusiastic French and Scandinavian campers. The almost continuous beaches are long, wide and not too heavily populated, except in August. *Tarragona* is the major city.

Costa de la Luz
Map 6I3. Along the SW Atlantic coast, from the Straits of

Gibraltar to the Portuguese border. Airport: Jerez de la Frontera.

Families and campers often prefer the relative solitude of this quiet stretch of coastline, whose major city is the attractive but industrial port of *Cádiz*. The Atlantic grows cool earlier than the Mediterranean, but the climate is comparable with the other coasts.

Costa del Sol

Map 7I5. The southern coast from Cabo de Gata to Algeciras. Airport: Málaga.

Although its boundaries have never been officially defined, *Málaga* is certainly the major city, *Torremolinos* the center of mass appeal, and *Marbella* the most stylish resort. The sea is perfect for swimming between Apr and Oct. Numerous commercial and resort developments mar much of the coast, but they are offset by unspoiled inland villages and centers of Moorish culture, such as *Sevilla*, *Granada* and *Córdoba*.

Costa Verde

Map 11B4&5. Along the Cantabrian (Bay of Biscay) coast from Vivero to Santander. Airports: Gijón, Salinas, Santander.

Atlantic rains ensure that this notched shoreline stays green, but also keep it raw and blustery or at least cool for nine months of the year. Campsites proliferate, and access roads are narrow and winding. The major cities are *Santander* and *Gijón*, and there are many appealing villages.

Cuenca

Map 13E7. Cuenca. 163km (101 miles) SE of Madrid; 201km (125 miles) NW of Valencia. Population: 45,000 **i** *Dalmacio García Izcara 8* ☎ *(966) 222 231.*

An unrecorded geological incident centuries ago heaved up the tip of a tongue of land, resulting in a town that creeps up a steep slope to the edge of a precipice 182m (600ft) deep. Two rivers cut through the gorges, joining at the SW border of what is now the old quarter. Houses teeter at the edge of the three-sided cliff, and belvederes, restaurants and a unique museum peer down at wheeling hawks.

Sights and places of interest

Casas Colgadas and Museo de Arte Abstracto 🏛 ★
Canónigos s/n 🖼 💻 *Open 11am-2pm, 4-6pm. Closed Mon, Sun afternoon.*

These "hanging houses" are cantilevered out over the river Huécar gorge, an engineering feat accomplished in the 14thC. But the appeal of Cuenca's most famous attraction exceeds the scenic and architectural, for most of the interior is devoted to a superb collection of Spanish contemporary art, featuring the work of Luis Feito, Antonio Tapies, Eduardo Chillida and Antonio Saura, and younger artists. Admirers of abstract art are delighted by the display, and even those who are indifferent find this showcase for Spain's living artists — most of whom found their first recognition abroad — a refreshing antidote to the succession of Crucifixions and Pietàs found in other Spanish museums.

The buildings dazzle the eye in other ways. Passages widen into large multi-level galleries, narrow into intimate cul-de-sacs, end in unexpected nooks. Platforms, balconies and staircases twist back upon each other, and windows above the gorge frame nothing but scudding clouds.

Cathedral †
Plaza Pio XII. Open 10am-1pm; 5-6pm.

The facade of the 12th-13thC cathedral encloses the E side of the sloping main plaza of the old town. Part of the wall and tower collapsed in 1902.

Most of the building is French Gothic, unusual this far south. In the **treasury** (▨) are two El Greco canvases and some Flemish tapestries.

Other sights
North of the **Casas Colgadas** is a pedestrian bridge reaching high across the river to the 16thC convent of San Pablo. The walk is not recommended for those who suffer from vertigo. On the opposite side of the old town is the **Convento de Descalzas**, from where there are breathtaking views of the Júcar gorge.

Sight nearby
Ciudad Encantada
36km (23 miles) N of Cuenca ▨ ✗
This "enchanted city" was created by wind and water, not man. Eroded rock formations uncannily suggest houses, people and animals.

▨ In the new town **Torremangana** (*San Ignacio de Loyola 19* ☎ *(966) 223 351* ▯▯ *to* ▯▯▯) is functional, efficient and comfortable; the best among the other hotels are **Alfonso VIII** (*Parque de San Julián 3* ☎ *(966) 214 325* ▯▯), overlooking a large park, and **Figon de Pedro** (*Cervantes 17* ☎ *(966) 224 511* ▯▯), near the Madrid-Valencia road; both are quite small. On the road to Buenache, 7km (4½ miles) E of Cuenca, is a restored 16thC manor house that is now called **Cueva del Fraile** (☎ *(966) 211 571* ▯▯ *to* ▯▯▯), a charming, quiet inn, where only the absence of air conditioning can be considered a drawback.

▭ Occupying a floor of the **Casas Colgadas**, with a bar on a lower level, is the rather formal **Mesón Casas Colgadas** (*Canónigos s/n* ☎ *(966) 210 876* ▯ *to* ▯▯). Plan to go for lunch, after a visit to the Museo de Arte Abstracto, and sit at a table on a balcony thrusting out over the gorge. The views are spectacular and the meals the tastiest available in the old quarter.
  In the new quarter, the restaurant of the hotel **Torremangana**, called **La Cocina** (*address and* ☎ *as hotel* ▯▯), is popular locally, featuring regional and national dishes; the hotel **Figon de Pedro** (*address and* ☎ *as hotel* ▯▯) also has a traditional restaurant.

Ecija
Map 6H4. Sevilla. 87km (55 miles) E of Sevilla; 51km (32 miles) SW of Córdoba. Population: 35,000.
Ecija was probably founded by the Greeks, and then occupied, in the usual order, by the Romans, Visigoths and Moors. The monuments bequeathed by each race include steeples, some Mudejar, some Gothic, others Baroque, that bristle above the rooftops. The churches in which they are incorporated are often ruined or under restoration. Although exaggerated, the town's notoriety for suffering a torrid climate in summer is a factor to be considered when planning a visit.

Sights and places of interest
Iglesia de Santa Cruz ▥ ✝
The multicultural tradition is manifest in this church with its 16thC Christian representation of *Nuestra Señora del Valle*, and Moorish tower and inscriptions. The church itself was not completed until the 19thC.
Iglesia de Santiago ▥ ✝
A 16thC Gothic church including portions of an earlier Mudejar building and an ornate Isabeline retable, it also has several Gothic paintings and a Renaissance patio.
Palacio de Peñaflor
Prominent among many great houses still extant in the city, this mansion captures attention with a facade of frescoes, ironwork and a classical Renaissance entrance.

▨ Slightly N of town on the main road, the modest **Astigi** (*Carretera Madrid-Cadiz km 450* ☎ *(954) 830 162* ▯▯) is small but has the most important requirement in this district, namely air conditioning.

Elche

Map 9G8. Alicante. 24km (14 miles) sw of Alicante; 60km (37 miles) NE of Murcia. Population: 165,000 ℹ Parque Municipal ☎(965) 545 2747.

The largely industrialized city in the SE corner of the peninsula has two distinctions. First, it was here that a remarkable 5thCBC bust of an Iberian woman with an unusual disc headdress was found in the 19thC. The 5thCBC **La Dama del Elche** is strong evidence of the sophistication of the pre-Roman peoples, and is now on display in the Museo Arqueológico in *Madrid*. Second, Elche contains the only large palm forest in Europe. First planted by Greek or Phoenician traders, it encircles much of the town; the almost continuous groves have a total of 120,000 date palms.

Event   In mid-Aug, annual mystery play, performed in the Basílica de Santa María (see below).

Sights and places of interest

Elche's two most significant sights are the large, 17thC **Basílica de Santa María**, with a lavish Baroque facade designed by Nicolás de Bari, and the **Huerto del Cura** (*Federico G. Sanchiz s/n* ☎ *open mid-June to mid-Sept 9am-8pm, mid-Sept to mid-June 9am-6pm*), a garden filled with flowers and shaded by majestic palm trees. Among them is a 150yr-old "Imperial" palm.

Designed to take full advantage of a setting among magnificent trees and gardens, **Huerto del Cura** 🏨 (*Av. Federco Garcia Sanchiz 14* ☎(965) 545 8040 ▮▮▮ *to* ▮▮▮) has bungalows scattered throughout the grounds. It is privately owned, but associated with the *parador* system, and adheres to its high standards.

Meals at **Huerto del Cura** (*address and* ☎ *as hotel* ▮▮▮) are usually excellent; **Parque Municipal** (*Paseo Alfonso XIII s/n* ☎(965) 543 3415 ▮▮) also has a superb setting amid palms, with a dining terrace that is open whenever the weather permits. The kitchen concentrates on fish and rice dishes of the region.

El Escorial

Map 12E5. Madrid. 55km (34 miles) NW of Madrid; 50km (31 miles) S of Segovia. Population: 10,000.

The great monastery-palace of San Lorenzo del Escorial was built on a remote site in the foothills of the Guadarrama mountains by Philip II, in thanksgiving for his victory over the French at St Quentin in Flanders in 1557. It was from his monastic cells here that the ascetic Philip II governed the great Spanish Empire for the last 14yrs of his life and here that he died in 1598. Designed by Juan Bautista de Toledo and completed by his gifted disciple, Juan de Herrera, the huge edifice is built in the shape of a gridiron to symbolize the martyrdom of St Lawrence, to whom it is dedicated. Hardly smaller than St Peter's and the Vatican, it breathes the spirit of the Counter-Reformation. Although praised by some for its massive simplicity, it is also thought to be glum and ponderous, especially when black storm clouds gather around the nearby mountain peaks and block the sun. Then, its sheer walls and 2,673 small windows seem more fitting to a fortress than a palace.

An agreeable town has grown up around the monument, interesting for casual strolls and largely avoiding the gimcrackery of other major tourist destinations. Tour groups from Madrid, only a short drive away, fill the streets and cafés on most fine days and especially on weekends.

Event   On Aug 10, St Lawrence's Day. Bullfights and celebrations in the streets.

El Escorial

Sights and places of interest

Casita del Príncipe (*Prince's Pavilion*)
SE on the road to the railroad station 🚻 *Open mid-Apr to mid-Sept Mon-Sat 10am-1pm, 4-7pm, Sun 10am-1pm; mid-Sept to mid-Apr Mon-Sat 10am-1pm, 4-6pm. Closed holidays.*

The Casita was built in the late 18thC by Juan de Villanueva for the Prince of Asturias, the future Charles IV. Light and airy in style, without the huge size or grandeur of the Escorial, it reflects the Prince's cultivated 18thC taste, with silk hangings, elegant furniture, carpets, locks and porcelain from the Buen Retiro factory.

The Monastery 🏛 ☆
🚻 *but* 🅿 *for formal gardens and courtyards. Open mid-Apr to mid-Sept Mon-Sat 10am-1pm, 3-7pm, Sun 10am-1pm; mid-Sept to mid-Apr 10am-1pm, 3-6pm, Sun 10am-1pm. Closed holidays.*

Flanking the church, the endless corridors and rooms of the **Palacios** ☆ (Royal Apartments), used by the Spanish Habsburgs and the Bourbons after them, are hung with splendid tapestries, both Flemish and from the Royal Tapestry works in Madrid. Among the most attractive are those based on Goya's lighthearted cartoons of pastoral scenes.

Philip II's apartments, in stark contrast to the splendor of the other rooms, are small, almost monastic chambers, from which Philip presided over Spain at its most glorious — and brief — moment of power. It was in his well-lit but mean workroom that he received the news of the defeat of the Armada, and in the bedroom adjoining, with a window giving on to the high altar of the church, that Philip died. The rooms contain a notable painting by Hieronymus Bosch, *The Haywain*, and the sedan chair in which the king was carried up to the Escorial from Madrid when he was too ill to walk.

The **church** ☆ is in the form of a Greek cross and is grandiose in scale, with four immense pillars supporting a cupola which rises to 92m (302ft). Red marble steps lead up to the sanctuary and high altar, with its columns of jasper, onyx and red marble, designed by Herrera. On either side are the royal stalls, backed by funerary sculptures by Pompeo Leoni of the Emperor Charles V and his family.

The entrance to the octagonal **Panteón de los Reyes** (Royal Pantheon) is down narrow stairs from the Patio de los Evangelistas. Lying below the high altar, it contains 26 sarcophagi in dark gray marble and bronze. With the exception of Philip V, Ferdinand VI, Amadeus of Savoy and Alfonso XIII, all the monarchs of Spain from the time of Charles V are buried here. It is a somber place. As Richard Ford remarked, "All to their wormy beds are gone — the ambition of Charles V, the bigotry of Philip II, the imbecility of Carlos II, the adulteries of María Luisa, the ingratitude of Ferdinand VII."

Tapestries and paintings, formerly hung throughout the Escorial, are found in the **Nuevos Muscos** ☆ (New Museums), which include some of Titian's greatest religious paintings and works by his successors such as Tintoretto, Veronese, Jacopo Bassano and Guido Reni. Spain is represented by Ribera, Velázquez — in particular his *Joseph's Tunic* — and El Greco, five of whose works are hung in a single gallery. An interesting exhibition in the basement illustrates the construction of the monastery and includes some of Herrera's original designs, bills, tools and materials.

In a sumptuous hall above the entrance gateway with a great curved ceiling decorated with frescoes by Tibaldi, the **Biblioteca** (Library) contains some 40,000 volumes, including St Teresa's diary and the illuminated velum manuscripts, which are priceless, and a great globe that belonged to Philip II.

Sights nearby

Valle de los Caídos
14km (9 miles) NE of El Escorial 🚻 *Open summer 10am-7pm; winter 9.30am-6.30pm.*

The Valley of the Fallen, high in the Guadarrama mountains, with splendid views, is a spectacular monument to the dead of the Spanish Civil War. Cut deep into the living rock, the 262m (860ft) nave of the basilica is longer than those of either St Peter's or St Paul's cathedrals. It is surmounted by a massive cross 125m (410ft) high. The crypt contains the coffins of 40,000 soldiers of both sides killed in the Civil War, but the principal positions go to heroes of the winning side, including General Franco.

🛏 **Victoria Palace** (*Juan de Toledo 4* ☎ (91) 890 1511 🛏) has a pleasant garden, a swimming pool and a restaurant.

≡ The atmospheric surroundings of **Mesón la Cueva** (*San Antón 4* ☎*(91) 890 1516* ▯) and the accomplished kitchen of **Charoles** (*Floridablanca 24* ☎*(91) 890 5975* ▯) compete for dining honors. **Casa Cipriano** (*Juan de Toledo 48* ☎*(91) 890 1783* ▯) continues to give good value for uncomplicated regional specialties; **Cervercería La Real** (*Del Rey 25* ☎*(91) 896 1357* ▯) sets out tasty snacks and *tapas*.

The Extremadura region
Map 6G4. In the w, bordering central Portugal.
Cáceres and Badajoz are the only two provinces within this region, yet it takes almost all day to drive across it. Unappealing references to its relentless heat and boundless aridity have discouraged visitors, which is regrettable, for there is a grandeur in these empty rolling plains and majestic mountain ranges. Vast fields of wheat ripple endlessly beneath a metallic sky, groves of cork trees have been stripped to russet sinew, knubbly rows of vegetation band the unexpected river valleys and lakes.

Population centers are spread far apart, as are the towns and small cities, such as *Guadalupe*, *Mérida*, *Trujillo*, Medellín, *Cáceres* and *Badajoz* — the birthplaces of the conquistadors, no doubt driven to daring exploits in the New World by the desperate poverty of their homeland. Many of them returned as wealthy lords, and bestowed their new-found riches upon the places of their youth. These towns are unsullied by the ravages of mass tourism and remain true to their heritage.

From late May to late Sept, Extremadura drowses beneath such a fierce sun that especially long siestas are vital. In Dec and Jan, temperatures drop well below freezing. Trout fishing and wild turkey, deer and boar hunting are the sports most eagerly pursued.

Formentera
Map 9J8. 175km (109 miles) NE of Alicante; 180km (112 miles) SE of Valencia. Ferry connections with Ibiza daily in summer. Population: 4,200.
Only avid seekers of seclusion are drawn to this tiny question mark of an island, the smallest inhabited of the *Islas Baleares*, which history has virtually bypassed and hoteliers have barely noticed. The so-called capital, **San Francisco Javier**, with two 19thC churches and a few windmills, is simply a widening in the only major road. There are long stretches of vacant sand.

≈ The facilities at **La Mola** (*Playa Mitjorn* ☎*(971) 320 050* ▯) exceed the requirements of the island; **Club Punta Prima** (*Es Pujols* ☎*(971) 320 368* ▯) is a comparable alternative.

Fuengirola
Map 7I5. Málaga. 32km (20 miles) SW of Málaga; 27km (17 miles) E of Marbella. Population: 32,000.
Not the gaudiest of the *Costa del Sol* resorts, Fuengirola doesn't enjoy the panache of *Marbella* either. Mass tourism has arrived, and there are signs touting restaurants, excursions and fiestas in as many as eight languages. A small commercial fishing fleet is based in a man-made inlet in the middle of the town, bracketed to E and w by crowded beaches. The only historical sight of note is a ruined 10thC Moorish castle on a bluff at the w end of the town.

≈ **Las Palmeras** (*Paseo Marítimo* ☎*(952) 472 700* ▯ to ▯). **Las Pirámides** (*Paseo Marítimo s/n* ☎*(952) 470 600* ▯ to ▯), and **El Puerto** (*Paseo Marítimo s/n* ☎*(952) 470 100* ▯) all provide good facilities, including large rooms, often with balconies.

≋ **Europa** (*Paseo Marítimo, Los Boliches* ☎(952) 470 591 **Ⅲ**) is the most sophisticated restaurant in the resort, with elaborate fixtures, live organ music on weekends and an international menu; the German owners of **La Langosta** (*Francisco Cano 1, Los Boliches* ☎(952) 475 049 **Ⅲ**) provide the international set with an appropriate variety of dishes ranging from *langosta* in several elaborate and costly guises to succulent *steak aux herbes*; **Mamma Mia** (*Italia s/n* ☎(952) 473 251 **Ⅲ**) is raucous and disorganized, but the pastas and pizzas are good; Greek food is the focus of **Sin Igual** (*Carretera de Málaga* ☎(952) 475 096 **Ⅰ**); the specialty of **El Caserío** (*Plaza Nueva* ☎(952) 462 474 **Ⅲ**) is Basque cuisine; **The Beefeater** (*Italia 20* ☎(952) 471 547 **Ⅲ**) describes itself; **China** (*Ramón y Cajal 27* ☎(952) 472 993 **Ⅲ**) provides conservative but good Cantonese and Indonesian dishes. Seafood restaurants abound along the Paseo Marítimo, most with outdoor tables. See *Migas* for other possibilities.

Nightlife
The Paseo Marítimo and Calle Ramón y Cajal are lined with bars catering for various nationalities, several of which feature live music nightly during the season. The disco of the moment appears to be **Pomelo** (*Paseo Marítimo s/n* ☎(952) 475 342).

The Galicia region
Map 10B3. At the NW corner of Spain, N of Portugal.
Airports: La Coruña, Santiago de Compostela, Vigo.
Consisting of the four northwesterly provinces, Orense, Lugo, Pontevedra and La Coruña, Galicia is as green as Southern Ireland, and is similarly beset by frequent rain for most of the year. The rocky coastline is deeply indented with estuaries and elongated bays called *rías*, which are bracketed by low mountains covered by forests of pine and stately eucalyptus.

Moorish occupation of the area lasted barely 30yrs, but the Phoenicians, Greeks, Romans and Visigoths all dropped by for a taste of either trade, pillage or empire-building. From the late 8thC onward, Galicia remained firmly Christian. Its Celtic heritage survives in the mournful wails of the bagpipes (*gaitas*).

Clusters of granite houses are scattered over the slopes that rise from the shore, their sides sometimes covered with scallop shells, their fronts and gardens shaded by arbors of tangled grapevines. Beside the houses are structures which look like sarcophagi; they are storage sheds called *hórreos*, but give a comforting ecclesiastical air to the countryside. ln the *rías*, floating platforms are permanently moored in curious flotillas; they are *bateas*, used in the thriving shellfish industry.

Gandía
Map 9G8. Valencia. 108km (68 miles) NW of Alicante; 68km (42 miles) S of Valencia. Population: 52,000 ℹ Plaza del Constitución s/n ☎(96) 287 1600.
The city is 4km (2½ miles) inland, and although it has its attractions, Gandía flourishes mainly because of the beach district called **Grao de Gandía**. The city is surrounded by *arrozales* and *huertas*, set aside for rice and oranges, which are shipped from the harbor formed by the mouth of the river Serpis. The so-called "Golden Beach" runs N of the port.

Sections of the original fortification remain, but Gandía's historical interest lies in its 15th-16thC tenure as a duchy of the infamous Borgia family (Borja in Spanish). St Francis Borja was more virtuous than most of his relatives and lived, like his corrupt ancestors, in the **Palacio de los Duques** (𝕏 *open summer Mon-Sat 10am-noon, 5-7pm, Sun 10am-noon; winter Mon-Sat 11am-noon, 4.30-5.30pm, Sun 11am-noon*), a fine Gothic-Renaissance building with lavish salons and an art gallery. Also in the town, not far from the ducal palace, is the Gothic **Iglesia Colegial**, which is being renovated.

➤ Head for the hotels near the beach, as those in the town center are unalluring. **Bayren 1** (*Passeig Maritím Neptú s/n* ☎(96) 284 0300 ▮▮▮) has good amenities and serves dinner on the swimming pool terrace, overlooking the beach with live music for dancing; **Los Robles** (*Formentera 33* ☎(96) 284 2100 ▮▮▯) and **Madrid** (*Castilla la Nueva s/n* ☎(96) 284 1500 ▮▮▯) are not as grand.

🍽 As is often true of resort restaurants, little is memorable. Choose the simpler fish dishes at **La Gamba** (*Carretera Jaraco-Gandía* ☎(96) 284 1310 ▮▮▯) and **As de Oros** (*Passeig Maritím Neptú s/n* ☎(96) 28401237 ▮▮▯); beef and pork head the menu at **Celler del Duc** (*Plaza Castell s/n* ☎(96) 284 2082 ▮▮▯).

Gibraltar

Map 6/4. 21km (13 miles) E of Algeciras; 70km (44 miles) SW of Marbella. For border opening times (pedestrians only) contact **i** *Muelle, Algeciras* ☎(956) 656 761. *Population: 30,000* **i** *Cathedral Sq.* ☎(9567) 76400.

A British possession since 1704 when Admiral Rooke captured it during the War of the Spanish Succession, the Rock is a persistent anomaly. Determinedly Anglophile in law and custom, with its tearooms and military pageantry, its citizens are principally of Mediterranean stock and are as likely to speak an Andalucian patois as English. Spanish governments of past and present regard the colony as an affront to their sovereignty. The Franco regime closed the border at La Línea in 1969, but it was reopened in 1982 by President Felipe González.

One of the Pillars of Hercules of the ancient world, the Rock was originally inhabited by prehistoric peoples. The name derives from a corruption of Jabal Tariq, the first Arab conqueror, and it was probably the Moors who introduced the famous Barbary apes still found here.

The town of Gibraltar is on the terraced W side of the Rock, facing *Algeciras* across the bay. Victorian-style houses with Spanish embellishments such as wrought-iron balconies crowd over steep streets clogged with cars. A cable car carries visitors to the splendid views at the crest of the Rock. Nearby is **St Michael's Cave**, a natural basilica in which summer concerts and sound-and-light shows are performed.

On the E bank of the Rock is the smaller settlement of **Catalan Bay**, and at the southernmost tip **Europa Point** is situated, with views of the African coast from its lighthouse and the chapel of **Nuestra Señora de Europa**. The fabled tunnels or **galleries** are better understood after seeing the scale model in the **Gibraltar Museum**. As Gibraltar is less than 6sq.km (2.32sq. miles) in area, the main sights and places of interest are easily covered in a couple of days, and for two or more people, taking a taxi for the day is not too expensive.

➤ **Holiday Inn** (*Governor's Parade* ☎70500 ▮▮▮) is representative of the multinational breed, comfortable enough and holding no surprises; **Rock** (*3 Europa Rd.* ☎73000 ▮▮▮) needs some cosmetic attention but nevertheless has good facilities and views from almost every vantage point; cheaper hotels include **Queen's** (*Boyd St.* ☎74000 ▮▯) and **Bristol** (*Cathedral Sq.* ☎2962 ▮▮▯).

🍽 For a break from the prevailing *paella* and *gazpacho* of the mainland, drop into one of the pubs in Gibraltar's main street for an inexpensive lunch of shepherd's pie, bangers and mash, fish and chips or a hamburger. The dining room at **Rock** (*address and* ☎ *as hotel* ▮▮▮) is known for its beef; **La Bayuca** (*21 Turnbull's Lane* ☎*5119* ▮▮▮) serves Spanish and international dishes; **Tony's** (*24 Main St.* ▮▮▮) imitates a Neapolitan trattoria.

Shopping

Stores observe approximately the same hours as on the mainland. Banks, however, are open Mon-Fri 9am-3.30pm. British currency as well as local notes are used.

Gibraltar is a free port, but savings on duties are not impressive. British products, electronic equipment and cameras are the best buys. Bargaining is expected in smaller stores.

Gijón

Map 11B5. Oviedo. 28km (17 miles) NE of Oviedo; 195km (121 miles) w of Santander. Population: 270,000 ℹ Marqués de San Esteban 1 ☎(985) 346 046.

Asturias' major port presumably existed even before the arrival of the Romans. Neither they nor the Visigoths made much impact still discernible today, and Moorish forays in the 8thC were brief. Vestiges of the late Middle Ages are concentrated in the warren of stepped alleys and leaning houses of the Cimadevilla *barrio*, which spills over the high knob of land called Santa Catalina jutting into the Atlantic to the N of the new city. To its w is the thriving port which serves the Asturian coal-mining and smelting industries.

To the s and w, a broad scimitar of sand attracts tens of thousands of Spanish and foreign tourists every year, a circumstance which encourages the substantial number of bars and nightclubs whose diversions cater to many tastes.

Sights and places of interest

Museo-Casa Natal de Jovellanos
Plaza Jovellanos ☎(985) 346 313. Open Tues-Sat 10am-1pm, 4-8pm, holidays 10am-1.30pm. Closed Sun and Mon.
The 18thC poet, educator and political activist Gaspar Melchor de Jovellanos was born in this house, which has now been restored and is used as a museum. Exhibits include paintings and polychrome woodcarvings by regional artists, and an intriguing model of the old city.
Termas Romanas
Camp Valdés s/n ✗ arranged through museum (above).
Although not extensive, these subterranean baths near the w end of the San Lorenzo beach, below the Cimadevilla quarter, are the principal surviving structures of the Roman settlers.

Other sights

In the Plaza del Marqués can be seen both the **Iglesia de San Juan Bautista**, a collegiate church built between the 15th and 18thC, and the **Palacio del Conde de Revillagigedo**. The latter, a 16thC residence which was renovated at the end of the 17thC, dominates the plaza.

🏨 As the name implies, **Parador Nacional Molino Viejo** (*Parque de Isabel la Católica s/n ☎(985) 370 511* ▮▮▮) was once an old mill; the present building is essentially new with 40 rooms and a beach and park nearby. All the rooms at **Príncipe de Asturias** (*Manso 2 ☎(985) 367 111* ▮▮▮ *to* ▮▮▮) face the beach, and the breakfast room at the top of the hotel has the grandest views of all. The usual comforts are provided by **Hernán Cortés** (*Fernández Vallín 5 ☎(985) 346 000* ▮▮▮ *to* ▮▮▮), a centrally located hotel built in the 1950s.

🍴 Skillful recipes with local seafood are on hand at **Casa Víctor** (*Carmen 11 ☎(985) 350 093* ▮▮▮), where the wine list excels; **El Retiro** (*Enrique Cangas 28 ☎(985) 350 030* ▮▮▮) is popular locally for its regional cuisine; the owner of **Casablanca** (*Av. García Gernardo s/n ☎(985) 365 869* ▮▮▮) is still experimenting, but it's worth a visit just to see what the chef is doing this week; **Juan del Man** (*Paseo de Begoña 30 ☎(985) 350 073* ▮▮▮) has been on the scene longer, but hasn't lost its capacity for innovation — romantics inquire about the private nooks available; **Casa Tino** (*Alfredo Truán 9* ☎*(985) 341 387* ▯ *to* ▮▮) caters to every taste.

Girona (*Gerona*)
*Map **16**D2. Girona. 96km (60 miles) NE of Barcelona; 92km (57 miles) SW of Perpignan. Population: 75,000* **i** *Ciudadanos 12* ☎*(972) 201 694.*

Capital of the province of the same name, Girona, situated off the A17 *autopista* from Perpignan to Barcelona and with an airport nearby, is a main access point for the popular *Costa Brava*. The city, strategically located at the junction of the Ter and Oñar rivers, was important long before Roman times, and its ramparts incorporate massive cyclopean blocks of uncertain origin. It has been much fought over during its history and was besieged three times during the Peninsular War, when, under the heroic Alvarez de Castro, the women joined in its defense, forming a battalion commemorated by the statue in the **Plaza de la Independencia**. The old town is a labyrinth of steep and narrow alleys, flanked by old stone houses with grilled windows; along the Oñar they form a continuous rampart.

Event In Holy Week, processions of barefoot penitents in black hoods, carrying burning tapers.

Sights and places of interest
Baños Arabes
▨ *Open Tues-Sat summer 10am-2pm, 4-7pm; winter 10am-1pm; Sun and holidays 10am-1pm.*
Just to the N of the cathedral, the Moorish baths dating from the 12thC are among the best preserved in Spain. They incorporate a large pool surrounded by columns, and smaller chambers for hot and steam baths.

Cathedral †
This impressive cathedral surmounts a beautiful 17thC flight of 90 steps. The facade, pierced by a single great oval rose window, is Baroque, but the rest is Gothic, dating from 1316 — although it was allegedly founded in 786 by Charlemagne, who is also credited with the great octagonal tower and campanile on the right-hand side. The most impressive feature is the single great nave, 60m (200ft) long, 23m (75ft) wide and 34m (110ft) high, with a chancel canopied in silver to resemble the sky and an altarpiece in silver gilt and enamel retracing the life of Christ.

The **treasury** ☆ (*open July-Sept 9.30am-8pm; Oct-June 9.30am-1.15pm, 3.30-7pm*) contains magnificent 14th and 15thC gold and silver plate, Mozarabic caskets, a Bible which belonged to Charles V of France, beautifully embroidered 12th-15thC altarfronts, and a superb tapestry of the *Creation* dating from about 1100.

Other sights
Apart from the old town, the most interesting sights to be found in this area are the former **collegiate church of San Félix**, of Romanesque foundation, and the **provincial archeological museum**. Both of these are situated near the cathedral.

☜ The best hotels are **Costabella** (*2km/1¼ miles outside Girona on the N11* ☎*(972) 202 524* ▮▮), and, in the city itself, **Inmortal Gerona** (*Carretera de Barcelona 31* ☎*(972) 207 900* ▮▮) and the picturesquely situated **Ultonia** (*Av. de Jaume I 22* ☎*(972) 203 850* ▮▮).

▧ The most sophisticated restaurant in the area is **Ampurdán** (*near Figueras, on the N11, km 763* ☎*(972) 500 662* ▮▮), the brainchild of Joseph Mercader. It has a splendid range of fish mousses, charcoal grills and sweets, including one of Mercader's greatest creations, the mint sorbet. For more simple fare two restaurants serving seafood and local specialties are **Cal Ros** (*Con Real 9* ☎*(972) 201 011* ▮▮) and **Cipresaia** (*Peralta 5* ☎*(972) 215 662* ▮▮).

Place nearby

Figueras (*37km/23 miles N of Girona*). Figueras was the birthplace of the surrealist painter Salvador Dalí and possesses the **Salvador Dalí museum** (*open 10.30am-12.30pm, 3.30-7.30pm; closed Mon in winter*).

Granada

Map 7H6. Granada. 126km (78 miles) NE of Málaga; 168km (105 miles) NW of Almería. Population: 285,000 i Casa de los Tiros ☎(958) 221 022.

For long a spiritless provincial capital of the Moors, Granada profited by the agonizingly slow advance of the Christian Reconquest. When *Córdoba* fell to Ferdinand II in 1236, the cream of its artisan and mercantile classes migrated to the last major Moorish city in the peninsula. With this injection of talent and treasure, Granada was to flourish for nearly 300yrs.

> Alms, lady, alms! For there
> is nothing crueler in life
> than to be blind in Granada.
>
> The appeal of De Izaca's blind beggar

Potentates of the Almoravid and Nasrid dynasties had the leisure and funds to build numerous reportedly exquisite mosques and palaces for themselves and their subjects. Most of these were razed over the centuries, first through the royal Muslim predilection for destroying the monuments of predecessors, and then through the vindictiveness of their conquerors. The fact that it is so rare enhances the aura of the **Alhambra**, the ultimate architectural achievement of the Moors in Spain. It ranks in near-mystical exuberance with the Taj Mahal, the Parthenon and Mayan Tikal. Not a single building, but a multi-level complex of castles, churches, fortifications and royal residences connected by tiers of gardens, massive gates, terraces, corridors and half-hidden staircases, it looms over the entire city.

Granada itself is only of fleeting interest. It huddles at the rim of a flat irrigated plain and is backed by the foothills of the Sierra Nevada, whose peaks are covered in snow well into late spring, which is surprising this far south. For much of the year, it is possible to ski in the morning and in the afternoon swim in the Mediterranean, little over an hour's drive away. The motive for staying, however, is not the city, but the Alhambra.

Events In Jan, celebration of the 1492 Christian Reconquest.

In Holy Week, extensive celebrations.

In late June or early July, festival of music and dance.

Sights and places of interest

Albaicín

The old Moorish quarter climbs the slope from the narrow river Darro, with a view up to the **Alhambra**. The picturesque houses with interior patios in this until now poor district are today being renovated by middle-class purchasers.

Alhambra 🏛 ★

▓ *Combined entry with Generalife ▣ for grounds ⚔ Open June-Sept 9am-8pm, Oct-May 9.30am-5.45pm. Illuminated visits on selected nights (ask at tourist information office).*

Water was such an elusive commodity in the Moors' arid homelands that they delighted in its abundance in the conquered Iberian territories. Nowhere in their building did they employ it with a more lavish hand than at the Alhambra.

Viewed from above, the walled complex at the top of the sloping table-rock resembles a pointing finger. At its tip is the 9thC **Alcazaba** that was itself constructed on the foundations of an earlier castle. Its attraction is the panorama of city, plain and mountains provided by the belvedere of the roof of its watch tower. But the real pleasure of the Alhambra lies in the **Casa Real** (Royal House) at the joint of the "finger." The best time to arrive is at the stroke of the opening hour, when relative solitude allows the quiet contemplation these buildings deserve.

The Casa Real unfolds itself slowly, but patience is soon rewarded. Across the small **Patio del Cuarto Dorado** is the **Barca Gallery** and, to the left, the **Hall of the Ambassadors**, where the emir granted twice-weekly audiences. This is the most beautiful room in the Alhambra, fairly small in floor dimension, but sweeping 18m (60ft) to a vault of carved cedar. Hills and ramparts are framed in scalloped windows. The walls, covered in intricately carved decorative Arabic, are anchored by dadoes of lustrous tiles that glow in the diffused light.

The portal to the right passes through a loggia to a court trisected by myrtle hedges. A long shallow pool in the center reflects the tower housing the Hall of the Ambassadors, its glassy surface stirred only by gold and crimson carp. At the far end, another opening on the left leads through a forest of incredibly slender columns to the **Court of the Lions**, probably the most photographed part of the palace. In the middle of the square, 12 stylized but robust stone lions make a circle, bearing a large basin on their haunches. Jets of water issue from their mouths. A colonnade surrounds the court, with porticoes projecting spectacularly toward the fountain from each end.

Off the Court of the Lions is the **Hall of the Two Sisters**, notable for thousands of sculptured protuberances dripping from above like dainty stalactites. The Moors built for their own amusement, not for the ages, and it is astonishing that these delicate plaster filigrees have weathered the centuries of neglect. A nearby staircase leads down to the tiled baths. Returning upstairs, you emerge in the tranquil **Patio de Daraxa**. While Ambassador to Spain from the United States, the author Washington Irving gazed down upon it from the apartments above, where he wrote *Tales of the Alhambra*. These apartments, designed for Charles V, have been destroyed by fire, vagabonds, royal caprice and time itself. For years they remained derelict, and only now are they undergoing restoration.

Return through the Patio de Daraxa, turn left into the **Jardines del Partal**, and on the left is the squat **Torre de las Damas**, with an open pavilion facing a rectangular pool with two spouting lions at the opposite end. Walk in their direction (s) through the terraced gardens and pools and bear back toward the **Palacio de Carlos V**. It is unlikely that the uncompleted Renaissance structure would be esthetically hospitable in any setting. Here, it is definitely out of place; grim, massive and ponderous amid the playful delicacy of the Moorish creation. Begun 34yrs after the victory of Ferdinand and Isabella, it was eventually abandoned, its roof left open to the sky.

In the galleries surrounding the circular courtyard are two museums (▨

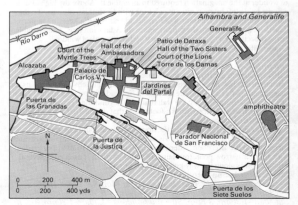

Granada

open 10am-2pm, closed Sun and holidays); the **Hispano-Moorish museum** displays objects from the Alhambra and other Moorish sites, the **fine arts museum** (on the first floor) exhibits religious paintings and sculptures of the late Gothic and Renaissance periods.

Baños Arabes
Carrera del Darro 31 🖼 *Open 9am-6pm.*
These 11thC Arab baths are among the few Moorish architectural remnants outside the boundaries of the Alhambra.

Capilla Real † ☆
Plaza de la Lonja 🖼 *Open 9am-6pm* 💵 *Enter from the alley leading from the Gran Via de Colón, three streets N of the intersection with Reyes Católicos.*
Ferdinand and Isabella commissioned this royal chapel-mausoleum once they had wrested Granada from the Moors. They died before its completion and were buried temporarily at the **Convento de San Francisco** in the **Alhambra**, which has now been converted into a *parador*. Because it was completed in a relatively short period of time, the Capilla Real is a building of rare harmony both inside and outside and, because the royal couple were to be buried there, its style is, appropriately, undiluted Isabeline.

The first room is the **sacristy**, in which paintings from Isabella's collection are displayed; they include works by Botticelli, Berruguete and Van der Weyden, among others. Also on view are Isabella's crown and scepter, Ferdinand's sword, several tapestries and military banners.

In the chapel itself is a splendid altarpiece composed of shallow boxes with realistic scenes in relief from the life of Christ. The kneeling figures to either side are the Catholic Monarchs. Their marble sarcophagi and those of Philip I and Juana the Mad are in the chancel, closed off by a remarkable wrought-iron grille, with cherubim and rampant eagles and lions, by Bartolomé de Jaén.

Cartuja
Real de Cartuja s/n 🖼 *Open June-Sept 10am-1pm, 4-6pm; Oct-May 11am-1pm, 3-6pm.*
This 16th-17thC Carthusian monastery, in the N of the city, has a Baroque church and Gothic rooms. A wildly Churrigueresque Baroque **sacristy** ☆ is the highlight.

Casa de los Tiros
Santa Escolástica. Open 9am-1pm, 5-7pm.
This 16thC Mudejar building contains the tourist office and a **museum** devoted to local history and crafts.

Cathedral †
🖼 *Opening times the same as Capilla Real. Enter through the Capilla Real.*
Largely Renaissance in style, it was begun as a Gothic cathedral in 1521 and work continued until 1714. It is perhaps the least satisfying of Spain's larger cathedrals; the execution of its parts appears heavy-handed and as a whole it lacks grace. Only the **capilla mayor** merits more than a quick glance, if only to wonder at the imagination required to assemble it. Above the high altar is a dome held aloft by twin rows of columns with Corinthian capitals. To the sides of the entrance are statues of Ferdinand and Isabella kneeling in prayer. The carved reliefs above the pulpits represent Adam and Eve. The available space is occupied by paintings, statuary and stained-glass windows. .

Generalife ☆
🖼 *Combined entry with Alhambra. Opening times same as Alhambra.*
Little remains of the royal summerhouse known as the Generalife (pronounced "hay-nay-rahl-ee-fay"), but its formal gardens and fountains are magnificent. After a visit to the **Alhambra**, instead of returning to the Palacio de Carlos V, continue along the wall that runs beyond the Torre de las Damas. At the end of the path is a footbridge that doubles back and climbs to the entrance of the gardens.

Beyond an open amphitheater the first garden and fountains are encountered. (The best time to go is in the morning as the fountains are often turned off in the afternoon.) Steps and terraces then rise to an upper garden, with another narrow pool, fountain jets, and a pavilion at each end. Several vantage points along the way give views of the city.

Monasterio de San Jerónimo
Rector López Argüeta 9 🖼 *Open summer Mon-Sat 10am-1pm, 4-6.30pm, Sun and holidays 11.30am-1pm; 4-6.30pm; winter Mon-Sat 10am-1.30pm, 3-6pm, Sun and holidays 11.30am-1.30pm, 3-6pm.*

In the church is a remarkably complex altarpiece, polychrome sculptures in pillared niches stacked one on top of the other all the way to the vaulted ceiling. One of the two cloisters is Renaissance with a large courtyard, the other a blend of Gothic, Mudejar and Renaissance motifs.

Museo Arqueológico
Paseo del Padre Manjón 🖼 *Open June-Sept Tues-Sat 10am-2pm, 6-8pm, Oct-May Tues-Sat 10am-2pm, 4-6pm; Mon 10am-2pm. Closed Sun and holidays.*
Housed in the Renaissance **Casa Castril**, this museum has a collection of Greek, Roman and Moorish archeological finds.

Hotels

Alhambra Palace
Peña Partida 2 🕿 *(958) 221 468* ☎ *78400* ▥ *124 rms* ▭ *124* ▦ ⊸ ⇌
▨ ⊕ ⊙ ▧
Location: Halfway down the hill from the Alhambra. King Alfonso XIII, Juan Carlos' grandfather, attended the opening of the hospital that was later to be converted into the Alhambra Palace. The building imitates the Moorish design, with spacious public and private rooms. From most vantage points the views of the city and mountains are superlative.
‡ ▱ ⥥ ◁ ⚐ ♈

Luz Granada
Av. Constitución 18 🕿 *(958) 204 061* ☎ *78424* ▥ *174 rms* ▭ *174* ▦
⊸ ⇌ ▨ ⊕ ⊙ ▧
Location: In the NW district, on the Córdoba road. The inconvenient location is a liability, unless you are staying only a night or two. Otherwise, plan to use taxis to and from the city center, as the traffic can be hectic. Views of the city and mountains are particularly enjoyable from the top-floor restaurant. Maintenance and staff are excellent, the bedrooms are rather small but attractive.
‡ ▯ ▱ ⁒ ◁ ⚐ ♈

Parador Nacional de San Francisco
Recinto de la Alhambra 🕿 *(958) 221 493* ▥ *32 rms* ▭ *32* ▦ ⊸ ⇌
▨ ⊕ ⊙ ▧
Location: In the Alhambra. As befits a mosque that has been turned into a convent, the bedrooms are simply furnished and the public rooms are not extravagant. The enclosed terrace, where Queen Isabella was once buried, is soothing, but the glory of this *parador* is its setting. Immediately outside, blooming vines cover the walls and leaves shimmer over secluded benches. Just beyond are the groves, courts, gardens, palaces and gateways of the Arab monarchs. The 32 rooms cannot begin to meet demand, and reservations must be made months in advance.
▣ ▱ ⁒ ⥥ ◁ ♈

🖙 Useful hotels include: **Carmen** (*Acera del Darro 62* 🕿 *(958) 258 300* ▥); **Guadalupe** (*Av. de los Alijares s/n* 🕿 *(958) 223 423* ▯); **Kenia** (*Molinos 65* 🕿 *(958) 227 506* ▯); **Meliá Granada** (*Angel Ganivet 7* 🕿 *(958) 227 400* ▥); **Washington Irving** (*Paseo del Generalife 2* 🕿 *(958) 227 550* ▯).

Hotel nearby
Sierra Nevada (*35km/22 miles SE of Granada*).

Parador Nacional Sierra Nevada
Carretera de Sierra Nevada, km 35 🕿 *(958) 480 200* ▥ to ▥ *33 rms*
▭ *33* ⊸ ⇌ ▨ ⊕ ⊙ ▧
Location: In the mountains. The mountain road eventually reaches the highest elevation of any in Western Europe, often wreathed in clouds. On the way, it passes this prototypical alpine chalet, a definite deviation from the *parador* norm. Locally, there is skiing well into April, most years.
▣ ‡ ▱ ⁒ ◁ ♈

⇌The *parador's* restaurant is exceptional — one wall is glass, so that diners can admire the spectacular views as they tuck into specialties such as roast kid sizzling in a garlic sauce, and toast their feet by the circular fireplace.

Restaurants

Cunini
Pescadería 9 ☎ *(958) 263 701* ‖▯ ▢ ▬ ▤ ⅄ ⒜Ɛ ⊕ ⓒⓓ 𝘝𝘐𝘚𝘈 *Last orders 11.30pm. Closed Sun dinner.*
Fish and shellfish in profusion are the specialty of this traditional bar-restaurant. Contemplate the possibilities in the popular *tapas* bar on the ground floor. The cooks are highly versatile; dishes range from the airy fried fish of Málaga, to the sturdy soup-stews of the Basque country, to the skewered grilled fish of Catalunya.

Sevilla
Oficios 14 ☎ *(958) 224 665* ‖▯ ▢ ▬ ▦ ▤ ⅄ ⒜Ɛ ⊕ ⓒⓓ 𝘝𝘐𝘚𝘈 *Last orders 11pm.*
Sevilla has been in business for over 50yrs and is Granada's most reliable restaurant; it neither excels nor disappoints. It contains the city's best *tapas* bar, and national dishes (monkfish, lamb and chicken) can be eaten either in the dining room or out on the terrace.

☰ **Hostal América** (*Real de la Alhambra 53* ☎ *(958) 227 471* ‖▯) provides unpretentious and abundant meals; **Los Leones** (*Av. José Antonio 10* ☎ *(958) 255 007* ‖▯) is basic but good value; **Torres Bermejas** (*Plaza Nueva 5* ☎ *(958) 223 116* ‖▯) aims higher, opting for stylishness in decor and services, but the food does not always measure up.

Nightlife
Nightlife in Granada centers on the Gypsy quarter of Sacramonte, the hillside opposite the **Generalife**. Here, in lurid rooms hollowed from the side of the hills, you may see impromptu flamenco dancing. Foreign visitors are vastly overcharged for drinks. You will be encouraged to go. Don't.

Guadalajara
Map 12E6. Guadalajara. 56km (35 miles) NE of Madrid; 265km (164 miles) SW of Zaragoza. Population: 58,000.
Originally an Iberian settlement, this small provincial capital has been bombarded and sacked repeatedly over the centuries, notably by the French in 1809 and during the Civil War. Little of its historical heritage survives in a now industrialized city dominated by its neighbor Madrid.

Palacio del Infantado
At the N entrance to the town ▦ *Open 9am-2pm, 4-9pm.*
Because of wartime depredations, much of the former grandeur of the interior has been lost and other parts have been reconstructed in this 15thC ducal palace; restoration continues. The facade retains its original graceful stonework and Mudejar windows, and with renovation the inner patio has regained a sense of its original Isabeline styling.

☞ A useful hotel on the main Madrid-Zaragoza/Barcelona road is **Pax** (*Carretera Madrid-Barcelona, km 57* ☎ *(911) 221 800* ‖▯ *to* ‖▯).

☰ **Minaya** (*Av. del Generalísimo Franco 23* ☎ *(911) 212 253* ‖▯), **El Ventorrero** (*López de Haro 4* ☎ *(911) 212 251* ‖▯), and the regional-style **Mesón Hernando** (*Carretera NII, km 52* ☎ *(911) 222 767* ‖▯ *on the Madrid-Zaragoza road SW of the city*) all provide traditional Castilian meals; their specialty is roast meat.

Place nearby
Mar de Castilla (*51km/32 miles SE of Guadalajara*).   This "Sea of Castile" is a string of artificial lakes formed by dams in the Tajo river. The road to **Sayatón** leads along the W shore, and from here there is a road traveling E to **Buendía**. There are many viewpoints on this excursion, with fine vistas of water and green countryside.

Guadalupe

Map 6F4. Cáceres. 128km (80 miles) SE of Cáceres; 181km (113 miles) SW of Toledo. Population: 2,800.

The empty steppe of *Extremadura*, as vast and majestic as an uncharted sea, supports fewer people than any other comparable region of Spain. Yet several of the towns and villages that make up its archipelago of isolated communities are of outstanding interest, neglected by tourists and therefore largely unspoiled. Of these none exceeds Guadalupe, situated on the undulating slopes of the Guadalupe sierra.

Overwhelming the orange-roofed houses around its walls is an extravagant **fortress-monastery** raking the sky with crenellated keeps, spiky cylindrical turrets with chequerboard tiles, belfries and octagonal towers. The richness of its architecture is almost equaled by the art treasures within.

Monastery 🏛 † ★
📷 ✗ *compulsory. Open 9am-1pm, 3.30-6.30pm.*

A reported appearance of the Virgin Mary in 1300 on this site was the reason for the construction of the original sanctuary. As you enter from the attractive *plaza mayor*, up balustraded stairs, it becomes clear that the complex does not follow a rigid rectilinear plan. Twin towers suitable for a castle frame an exuberant Gothic portal with doors in bronze relief depicting Biblical scenes. An exceptional 16thC iron grille encloses the *capilla mayor*, with a 17thC retable partly sculpted by El Greco's son, Jorge Manuel Theotokopoulos.

The **Mudejar cloister** is a large patio garden of orange trees and scrupulously tended box hedges, surrounded by two tiers of horseshoe-arched galleries. In the middle is an ornate tabernacle, a graceful blend of Mudejar, Gothic and Renaissance themes. Pointed arches on each of the four sides contain two smaller arches supported by slender central columns. They are surmounted by stone petals like artichokes, with tile traceries, tapering to a spire. Off to the left you will find a **museum** containing vestments and embroidery.

Almost every inch of the long vaulted **sacristy** is adorned with intricate gold figuring on plaster, tiles, marble and glowing wood cabinetwork, all of which acts as setting for a series of large Zurbarán paintings. There are more canvases by Zurbarán in the **chapterhouse**.

On the first floor there is a room called the **Camarín**, a showcase for a carved blackened wood statue of the *Virgin of Guadalupe*. Take a special look at her garments, which are lavishly embroidered. Also on display are polychrome sculptures, crucifixes and paintings by the 17thC Italian, Luca Giordano.

Ask the guide to make a detour to the 16thC **Gothic cloister** as it is worth a visit.

❧ Parador Nacional Zurbarán
Marqués de la Romana 10 ☎ *(927) 367 075* ▥ *20 rms* ⬚ *20* 🍴 ⬛
⬛ AE ⬤ VISA
Location: Near the plaza mayor. The roof of this former 15thC hospital bristles with bleached white chimney pots and air vents, enclosing a lovely courtyard. Inside, latticed shutters filter the sun.
⌂ ‡ 📷 ⚐ ⚲ ≪ ☿

❧ Hospederia del Real Monasterio
Plaza Juan Carlos I ☎ *(927) 367 000* ▥ *40 rms* ⬚ *40* 🍴 ⬤ VISA
A Gothic cloister attached to the monastery was converted into a modern hospice by the monks who oversee the fortress monument. The Hospederia is nearly as appealing as the *parador*, with similar facilities, and at half the cost.
⌂ ‡ ▦ ⚲

≡ The dining rooms of the *parador* and *hospederia* are superior to anything else in town, but for variety, there is **Mesón El Cordero** (*Convento 11* ☎ *(927) 367 131* ▥), near the main square. It has an attractive *tapas* bar in front.

Guernica *(Guernika y Luno)*

Map 13B7. Vizcaya. 36km (23miles) E of Bilbao; 84km (53 miles) W of San Sebastián. Population: 18,000.

If Guernica once possessed a lively *ambiente*, no living person under 50 can recall it. The Basques have been a thorn in the side of every aspiring ruler and government of Iberia since history was first recorded, and this town has been considered their spiritual capital for much of that time. This is the reason why (in April 1937) it was subjected to the infamous terror bombing by the Germans in support of the Falangist rebels. The town had little military value for either side, so the attack was intended only to crush the morale of the Loyalists. At least 2,000 civilians – about 20 percent of the population — were slaughtered in a single raid. Picasso's harrowing depiction of this event is displayed in the Casón del Buen Retiro in *Madrid*.

The present town attempts to emulate the one that was destroyed, but the effect is bleakly modern. An oak tree, grown from an acorn of a tree that once stood on this site, marks the place where medieval lords assembled to conduct the business of the region. It acts as a symbol of Basque nationalism. The **Casa de Juntas** preserves a fragment of the original tree and has an assembly room of the old parliament.

Guernica is near the Cantabrian Sea, so choose the fish dishes at **Faisen de Oro** (*Adolfo Urioste 4* ☎(94) 685 1001 ▮▮▮), or at **Zimela** (*Carlos Gangoiti 57* ☎(94) 685 1012 ▮▮▮), where the Basque specialties may not astound, but where the standard rarely falls below the acceptable.

Huelva

Map 6H3. Huelva. 87km (55 miles) W of Sevilla; 60km (37 miles) E of the Portuguese border. Population: 135,000 i Plas Altra 10 ☎(955) 245 092.

The prosperous Atlantic port city exports copper and other metals and imports crude oil for the nearby refineries. It dates back at least to the Phoenicians, but the 1755 Lisbon earthquake devastated the city, and very little remains from Roman times or the period during which it was a primary landfall of the conquistadors. Columbus set sail on his first quest for a westerly route to the Orient from **Palos de la Frontera**, a few miles up the Tinto river.

Sights and places of interest

Two 16thC churches are among the few survivors of the 1755 earthquake; **Iglesia de la Concepción** contains two paintings by Zurbarán, and **Iglesia de San Pedro** incorporates parts of an earlier mosque. The **archeological museum** (*Alameda Sundheim 13* ▨ but ⌖ on Sat; *open 10am-2pm, 4-7pm, closed Mon and Aug*) has artifacts from the Roman copper mines at nearby Tharsis on view, together with a gallery of medieval and Renaissance paintings and artworks.

Sight nearby

La Rábida

4km (2½ miles) SE of Huelva ✗ compulsory. Open 10am-1.30pm, 4-8pm.

Columbus was sheltered at this Franciscan monastery by a sympathetic prior in 1491, before the would-be explorer had persuaded Isabella of his radical idea about the shape of the earth. A garrulous monk shepherds groups through the 14th-15thC building, where the most interesting exhibits are models of Columbus' ships.

The four-star **Luz Huelva** (*Alameda Sunheim 26* ☎(955) 250 011 ▮▮▮▮ to ▮▮▮▮) has all the usual comforts.

Hotel nearby
Mazagón (*23km/14 miles* SE *of Huelva*).

Parador Nacional Cristobal Colón (*Carretera Mazagón-Moguer* ☎(955) 376 000 ▮▮▮▮) is a very agreeable modern *parador*, where the grounds are planted with pines leading down to an almost always deserted beach.

▤ A cooling bowl of *gazpacho* is an ideal starter at **Los Gordos** (*Carmen 14* ☎(955) 246 266 ▮▮▮), followed by mixed vegetables with ham or grilled hake. The ingredients are always fresh and of a high quality.

Huesca
*Map **14**C8. Huesca. 71km (45 miles)* NE *of Zaragoza; 120km (74 miles)* NW *of Lleida. Population: 42,000* ℹ *Coso Alto 23* ☎(974) 225 778.

The Roman Quintus Sertorius established this town as the center of an autonomous state and founded a college here *c.*76BC, after fleeing the hostile forces of the rival Sulla faction. His own men did not appreciate his efforts and murdered him a few years later. In 1096, Pedro I reclaimed Huesca from the Moors, who had held it for over three centuries. The Falangists occupied the city during much of the Civil War and it was subject to continuous bombardment for 2yrs by the Loyalists. Although many buildings were lost, it remains a pleasant, relaxed provincial capital.

Sights and places of interest
The florid 16thC Gothic **cathedral** (*Plaza de la Catedral*) has a 14thC W facade, surmounted by an Aragonese Mudejar gallery. Huesca's oldest church is the 13thC **Iglesia San Pedro El Viejo** (*Cuarto Reyes* ▩ *open Mon-Sat 9am-1.30pm, 4-6pm, Sun 10am-1.30pm*), painstakingly restored and a fine example of the Romanesque. The capitals are carved with creatures and vivid nightmarish scenes. The **provincial museum** (*Plaza de la Universidad* ▩ *open Tues-Sun 10am-2pm, 4-6pm, Sun 10am-2pm, closed Mon*) is housed in a 17thC university building and displays, among other artworks, a collection of 13th-16thC Aragonese paintings. **Pabellón de Deportes** is the main park, with fountains, flowerbeds, peacocks, bands which play in summer, and café tables set out on shaded patios.

🗪 **Pedro I de Aragón** (*Calle del Parque 34* ☎(974) 220 300/220 304 ▮▮▮) is near the park and is the best hotel in Huesca.

▤ Shellfish and beef are the specialties at **Navas** (*San Lorenzo 15* ☎(974) 224 738 ▮▮▮).

Ibiza
*Map **9**I8. 260km (162 miles)* S *of Barcelona; 112km (70 miles)* SW *of Palma. Airport:* S *of Ibiza town. Population: 50,000.*

Third largest of the *Islas Baleares*, Ibiza is far smaller than *Mallorca* but second to it in touristic importance. Its first known habitation was in the 10thCBC by Phoenician traders, who were followed by the Carthaginians and then by the Romans. After consolidating their hold on the mainland, the Moors occupied the island in the 8thC — a heritage that accounts for the African character of the houses that gave rise to the nickname Isla Blanca (White Isle). Square houses, with flat roofs to collect rainwater, are painted a dazzling white, reflecting the sun and helping to keep the interiors cool.

Ibiza came under the authority of the various Christian successors to the Arabs, but avoided serious involvement in most of their wars. It lazed in sun-drenched somnolence until the 1960s, when it began to pick up the overflow of the tourist trade from

Ibiza

Mallorca. First came the writers and artists, then the hippies and package tours. Despite tourism, the customs, folklore and local dialect persist.

With only a little over 570sq.km (220sq. miles) of land, Ibiza can support only two towns of any size — **Ibiza** on the E shore and **San Antonio** on the w, although resort hotels crop up near every beach along the indented coast. The haphazardly hilly terrain is patterned with groves of olives, figs, almonds and pine trees. Sailing, swimming, golf, tennis, riding and windsurfing are among the many diversions.

Ibiza

Map 9/8. Population: 25,000 i Plaza Vara del Rey 13 ☎ (971) 301 900.
With as many as 60 jumbo-jet arrivals every day in high season, the population of the island's largest town and of the suburban resort communities can easily grow to ten times the permanent size. Astonishingly, the old *barrio* of **Dalt Vila**, behind 16thC fortifications halfway up the slope on which the town is built, clings to much of its Arabic charm. Below is the Marina quarter, a predictable conglomeration of boutiques, bars and restaurants similar to every other Mediterranean vacation port.

Sights and places of interest

Barrio de La Penya
The fishermen's quarter to the E of the main port district is an enchanting jumble of houses that suggests a Moroccan *souk*.

Cathedral †
Plaza de la Catedral ◁ᠼ
The 14thC bell tower, which can be seen from every part of the town, is a remnant of the medieval fortress-cathedral. Interior restoration took place from then until the 18thC, resulting in the present and rather unfortunate Baroque overlay. There is a good view over the town from a terrace at the E end.

Museo Arqueológico
Plaza de la Catedral 3 ▨ includes entrance to the necropolis in Puig des Molins, w of the old town. Open 10am-1pm.
This is one of the few places in Spain in which it is possible to view substantial remains of the pre-Christian Carthaginian epoch. There are galleries displaying terra-cotta sculptures, glassware, jewelry and some Roman artifacts excavated on the island. The nearby **necropolis** is a stunning reminder of a history of habitation reaching back to the edge of recorded time.

Museo de Arte Contemporáneo
Plaza de Armas s/n ▨ Open 10.30am-1pm, 6-8.30pm. Closed Sun, Jan and Feb
Works by important present-day Spanish painters and sculptors are on display here.

☞ There are very few luxury hotels in this area. Therefore, anticipate simple settings and basic necessities, which in this case mean swimming pools and gardens of tropical flowers. Very similar and barely 10yrs old are **Los Molinos** (*Ramón Muntaner 60* ☎ (971) 302 250 ▮▮▮▮ to ▮▮▮▮) and **Torre del Mar** (*Playa d'En Bossa* ☎ (971) 303 050 ▮▮▮▮ to ▮▮▮▮), both air conditioned and near beaches to the s of Ibiza town. In San Antonio is the comfortable **Palmyra** (*Av. Dr. Fleming s/n* ☎ (971) 340 354 ▮▮▮▮ to ▮▮▮▮), well-situated on the bay. Outside the hamlet of San Miguel, **Hacienda** ▨ (*Na Xamena s/n* ☎ (971) 333 046 ▮▮▮▮) is several steps up in cost and luxury; chic prevails in this attractive setting of rambling mock-Ibizan houses, and advance reservations are essential.

☴ Ibiza town has a restaurant at every corner, few of them offering more than sustenance. Among the exceptions, **Ama-Lur** (*Carretera San Miguel 2.3* ☎ (971) 314 554 ▮▮▮▮) impresses with "New Basque" cuisine, a close cousin of the French *nouvelle cuisine*. It caters to a fashionable clientele attracted by lovely setting and solicitous service. The wine cellar is perhaps the best on the island. Not far away on the same road toward San Miguel is **La Masia D'en Sort** (*Carretera San Miguel 3.5* ▮▯ *closed Nov-Mar*). Considerably less ambitious, it chooses instead to highlight precisely grilled meats. It borders a pretty garden. **Grill San Rafael** (*Carretera San Antonio, km 6* ▮▯ ☎*(971) 314 475*) blends an eclectic menu with lovely decoration, above-par service and a terrace for taking in the fragrant air and pleasant views of the hills and town.

In San Antonio, **Raco de's Pins** (*Port de's Terrent* ▮▯) features traditional Ibizan food composed largely of conspicuously fresh fish. In Santa Eulalia del Río, **Can Pau** (*Santa Gertrudis s/n* ▮▯) was originally a farmhouse and now comprises several pleasant rooms and a dining terrace, where frequently excellent Catalan entrées are served to stylish people who make it their permanent club.

Nightlife

Ibiza basks by day, bubbles at night. Bars to try are **Zoo**, **Los Valencienos** and **Graffiti**, all near each other in the center of town. **La Tierra** (*Callejón Trinidad*) is the trendiest nightspot at present, so the drinks are expensive. There is also the **Casino de Ibiza** (*Paseo Marítimo* ☎*(971) 313 312*) which is open from 9pm-5am.

Islas Baleares *(Balearic Islands)*

Map 9I8&9. In the Mediterranean, 160km (99 miles) SE of Barcelona. Airports: Ibiza, Menorca, Palma de Mallorca. Ferry connections with Alicante, Barcelona, Valencia and between Ibiza, Mallorca and Menorca. Railroad and bus connections on Mallorca. Population: 560,000.

An archipelago comprising four main islands and numerous smaller islands, the Baleares in total constitute a separate province. The capital, **Palma**, is on the largest island, Mallorca. Menorca, Ibiza and Formentera, in that order, are next in size.

Tourism concentrates on Mallorca and Ibiza. Mallorquín, a dialect related to Catalan, is widely spoken, accounting for two spellings of nearly every proper name. Almost every Mediterranean trader, conqueror and brigand since the Bronze Age has stopped on the Baleares and most have left evidence of their habitation. Olives, fruit and almonds are the principal agricultural products. (See also individual entries on *Formentera, Ibiza, Mallorca* and *Menorca*.)

Jaca

*Map 14C8. Huesca. 91km (56 miles) N of Huesca; 111km (68 miles) SE of Pamplona. Population: 11,500 **i** Av. Regimiento de Galicia 2* ☎*(974) 360 098.*

Jaca did not remain for long under the suzerainty of the Moors, who captured it in 716. The doughty Aragonese threw the invaders out only 45yrs later and never again lost their grip, although it was to be another seven centuries before the Moors finally withdrew from the peninsula. For her efforts, Jaca was awarded the status of a kingdom.

Presumably of Celtiberian origin, the city still has parts of a Roman wall dating back to the 2ndCAD. Most of the extant fortifications that bristle throughout the hillside town are of the Middle Ages. On the pilgrim route from Northern Europe to *Santiago de Compostela*, it remains a pleasant stopover for travelers crossing the Somport pass.

Event On the first Fri in May, celebration recounting the role of the women of Jaca in repelling an Arab attack in 795.

Sights and places of interest

Jaca's major sights are the 15thC **Castillo de San Pedro**, unusual because of its pentagonal design, and an 11thC Romanesque **cathedral**; despite later renovations, it retains its former simple grace.

Sights nearby
Santa Cruz de la Serós
16km (10 miles) sw of Jaca, off the Pamplona road.
Of the 10thC monastery abandoned in the 16thC, only a Romanesque church of admirable simplicity survives. It stands in the middle of a small village.

Gran Hotel (*Paseo del Generalísimo Franco 1* ☎(974) 360 900 ▥ *to* ▥) strives to live up to its name, with more facilities than is usual in this region, and attentive service; the small, utilitarian **Conde Aznar** (*General Franco 3* ☎(974) 361 050 ▥ *to* ▥) takes the overflow.

La Cocina Aragonesa (*Cervantes 5* ☎(974) 361 050 ▥ *to* ▥) changes its menu with the season, and has additional daily specialties to make the most of freshly harvested ingredients; the closest competitor in quality and price is **José** (*Av. Domingo Miral 4* ☎(974) 361 112 ▥ *to* ▥), which features *paella* and a mixture of fish and meat dishes.

Jaén
Map 7H5. Jaén. 96km (60 miles) N of Granada; 109km (68 miles) SE of Córdoba. Population: 105,500 **i** *Arquitecto Bergés 3* ☎(953) 222 737.
The name of this provincial capital derives from the Moorish "Gaen," which means "route of the trailer." To its s is the Sierra de Jabalcuz, and to the N a rolling plain that rises beyond the river Guadalquivir to the central Meseta. Historically, Jaén came under the sway of the Carthaginians, followed by the Romans and then the Moors. Today, it bustles at the center, drowses in the residential quarters and finally fades into olive groves.

Sights and places of interest
Cathedral †
Plaza de la Catedral. Open 8.30am-1.30pm, 4.30-7pm.
Although it overwhelms its neighborhood, the massive 16thC basilica is almost pure Renaissance, not the typical patchwork of most Spanish churches. The two towers, with cupolas, at each corner of the main facade are nearly 61m (200ft) high. They were completed in 1688 to frame an assemblage of fluted columns, round-arched doors and windows, niched statues, balconies, balustrades and triangular pediments. A cabinet beside the main altar contains a cloth with which St Veronica is said to have dried the brow of Christ. In the **museum** (▨) there are paintings by Ribera and Sebastián Martínez.

Other sights
The **provincial museum** (*Paseo Estación* ▨ *open 10am-2pm, 4-7pm, closed Mon*) features a Palaeo-Christian sarcophagus, Roman mosaics, and Celtiberian and Greek ceramics. The oldest church in the city, the Gothic **Iglesia de la Magdalena**, is temporarily closed, but there is the 13thC **Monastero de Santa Clara**, with a lovely cloister and an *artesonado* ceiling in the chapel. The crumbling **Castillo de Santa Catalina**, on a towering cliff to the w, has disintegrated beyond significance but offers impressive vistas; parts of the ruins have been reconstituted as a *parador*.

Parador Nacional Castillo de Santa Catalina
☎(953) 264 411 ▥ 43 rms ▭ 43 ▦ ▬ ▭ Æ ⊕ ⊙ VISA
Location: On a cliff high above the city. Although installed within the ruins of Jaén's 13thC Moorish castle, this *parador* is a modern evocation of the period with no direct relation to previous structures. The windswept hilltop offers solitude as well as splendid views of miles of countryside. The kitchen is competent, and rooms are spacious and tidy.
▨ ▨ ▨ ▨ ▨ ▨ ▨

Condestable Iranzo (*Paseo Estación 32* ☎(953) 222 800 ▥) is a high-rise building (1975) lacking in distinctiveness but not in contemporary comforts; as central and as unsurprising is **Xauen** (*Plaza Deán Mazas 3* ☎(953) 264 011 ▥).

Hotel nearby
Bailén (*39km/25 miles* N *of Jaén*).

A useful stop on the Granada-Madrid road is **Parador Nacional de Bailén**
(☎(953) 670 100 ▮▯).

≡ It isn't in the same league as its Madrid namesake, but the **Jockey Club**
(*Paseo de la Estación 20* ☎(953) 211 018 ▮▯) makes a stout effort. Specialties
cover the whole range of national gastronomy, with selections from France
and Italy as well. At **Los Mariscos** (*Nueva 2* ☎(953) 231 910 ▮▯), shellfish
are paramount.

Jerez de la Frontera
Map 6I3. Cádiz. 36km (23 miles) NE *of Cádiz; 90km (56 miles)*
s *of Sevilla. Population: 176,000* **i** *Alameda Cristina* ☎(956)
342 037.

The Moors called their white city Sherish, which the conquering
Christians transformed into Jerez (pronounced "haireth"). It is
perhaps not surprising that the British merchants who came in the
early 17thC to produce and ship a unique fortified wine managed to
corrupt the word into "sherry." Many *bodegas* still carry the
British names of their founders and descendants: Sandeman,
Williams & Humbert, Osborne and Duff Gordon. Other famous
names include González Byass and Pedro Domecq. Jerez is still the
center of sherry production in Spain, and the wine has yet to be
reproduced with comparable success in any other country. (For
more information on sherry and the *bodegas*, see *Spanish Wines* in
Special information.)
Events In Apr, Feria del Caballo (horse fair). This joyous
celebration includes dressage competitions and races.
   In Sept, Fiesta de la Vendimia. A colorful wine festival to
celebrate the harvest, with flamenco and *sevillana* dancing.

Sights and places of interest
Above the 17th-18thC Renaissance-Baroque **cathedral** (*Plaza de la
Encarnación*) is the 12thC Moorish **Alcázar** (*Fortún de Torres*), surrounded by
gardens. In Plaza de la Asunción, a 16thC Renaissance mansion (*open
10am-1pm, closed Aug and Sun*) now houses a **public library** and an
archeological museum with prehistoric, Greek and Roman finds. The
Gothic-Baroque **Iglesia de Santiago** (*Plaza de Santiago*) is notable for the
intricate Isabeline decoration of its main facade.

⌘ **Jerez** (*Av. Alcalde Alvaro Domecq 35* ☎(956) 330 600 ▮▮▮ *to* ▮▮▮▮), a
contemporary hotel with a terrace that surrounds the swimming pool, is the
best of a weak lot; **Capele** (*General Franco 58* ☎(956) 346 400 ▮▯) is a
no-frills alternative.

≡ It is an oddity of the major Spanish wine-growing regions that they boast
very few restaurants of true distinction. That is not to suggest, however, that
Gaitán (*Gaitán 3* ☎(956) 345 859 ▮▯) does not offer good value, because it
does, with authentic regional dishes incorporating both seafood and roast
meat. Alternatively, **El Bosque** (*Av. Alcalde Alvaro Domecq 28* ☎(956) 333
333 ▮▯) is the most stylish recommendation, with national recipes and a few
foreign dishes, and dining in the garden when the weather is fine. **El Ancla**
(*Beato Juan Grande 13* ☎(956) 340 352 ▮▯) has an excellent *tapas* bar, as
well as a dining room.

León
Map 11C4. 317km (197 miles) NW *of Madrid; 118km (73
miles)* s *of Oviedo. Population: 132,000* **i** *Plaza de la Regla 4*
☎(987) 237 082.

The 7th Roman Legion effectively founded León in the 1stCAD,
with an instant population of perhaps 15,000, including soldiers,

camp followers and merchants. The old city hugs the E bank of the Río Bernesga and contains all that is of interest to the tourist, although the modern W bank is evidence of the prosperity brought by coal and mineral development.

...although...León Cathedral was entirely French in concept, with the best stained glass in Spain, I was entirely unprepared for the iridescent blaze of coloured lights all around me: it was like stepping into a spotlit jewel-box.

Elisabeth de Stroumillo,
The Tastes of Travel, Northern and Central Spain, 1980

Walls with closely spaced semi-circular towers date from the 3rdC. Despite these fortifications, Goths conquered the city in the late 6thC and the ruthless Moor Almansor ransacked much of it in 996. For a while the capital of the kingdom of León, it subsequently served as a major stopping place along the Camino de Santiago (the way of St James) during the Middle Ages.

Sights and places of interest

Basílica de San Isidoro † ☆

Plaza de San Isidoro *Open 9am-2pm, 4-6pm.*

A section of the city wall was incorporated into this Romanesque church in the 11thC. Some of the original structure and embellishment survive, notably in the main S entry and W portico. The rest of the building is primarily of the 12thC with Gothic and Renaissance additions, including a *capilla mayor* by Juan de Badajoz, who was responsible for the sacristy at the **Monasterio de San Marcos** (see below). The **panteón** to the left of the front entrance has 12thC vault frescoes and capitals, intricately carved in animal and floral motifs and Gospel scenes. An 11thC chalice, created for Queen Urraca, which combines two Roman onyx bowls in a gold framework with gems, is the highlight of the **treasury**.

Cathedral 🏛 † ★

Plaza de Regla *Open 8.30am-1.30pm, 4-8pm.*

The glory of the Pulchra Leonina, as the Gothic cathedral is known, is in the blaze and glow of its 128 stained-glass windows, so many and so large that they threaten the structural integrity of the walls. Essential restoration is under way, critical for both esthetic and pragmatic reasons. The sandstone used on the exterior is so weather-worn that many of its sculptures and decorative details have been nearly obliterated.

The 13thC rose window over the main W portal is magnificent, and the two towers of the main facade, while not nearly so dissimilar as those at Chartres, are nonetheless distinct; the pierced S spire is barely more than a stone filigree. The finely tooled silver chest in the *capilla mayor* contains relics of the patron saint Froilán, and is backed by a tall triptych depicting scenes from his life, painted in the 15thC by Nicolás Francés.

Superbly carved wood doors in the N transept lead to the **cloisters**, where faded frescoes decorate 14thC Gothic walls beneath vaulted Renaissance ceilings. If the doors are locked, as is often the case, they can be reached through the museum (see below).

Monasterio de San Marcos 🏛 † ☆

Plaza de San Marcos

The richly detailed Plateresque facade draws the eye immediately upon entering the city of León. It was commissioned by King Ferdinand in 1513 to honor the Order of St James for its part in the protection of pilgrims and in the Catholic Reconquest, it was essentially complete by 1549. It is the equivalent of a full soccer field in length, and the central portion is two stories high, surmounted by a Baroque pediment added in the 18thC. Stone garlands, scallop shells, pilasters and medallions — balanced components of a particularly harmonious whole — decorate the facade. Above the main entrance, which leads into that part of the building now used as a luxury hotel, is an elaborate equestrian relief of the miraculous intervention of St James at the Battle of Simancas with the Moors. Supporting scenes illustrate other events in his life. The church at the E end of the structure is unfinished and of rather clumsy proportions.

Museo Arqueológico and Sacristy †
Inside Monasterio de San Marcos church. Museum 🖾 ✗ *compulsory for sacristy. Open Mon-Sat 10am-2pm, 4-6pm, Sun and holidays 10am-2pm. Closed Jan 15-Feb 15.*

The religious art objects and paintings on view are dominated by an exquisite ivory crucifix of the 11thC, a figure of Christ rendered with such dignity that its compelling presence outshines its surroundings. The imposing vaulted sacristy, built by Juan de Badajoz in the 16thC, now houses an assortment of religious and secular items, including Roman statues.

Museum
🖾 *Open Mon-Thurs, Sat 9am-1.30pm, 4-7.30pm, Sun 9am-2pm, closed Fri. Leave the cathedral by the main entrance, turn right, then left for the entrance to the museum.*

This small repository of religious objects contains representations of Christ, St Sebastian, various crucifixes, a 16thC Plateresque staircase by Juan de Badajoz, an illuminated 10thC Bible, and a letter dated 1494 and signed by Ferdinand and Isabella.

Other sights

Students of the visionary Catalan architect Antonio Gaudí will be interested in his Neo-Gothic **Casa de Botines** in the Plaza de Santo Domingo, although it betrays little of the structural surrealism for which he is known. Adjacent, on the NE side of the square, is the Italianate **Palacio de los Guzmanes**, built in 1560 and now a municipal building. The nearby **Iglesia de San Marcelo** is also of the late 16thC, with relics of the eponymous saint. In the *plaza mayor*, the **Ayuntamiento** (1667) is the predominant building.

Hotels

Conde Luna
Independencia 7 ☎ *(987) 206 600* ☎ *89888* ▥▥ *to* ▥▥▥ *152 rms* 🛏 *152*
▤▤ 🍴 ⬛ ⚊⚊ AE ⓘ 💳

Location: Near the Plaza Santo Domingo. Although it can't compete with the **San Marcos** for glamor or heritage, there is an indoor pool, a bingo parlor and a sauna, and the staff are equally capable. In most provincial capitals, this hotel would rule the roost.

≋ 🖾 �_≈≈ ☂ Ŷ

Quindós
Av. José Antonio 24 ☎ *(987) 236 200* ▥▥ *to* ▥▥▥ *96 rms* 🛏 *96* 🔥 ⚊⚊ ⚊⚊
ⓘ *VISA*

Location: Three streets s *of the Plaza de San Marcos.* Although ordinary in most respects, the Quindós is a lesson to more ambitious hotels. The owner is an *aficionado* of contemporary art and has hung original prints and collages on the walls of every room. The bedrooms are snug and unremarkable.

≋ 🖾 Ŷ

San Marcos 💳 ❀
Plaza de San Marcos 7 ☎ *(987) 237 300* ☎ *89809* ▥▥ *to* ▥▥▥ *258 rms*
🛏 *258* 🔥 ⚊⚊ ⚊⚊ AE ⓘ 💳 *VISA*

Location: On the E *bank of the Río Bemesga.* The Monasterio de San Marcos was a logical candidate for conversion, since it had been built in part as a hospice for medieval pilgrims. Certainly they did not enjoy the pampering accorded present-day travelers, although they would recognize the Plateresque exterior, coffered ceilings and grand staircases. Attendance to needs and whims is at least correct and often anticipatory. Any list of distinguished Iberian hotels must include this one.

⌂ ≋ □ 🖾 🌸 ⚘ ☂ Ŷ

Restaurants

Adonias
Santa Nonia 16 ☎ *(987) 206 768* ▥▥▥ ⌷ ▰▰ ☰☰ Ŷ AE ⓘ *VISA Last orders 11pm. Closed Sun.*

Care is evident in every detail, from fish smoked on the premises to meat grilled precisely to order. *Chuletón* and *entremeses ahumados* are among the specialties.

Bodega Regia
Plaza de San Martin 8 ☎ *(987) 254 151* ⅢⅡ ▯ ▰ ▤ ⅄ ⓒⓓ ⱽⁱˢᵃ *Last orders midnight. Closed Sun dinner.*
The allegedly 13thC building is decked out with Castilian oddities, an appropriate environment for sampling regional specialties, which include *perdiz estofada*, *sopa de ajo* and *lubina*. Don't let the raucous room at the front deter you.

Novelty
Independencia 4 ☎ *(987) 250 612* ⅢⅡ ▯ ▰ ▰ ▤ ⅄ ⓒⓓ ⱽⁱˢᵃ *Last orders 11.30pm.*
The Novelty ladles modernity and stylish dishes in equal measure. Try one of its specialties, such as *jabalí* or *morcilla*, and treat yourself to a good bottle of wine, for the food deserves it and the cellar is abundantly stocked with the finest Riojas.

━━ The restaurants already mentioned, the dining rooms of the recommended hotels and the *tapas* bars in and near the tacky, sprightly Plaza de San Martin will probably cover eating requirements for the average stay; alternatively, there is **Grandigione** (*Arco de Animas 1* ☎ *(987) 208 511* ⅢⅡ) for satisfying Italian dishes; **Patricio** (*Condesa de Sagasta 24* ☎ *(987) 241 651* ⅢⅡ) for selections of international cuisine; or **Las Redes** (*Carretera Astorga km 5* ☎ *(987) 300 164* ⅢⅡ) for fish specialties, with some meat dishes for non-enthusiasts. Telephone in advance on Sun and Mon, when restaurants are frequently closed.

Place nearby
Astorga (*47km/30 miles* SW *of León*).   One of the primary stops on the Camino de Santiago, this fortified city boasts substantial **Roman walls**, a late 15thC **cathedral**, a 17thC **Ayuntamiento**, a Neo-Gothic **Palacio Episcopal**, designed by Gaudí but completed by Ricardo Guereta, and a magnificent location facing the León mountains.

☞ Five km (3 miles) N on the Madrid-La Coruña road, **Pradorrey** (☎ *(987) 615 929* ⅢⅡ) is hardly a typical motel, although that is what it calls itself; simulating a medieval manor house inside and out, it nevertheless has ample modern comforts.

━━ **La Peseta** (*Plaza San Bartolomé 3* ☎ *(987) 617 275* ⅢⅡ) presents sturdy traditional dishes.

The León region
Map 11C4. In the NW, *bordering* N *Portugal.*
The old Kingdom of León is represented now by the provinces of Zamora, Salamanca and León. Running from N to S, they constitute a topographical cross-section of the central Iberian tableland called the Meseta. Arid and bleak throughout much of its length, the land imperceptibly climbs upward to the abrupt alpine ridge at the border with *Asturias*. Although the countryside is harsh and often lacking in vegetation, its few rivers provide irrigation for cereal crops. Cattle and sheep have grazed here for centuries, and the bulls of Salamanca are prized by *aficionados* of the *corrida*.

Salamanca, the seat of a medieval university that influenced scholarship throughout Europe, is a lesson in Romanesque, Renaissance and Churrigueresque architecture; *Zamora* is noted for its Romanesque structures and a moving Holy Week celebration; and the capital, *León*, for its cathedral with magnificent stained-glass windows.

After Asturias had succeeded in repelling the Moors in the 9thC, the Christians continued to advance south. Conflicts with other Catholic kingdoms slowed the Reconquest, but eventually,

episodes of its warlike past was the prolonged siege in 1487 by the Catholic Ferdinand, undertaken as a preliminary to the onslaught on Granada. It is not, however, a city of great artistic or architectural interest; the old quarter is now ringed by high-rise apartments and factories and the romantic Málaga of García Lorca's *Canto Nocturno* is sadly a place of the past.

Event   In Aug, celebrations with parades and bullfights.

Sights and places of interest

Alcazaba 🏛

Plaza de la Aduana 🔁 *Open July-Sept Mon-Fri 10am-1pm, 5-7pm; Oct-June Mon-Fri 10am-1pm, 2-7pm; Sun and holidays 10am-2pm.*

The remains of the twin fortresses from which the Moors conducted their last desperate resistance to the encircling Christian army, the Alcazaba and Gibralfaro (which means hill of the lighthouse and is now the site of the **parador** — see below) crown a hill 130m (300ft) high, rising abruptly from the center of the city and approached by a long winding road. Inside the perimeter of the Alcazaba then are **Moorish gardens**; the former palace, incorporating two patios with 11th and 12thC Moorish decoration and a room with an *artesonado* ceiling, is a museum of Moorish art. The views across the city and its port are spectacular.

Cathedral †

Molina Larios.

Begun in the 16thC and built in Renaissance style, the cathedral still lacks a south tower. The three aisles, supported by Corinthian columns, are covered with cupolas decorated with palm fronds and shells. On no account miss the **choirstalls**, delicately and beautifully carved by the 17thC artist, Pedro de Mena. There are also paintings by Alonso Cano, architect of the cathedral, Morales, Van Dyck and Andrea del Sarto. The **chapterhouse** has a fine *artesonado* ceiling.

Museo de Bellas Artes

Molina Larios 🔁 *Open summer Tues-Sat 10am-1.30pm, 5-8pm; winter Tues-Sat 10am-1.30pm, 4-7pm; Sun and holidays 10am-1.30pm. Closed Mon.*

This former Moorish palace houses paintings by Ribera, Murillo, Morales, Cano and Jordán, as well as local artists. One gallery is devoted to Picasso, who was born in Málaga.

Other sights

The most interesting area in which to spend a few hours in Málaga is the network of narrow alleys and old streets lying immediately behind the port, where most cafés set out tables on the sidewalk. The port, which often plays host to foreign warships, is also worth a visit.

🍴 **Parador Nacional de Gibralfaro**

Paseo García del Olmo s/n ☎ *(952) 840 901* ▥ *12 rms* ▭ *12* 🛏 ≋
AE ⊕ ⊙ VISA

Location: 3km (2 miles) from the city center at the top of Gibralfaro. Splendidly located in the gardens of Gibralfaro above the city with wide views across the port and out to sea, this is the quietest and most picturesque place to stay. It is often difficult to make reservations since there are few rooms, but the drive to the summit is well worthwhile if only to lunch or dine on its open-air terraces. Avoid Sundays, when the rest of Málaga has the same idea.
🍴 🎞 🚿 ⚓ ⛵ ⛄ 🍸

🍴 **Casa Curro** (*Sancha de Lara 7* ☎ *(952) 227 200* ▥) is modern, comfortable and centrally located. **Holiday Inn** (*Urbanización Guadalmar* ☎ *(952) 319 000* ▥) is a luxury hotel, with a garden, tennis courts, swimming pool and disco, just outside the city center. **Málaga Palacio** (*Cortina de Muelle 1* ☎ *(952) 215 185* ▥) is the largest and most elegant of Málaga's hotels. Another pleasant hotel is **Los Naranjos** (*Paseo de Sancha 35* ☎ *(952) 224 319* ▥), easily accessible to central Málaga by bus.

🍴 Both the food, Andalucian and otherwise, and the service are first-rate at **Café de Paris** (*Vélez-Málaga* ☎ *(952) 225 043* ▥). Try cold melon and shrimp soup, the excellent hors d'oeuvres, and fresh local fish or game in season. Overlooking the sea, **Casa Pedro** (*Playa del Palá, just E of Málaga*

☎ *(952) 290 013* ▮▯) is the restaurant most popular with Malagueños. Large and always full, it serves a magnificent variety of fresh seafood. The sophisticated **Escorpio** *(Ventaja Alta 12* ☎ *(952) 258 494* ▮▮▯) serves well-prepared French food.

Shopping

The best and most typical shopping area is behind the port, where you may buy anything from *charcuterie* and pastries to dresses and souvenirs. Shoes, as elsewhere in Spain, are elegant and excellent value. Don't miss the great open market, where, if catering for yourself, fish, vegetables and fruit in enormous variety are cheaper than elsewhere. Also, to take home, spices are fresh and inexpensive. Local craftwork includes pottery and tooled leather.

Mallorca *(Majorca)*

Map 9/9. 180km (112 miles) SE of Barcelona; 325km (200 miles) NE of Alicante. Boat connections with Alicante, Barcelona, Ibiza, Valencia. Airport: Palma. Population: 525,000.

Largest of the *Islas Baleares*, Mallorca comprises 3,639sq.km (1,400sq. miles) of mountains and fertile plain girdled by beaches. **Palma de Mallorca**, in the SW, is the largest city and the capital of the Baleares province. Wheat, olives, almonds and grapes are the principal crops, but tourism is the main industry.

Resort development is concentrated near Palma, around Bahía de Pollensa in the N, and along the SE shore. A spine of mountains reaching peaks of 1,444m (4,750ft) runs along the NW coast, parallel with a range of lower hills on the opposite shore. They cradle a fertile central plain devoted almost entirely to cultivation.

With its consistently mild climate and host of sights, including those in Palma and the caves along the SE coast, Mallorca is an island that gratifies all the senses.

Cabo de Formentor

Map 9/9. 78km (49 miles) NE of Palma; 20km (12 miles) NE of Puerto de Pollensa.

Those who brave the hair-raising drive to the tip of this peninsula are rewarded with stunning views of sea, and sheer cliffs covered in pine and cypress trees.

☞ Formentor ▥

Puerto de Pollensa ☎ *(971) 531 300* ❼ *68523* ▥▥▥ *131 rms* ▤ *131* ▦▦
▱▱ ▣ ⓐ ⑩ VISA

Location: On the Bay of Pollensa, halfway along the cape. Surpassing its rival, the Son Vida in **Palma**, this splendid hotel deserves the kudos showered upon it. Luxuriant gardens rise in tiers from the gin-clear water of the bay to meet the pine-covered lower slopes of the mountain that form this wild scenic cape. Windsurfing, waterskiing, boating, fishing, riding, tennis (two courts are floodlit) and dancing fill the day. Rooms are routinely comfortable, but throw open the shutters for bougainvillea-framed panorama of sea or peaks. With advance notice, guests will be met at Palma airport by a private car.
▨ ‡ ▢ ▧ ⎯ ⸙ ≈ ⬟ ⤳ ⮜ ⛳ ▰ ⛴ ☗ ⓞ

Cala Ratjada

Map 9/9. 80km (50 miles) NE of Palma.

Originally a fishing hamlet, Cala Ratjada is now an international resort. East of the town a lighthouse on a promontory enjoys superb views of the coast. The exposed position confines swimming to the summer months.

Sight nearby

Artá Caves

12km (7 miles) S of Cala Ratjada ▨ *Open Apr–Oct 9.30am-7pm; Nov-Mar 9.30am-5pm. Closed Christmas.*

These extensive caves, which were hollowed out by the sea, enjoy a stunning location, piercing the sheer cliff that rears above an inlet. The chambers themselves are of impressive cathedral dimensions.

♋ Ses Rotges

Alsedo ☎*(971) 563 108* ▥ *12 rms* ▭ *12* ⇒ *[VISA] Closed Nov-Mar.*
Location: *To the right off the C715, just before the town center.* This rustic stucco and beam country inn with its crisply furnished rooms is a refreshing contrast to the gaudy resort community it serves. (See also restaurant, below.)

⌂ ⚓ ⛵ 🎣 ⅄

♋ The spacious rooms of **Son Moll** (*Tritón s/n* ☎*(971) 563 100* ▥) overlook the adjacent beach and sea; **Aguait** (*Av. de los Pinos s/n* ☎*(971) 563 408* ▥ *to* ▥▥) has comparable views and good facilities.

⇒ Ses Rotges

Address and ☎ *as hotel* ▥▥▥ ▭ ■ ⚘ ⅄ *[VISA] Last orders 11pm. Closed Nov-Mar.*
The French chef mixes dishes from France and Spain, basing his superb specialties on abundant local ingredients; try *conejo a la mostaza, mejillones con salsa "poulette," gallo San pedro a la parrillada, pollo al vino,* or the house *terrine,* cradled in a napkin with a rose. (See also hotel, above.)

Inca

Map 9I9. 28km (17 miles) NE of Palma; 24km (14 miles) SW of Pollensa.
A stop on the road between Palma and Pollensa, Inca has an 18thC Baroque church of **Santa María la Mayor,** which was built five centuries earlier but shows little of its origins.

⇒ In attractive surroundings, **Celler C'an Amer** (*Miguel Durán 39* ☎*(971) 501 261* ▥) provides classic Mallorquín food.

Palma de Mallorca

Map 9I8. 30km (19 miles) S of Soller; 49km (31 miles) W of Manacor. Population: 307,000 ℹ *Av. Jaime III 10* ☎*(971) 212 216.*
Known as "Ciutat de Mallorca" in the local dialect, this capital city is populated by over half the inhabitants of the Baleares. It crowds the edge of a broad bay enclosed on the N side by a hook of rock and sand, flattening in the SE to coastal plain. The promenade beside the harbor is its most agreeable feature, passing the looming cathedral, moored yachts, commercial fishing boats, corridors of sentinel palms and a few of the characteristic Mallorquín windmills.

A key link in the Kingdom of Aragón, Palma enjoyed particular influence from the 13th to the 16thC, a period which saw the appearance of many Italianate mansions built by noblemen and merchants who fed on the island's prosperity.

Sights and places of interest

Baños Arabes

Serra 3 ▧ *Open Mon-Fri 10am-1.30pm, 4-6pm, Sat 10am-1.30pm. Closed Sun.*
The only existing Moorish buildings in Palma, these bath houses remain essentially as they were under the Caliphate.

Barrio Antiguo

A section of the Moorish town wall is preserved, running along the coast from the **Palacio de la Almudaina** and the **cathedral** to the Avenida Gabriel Alomar Villalonga. Behind it is the old town. To reach this quarter, pass through an arch halfway along the Paseo Uruguay, and immediately beyond is **La Portella,** the former Jewish *barrio.* Follow Calle Portella until you come to **Museo de Mallorca** (▧ *open 10am-1pm, 4-6pm, closed Sun and holidays*), on the left, where Renaissance paintings and church sculpture are exhibited.

Mallorca

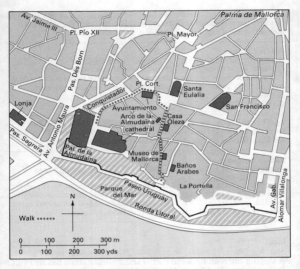

After the museum turn right and then left at the first corner. At the next intersection is the **Casa Oleza**, a 17thC residence with a graciously proportioned courtyard. Turn right (N) into Calle Morey, glancing left for a view of the **Arco de la Almudaina**. The street opens onto the Plaza Santa Eulalia, and directly ahead is the Gothic church after which it was named; on the left is the handsome Renaissance **Ayuntamiento**. Pass it on the right to reach the Plaza Cort. The street on the left leads back to the cathedral, skirting a small tree-shaded square with tables, an ideal place to stop for a rest and a drink.

Basilica de San Francisco †
Plaza San Francisco 6 🖼 *Open 9.30am-1pm, 3.30-7pm. Closed Sun and holidays.*

A Baroque facade was imposed on this large Gothic basilica in the 17thC. Inside is the tomb of the noted medieval theological philosopher Ramón Llull (1235-1315).

Castillo de Bellver ☆
Toll road to the castle off Calvo Sotelo in the Terreno district 🖼 ✱
◁**€** *Open 9am-sunset. Closed some holidays.*

On a hill to the NW, the very unusual circular fort affords spectacular views of Palma and the harbor. Erected in the 14thC, it is in a wonderful state of preservation, with a scalloped moat, three semi-circular towers and a higher, detached cylindrical keep. The round open courtyard has an ancient well and a number of Roman statues. The **Museo Municipal de Historia** exhibits archeological relics and early Mallorquín ceramics. Try to go just before sunset and stay until the doors are closed.

Cathedral † ☆
Plaza Almoina 🔲 🖼 *for museum. Open 10am-12.30pm and 3.30-7pm. Enter through the N door.*

The imposing Gothic 13th-16thC basilica has an appropriately dramatic location on raised ground. Honey-colored limestone is the facing material, worked into filigree on the uniform W towers that flank the noble rose window. Closely spaced flying buttresses, topped by turrets, double the visual bulk of the apse. Above the main altar is a fantastical 19thC iron **canopy** designed by Antonio Gaudí, oddly suitable in a church completed 400yrs earlier.

A small **museum** (🖼 *open Mon-Fri 10am-12.30pm, 4-6.30pm, Sat 10am-2pm, closed Sun and holidays*) in the **chapterhouse** displays late Gothic and early Renaissance paintings, religious and secular silverware, ancient coins and prehistoric objects.

Lonja 🏛 ☆

Paseo Sagrera 🅿 *Open only during exhibitions.*

Guillermo Sagrera's 15thC stock and commodity exchange has debts to military and ecclesiastical Gothic design, with turrets, mock battlements and buttresses. It only served commerce, however, and is now an exhibition hall where shows are mounted beneath the graceful vaulting.

Palacio de la Almudaina

Plaza Almoina 🕿 *Open 10am-1pm, 3.30-6pm. Closed Sun and holidays.*

The severe walls of this former Arab castle form the shell for an interior of Gothic vaultings and traceries installed for the Christian kings of the 15thC. Today, part of the building is set aside for the **Museo del Patrimonio Nacional**, devoted to furniture, tapestries, paintings and armor.

Pueblo Español ☆

Palacio de los Congresos 🕿 *(971) 237 070* 🕿 💻 ✦ *Open 9am-6pm.*

Similar to the Pueblo Español in *Barcelona*, this skillful accumulation of the architectural styles found throughout the country includes scaled-down representations of the Torre del Oro in *Sevilla* and part of the Alhambra in *Granada*. They lack the grandeur and delicacy of the originals, of course, but these reproductions underscore the rich diversity of Spanish domestic and public architecture. There are also bars, a restaurant and many craft and souvenir stores.

Hotels

Maricel

Carretera de Andraity, Palma de Mallorca 15 🕿 *(971) 402 712* 🎢 *to* 🎢 *55 rms* 🛏 *55* 🍽 🍴 AE ⊙ 🗲 VISA

Location: *On the sea, 15km (9 miles) w of the city center.* Although some distance from Palma's main attractions, the Maricel is a charming, quietly stylish hotel, which tastefully evokes a country estate.

‡ ☑ 🦢 ⚓ ⟨⟨ ⇌ 🐟 ⅍ ♉

Son Vida 🏰 🏛

Palma de Mallorca 13 🕿 *(971) 451 011* ☎ *68651* 🎢 *175 rms* 🛏 *175* 🍽 🍴 AE ⊙ 🗲 VISA

Location: *10km (6 miles) NW of the center of Palma.* One of Spain's most honored hotels, awarded the rare five-star *Gran Lujo*. There are minor irritations, however. Standard rooms lack elegance, often with tatty furnishings. Service standards are generally high, but with occasional lapses. However, the public rooms are grand, even opulent, with collections of antiques dotted about and delightfully overblown 19thC landscapes and battle scenes in the corridors. Marble, brocades, pecan paneling and fine leathers are skillfully used, and hints of the 13thC castle that was the inspiration of the hotel remain.

☑ ‡ ☑ ⚓ ⟨⟨ ⇌ ⅍ ✓ 🏌 ⛳ ♉

Valparaíso Palace 🏰

Francisco Vidal 23, Palma de Mallorca 15 🕿 *(971) 400 300* ☎ *68754* 🎢 *150 rms* 🛏 *150* 🍽 🍴 🍴 ⊙ 🗲 VISA

Location: *In La Bonanova district, w of the city center.* No hotel surpasses the Valparaiso for unleashed mid-20thC Rococo excess either in spaciousness or extravagant trappings. Bedrooms are capacious, most with extensive vistas of the city and harbor, the facilities are excellent and the staff is attentive.

☑ ‡ ☑ ☑ 🦢 ⚓ ⟨⟨ ⇌ 🐟 ⅍ 🏌 ♉ ⊙

Victoria Sol 🏰

Av. Joan Miró 21, Palma de Mallorca 14 🕿 *(971) 232 542* ☎ *68558* 🎢 *171 rms* 🛏 *171* 🍽 🍴 AE CB ⊙ 🗲 VISA

Location: *On the w side of the bay, just outside the city center,* easily one of the three top hotels in Palma, with fine views of the bay, precise if rather dour service and well-decorated bedrooms (many with balconies flowing with blossoming vines). Although it is next door to the Plaza Gomila nightclub quarter, no tawdriness spills over into these spacious halls. Only the noise from the gigantic Tito's club intrudes, so make sure you choose a room facing another way. There are two swimming pools, and open-air dancing in summer.

‡ ☑ 🦢 ⚓ ⟨⟨ ⇌ 🏌 ♉ 🍴

↝ Recommended alternatives include: **Almudaina** (*Av. Jaime III 9, Palma 12* 🕿 *(971) 225 943* 🎢); **Bellver Sol** (*Paseo Marítimo 11, Palma 12* 🕿 *(971) 235 142* 🎢); **Cala Blanca-Sol** (*Paseo Duque de Estremera, Palma Nova* 🕿 *(971) 680 100* 🎢); **Comodoro Sol** (*Paseo*

133

Mallorca

Calablanca, Palma Nova ☎*(971) 680 200* ▮▮▯ *to* ▮▮▮▯); **Coral Playa Sol** (*Goleta, Magaluf* ☎*(971) 680 562* ▮▮▯); **Delfin Playa Sol** (*Hermanos Moncada 32, Palma Nova* ☎*(971) 680 100* ▮▮▮▯); **Jaime III Sol** (*Paseo Mallorca 14, Palma 12* ☎*(971) 725*

943 ▮▮▯); **Meliá Mallorca** (*Monseñor Palmer 2, Palma 14* ☎*(971) 233 740* ▮▮▮▯); **Palas Atenea Sol** (*Paseo Marítimo 200, Illetas* ☎*(971) 281 400* ▮▮▮▯); **Saratoga** (*Paseo Mallorca 6, Palma 12* ☎*(971) 227 240* ▮▯ *to* ▮▮▯).

Restaurants

Ancora
Ensenada C'an Barbara ☎*(971) 401 161* ▮▮▮▯ ▭ ▬ ⁉ AE ⊙ VISA *Last orders midnight. Closed Mon lunch, Sun.*
Set among the flowers and boats of an enclosed inlet, with solicitous service and a comprehensive wine list, Ancora is one of the most agreeable (and pricey) restaurants on the island. The essentially Mallorquín food has a *nouvelle* bias. Fish and poultry prevail in innovative combination — for example, *corzo a la pimienta roja* and *crepes de verdura y pescados*.

Le Bistrot
Teodoro Llorente 4 ☎*(971) 287 175* ▮▮▮▯ ▭ ▬ ⁉ ▤ *Last orders 11pm. Closed July and Sun.*
This French-style bistro provides familiar preparations such as Burgundian snails and pepper steak, in an atmosphere reminiscent of the Parisian Left Bank.

Casa Eduardo
Industria Pesquera 4 ☎*(971) 221 182* ▮▮▯ ▭ ▬ ⁉ *Last orders 11pm. Closed mid-Dec to mid-Jan, Sun, Mon.*
"Cantina de la Lonja de Pescados-Casa Eduardo," located on the main pier of the fishing fleet, serves fresh seafood. The two dining rooms, with views of the bay and the illuminated cathedral, are simply decorated. Specialties include *zarzuela, bullabesa, calamares "Mollet," rape en salsa de mariscos* and *mero Mallorquína*.

El Pilón
Cifre s/n ☎*(971) 226 034* ▮▯ ▭ ⁉ ⊙ *Last orders midnight.*
Down an unpromising alley off the central Plaza Pío XII is a small *taberna* crowded with Mallorquínes sampling the tastiest *tapas* on the

island, which include grilled mushroom caps, baby clams in spicy tomato sauce, large sautéed prawns and skewered beef and sausage.

Plat Pla
Av. Joan Miró 50 ☎*(971) 232 066* ▮▮▮▯ ▭ ▬ ▤ ⁉ AE ▨ ⊙ VISA *Last orders midnight. Closed last two weeks in Nov, Sun, Mon lunch.*
One of Palma's most "chic" restaurants, Plat Pla is frequented by stylish people and the food is of secondary importance. The largely Italian dishes include *dorada al limón, raviolis mantecados* and *escalopines a la romana*.

El Portalón
Bellver 9 ☎*(971) 237 866* ▮▮▮▯ ▭ ▬ ▲ ⁉ AE CB ⊙ ⊙ VISA *Last orders 11.30pm.*
The romantic inner courtyard of tiles and plants compensates for the kitchen's occasional lapses. *Pastel de puerros y gambas con salsa marisquera* and *rape can salsa de cangrejos* are among the *nouvelle* Iberian specialties.

⟰ Among the numerous other restaurants are: **Caballito de Mar** (*Paseo de Sagrera 5* ☎*(971) 221 074* ▮▯ *to* ▮▮▯); **Fonda El Puerto** (*Paseo de Sagrera 3* ☎*(971) 213 537* ▮▯ *to* ▮▮▯); **Gina** (*Plaza de la Lonja 1* ☎*(971) 217 206* ▮▯ *to* ▮▮▯); **Mario's** (*Bellver 12* ☎*(971) 281 814* ▮▮▯); **El Patio** (*Consignatario Schembri 3* ☎*(971) 232 441* ▮▮▮▯); **Pizzera El Padrino** (*Juan de Saridakis 2* ☎*(971) 401 962* ▮▮▯); **Porto Nova** (*Paseo del Mar 2, Palma Nova* ☎*(971) 681 512* ▮▮▯); **Le Relais del Club de Mar** (*Paseo Marítimo* ☎*(971) 403 611* ▮▮▯); **Rififi** (*Av. Joan Miró 186* ☎*(971) 402 035* ▮▮▯); **Samantha's** (*Plaza Mediterráneo s/n* ▮▮▯).

Nightlife
Nightclubs cluster around the Plaza Gomila, in the throbbing Terreno district. **Tito's** (☎*(971) 235 884*), a vast glass building, impossible to miss, offers elaborate live shows catering to many nationalities. **Jack el Negro's** is a heavily advertized club, where Jack sings with his band when the mood takes him. The young are drawn to the disco **Bésame Mucho** (☎*(971) 283 616*);

and **Bar Bellver**, which has tables across the plaza, is the place to contemplate the funseekers.

Club de Mar (*Muelle Pelaires*) is currently the top disco. **El Hexágono** (*address and ☎ as for Palas Atenea Sol hotel*) is more exclusive and sedate. For live rock music without dancing, there is **Studio B** (*Av. Joan Miró 20*), and there is a casino just E of Palma (*Carretera Cala Figuera*).

Porto Cristo

Map 9I9. 62km (38 miles) E of Palma; 27km (16 miles) SE of Cala Ratjada.

This fishing village halfway down the E coast attracts visitors because of its proximity to **Drach** and **Hams** caves.

Sights nearby

Auto Safari Mallorca ☆

11km (7 miles) N of Porto Cristo ▓▓ ▣ ⚘ Open Apr-Oct 9am-7pm; Nov-Mar 9am-5pm.

Visitors remain in their cars and drive the hour-long winding route through a facsimile of the African veldt in which zebras, ostriches, impalas, springboks, giraffes, baboons, gnus, elephants and flamingos wander at will. At the end, there is a small zoo of lemurs, parrots and tortoises, some of which can be fed. All the animals seem to be humanely treated, and for obvious reasons there are no big cats.

Drach Caves

Just S of Porto Cristo ▓▓ 𝑋 compulsory May-Oct Sun-Fri 11am-noon, 2-3pm; Sat noon-2pm; Nov-Apr noon-2pm; musical visits Mon-Fri at noon.

Only discovered 60yrs ago and covering a vast area of 2km (1¼ miles), Drach Caves boast highly elaborate concretions and still, glassy pools. Noon tours feature a small orchestra playing classical music as it glides by in a dimly lit boat.

Hams Caves

1km (½ mile) NW of Drach Caves ▓▓ 𝑋 compulsory 10am-5pm.

Visit these caves to see the beautiful white stalactites in one of the chambers.

Puerto de Pollensa (*Pollença*)

Map 9I9. 58km (36 miles) N of Palma; 6km (4 miles) NE of Pollensa.

Sprawled across one corner of a rectangular bay, this resort is less frenetic than those in the SW and is therefore popular with long-term foreign residents. Windsurfers, waterskiers and sailing boats dart over the cobalt water against the backdrop of a craggy peninsula.

≈ **Illa d'Or** (*Paseo Colón s/n* ☎(971) 531 100 ▐▐▐) and **Uyal** (*Paseo de Londres* ☎(971) 531 500 ▐▐▐) are better than adequate; **Daina** (*Teniente Coronel Llorca s/n* ☎(971) 531 250 ▐▐▐) is smaller, but has good amenities.

═ Try the grilled meat at **Bec Fi** (*Paseo Anglada Camarasa 91* ☎(971) 531 040 ▐▐▐) or seafood at **Lonja del Pescado** (*Muelle Viejo* ☎(971) 530 023 ▐▐▐).

Places nearby

Alcudia (*8km/5 miles S of Puerto de Pollensa*).   A ruined Roman theater and medieval fortifications are in excellent repair.
Pollensa (*6km/4 miles SW of Puerto de Pollensa*).   An inland town with a number of 14thC buildings in varying states of preservation, including a *Calvary* reached by a staircase with 365 steps, providing a spectacular view from the top.

Sóller

Map 9I8. 30km (19 miles) N of Palma.

The mountain road descends to Sóller through pines, steeply terraced orchards and gardens. **Puerto de Sóller**, only 4km (2½ miles) N, is lined with small hotels and cafés. An amusingly old-fashioned tram connects the port and the town.

Marbella

Espléndido (*Marina Es Traves 23* ☎(971) 631 850 🔲) is right on the bay and enjoyable for a relaxed night or two.

≡ Mallorquín seafood dishes are the offerings of the family-run, unpretentious **El Guía** (*Castañer 3* ☎(971) 630 227 🔳).

Valldemosa
Map 9/8. 17km (10 miles) N of Palma.
The prettiest village on Mallorca, Valldemosa is a web of tidy lanes of honey-colored stone terraced houses with green shutters and an abundance of plants and flowers. Near the center is a 14thC **Cartuja** (🔳 *open Apr-Sept 9.30am-1.30pm, 3-7pm; Oct-Mar 9.30am-1.30pm, 3-6pm; closed Sun*), vacated by the monks early in the 19thC, permitting Chopin and George Sand to spend an unhappy winter there in 1838. The cells which they rented are charming, each with compact terraces overlooking the mountains and furnished with mementos of their lives, including the composer's two pianos.

≡ Near the edge of the village is **Ca'n Pedro** (*Av. Archiduque Luis Salvador s/n* ☎(971) 612 170 🔳), a conventionally rustic family restaurant serving typical Mallorquín and Spanish dishes.

Marbella
Map 6/4. Málaga. 59km (37miles) SW of Málaga; 79km (50 miles) NE of Algeciras. Population: 72,000 i Av. Miguel Canol ☎(952) 771 442.
The most fashionable resort of the *Costa del Sol* and the destination of sophisticated travelers, Marbella has some of Spain's best hotels and most stylish stores and discos, restaurants of distinction, luxurious villas, and extensive golf and tennis facilities. Only the old *barrio*, N of the main road, and the Moorish castle above it are of historic interest. Bullfights are held throughout the year.

Puerto Banús, 8km (5 miles) W of the center, has an astonishing collection of yachts, rows of Rolls-Royces and Lamborghinis to shuttle their passengers to and from the nearby casino, and shoulder-to-shoulder bars and bistros. At least 30 charter cruisers take anglers out to fish for shark; the nearby Sierra Blanca provides quail and partridge shooting; there are eight challenging golf courses within easy reach and 28km (17 miles) of nearly uninterrupted beach.

Hotels

El Fuerte
Castillano De San Luis ☎(952) 771 500 ☎ 77523 🔳 to 🔳 146 *rms* 🔲 146 ⚓ ≡ AE ⦿ VISA
Location: In the town, near the beach. This is the best of the central hotels. Its facilities cannot compare with the luxury hotels to the E and W, but prices are reasonable and guests cannot complain of being denied many comforts.
♨ 📷 🏄 ⛷ ≋ 🎿 ☂ 🍷

Golf Hotel Nueva Andalucía
Urbanización Nueva Andalucía ☎(952) 780 300 ☎ 77783 🔳 to 🔳 21 *rms* 🔲 21 ⊞ ⚓ AE ⦿ ⦿ VISA

Location 4km (2½ miles) E of Marbella. A small, placid five-star hotel near the Puerto Banús casino, with access to two golf courses.
⊟ 🍴 📷 🏄 ⛷ ≋ 🎿 ✓ 🍷

Marbella Club 🏨
Carretera Cádiz-Málaga, km 178 ☎(952) 771 300 ☎ 77319 🔳 72 *rms* 🔲 72 ⊞ ⚓ ≡ AE CB ⦿ ⦿ VISA
Location: 3km (2 miles) W of Marbella. The only failing of this smart retreat is the coolness of the staff at the reception desk. The beautiful, landscaped grounds are carefully tended and, in addition to the usual

rooms, there are 22 suites and 12 bungalows. The recreational facilities are shared with **Puente Romano** nearby.

🏠 🏊 🏋 🚲 ≈ 🎾 ✈ ✓ 🍴 🐎
🍷 ⊙

Los Monteros 🏨
Carretera Cádiz-Málaga 187
☎*(952) 771 700* ☎ *77059* ▥ *168*
rms ▭ *168* ▦ ▬ ═ 🆎 ℃🅱 ⊙
🍷 🆅🆂🅰

Location: 5km (3 miles) E *of Marbella.*
Flamingos stalk the gardens, and should the temperature drop there is an indoor pool to supplement the ones outside. Its excellent amenities make this acclaimed resort hotel the closest rival of the supreme **Puente Romano**. (See also **El Corzo** restaurant.)

🏠 🏊 🏋 🚲 🍴 🏋 ⛳ ≈ 🎾 ✈ ✓
✈ 🍷

Puente Romano 🏨
Carretera Cádiz-Málaga, km 184
☎*(952) 770 100* ☎ *77399* ▥ *200*
rms ▭ *200* ▦ ▬ ═ ═ 🆎 ℃🅱
⊙ ℃ 🆅🆂🅰

Location: 3.5km (2¼ miles) W *of Marbella.* If there is a finer resort hotel in Spain, it has yet to be found. The exterior design is mock Andalucian *pueblo*; its clustered buildings enclose luxuriant gardens, with a brook, spanned at one point by the Roman bridge that inspired the hotel's name. The international clientele are pampered with twice-daily maid service, four-channel TV in a two-channel country, two swimming pools, a beach club, four

restaurants, seven tennis courts, **Regine's** nightclub, and security patrols for protection. The service excels; order breakfast as you step into the shower and it arrives before you've reached for the towel.

🏠 ▢ 🌊 🚲 ≈ 🎾 🍴 ✓ 🏋 🍷
⊙

Skol
La Fontanilla s/n ☎*(952) 770*
800 ▥ *320 rms* ▭ *320* ⬤ ═ 🆎
🆅🆂🅰

Location: In the town, two streets from the beach. Should the five-star alternatives seem too distant from the action or provide unnecessary and expensive facilities, the central and cozy Skol might fit the bill. Comprising only of apartments, especially suitable for families staying for a week or more, minimal services keep costs low.

▢ 🚲 ⛳ ≈ 🎾 🍷

🐦 Other hotels just outside the center of Marbella include:
Andalucía Plaza (*Urbanización Nueva Andalucía* ☎*(952) 782 000*
▥ *to* ▥); **Artola** (*Carretera Cádiz-Málaga, km 194* ☎*(952) 831 390* ▢ *to* ▥); **Las Chapas** (*Carretera Cádiz-Málaga, km 198* ☎*(952) 831 375* ▥); **Don Carlos** (*Carretera Cádiz-Málaga, km 198* ☎*(952) 831 140* ▥ *to* ▥); **Guadalpín** (*Carretera Cádiz-Málaga, km 186* ☎*(952) 771 100* ▢); **Marbella Dinamar** (*Carretera Cádiz-Málaga, km 175* ☎*(952) 780 500* ▥ *to* ▥); **Meliá Don Pepe** (*Carretera Cádiz-Málaga, km 186* ☎*(952) 770 300* ▥).

Restaurants

El Corzo △
Address and ☎*same as Los Monteros hotel* ▥ 📖 🍴 ▦ ⬤
🍷 🆎 ⊙ ℃ 🆅🆂🅰 *Last orders 11.30pm.*
The heady praise lavished on this restaurant is mostly justified. The specialties of the house, which include *pastel de anguilas y salmón ahumado, carré de cordero chateaubriand* and *lubina al hojaldre* (sea bass in puff pastry), are often exemplary. The garden setting is extremely pretty, and even hotel guests must reserve in advance. (See also **Los Monteros** hotel).

La Fonda
Plaza Santo Cristo 9-10 ☎*(952)*
772 512 ▥ 📖 🍴 🍷 🆎 ⊙ *Last orders 11.30pm. Closed lunch, and Sun Sept-June.*
The patio shimmers with candlelight

and fragrant blossoms and the kitchen is far more imaginative and accomplished than is usual in this area, featuring *sopa de melón, lenguado a la naranja* and *ragout de vieiras*. Make sure you reserve ahead and arrive early, in time for a cocktail in the attractive Edwardian-style lounge.

Gran Marisquería Santiago
Paseo Marítimo ☎*(952) 770 078*
▥ 📖 🍴 🍷 🆎 ⊙ ℃
🆅🆂🅰 *Last orders 11.30pm.*
Gran Marisquería Santiago is among the worthiest of the Costa del Sol's seafood restaurants, crustaceans and molluscs of every kind are on hand, including lobster of several varieties, kept alive in a tank. Be certain of the price of the rarer sea creatures, or the bill can shoot from reasonable to breathtaking.

La Hacienda ⌂
Carretera Cádiz-Málaga, km 193
☎ *(952) 831 116* ▥ *to* ▥ ▭ ▰
▰ ▰ ▰ ⚲ Æ ● ⤢ *Last orders
11.30pm. Closed Tues Oct-May,
Mon and lunch June-Sept.*
Just outside Marbella in the
Urbanización Las Chapas, with a
view of the African coast, this serious
dining establishment has an excellent
reputation, so be certain to reserve in
advance. French dishes interpreted
by a Belgian owner-chef combine
flair and finesse. Fish mousse, guinea
fowl and red mullet are recommended.

▰ Among the alternative
restaurants and bistros are: **El Beni**
(*Muelle Benabola* ☎ *(952) 811 625*
▥); **Don Leone** (*Muelle Ribera*
☎ *(952) 781 727* ▥); **Mamma Rosa
Old Spaghetti House** (*Paseo
Marítimo* ☎ *(952) 776 389* ▥);
Mena (*Plaza de los Naranjos 10*
☎ *(952) 771 597* ▥); **Mesón del
Conde** (*Av. José Antonio 18* ☎ *(952)
771 057* ▥ *to* ▥); **Pepito** (*Muelle
Ribera* ☎ *(952) 812 965* ▥); **Plaza**
(*Plaza de los Naranjos s/n* ☎ *(952)
771 819* ▥); **La Poularde** (*Muelle
Ribera* ☎ *(952) 812 757* ▥).

Nightlife

There are two casinos within a few kilometers of Marbella: **Casino Nueva
Andalucía** (*Puerto Banús* ☎ *(952) 811 344*) and **Casino de Juego de
Torrequebrada** (*Benalmádena* ☎ *(952) 442 545*), which incorporates a
nightclub, **La Fortuna**. The most elegant nightclub in Marbella itself is the
celebrity-haunt, **Mau Mau** (*Puerto Banús Carretera N340, km 182*).
    Other nightspots include: **Vicy Peter** (*Puerto Banús* ☎ *(952) 812 103*);
Fiesta (*Valentuñana 8* ☎ *(952) 773 743*), where you can watch flamenco
dancing; and the disco, **Kiss** (*Av. Ricardo Soriano y Ansol* ☎ *(952) 774 694*).

Shopping

Apart from the ubiquitous supermarkets, which are useful if you have an
efficiency villa or apartment, Marbella has numerous elegant stores selling
stylish beachware and sports equipment. There are few bargains, however.
English and American newspapers and novels are available.

Places nearby

Estepona (*26km/16 miles SW of Marbella*).   A typical Andalucian
town where black-grilled, whitewashed, orange-tiled houses
enclose winding streets that lead to an attractive leafy plaza.

▰ Solid bistro dishes are available at **Costa del Sol** ♣ (*San Roque s/n*
☎ *(952) 801 101* ▥); **La Fuente** ☂ (*San Antonio 48* ▥) is a rustic
restaurant, run by a British couple.

Ojén (*9km/5½ miles N of Marbella*).   A classic "white village of
Andalucía," unspoiled despite its proximity to Marbella.

☜ A former hunting lodge in what is now a national game reserve, **Refugio
Nacional de Juanar** (*10km/6 miles NW of Ojén* ☎ *(952) 881 000* ▥) provides
parador comforts in a wilderness setting.

San Pedro de Alcántara (*10km/6 miles W of Marbella*).   Once a
sleepy fishing village, today it aspires to Marbella's glamor.

☜ **Golf Hotel Guadalmina** (*Urbanización Guadalmina* ☎ *(952) 781 400* ▥
to ▥) provides excellent sporting facilities.

Menorca (*Minorca*)

*Map 9/9. 37km (24 miles) NE of Mallorca; 205km (127 miles)
SE of Barcelona. Airport: Mahón. Boat connections with
Barcelona, Palma de Mallorca. Population: 55,000* **i** *Plaza
Constitución 13, Mahón* ☎ *(971) 363 790.*
Second largest of the *Islas Baleares*, Menorca is less than 50km
(31 miles) long and 15km (9 miles) wide. The most attractive
scenery is found along its indented coastline, for the interior is flat.
The island is still unspoiled, although the growing numbers of

northern escapists, who cherish over 100 often deserted beaches,
are an ominous sign.

Although all the traders and colonizers of the ancient world
landed here, the hundreds of dwellings and monuments of Bronze
Age inhabitants are the most intriguing architectural records.
They remain as mysterious to scholars as Stonehenge. In the larger
settlements there are numerous conical stone structures called
talayots that are surmised to be either roofs of burial vaults, or
foundation pillars for houses that no longer exist, or silos. *Navetas*
are piled stone structures which resemble overturned boats and
were probably tombs. The high vertical slabs topped by flat stones
are called *taulas*, and are assumed to have served a religious
function. All these feats of megalithic engineering can be seen
throughout the island. Troglodyte homes are an equally ancient
tradition, and many are still in use in the countryside.

Mahón, at the end of a narrow bay denting the eastern tip of the
island, is the capital and has a population of 25,000. Throughout
most of the 18thC it was held by the British, and their influence is
seen in casement windows instead of shutters, in Georgian houses,
and in a potent local gin. There is a small **archeological museum**
concerned with the island's prehistoric period. A drive along the s
shore of the harbor is visually rewarding, especially the tiny village
of **Villacarlos**.

Ciudadela, at the other end of the island, is distinctly Spanish
and protected by extensive 16thC fortifications. The almost
enclosed bay of **Fornells**, on the N coast, shelters a fishing village
and is popular for water-sports.

Events   Throughout summer, fiestas; the most prominent is a
music festival in Mahón in Sept.

Port Mahón (*Fort de l'Eau s/n* ☎*(971) 862 600* ▥) observes mainland
standards of comfort; in Ciudadela, the comfortable and well-equipped
Almirante Farragut (*Los Delfines* ☎*(971) 382 800* ▯) is named after an
American admiral who stayed here in 1868; **Cala Blanca** (*Urbanización Cala
Blanca* ☎*(971) 380 450* ▥) provides similar amenities in a modern
Andalucian vacation development.

(*For information about hotels along the coasts, contact* **i** *Mahón — see above
— or* **i** *Conquistador 81, Ciudadela* ☎*(971) 381 174.*)

In Mahón, **Rocamar** (*Fonduco 32* ☎*(971) 365 601* ▥) must be judged
the best against indifferent competition — don't expect especially adroit
service, but revel in absolutely fresh seafood, prepared simply; **El Mero**
(*Andén de Levante 227* ☎*(971) 367 804* ▥) specializes in Basque cookery,
almost always of a high standard; despite the name, **El Greco** (*Dr Orfila 49*
☎*(971) 364 367* ▯) features standard Gallic dishes, and has an amiable bar
in which to meet friends and consider the specialties of the day; onion soup
and pepper steak underline the Provençal flavor of **Chez Gaston** (*Conde de
Cifuentes 13* ☎*(971) 360 044* ▯); in Ciudadela, **Casa Manolo** (*Marina 103*
☎*(971) 380 003* ▥) is the place for fish and crustaceans, in stews, soups or
simply grilled.

Mérida
*Map 6F3. Badajoz. 201km (125 miles) N of Sevilla; 70km (44
miles) s of Cáceres. Population: 42,000* **i** *Puente 9* ☎*(924)
315 353.*

Gypsies camp beneath the 81-arch bridge across the Guadiana
river, as they have probably done since the Romans left. That the
bridge is still in use as a link in the main Madrid-Lisbon road is
testimony to the skill of the imperial engineers. It is just one of the
preserved structures in Mérida, a repository of extant monuments
of Roman Iberia that surpasses any in the country.

Although a Celtiberian settlement apparently existed on the site, its history can be dated from 25BC, when Augustus proclaimed it a colony for his retired soldiers. The bridge, an amphitheater, an aqueduct and a circus were completed in a matter of years thereafter. Only in the 20thC have excavations shown the extent of this historical bounty.

Sights and places of interest

Alcazaba
🕿 *8am-1pm, 4-7pm.*

At the N end of the Roman bridge are the walls of a fortress, erected by the Moors on a site previously utilized by the Visigoths and Romans and incorporating elements of those buildings. Floor mosaics and decorated pilasters remain from the earlier structures, but relatively little of interest was left by the Arabs. There is a small **museum** here.

Anfiteatro ☆
Intersection of Suárez Somonte and J. Ramón Mélida 🕿 *Open summer 8am-8pm, winter 8am-7pm.*

The elliptical arena, only a few meters from the theater, seated 14,000 for the favored Roman entertainments of imaginative blood-sports. Lions fed on slaves and captives, gladiators dispatched each other, violent chariot races were held. Completed in about AD8, most of the ornamental stonework is lost, together with the wall that presumably contained the amphitheater. But it requires no great leap of fantasy to imagine thousands of citizens roaring their approval or disdain. Nearby are the remains of a nobleman's villa, with large mosaic panels.

Museo Arqueológico ☆
Plaza Santa Maria 🕿 *Open Tues-Sat 10am-2pm, 4-6pm, Sun 10am-2pm, Mon 4-6pm. Closed holidays.*

Statuary and relics of the Roman and Visigothic occupations, too fragile or valuable to remain where they were found, are housed in this small museum, which was once a convent. Originals of sculptures found in the theater are on display here, as well as busts of several emperors, and architectural fragments left by the Visigoths.

Teatro Romano † ★
See Anfiteatro for entry details.

Follow the signs through a vaulted granite passage, turning right beneath a brick portal onto the floor of the theater. On the right-hand side are two tiers of white marble pillars topped with Corinthian capitals and interspersed with statuary. Actors made appearances on these balconies in counterpoint to the chorus in the pit below. Although Agrippa built the theater in 23BC, the columns were added after a fire during Hadrian's rule in the 2ndCAD. Raised semi-circular seating could accommodate at least 6,000 spectators. From the last row there are fine views of the city and its other ruins.

Other sights

At the edge of the town, along the road that leads N to Cáceres, is the **Acueducto de los Milagros**. Only a shadow of its former structure, it nonetheless gives a more complete impression of its scope than the few pillars remaining of its twin **Acueducto de San Lázaro**, which crosses the Trujillo road. Close to the latter is the old **Circus Maximus** or Circo Maximo, although only outlines in stone and earth still remain, they are just enough to discern an arena for up to 30,000 spectators to witness mock naval battles and chariot races. Near the archeological museum is the Trajan triumphal **Arco de Santiago**.

🕿 **Parador Nacional Vía de la Plata**
Plaza de la Constitución 3 🕾 *(924) 313 800* ▥ *to* ▥ *50 rms* 🛏 *50* ▦
🗪 🗪 AE ● ● VISA

Location: In the center of the town. Marble pillars with Arabic markings surround the inner patio where there is a well which may have been dug by the Romans. Older parts of the *parador* have seen service as a convent, a prison and a church. There are many public rooms, including a former chapel, and some of the bedrooms are large. The garden has been planted out with great imagination.
🖼 🗪 ⚓ ☕

🕿 Complementing the main square is **Emperatriz** (*Plaza de España 19*

☎*(924) 313 111* ■■), a 16thC mansion which has undergone substantial renovations in keeping with its period style.

Place nearby
Medellín (*39km/25 miles E of Mérida*).   A turreted castle covers a flat hill behind the village. It was built in the l4thC on Roman foundations. The heroic statue of *Hernán Cortés*, born here in 1485, is said to be an exact replica of the conqueror of Aztec Mexico.

Mijas
Map 7|5. Málaga. 8km (5¹/₂ miles) N of Fuengirola; 30km (19 miles) sw of Málaga. Population: 17,000.
Splashed across the mountainside rising behind the *Costa del Sol*, Mijas suffers the advantage of proximity to those teeming resort towns, a target for tourists intent upon visiting a "typical Andalucian hill town" with minimum inconvenience. The result is that it is no longer typical, awash in such kitsch as nonindigenous *burro* taxis, and heaps of leather goods and pottery spilling across streets from store fronts. However, the village clings tenaciously to its heritage in black alleys and remote *barrios* farther up the mountain. There are several belvederes offering vistas of peaks and coastline, as from the **Hermitage of the Pass** next to the unusual square bullring.

☜ Mijas
Urbanización Tamisa ☎*(952) 485 800* ❿ *77393* ▥▥ *106 rms* ▭ *106* ⬤
▱ ▱ *after two days* ᴀᴇ ⊙ ⊚ ᴠɪsᴀ
Location: On the outskirts of Mijas, 8km (5 miles) N of Fuengirola. Although it possesses twice the appeal of most conventional Costa del Sol hotels, the Mijas receives half the attention it deserves. All is quiet elegance, invoking the best of Andalucian style while avoiding the clichés. Many of the bedrooms have balconies facing Fuengirola and the Mediterranean, and their furnishings include potted plants and comfortable seating. The housekeeping is exemplary; mountain breezes keep the nights pleasantly cool.

⌂ ❁ ☞ ☂ ↯ ⟨⟨ ⇌ ℒ ✓ ☗

☰ El Mirlo Blanco
Plaza de la Constitución 13 ☎*(952) 485 700* ■■ ☐ ▆ ☖ *Last orders 11pm.*
Authentic Basque cookery survives here, amid the tourist hordes on day-trips into the mountains backing the Costa del Sol. Try any of the regional specialties: *chipirones*, *bacalao*, *cordero asado* or *almejas*.

☰ Molina del Cura
Carretera de Mijas ☎*(952) 485 813* ■■ ☐ ▆ ☖ ☗ ⊙ ᴠɪsᴀ *Last orders 11.30pm. Closed Mon, and Tues-Sun lunch.*
This converted 17thC flour mill is perfect for romantic liaisons. The surroundings and warmth of the welcome compensate for the inadequacies of the kitchen. Sunday brunch is popular, as are weekend concerts. The specialty of the house is chicken stuffed with spinach, cheese, mushrooms, nuts and mixed herbs.

☰ Valparaiso ❁
Carretera de Mijas ☎*(952) 485 996* ■■ ☐ ☖ ⬤ ☗ ♫ ⟨ ᴀᴇ ⊙ ⊚ ᴠɪsᴀ *Last orders 11.30pm Oct-June, midnight July-Sept. Closed Sun, and Oct-June lunch.*
Beef of sublime tenderness, prawn cocktails of prodigious proportions, live music every night and warm welcomes from the young multilingual Spaniards who run this large hillside retreat attract a faithful following from the Costa del Sol foreign community. To take full advantage of the food avoid eating during the preceding 24hrs; enjoy specialties such as stuffed mussels, duck *à l'orange*, veal marsala, spring lamb and steak, and plan to spend the evening here.

Murcia

Map 9H8. Murcia. 84km (52 miles) SW *of Alicante; 391km (243 miles)* SE *of Madrid. Population: 300,000* **i** *Alejandro Séiquer 4* ☎*(968) 213 716.*

The arid and mountainous region of Murcia is a favorite location for "spaghetti" Westerns because of its similarities to Arizona. The city was founded on a Roman site by the Moors in the 8thC and straddles the river Segura; little remains of old Murcia except for the cathedral and some dilapidated houses by the river, and it is now a commercial and industrial center best known for fruit-canning and its university.

Events   In Holy Week, processions of penitents in purple robes.
  In the week after Easter, battles of flowers and the ritual burial of a sardine to symbolize the end of Lent.

Sights and places of interest

Cathedral †
Plaza Cardenal Belluga.
Although work began in the 14thC, the elaborate Baroque facade was not added until 1737. The interior is mostly Gothic, and its most notable feature is the splendid **Capilla de los Vélez** with its fine vaulting and murals in Renaissance and Mudejar styles. The **sacristy** is approached by two paneled Plateresque doors, and there is more magnificently carved Plateresque and Baroque paneling on the walls. There are panoramic views of the city and mountains from the **belfry**.

Museo Arqueológico
Gran Via Alfonso X 🖼 *Open Tues, Thurs-Sun 9am-2pm, Wed 9am-2pm, 5-9pm. Closed Mon.*
Housed in the Casa de Cultura is an interesting collection of Hispano-Moresque and 17th-18thC Spanish ceramics.

Museo Salzillo
Antonio García Alix 🖼 *Open Apr-Sept 9.30am-1pm, 4-7pm; Oct-Mar 9.30am-1pm, 3-6pm; holidays 9.30am-1pm; Sun 10am-1pm.*
The 18thC sculptor Salzillo was responsible for the most vivid of the sculptures in the **cathedral**, and this museum contains examples of his polychrome wood carvings of figures carried in the Holy Week processions, and a large number of terra-cotta figurines depicting episodes from the Gospels and the daily life of the Murcian peasants.

Traditional Costume Museum
Acisclo Díaz 🖼 *Open Tues-Sat 10am-1.30pm, 5-8pm; Sun and holidays 10am-1pm. Closed Mon.*
In the College of San Estéban, this museum houses displays of regional costume.

☞ Conde de Floridablanca (*Corbalán 7* ☎*(968) 214 624* ▥) is a comfortable hotel in a historic building; **Fontoria** (*Madre de Dios 4* ☎*(968) 217 789* ▥) is a three-star hotel, but has no restaurant; **Siete Coronas Meliá** (*Ronda de Garay 3* ☎*(968) 217 771* ▥), large, modern and comfortable, is the best hotel in Murcia.

⇌ El Rincón de Pepe
Apóstoles 34 ☎*(968) 212 249* ▥ ▤ AE ⓞ ⓒⓓ VISA *Closed Sun dinner, Mon in summer.*
This restaurant, in a three-star hotel, is one of the best in Spain. Raimundo Frutos insists on the freshest of ingredients, and the vegetables, grown without chemical fertilizers, are from the restaurant's own farm. There are three regional menus, featuring such dishes as angler fish pie, fish baked in salt paste, *menestra* and Murcian-style rice.

⇌ Hispano (*Lucas 7* ☎*(968) 216 152* ▥) is a first-rate restaurant, with rapid, efficient service and excellent specialties such as *paella murciana*, langoustine and leek pie, baked bass, roast lamb and a variety of fruit tarts. **Los Apóstoles** (*Plaza de los Apóstoles 1* ☎*(968) 212 197* ▥), an agreeable restaurant with old tiled walls and a menu based on fish and vegetables in season, is run personally by the owner and his family; it goes from strength to strength.

Nerja
Map 7I5. Málaga. 52km (32 miles) E of Málaga; 169km (105 miles) w of Almeria. Population: 12,000.

A pretty town perched over the sea on the slopes of the steep foothills of the Sierra Almijara, Nerja meant "rich spring" in Arabic. Old houses mingle with resort hotels around the high point of land known as the **Balcón de Europa**, splitting the beaches to both E and W. The only notable buildings are the 18thC **Ermita de Nuestra Señora de las Angustias**, which displays paintings of the same period, and the 17thC **Iglesia del Salvador**.

Sight nearby
Cueva de Nerja ☆
4km (2½miles) NE of Nerja ▨ Open May to mid-Sept 9am-9pm; *mid-Sept to Apr 10am-1.30pm, 4-7pm.*
The stalactite caves reveal traces of Stone Age habitation, in wall paintings for example, and also serve as an auditorium for concerts and ballets. A small **museum** displays prehistoric pottery, on site when the caves were discovered in 1959.

◆ At **Balcón de Europa** (*Paseo Balcón de Europa* ☎(952) 520 800 ▮▯ to ▮▮▯), the fixtures and furnishings are a little worn, but the location and price are right. In keeping with the resort environment, **Parador Nacional de Nerja** (*El Tablazo s/n* ☎(952) 520 050 ▮▮▮▮) has more recreational facilities than most *paradores*. Check ahead, as it was scheduled to close for renovations.

▧ Expect only sustenance and good views at **Rey Alfonso** (*Paseo Balcón de Europa* ☎(952) 520 195 ▮▮▯), where the dishes are international.

Orense (*Ourense*)
Map 10C3. Orense. 105km (65 miles) E of Vigo; 173km (108 miles) w of Ponferrada. Population: 95,000 **i** *Curros Enriquez 1* ☎(988) 234 717.

This provincial capital has been known for its hot springs for centuries. The only significant remnant of Roman occupation is a bridge over the river Miño, and the Moors only stayed long enough to destroy, not to build.

Sights and places of interest
Cathedral †
Plaza del Trigo s/n. Open 10.30am-1pm, 3.30-7.30pm.
A church was first erected here in the 6thC by the converted Suevi, who preceded the Visigoths. Most of the present building, however, dates from the 13thC. Entrance is through the transept door, for the main facade has been closed in by later buildings. The highlight is the **Pórtico del Paraíso** at the W end, modeled on the **Pórtico de Gloria** in the cathedral in *Santiago de Compostela*. There is a 16thC Gothic retable in the *capilla mayor* and a small **museum** (▨) housed in the chapterhouse off the S aisle.
Museo Arqueológico
Carrascosa s/n. May be closed for renovation.
The 12thC episcopal palace contains an array of historic archives, pottery, archeological artifacts ranging from the Neolithic to the Roman era, and religious art.

◆ **Padre Fejióo** (*Plaza Eugenio Montes 1* ☎(988) 223 100 ▮▯ to ▮▮▯) is adequate for a night; **San Martín** (*Curros Enriquez 1* ☎(988) 235 611 ▮▮▮▮), the old quarter, is modern and functional.

▧ **Sanmiguel** (*San Miguel 12* ☎(988) 221 245 ▮▮▯) surpasses its local competitors with sensitive Galician dishes, understated decoration and a summer terrace. **Martín Fierro** (*Sáenz Diez 65* ☎(988) 234 820 ▮▯) is in distinct second place, but enlivens its Galician menu with a few Argentine grilled meat dishes.

Oviedo

Map 11B4. 118km (73 miles) N of León; 28km (18 miles) S of Gijón. Population: 190,000 **i** *Cabo Noval 5* ☎*(985) 213 385.*

The capital of the Kingdom of Asturias, Oviedo was razed in the 8thC during the Reconquest. It was quickly rebuilt, and an architectural style known as Asturian Pre-Romanesque is evident in a number of buildings constructed in the 8th-9thC. They are of particular interest, representing the earliest stirrings of a native esthetic movement which predated many of the Moors' greatest achievements. The short but destructive workers' revolt of 1934 caused extensive damage to the cathedral and 17thC university. The largely modern city that survives still contains a sizeable ancient quarter as well as a singularly attractive and spacious central park.

Event In Sept, Día de las Américas, with dancing, parades and bullfights.

Sights and places of interest

Cámara Santa ☆
Plaza Alfonso 11 🖾 ✗ *Open summer 10am-1pm, 4-8pm; winter 10am-1pm, 4-6pm. Entrance is through the cathedral.*
Frequently damaged, altered and restored over the centuries, this 9thC shrine was first commissioned by Alfonso II to house Christian relics of the Visigothic era. Six double columns at the entrance incorporate sculptured heads of the 12 Apostles; they are superb examples of the 12thC Romanesque. Caskets in the **treasury** contain objects made of jewels and precious metals.

Cathedral ☆ †
Plaza Alfonso II 🖾 *Open summer 4-8pm, winter 10am-1pm, 4-6pm.*
This Flamboyant-Gothic cathedral has an asymmetrical main facade with only one tower. While its ornamental traceries are relatively restrained, the florid pierced steeple is in marked contrast to the simplicity of its lower components.

Museo Arqueológico
San Vicente s/n ☎*(985) 215 405* 🖾 ✗ *Open 11.30am-1.30pm, 4-8pm. Shorter hours in winter. Closed Mon.*
Housed in a former convent which was built in the 15thC and renovated in the 18thC, this museum highlights prehistoric artifacts from Asturias and pre-Romanesque sculptures and architectural fragments.

Sights nearby

In a suburban village on the slope rising beyond the railroad tracks 2km (1 mile) NW of the center of Oviedo is **Santa María de Naranco** (*open Apr-Sept 10am-1pm, 4-7pm, Oct-Mar 10am-1pm*), a 9thC palace with views of the city and the snowcapped **Picos de Europa**. Three streets farther N you will find the **Iglesia de San Miguel de Lillo** (*same opening hours as Santa María del Naranco*), which was built to order by the monarch who was responsible for the palace, Ramiro I. Although the church was ineptly altered by 15thC meddlers, the remaining stone carvings are exemplaary.

⋐ La Reconquista
Gil de Jaz 16 ☎*(985) 241 100* ☎ *87328* ⅢⅢ *139 rms* 🖾 *139* 🖾 ⇌ ⇌ ⇌ 🖾 ⓐ ⓔ ⓞ ⓞ 𝗩𝗜𝗦𝗔
Location: Three streets N of the Parque de San Francisco. An effusively restored 17thC hospice with 20thC comforts, this is the kind of hotel that inspires longer stays than can be justified by the demands of a business or sightseeing trip. The restaurant and bar are local gathering places.
⇕ ☐ 🖾 🕸 ♨ ♟ ▼ ●

⋐ Sober decor, good views and inconsistent staff are typical of **La Jirafa** (*Pelayo 6* ☎*(958) 222 244* ⅢⅢ); the up-to-date **Ramiro I** (*Av. Calvo Sotelo 13* ☎*(985) 232 850* ⅢⅢ *to* ⅢⅢ) is located uphill from Oviedo''s main attractions, but offers easy access to the Madrid road; the shiny new **Regente** (*Jovellanos 31* ☎*(985) 222 343* ⅢⅢ) takes no awards for imagination, but supplies modern comforts and a good position for sightseeing.

Casa Fermín
San Francisco 8 ☎ *(985) 216 452* 📶 🖵 🍴 🛋 🗔 ⟡ AE ⊕ ⊙ VISA
Last orders 12.30am.

For over 50yrs the Casa Fermín, regarded by some as Oviedo's best restaurant, has been gathering a loyal clientele, although most of the present staff are young. It is attractive both inside and out, and the wine cellar is exceptional. Regular specialties, which include *lomo de merluza con salsa de almejas*, *entrecôte al queso* and *fabes con almejas*, are almost unfailingly good.

Marchica
Dr Casal 10 ☎ *(985) 213 027* 📶 *to* 📶 🖵 🍴 🗔 ⟡ AE ⊕ ⊙ VISA *Last orders 11.30pm.*

With an animated *tapas* bar and two dining rooms, Marchica caters for every need. Go for a speedy snack or a leisurely three-course meal. Seafood is paramount and beef is at least standard. Specialties include *callos a la Asturiana* (tripe stewed with pigs' trotters, calves' feet, *chorizo* sausage, ham, red peppers, onion and garlic) and *fabes con almejas*.

Pelayo
Pelayo 15 ☎ *(985) 212 652* 📶 🖵 🍴 🗔 ⟡ AE ⊕ ⊙ VISA *Last orders 11.30pm.*

Someone in the kitchen knows exactly what he or she is doing, especially with such robust Asturian specialties as *fabada*, *lubina con verduras* and *fabes con almejas*. If only the head waiter and harried waitresses could remember who ordered what!

Alternatives include: **Casa Conrado** (*Argüelles 1* ☎*(985) 223 919* 📶); **La Goleta** (*Covadonga 32* ☎*(985) 220 773* 📶); **La Gruta** (*Alto de Buenavista s/n* ☎*(985) 232 450* 📶); **Principado** (*San Francisco 6* ☎*(985) 217 792* 📶).

Pajares
Map 11B4. León and Oviedo. 59km (37 miles) s of Oviedo; 59km (37 miles) N of León.

A handful of houses straddle this pass through the Cantabrian Mountains. If possible, approach it from the s, for on that side the central plateau rises gently to its 1,379m (4,524ft) height and the corniche on the N face is easier to negotiate when going downhill. Furthermore, the drama of this awesome alpine stronghold is enhanced when encountered after the drive through pleasant but unremarkable plains. The pass is signalled by an intriguing Romanesque **collegiate church**, 1km (½ mile) s. It is worth a visit to see the porch and vaulting, both additions of the Renaissance, and the capitals, carved in a stylized Far Eastern motif. Unfortunately, the Parador Nacional Puerto de Pajares, at this site, has been closed permanently.

Palencia
Map 12C5. Palencia. 84km (52 miles) SW of Burgos; 44km (27 miles) NE of Valladolid. Population: 76,000 i Mayor 105 ☎*(988) 740 068.*

Palencia is a 10km (6 mile) detour off the Valladolid-Burgos road. Admittedly lively, its streets filled with people at all hours, there is in fact remarkably little of interest to visitors, considering that this is, after all, a provincial capital. The only museum is temporarily closed. The principal sights are the cathedral, built between the 14th and 16thC in Transitional style, and three smaller churches.

The choice lies between **Rey Sancho de Castilla** (*Av. Ponce de León s/n* ☎*(988) 725 300* 📶 *to* 📶) and the newer, smaller **Castilla Vieja** (*Casado del Alisal 26* ☎*(988) 749 044* 📶 *to* 📶).

Lorenzo (*Av. Casado del Alisal 10* ☎*(988) 743 545* 📶) and **Casa Damian** (*Ignacio Martínez de Azcoitia 9* ☎*(988) 743 870* 📶) are Palencia's best restaurants.

Pamplona (Iruña)

*Map 13C8. Navarra. 94km (59 miles) se of San Sebastián;
96km (58 miles) e of Vitoria. Population: 180,000* **i** *Duque de
Ahumada 3* ☎*(948) 211 287.*

This is the city that Ernest Hemingway made famous in his novel
The Sun also Rises. His characters Jake Barnes, Lady Brett and
friends carried their understated *angst* to the **Feria de San Fermín**
in July — the time when everyone should go. At other times,
Pamplona is a gray, dispirited city, with nearly continuous political
ferment and outbursts of Basque separatist terrorism.

"Pompaelo" was founded early in the Roman era. When the
Moors occupied it for a decade in the 8thC, Charlemagne helped
the Spaniards to push them out, but then sacked the city and tore
down its walls. It was the capital of the kingdom of Navarra from
the 10thC until it was subjugated by Ferdinand II in 1512.
Event   In July, Feria de San Fermín. Celebrations involve 15
days of parades, music, fireworks and the main event which is the
running of the bulls. These massive sacrificial brutes, each
weighing 400kg (882lbs) or more, are delivered to a pen the night
before the event. A route of about 2km (1¼ miles) is laid through
the city from the pen to the Plaza de Toros.

In the morning, the men position themselves along the route,
the daring nearest the gate, the slower nearest the ring entrance. At
approximately a minute to 7am a warning rocket is sent up. A
second rocket is the signal for the gate to be opened. The *encierro*
has begun. The idea is to remain as close to the horns as courage
permits for the length of the course.

Once the bulls arrive at the ring, they are promptly herded out.
Cows with protective sheaths on their horns are released into the
ring so that the surviving runners may play *matador.* The bulls
meet their preordained fate in the ring that evening, to the music
of the several bands sponsored by neighborhood and fraternal
organizations.

Sights and places of interest

Cathedral † ☆
Plaza de la Catedral.
The French Gothic cathedral was founded by Charles III in 1416. The 18thC
architect Ventura Rodríguez is responsible for the gaudily Baroque w facade.
The **cloister** displays the familiar delicacy of detail for which the Gothic style
is known. The **Museo Diocesano** (☎ *open mid-May to mid-Oct 10.30am-
1.30pm, 4-7pm*) contains polychrome sculptures of sacred figures and other
religious relics.

Museo de Navarra ☆
Santo Domingo s/n ☎ *Open Mon-Sat 10am-1.30pm; Sun and
holidays 11am-1.30pm. Closed Mon.*
Archeological and cultural exhibits include Roman mosaics, armor and
weaponry, paintings from the Gothic to the Renaissance period, including a
Goya portrait, and handsomely detailed capitals from the 12thC Romanesque
cathedral that was replaced by the present structure.

☎ Tres Reyes
Jardines de la Taconera s/n ☎*(948) 226 600* 🕾 *37720* ▥ *168 rms*
▭ *168* 🍽 ⇌ ⇌ ⇌ AE ⊚ 🌐 VISA
Location: At the edge of the Jardines de la Taconera. Pamplona's only luxury
hotel cannot be seriously faulted. Backed by a large park, it is a stroll from
the main plaza, has a heated pool, an attentive staff and an above average
restaurant that attempts elegance.
⚓ ▢ ▱ ⚞ ⚒ ⚓ ⚓ Ⓨ

☎ **Ciudad de Pamplona** (*Iturrama 21* ☎*(948) 266 011* ▥) is the newest
hotel, slightly removed from the city center in a modern district. **Nuevo
Hotel Maisonnave** (*Nueva 20* ☎*(948) 222 600* ▥) is a traditional favorite

and very central. The virtue of **Orhi** (*Leyre 7* ☎*(948) 228 500* ▮▮▯) is its proximity to the bullring.

▃Hartza
Juan de Labrit 19 ☎*(948) 224 568* ▮▮▮▮ ▬ ▭ ▤ *Last orders 11.30pm. Closed Mon, Christmas week, mid-July to mid-Aug.*
One of Pamplona's most honored restaurants bestows hearty portions of sophisticated provincial food. Book ahead or arrive early, for it is small and very popular. Consider *merluza de la casa*, tournedos or *besugo à la bermeana*.

▃Josetxo
Plaza Príncipe de Viana 1 ☎*(948) 222 097* ▮▮▯ ▭ ▬ ▤ ⊕ ⓒⓓ 𝘝𝘐𝘚𝘈
Last orders 11pm. Closed Aug and Sun.
Imaginative Basque dishes reveal their debt to *nouvelle cuisine* imported from France. The combination is irresistible. Specialties include *crema de cangrejos*, *merluza con salsa de salmón* and *lubina a la parrilla*.

▃ **Hostal del Rey Noble** (*Paseo de Sarasate 6* ☎*(948) 122 214* ▮▮▮▮), a.k.a. **Las Pocholas**, shares in local esteem with the two above, but price is not always consistent with quality. Other possibilities are **Rodero** (*Arrieta 3* ☎*(948) 228 035* ▮▮▮▮) and **Alhambra** (*Bergamin 7* ☎*(948) 245 007* ▮▮▮▮).

Places nearby
Estella (*45km/28 miles sw of Pamplona*). A pilgrimage stop on the way to Santiago and an occasional residence of Navarra royalty, Estella has an uncommon number of Romanesque churches and Renaissance palaces. Just se of the town there is a 12thC Benedictine monastery, **Monasterio de Santa María de Irache**, which was a university from the 16thC until 1833.
Roncesvalles (*47km/30 miles ne of Pamplona*). The mountain pass was the site of the battle between Basques and the rearguard of Charlemagne's army in 778, later glamorized in an epic poem. The restored 12thC abbey sheltered pilgrims on the way to Santiago.

Peñíscola
*Map **14E9**.Castellón. 124km (76 miles) s of Tarragona; 76km (48 miles) n of Castellón de la Plana. Population: 3,500.*
A high knob of land with a narrow isthmus and inlet made this a logical vantage point for feudal lords. Existing fortifications include the walls and a restored 14thC **citadel**, occupied at one time by the antipope Pedro de Luna. Resort development is creeping n up the long beach and the steep village streets. A stroll beneath a full moon out of season is the best way to capture the ghostly aura of the village.

☛ On the Benicarló road, 1km (½ mile) n, the privately owned **Hostería del Mar** (☎*(964) 480 600* ▮▮▮▮) is linked to the *parador* chain and observes its standards of restrained decor and immaculate housekeeping.

Plasencia
*Map **11E4**. Cáceres. 79km (50 miles) ne of Cáceres; 135km (84 miles) sw of Salamanca. Population: 32,000* ℹ *Trujillo 17* ☎*(927) 417 766.*
Founded by Alfonsŏ VIII in 1180, there is evidence of previous occupation by the Romans and Moors, but the town is notable for its collection of Gothic and Renaissance structures, most of which are enclosed within towered medieval walls.

Sights and places of interest
Just outside Plasencia on the road to Salamanca there is an imposing 13thC **aqueduct** which boasts 53 arches. In the town there is a **cathedral**, most of

which belongs to the 16thC, including the Plateresque main portal, although parts are three centuries older. Inside, the vaulting is remarkably graceful and the carvings on the choir stalls and retable — of the 16th and 17thC respectively — are a joyous blend of Biblical and contemporary scenes. To the left of the main altar is the tomb of Ponce de León, the explorer who discovered the Florida peninsula in 1513 while searching for the Fountain of Youth. The 13thC **Iglesia de San Nicolás** is located in a square where there are also a number of Renaissance mansions; on the N side is the **Palacio del Marqués de Mirabel**, with a Plateresque balcony and a large tower at its side.

❧ **Alfonso VIII**

Alfonso VIII 32 ☎ *(927) 410 250* ⬛ *to* ⬛ *56 rms* ▭ *56* ▦ ▬ ⇌
Location: s of the plaza mayor. While there are other modest hotels and humble restaurants in the area, they are no competition for this one. The dining room, on the top floor, is a favorite place for birthday and business celebrations. Rooms, public and private, are above average.
↕ ▱ ✿ ⚇ ♈

⇌ The menu at **Alfonso VIII** (see above) is dominated by Extremaduran specialties such as *pierna de cabrito* (leg of kid) and *lagarto en salsa verde* (lizard in a green sauce); snacks as well as filling, informal meals can be taken at **La Caña** (*Reyes Católicos* ⬛) and the nearby **Mi Casa** (*Maldonado 13* ☎ *(927) 411 450* ⬛).

Ponferrada

Map 11C4. León. 105km (65 miles) w of León; 170km (106 miles) E of Orense. Population: 55,000.
Surrounded by verdant countryside, Ponferrada was important as a pilgrim town; the castle of the Knights Templar offered refuge to pilgrims on their way to Santiago de Compostela. Today the chief concern is iron mining and related industry.

Sights and places of interest

The 16thC **Basilica de Nuestra Señora de la Encina** is Transitional Gothic and contains a figure of the *Virgin* dating at least to the 15thC. **Castilio de los Templarios** (⬛ ◁€ *open 9am-1pm, 3-7pm; closed Sun in winter, Tues in summer*) is customarily dated to the 12thC when it was reconstructed for the Knights Templar, but it has far earlier origins, possibly Moorish or even Roman. Now a ruin, it is nevertheless a commanding complex, with fine views of the town and valley.

Sight nearby

Iglesia de Santo Tomás de las Ollas ✝
1.5km (1 mile) E of Ponferrada, off the NVI.
This compact 10thC church created by Mozarabic artisans is an adulterated example of Moorish architecture including horseshoe arches and an oval apse.

❧ The medieval-style **El Temple** (*Av. Portugal 2* ☎ *(987) 410 058* ⬛ *to* ⬛) is adequate for an overnight stay.

⇌ **Azul** (*Camino de Santiago 40* ☎ *(987) 411 109* ⬛ *to* ⬛) provides simple sustenance.

Pontevedra

Map 10C2. 57km (36 miles) s of Santiago de Compostela; 25km (15 miles) N of Vigo. Population: 67,000 **i** *Galerías Oliva* ☎ *(986) 850 814.*
The ancient city at the end of the Ría de Pontevedra is no longer important as a shipping port, for the estuary began to silt up in the 17thC. Approaches from the N or s pass factories and ill-conceived housing developments, but press on, for the sizeable old *barrio* near the Burgo bridge is largely unspoiled and well worth a

leisurely inspection. It has delightful granite houses with green window frames, silver-painted grilles, arches, loggias, unexpected gardens and fountains, and many amiable bars and cafés.

Event In late May or early June, round-up of wild horses.

Sights and places of interest

Begin your exploration of the old *barrio* at the **Plaza de la Herrería**, a large square with an arcade to the w and the Gothic **Convento de San Francisco** opposite, which is now a church. To the s, the gardens shaded by vines lead to **La Capilla de la Peregrina**, an 18thC church with a narrow semi-circular facade joined to a rotunda and surmounted by twin towers.

Returning past the front of the convent, follow Calle Pasantería to the compact **Plaza de la Leña**, a microcosm of local architectural preferences. On its E border is the **provincial museum** (🖾 *open 11am-1.30pm, 5-8pm; holidays 11am-1.30pm*), two 18thC houses joined by a bridge and enhanced by a vine-covered terrace. Its contents focus on Galician history, beginning with the Celts and carrying on into the 19thC, and include maritime exhibits.

After the museum, turn left into Calle de Sarmiento and continue walking w until you reach the back of the 16thC **Basílica de Santa María**. Walk around to the front, where adornments are simple, even crude, variations of the usually intricate Plateresque style, but no less pleasing. Continue down the steps and turn left into the Calle Arzobispo Malvar; a short way along this street are the ruins of the 14thC **Convento de Santo Domingo**. The surviving E wing now houses part of the provincial museum's collection (*opening hours are the same as the museum*).

♨ Parador Nacional Casa del Barón
Maceda s/n ☎(986) 855 800 ▮▮▯ to ▮▮▮▮ 47 rms ▭ 47 ⚊ ⇌ AE CB ⊕
CD VISA

Location: Near the w end of the Burgo bridge. This 16thC baronial manor house serves as an architectural lesson as well as an inn. It is representative of the Galician *pazo*, with an austere granite exterior and imposing halls arranged in rectangular fashion. Some windows have balconies and carved stone balustrades, while arches and heavy ceiling timbers define the interior.
▨ ▨ ▨ ☙ ☙ Υ

♨ The principal alternative is the central and modern **Rías Bajas** (*Daniel de la Sota 7* ☎(986) 855 100 ▮▮▯).

⫞ Casa Solla
Carretera de La Toja, km 4 ☎(986) 852 678 ▮▮▮▮ ▭ ▬ ⇔ ▦ ⚊ Υ
Last orders 11pm. Closed Thurs, Sun dinner.

Enter through a walled, vine-covered courtyard into a paneled dining room, and if you like, out onto a broad, covered terrace. *Lenguado* and other seafood of the *rías* are featured here, as well as *chuletón* and *paella*, all correctly cooked and above standard for this district.

⫞ Useful alternatives include **Calixto** (*Benito Corbal 14* ☎(986) 856 252 ▮▯) and *Casa Roman* (*Augusto García Sánchez 12* ☎(986) 843 560 ▮▯).

Place nearby

La Toja (*33km/21 miles NW of Pontevedra*). Thermal springs here were used by the Romans, and today this islet is a resort colony making the most of the alleged health-giving waters.

♨ **Gran Hotel** (☎(986) 730 025 ▮▮▮▮) comes close to being the complete resort hotel; its facilities are shared by **Louxo** (☎(986) 730 200 ▮▮▮▮ to ▮▮▮▮), the second choice. There is a casino.

Ronda
Map 6I4. Málaga. 65km (40 miles) NW of Marbella; 152km (94 miles) SE of Sevilla. Population: 33,000 ℹ Plaza España 1 ☎(952) 871 272.

The road to Ronda from the Costa del Sol, which has recently been improved, affords snatched glimpses of mountain crags and brooks. The grandeur of Ronda's situation is undeniable; the flat-topped cliff it occupies is split across its breadth by the narrow Guadalevin gorge, more than 150m (490ft) deep. The western half of the town dates from the time of the Moors, while in the "new" section the Plaza de Toros, built in 1785, is among the oldest in the country.

Sights and places of interest

Evidence of the Moors can still be seen in the 13thC **Baños Arabes** (*apply to the caretaker for entry*). The Renaissance **Casa de Mondragón** was converted from a Moorish residence into one of the summer homes of the Catholic Monarchs and enjoys a fine view of the valley from its terrace. In the 15thC **Colegiata de Santa María la Mayor**, two arches, a minaret, a *mihrab* and four domes remain from the mosque that preceded the church. The naves are Gothic and the high altar is Plateresque. The **Plaza de Toros** (*open 10am-6pm*) is claimed to be the oldest bullring in Spain (its rival is in *Sevilla*); the handsome Neoclassical interior and Baroque main portal are of considerable interest.

Sights nearby

Pileta Caves
29km (18 miles) E of Ronda ✗ Tours usually 10am-1pm, 3-5pm. Open sunrise-sunset. Take the Jerez de la Frontera road N for 14km (9 miles), then turn S at the sign for Montejaque along a desolate road for 15km (9 miles).
Pottery and drawings in these magnificent caves attest to a history of 25,000yrs of occupation.

Ronda la Vieja
Just before the turnoff for the Pileta Caves take a rough road N.
The ruins of the Roman town of Acinipo include a well-preserved amphitheater.

≈In the old town, **Reina Victoria** (*Doctor Fleming 25* ☎(952) 871 340 ▥) is quiet and enjoys an arresting view over the valley from its terrace.

≈ The unexceptional meals at **Don Miguel** (*Villanueva 4* ☎(952) 871 090 ▥) are spiced by its position at the lip of the gorge; **Mesón Santiago** (*Marina 3* ☎(952) 871 559 ▥) is a simple, pleasant restaurant featuring regional specialties.

Salamanca

Map 11D4. Salamanca. 210km (130 miles) NE of Madrid; 113km (70 miles) SW of Valladolid. Population: 152,000
i *España 39* ☎(923) 243 730.
Two faiths — religion and intellectualism — coexist in Salamanca, often uneasily. This attractive city is the seat of a distinguished medieval university and the site of active monasteries and two cathedrals. The combination has produced a living architectural treasure-trove with few peers in Spain.

Hannibal arrived in the 3rdCBC to discover an already flourishing Celtiberian city. After the Romans took over, they constructed a bridge across the Tormes river that is still intact and in use. The other surviving buildings in central Salamanca are examples of the Romanesque, Gothic, and, most especially, the flowering of the Spanish Renaissance. With the establishment of the university in the early 13thC, important families settled here, contributing to the colleges and religious orders and erecting noble mansions.

In the unprecedentedly destructive War of Independence, neither the French nor British forces demonstrated the slightest regard for the irreplaceable architectural heritage of the city. The critical Battle of Salamanca in July 1812 was won by an army under the command of Wellington.

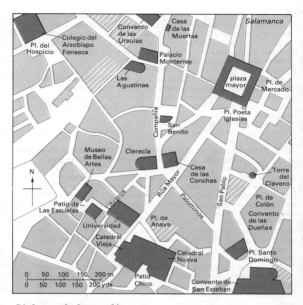

Sights and places of interest

Casa de las Conchas ☆

Rúa Mayor s/n. Renovations underway.

Scallop shells were the symbol of the Santiago pilgrims, adopted by the locally important Pimentel family. At least 400 stone shells cover the exterior walls of their 15thC mansion, one of the most photographed buildings in Salamanca. The fleur-de-lys, crest of the equally noble Maldonado family, is also depicted. Their joint presence celebrates the marriage of daughter and son at a time when family rivalries were a cause of frequently violent antipathies. The tubular Gothic iron window grilles at ground level and Isabeline decorations above add great visual interest.

Catedral Nueva ▥ † ★

Plaza de Anaya ◻ ◼ *Open May-Sept 10am-1pm, 3.30-6pm, Oct-Apr 9.30am-1.15pm, 3.30-5.45pm.*

The "new" cathedral was begun in 1513 and was in use by 1560, although another 173yrs passed before it was consecrated. One of the last of the pure Gothic structures in Spain, it disappoints in some details, delights in others. The w door falls into the latter category. Biblical scenes in deep relief are enclosed with ornamental bands and arches so luxuriant in detail that mind and eye are strained to absorb it all. Among the Renaissance and Baroque architects and artists who contributed to the building in later decades were the Churriguera brothers, Rivero Rada, and Juan Rodríguez.

Catedral Vieja ▥ † ★

Off Catedral Nueva ◻ ◼ *Open May-Sept 10am-1pm, 3.30-6pm, Oct-Apr 9.30am-1.15pm, 3.30-5.45pm.*

Many visitors prefer the old cathedral, perhaps because it is simpler and smaller in scale. Certainly devotion seems better served by the robustly stolid Romanesque style in which it was constructed. Built entirely in the 12thC, apart from minor later modifications, it has defied the years, weather and the earthquake of 1755.

Although Romanesque is usually associated with round arches, the vaulting here is pointed, probably a result of the emerging Gothic influence. The main retable comprises 53 paintings by the 15thC artist Nicolás Florentino; There is a revered 12thC gilded statue of the *Virgen de la Vega* in the center, above the altar. Off the s transept is the entrance to the **cloister**, where a few Romanesque elements remain. In the chapterhouse is a **museum**

151

displaying an interesting triptych by the Salmantino Fernando Gallego.

Outside in the Patio Chico, glance up to the scaled pointed dome known for its weathervane as the **Torre del Gallo** (*Tower of the Cock*), with a handsome perimeter of turrets, pediments and arches. Looming above it is the more sophisticated but less satisfying dome of the new cathedral.

Colegio del Arzobispo Fonseca
Plaza del Hospicio 🚽 *Open 9am-2pm, 4-8pm.*

Also known as the Colegio de los Irlandeses, for it housed Irish students in religious training, it has an especially fine Renaissance courtyard. A Plateresque portal leads into the 16thC Gothic chapel, in which the novices were said to have spent 10hrs every day. Alonso Berruguete is credited with the retable.

Convento de San Esteban ☆
Plaza Santo Domingo 🚽 *Open summer 9am-1pm, 4-7pm; winter 9am-1pm, 4-6pm.*

More church than convent, the main w portal is another brilliant Plateresque achievement, comparable to that of the **Universidad**. The high arch is divided into three sections. A relief portrait of St Stephen is in the middle, above the door. At the top, within the semi-circular arch, is an elaborate *Calvary* by Cellini. The incomparable detailing required from 1524 until 1610 to complete, the last part of an otherwise largely Gothic structure. To the right, the portico with ten arches, designed by Juan del Ribero, contains the entrance to the convent.

Within the cloister is a 16thC grand staircase leading up to a gallery where there is a fresco by Palomino. From the cloister is a door into the s wall of the church. Its principal feature is a retable by José Churriguera beneath a painting of the *Martyrdom of St Stephen*.

Plaza mayor
This is the most beautiful square in Spain, lined with cafés, the stage of fiestas and superior even to Madrid's famous *Plaza Mayor*. Enclosed on four sides, the arcaded ground level has 88 arches, topped by three stories of balconies and tall shuttered windows. This perfect harmony is enhanced rather than disturbed by the slightly higher and more ornate facade of the **Ayuntamiento** on the N side and by the **royal pavilion**, opposite. Philip V commissioned the Churriguera brothers to complete much of the design, and construction took from 1729 until 1755.

Universidad 🏛 ★
Liberos s/n 🚽 *Open Mon-Fri 9.30am-1.30pm, 4-6pm, Sat, Sun and holidays 9.30am-1.30pm.*

The main building of the ancient university is on the w side of the Plaza Anaya, but its masterpiece is on the other side, in the Patio de Las Escuelas. Above the two plain wooden doors of the principal entrance is a disciplined riot of sculptural ornamentation: shields, gods, medallions, animals, crests, busts, scallop shells, arches, columns, garlands, cornices, capitals. This effusive Plateresque decoration is reminiscent of the work of gold- and silversmiths of the time. The two figures represented in the circle just above the place where the two doors meet are *Isabella* and *Ferdinand*, who contributed to the construction of this 16thC structure.

Compared with the facade, the interior is rather an anticlimax. In keeping with medieval notions on the rigors of learning, the lecture hall off the interior court, named after the 16thC scholar Fray Luis de León, has only logs for seating, with a canopied pulpit for the professor. On the s side of the court, a staircase leads up to the old **library**, with nearly 140,000 books and manuscripts dating as far back as the 11thC.

Other sights
The former college, **Clerecía** (*Compañia; may be closed for restoration*) has 18thC Baroque towers although most of the rest of the building is 17thC. The humble **Convento de las Dueñas** (*Plaza de Santo Domingo* 🚽 *open summer 10am-1pm, 4-7pm; winter 10.30am-1pm, 4-5.30pm*) has a 16thC cloister with intriguingly carved capitals on the upper floor. The 16thC **Convento de las Ursulas** (*Compañia* 🚽 *open summer 9.30am-12.30pm, 4-8pm; winter 9.30am-12.30pm, 4-6.30pm*) has a shallow-buttressed circular tower at the SE corner, and, opposite, **Casa de las Muertas** has a Plateresque facade.

At the s end of Calle de la Compañia is the 15thC church of **San Benito** and mansions of the same period enclosing a small plaza. The 17thC church of **Las Agustinas** (*Compañia; open 9.30am-12.30pm, 4-6pm*) contains a number of paintings by Ribera. The grand Renaissance **Palacio de Monterrey** (*Compañia*) is currently being restored. The turreted **Torre del Clavero**

(*Plaza de Colón* ▓ *open Tues-Fri 10am-2pm, 4.30-7.30pm, Sat-Mon 10am-2pm*) was part of a 15thC fort and now serves as a museum of the history of the city.

Sight nearby

Alba de Tormes
19km (12 miles) SE of Salamanca.
A tower remains of the fortress which belonged to the ducal family of Alba. St Teresa founded the convent that still stands; she is buried in its church.

☞ Parador Nacional de Salamanca
Teso de la Feria s/n ☎ *(923) 228 700* ▓▓▓ *108 rms* ▭ *108* ▤▤ ⟵ ⟶ ▣
▣ ▣ ▨
Location: S of the river Tormes, facing the city. This *parador* was opened in 1981 in response to the mediocrity of the city's private hotels. Typically high standards apply. Rooms have glass-enclosed balconies with cushioned bamboo chairs. The public areas have glorious views.
⌂ ☼ ⌨ ☎ ⚓ ⫶ ⇌ ☂ ▓

☞ Despite its name, **Gran Hotel** (*Plaza Poeta Iglesias 3/5* ☎ *(923) 213 500* ▓▓▓) is more dowdy than luxurious, but it has an excellent location, with everything of interest within easy walking distance. **Monterrey** (*Azafranal 21* ☎ *(923) 214 400* ▓▓▓) has adequate facilities, which are shared by its immediate neighbor, **Alfonso X** (*Toro 64* ☎ *(923) 214 401* ▓▓▓).

═ Chez Victor ⌂
Espoz y Mina 26 ☎ *(923) 213 123* ▓▓▓ ▭ ▣ ▨ *Last orders 11.30pm. Closed Aug and Mon.*
Chez Victor so outshines its competitors in taste, performance and quality that it is in a category of its own. The tables, well-spaced and well-lit, are attractively set with yellow tablecloths and napkins, flowers in ceramic pots and balloon glasses. The menu is French, with few concessions to Spanish cuisine. Specialties such as *solomillo* and *estofado de rape* are cooked exactly as you like. Vegetables retain their identity, and the presentation is so artistic that it seems a pity to disturb the arrangements. Try the *pâte del chef* and the sherbert in a pastry shell.

═ Although **Venecia** (*Plaza de Mercado 5* ☎ *(923) 216 744* ▓▓▓) has an Italian bias, the Spanish dishes are preferable; light meals and a view of the *plaza mayor* are offered by **Cafetería Las Torres** (*Plaza Mayor 26* ☎ *(923) 214 470* ▓▓▓); **La Covachuela** (*Plaza de Mercado 24* ▓▓▓) is a tiny, determinedly atmospheric bar with a good selection of *tapas*; otherwise, eat at the **Parador** (*address and* ☎ *as hotel* ▓▓▓).

Nightlife

Rojo y Negro (*Espoz y Mina 10* ☎ *(923) 218 894*) is red, black, brassy and expensive. It offers entertainment for the late night hours with four bars, a disco downstairs and a piano player upstairs banging out several decades of American pop songs. It stays open until 4.30am.

San Sebastián (*Donostia*)

Map 13B7. Guipúzcoa. 54km (33 miles) SW of Bayonne; 99km (62 miles) E of Bilbao. Population: 172,000 **i** *Andia 13* ☎ *(943) 426 282.*
San Sebastián is the gem of the Cantabrian coast. Turn a blind eye to the sprawling industrial outskirts and drive straight to the resort area, spread out between two hilly promontories and flanking the beautiful Bay of La Concha. Behind the city's two long sandy beaches are gardens, promenades, stately apartment blocks and grand residences from the last century.
    The remains of the old town lie at the base of Monte Urgull. With its narrow streets, bars and small restaurants, this district has considerable character, but dates only from 1813 when the area was devastated by fire during the Peninsular War. Modern San Sebastián became a fashionable international resort when, from the

San Sebastián

late 19thC, the Spanish Royal Family, and then Franco, began coming here for the summer.

Together with Bilbao, San Sebastián is the gastronomic center of the Basque country, rich in culinary resources: fish from the Bay of Biscay (known to Spaniards as the Cantabrian Sea), dairy produce and meat from the lush mountain pastures. The city boasts numerous gastronomic fraternities, open only to men, who do all the cooking.

Events In Aug, a music and an international film festival.

In Sept, Basque week. This centers on folklore and sporting events of all kinds.

Sights and places of interest
Castillo de Santa Cruz de la Mota
Monte Urgull 🖼 *Open summer Mon 3.30-7pm, Tues-Sat 10am-1pm, 3.30-7pm; winter Mon 3.30-5.30pm, Tues-Sat 10am-1pm, 3.30-5pm; holidays 10am-1pm. Closed Sun.*

The castle, crowning Monte Urgull which is now a public park, has been converted into a **military museum**. On the ground floor there are displays of artillery, and above, of swords and pistols dating from the 15th-18thC.

Paseo Nuevo (*Paseo de José Antonio*)
This wide promenade almost encircles Monte Urgull, affording long views of the sea and bay and terminating at the **Palacio del Mar** (*open summer 10am-2pm, 3.30-8.30pm; winter 10am-1.30pm, 3.30-8pm*), an oceanographic museum and aquarium.

Museo de San Telmo
Pl. Ignacio Zuloaga 🖼 *Open Tues-Sat 10am-1.30pm, 3.30-5.30pm, Sun, 10am-1.30pm, Mon 3.30-5.30pm.*

In the old town at the base of Monte Urgull, the museum is housed in a 16thC monastery. The Renaissance cloisters contain Basque funerary crosses of the 15th and 17thC. The galleries feature exhibits of traditional Basque costume and furnishings, and there are also rooms with paintings by Spanish artists such as Zuloaga, Ribera and El Greco.

Sight nearby
Monte Igueldo
4.5km (3 miles) sw of San Sebastián 🖼

The ascent is either by a toll road or by funicular, and at the summit there are magnificent views, and a hotel, restaurant and amusement park.

🐚 Reportedly lavish renovation of **Maria Cristina** (*Plaza de la República Argentina s/n* ☎(*943) 293 300* ▮▮▮▮) was intended to provide the city with its only five-star luxury hotel, but opening day has been repeatedly delayed. In the meantime, the choice is the strand-side **Londres y de Inglaterra** (*Zubieta 2* ☎(*943) 426 989* ▮▮▮▮), a gracious hotel with great charm, beautiful views and excellent service. The cooking in its restaurant, "La Pecera," is sophisticated. **Costa Vasca** (*Avenida de Pio Baroja 9* ☎(*943) 211 011* ▮▮▯) is new, comfortable, quiet, but rather lacking in character.

▭ Akelarre ✿
Barrio Igueldo ☎(*943) 212 052* ▮▮▮▮ ▭▭ ━ ◁€ AE ⓪ ⓪ VISA *Last orders 11pm. Closed Oct, Holy Week, Mon, Sun dinner.*

Picturesquely situated on the slopes of Monte Igueldo, the restaurant is run by Pedro Subijana, voted best chef in Spain in 1979. The menu is limited to what is in season and includes specialties like *ensalada templada con pasta*, *angulas* and *piparras*, *osso-buco*, *lenguado con salsa de erizos* and *solomillo de las pimientas*.

▭ Arzak ✿
Alto de Miracruz 21 ☎(*943) 278 465* ▮▮▮▮ ▭▭ ━ AE ⓪ ⓪ VISA *Last orders 11pm. Closed Sun and Mon dinner from mid-June to mid-July.*

This is one of the best restaurants, not only in the Basque country, but in Spain. Its chef and maître d', Juan Mari Arzak, is a legend and one of the pioneers of *nueva cocina*. Try such famous dishes as his *foie*, fish steamed with seaweed, Bidasoa salmon in pastry, woodcock, wild boar and venison in season, and the delicious fruit soufflés and sorbets, among a host of others.

≕ **Panier Fleuri**
Paseo de Salamanca 1 ☎ *(943) 424 205* ⬛⬛⬛⬛ ▤▤ 𝗔𝗘 ⓪ ⓪ 𝗩𝗜𝗦𝗔
From the gracious reception to the moment the waitress brings the coats,
patrons know they are in the hands of people who care about their
satisfaction. Basque dishes are accorded the voguish light touch. Memorable
among them are *merluza a la vasca* or *pimientos de pacalao*. All is cooked
within a centimetre of perfection.

≕ **Nicolasa** (*Aldamar 4* ☎ *(943) 421 762* ⬛⬛⬛⬛) is nearly as good as the three
described above. Other restaurants, rating one or two stars, include: **Casa
Paco** (*31 de Agosto 28* ☎ *(943) 422 816* ⬛⬛⬛); **Chomín** (*Infanta Beatriz 14*
☎ *(943) 210 705* ⬛⬛⬛⬛); **Patxicu Quintana** (*San Jerónimo 22* ☎ *(943) 426 399*
⬛⬛⬛⬛); **Recondo** (*on the ascent to Monte Igueldo* ☎ *(943) 212 907* ⬛⬛⬛).

Santander

*Map 12B6. 107km (67 miles) w of Bilbao; 205km (127 miles) E
of Oviedo. Population: 190,000* **i** *Plaza Velarde 1* ☎ *(942)
211 417.*
In 1941 the city was blitzed by a killer tornado, followed by fires
that leveled many streets in the central medieval quarter. The
spirited modern metropolis that rose from the ashes can boast
relatively few of the antiquities distinguishing other provincial
capitals. A heritage remains, however, in the relics of allegedly
prehistoric origin recovered from the foundations of the city hall.

The fine beaches that run to the E and the N of the city are
responsible for the substantial tourism Santander has enjoyed since
the end of the 19thC. The resort and residential district to the N is
known as **El Sardinero**. At the easternmost point of the city is a
knob of land, **Península de la Magdalena**, jutting out into the sea;
a palace was built here for the royal family in 1912, which is now
part of the university.

The heart of Santander is concentrated at the point where the
Avenida de Calvo Sotelo becomes the Paseo de Pereda.

Sights and places of interest

Severely damaged in the 1941 fires, the 13thC Gothic **fortress-cathedral** has
now been completely restored. Entrance is through a vaulted corridor
leading past an earlier crypt, now a parish church. In the main building is the
tomb of the historian and writer Marcelino Menéndez y Pelayo (1856-1912).
The most impressive exhibits at **Museo Provincial de Prehistoria y
Arqueología** (*Hernán Cortés* ▨ *open Tues-Sun 9am-2pm, closed Mon*) are the
Palaeolithic circular stelae, Roman artifacts, prehistoric carved antler batons,
flint weapons, bronze jewelry and reproductions of cave paintings. Notable
among the 17th and 18thC Italian, Spanish and Flemish artworks on view at
Museo Municipal de Bellas Artes (*Rubio; open Mon-Sat 11am-1pm, 5-9pm;
closed Sun, holidays*) are Goya's portrait of *Ferdinand VII* and paintings by
Zurbarán. Housed in the same building is the **Menéndez Pelayo Library**
(*Rubio* ✗ *compulsory. Open Mon-Sat 9am-1.30pm; closed Sun, holidays*) of
over 40,000 books (including first editions) and manuscripts given by the
writer to the city of his birth. The guided tour includes his nearby home.

Ɀ **Real**
Paseo de Pérez Galdós 28 ☎ *(942) 272 550* ⬛⬛⬛⬛ *124 rms* ▭ *124* ⟷ ≡
≕ 𝗔𝗘 ⓪ ⓪ 𝗩𝗜𝗦𝗔 *Closed mid-Sept to June.*
Location: Overlooking the beach nearest the city center. With its splendid vistas
of the bay, tranquil residential surroundings, lovely terraced gardens,
attentive staff and plush rooms, it is unfortunate that the Real is only open
during the summer months. Of World War I vintage, it breathes the gracious
elegance of that epoch, but is not allowed to show its age in any other respect.
⌂ ♨ ⊠ ⚗ ⚲ ⟨ ⚘ ♟ ⚓ ♟

Ɀ **Bahía** (*Av. de Alfonso XIII 6* ☎ *(942) 221 700* ⬛⬛⬛ *to* ⬛⬛⬛⬛) has a central
location which compensates for its cool *ambiente* and small rooms;
Santander's newest and largest hotel, **Santemar** (*Joaquín Costa 28* ☎ *(942)
272 900* ⬛⬛⬛ *to* ⬛⬛⬛⬛), well-located near El Sardinero beach, is short on charm,

but has ample modern conveniences; always animated, especially in summer, **Sardinero** (*Plaza de Italia 1* ☎(942) 271 100 ▯) has recently been renovated as an attractive alternative.

☰ La Sardina ♣
Dr Fleming 3 ☎(942) 271 035 ▥▥ ▭ ▩ ▤▤ ⬛ ▼ 𝖵𝖨𝖲𝖠 *Last orders midnight. Closed Mon.*
For good value, no restaurant in Santander equals La Sardina. Although it has been in business for many years, it is well known for its experimental cuisine. Specialties include *merluza al horno, pimiento relleno de pescado, lubina al vapor, pastel de pescado y gambas, nécoras* and *solomillo al vino tinto.* Even the wine cellar excels. Make sure that you have at least one meal in this nautical-style restaurant.

☰ Chiqui (*Av. Manuel García Lago s/n* ☎(942) 271 008 ▥▥) has a beachside address and pleasing decor, which mask the inconsistencies of the kitchen; sit at a table overlooking Sardinero bay. At **Bar del Puerto** (*Hernán Cortés 63* ☎(942) 213 001 ▥▥), you can guarantee that the main ingredients have come straight off the boat; fresh meat is also on the menu for those who are unenthusiastic about seafood. **La Cigaleña** (*Daoíz y Velarde 19* ☎(942) 213 062 ▯) and **Maclem** (*Vargas 55* ☎(942) 238 611 ▯) boast substantial wine lists and focus on meat dishes; **Rhin** (*Plaza de Italia 2* ☎(942) 273 034 ▥▥), which enjoys vistas of the beach and bay and is close to the casino, has a long menu covering possibilities for all tastes; the tiny chef-owned **Cañadio** (*Gómez Oreña 15* ☎(942) 314 149 ▯) concentrates on fish, with tasty samples available at the bar in front.

Restaurant nearby
Puente Arce (*12km/7 miles sw of Santander*).

El Molino (☎(942) 574 052 ▯) is a superb restaurant where *nouvelle cuisine* is capably presented in a setting of antiques and works of art, and wine selections are admirable.

Places nearby
Good beaches abound along the coasts to the E and W, in between medieval villages, estuaries and fishing ports. The following two trips can each be accomplished in one day.

The eastern environs
Head S from Santander along the N634, which curves to the E and then passes the inland resort of Solares. After 21km (13 miles) take the road N to **Santoña**, where the fort overlooking the bay was erected by Napoleon's forces during the Peninsular War. If the area appeals to you, take a detour W along the coast and the successive beaches from **Noja** to **Isla**. Return to the N634 and continue E toward **Laredo**, an increasingly popular resort that combines new development with a picturesque old quarter. An exploratory climb affords fine views of the bay and local village life.

☰ There are a number of good restaurants here, including the rustic **Mesón Sancho** (*Santa María 12* ☎(942) 607 088 ▯).

Continue E to **Castro Urdiales**, a fishing village and tranquil resort that takes full advantage of an impressive setting of a bay backed by high mountains. Head S toward the crumbling castle on the point for a closer look at the old town.

☰ Mesón El Marinero (*Correría 23* ☎(942) 860 005 ▯) offers both snacks and full meals of great diversity.

From here, you can return to Santander on the N634.

The southwest

Leave Santander on the N611 toward Torrelavega, which passes Puerte Arce and has superb views of the snow-dusted **Picos de Europa**. At Barreda, turn w on the C6316, heading toward Santillana del Mar. While the road leading w is narrow and busy, the countryside is an expanse of lush green fields enlivened by tidy farm villages and sheltered coves. Campsites increase in number and intensity near **Comillas**, where royal pavilions and a curious building by Antonio Gaudí are arresting visual diversions.

≋ **Fonda Colasa** (*Antonio López 9* ☎(*942*) *720 001* ▯▯) has acceptable dining.

San Vicente de la Barquera is 10km (6 miles) w. Enormously popular with northern Europeans, it has a long beach, complemented by remnants of the medieval town, a 15thC bridge supported by more than a score of arches, and a striking setting at the mouth of a wide estuary.

≋ The best place to eat in town is the dining room of the hotel **Boga-Boga** (*Plaza José Antonio 10* ☎(*942*) *710 135* ▯▯ *to* ▯▯), which concentrates on seafood.

Return to Santander along the N634, a longer but speedier route.

Sant Feliu de Guíxols (*San Felíu de Guixols*)

Map **16**D3. *Girona. 35km (22 miles)* SE *of Girona; 100km (62 miles)* NE *of Barcelona. Population: 15,000.* **i** *Plaza España 1* ☎(*972*) *320 380*.

Sant Feliu is one of the largest of the fishing ports that have become resorts along the *Costa Brava*. Readily accessible from the *autopista*, it serves as a good base for excursions along the coast. Despite overdevelopment and the surge of visitors in the warmer months, Sant Feliu still possesses a certain ragged charm.

Museo Municipal
Plaza del Monasterio ▱ *Open Mon-Sat 10am-1pm, 4-8pm, Sun, holidays 10am-1pm.*
Iberian, Greek and Roman artifacts are exhibited, together with medieval artworks from the monastery that once stood nearby.

≈ Useful local hotels include **Montjoi** (*Sant Elm s/n* ☎(*972*) *320 300* ▯▯ *to* ▯▯) and **Murlá Park** (*Passeig dels Guíxols 22* ☎(*972*) *320 450* ▯▯).

Hotels nearby

Aiguablava (*23km/14 miles* NE *of Sant Feliu*).

Parador Nacional de la Costa Brava (*Playa de Aiguablava* ☎(*972*) *622 162* ▯▯▯ *to* ▯▯▯), the only *parador* on the Costa Brava, has a wild location above an isolated bay.

S'Agaró (*2km/1¼ miles* NE *of Sant Feliu*).

Hostal de La Gavina (*Plaza de la Roselada* ☎(*972*) *321 100* ▯▯▯) was lovingly assembled by a Girona industrialist and has become one of the finest luxury hotels in Spain. Rooms have silk-covered walls and are filled with antiques, the service is immaculate and every facility is available for a splendid vacation. The restaurant is one of the most accomplished in Catalunya.

≋ **Can Toni** (*Garrofers 54* ☎(*972*) *321 026* ▯▯) has a Catalan kitchen and excellent staff; the *bogavante* (large clawed lobster), *merluza* and roast kid are particularly memorable. The management of **Eldorado Petit** (*Rambla Vidal*

11 ☎*(972) 321 818* **⬛⬜** *to* **⬛⬜**) is caring and attentive, and the menu imaginative, spanning a European repertoire from tender strips of lean beef to wisps of snowy crab.

Places nearby

Begur (*26km/16 miles NE of Sant Feliu*).   A ruined castle squats on a hill slightly inland, with stunning views from its parapets. In the town itself is an interesting 18thC church.

≅ Good local restaurants include **Plaja** (*Calvo Sotelo 4* ☎*(972) 622 197* **⬛⬜**) and **Sa Punta** (*Platja de Pais s/n* ☎*(972) 636 410* **⬛⬜**).

Blanes (*41km/26 miles SW of Sant Feliu*).   Pause here for views of sandy coves, bobbing fleets of small fishing boats and craggy headlands, and visit the botanical garden, harbor, Romanesque castle, and aquarium.
Lloret de Mar (*34km/22 miles SW of Sant Feliu*).   A popular resort with an attractive crescent-shaped beach and harbor.
Palamós (*13km/8 miles NE of Sant Feliu*).   Cork manufacture and tourism are the principal industries here. **Museo Costa Brava** exhibits ancient ceramics and contemporary works of art.
Tossa de Mar (*22km/13 miles SW of Sant Feliu*).   Stop on the winding road to Tossa de Mar to take in the spectacular views. The town retains its 12thC **walls** and parts of a **castle** near the fishermen's *barrio*. A **municipal museum** displays local archeological objects and artworks.

≅ Try **Bahía** (*Socorro 4* ☎*(972) 340 322* **⬛⬜**) for grilled seafood and *zarzuela*.

Santiago de Compostela

Map 10B2. La Coruña. 74km (47 miles) S of La Coruña; 91km (57 miles) N of Vigo. Population: 90,000 **i** *Rúa del Villar 43* ☎*(981) 584 081.*
For the Catholic faithful, Santiago is a destination of holy pilgrimage almost as important as Jerusalem and Rome. For the visitor, it is a city as enchanting as any along the heavily traveled circuits of the S. Its damp climate and isolation did not deter legions of the devout from making the long and dangerous trek from points far N and E — the route known as *El Camino de Santiago* (The Way of St James). Up to two million pilgrims a year arrived to worship at the tomb of St James from the end of the 9thC until well into the 16thC.

... two staircases rise so jauntily from the level of the square that they seem to be leading you to some blithe belvedere ... the twin west towers of the cathedral soar into the blue in a sensational flourish of Baroque ...

Jan Morris, Spain, 1979

According to legend the remains of St James were found in the vicinity of the present city of Padrón. The Apostle had spent some years in Spain on an evangelical mission. After his death at the hands of the Romans, his followers returned his body to *Galicia*. The site of the grave, so the story goes, was lost until a miraculous star led to its rediscovery. By 899, a cathedral had been built to house the relics; it was razed by invading Moors in 997, but was replaced between the 11th and 13thC.
Events   No other Saint's Day celebration equals the elaborate religious observances and parades which mark the Feast of St

James on July 25. Festivities are intensified when the 25th falls on a Sunday; on that occasion, the Puerta Santa at the E end of the cathedral is opened.

Sights and places of interest
Cathedral � † ★
🔟 *but museum, treasure room, chapterhouse all* 🚫 *Open 10am-1.30pm, 3.30-7.30pm.*

Alfonso II constructed a modest *capilla* to house the newly discovered remains of St James in the early 9thC, and his successor, Alfonso III, ordered its expansion into a cathedral, completed in 899. Almansor, the Moor, destroyed all but the tomb in 997, and the present building was begun c.1075. Most of it had been completed by 1128.

The exterior is, in effect, a Baroque shell fitted around the Romanesque interior. At ground level, there is an entrance between the stairs leading to a 12thC crypt. Above is the Churrigueresque facade framing the principal entrance. It is an exuberant montage of niches, channels, arches, minor towers, statues, obelisks and floral motifs.

Inside the entrance is the unsurpassed sculptural masterpiece of the original Romanesque cathedral, the **Pórtico de la Gloria ★** by the celebrated Mateo. It comprises three massed sets of slender columns supporting a semi-circular grouping of deeply incised symbolic figures of the *Vices and Sins* contrasted with holy men and a seated *Christ*. High on the center column is *St James*, with scroll and staff. Beneath him is a representation of *Mateo*, his forehead dark from the touch of the foreheads of those who seek to absorb his genius. The bases are squatting monsters. Some of the figures have retained tints applied in the 17thC.

Structural elements in the main areas beyond the portico are unexpectedly austere, setting off the ornate Baroque chapels and the dazzling **high altar ☆** which blazes with silver, gemstones, bronze pulpits and intricate metalwork, and surrounding the shrine with its seated figure of *St James*. In the transept in front of the *capilla mayor*, a ceremony is performed as part of the Mass on the most important occasions, such as the Feast of St James. An incense burner called the *botafumeiro* is suspended from the dome and set swinging in great arcs, like a pendulum, from ceiling to ceiling by eight sturdy men in wine-red cloaks, trailing billows of incense.

Beneath the altar lies the **crypt** of St James and his two disciples, St Theodore and St Athanasius, which can be entered from the left side of the altar. Off the right (s) aisle of the transept are the entrances to the **sacristy** and **cloister**. Doors at the far w side of the cloister lead to the **library** and **chapterhouse**, where there is a collection of tapestries, some of them 17thC Flemish. A small **archeological museum** in the cellar displays articles discovered in excavations beneath the cathedral. Toward the main exit are doors to the **treasury** and **reliquary** on the right (s) of the nave.

Other sights
A walking tour is the best way to appreciate the **old town**, and the following route will lead you to all the most important sights.

Begin at the **Plaza de España**, also known as Plaza del Obradoiro, a graceful square, whose dimensions are delineated by four major buildings. On your left as you face the cathedral is the early 16thC **Hospital Real**, originally a shelter for pilgrims which was converted into a luxury hotel in 1954. On your right, the 17thC **Colegio de San Jerónimo** incorporates a 15thC Romanesque portal, and opposite the cathedral is the 18thC **Palacio de Rajoy**, which now functions as the town hall. The structure adjoining the cathedral on the N side of the square is the **Palacio de Gelmírez** (🚫 *open Apr to mid-Oct 10am-1.30pm, 4-7pm, closed mid-Oct to Mar*), a bishop's residence whose 12thC apartments are open to view.

To find the head of the old town, turn right (s) before the main entrance to the cathedral, taking the narrowing Calle de Franco, which passes the snug Plaza Fonseca on the left and the *colegio* of the same name opposite. Cafés and stores entice the eye all the way to the crowded pedestrian intersection with Calle Bautizados and the Avenida de Figueroa. If you cross the *avenida* there is a park called the **Paseo de la Herradura**, with attractive vistas from its upper slopes. Then return along Calle Bautizados (to the right of Calle de Franco), to the Plaza del Toral, where students, artists and ice cream vendors mingle around the central fountain. Bear left along Rúa del Villar, with its arcaded houses and glazed balconies, which ends at the Plaza de las Platerías where there is another fountain named after the four rearing horses at its base.

Straight ahead, wide steps lead to the **Puerta de las Platerías** ✪ at the SE corner of the cathedral. Intricately carved in the Romanesque manner, it is one of the few elements of the original building not hidden behind the 18thC Baroque overlay. Walk past the 17thC clock tower to its right and then bear right into the Plaza de la Quintana. In the looming E facade of the cathedral is another portal, the 17thC **Puerta Santa**, also executed by Mateo.

Continue in the same direction, bearing slightly left down another flight of stairs. Ahead is the Plaza de la Inmaculada, bordered on its far N side by the massive **Monasterio de San Martín Pinario**. Attached to the right-hand side of its facade is a church with an impressive Baroque interior. Return past the cathedral, through the Plaza de la Quintana, this time bearing left into the Rúa Nueva, another picturesque and essentially pedestrian street with a splendidly vivid sense of the Middle Ages in every balcony and loggia. Farther, on the left, is the **Iglesia de Santa María Salomé**, which has a Romanesque portico and wild flowers poking out between its stones.

In the Calle Castrón D'Ouro, **Iglesia Santa María del Sar** ✪ is a 12thC Romanesque collegiate church, unusual primarily because of the way in which its columns slant inward at sharp angles to their bases.

Los Reyes Católicos ✿ ▥

Obradoiro ☎(981) 582 200 ☏ 86004 ▥▥▥ to ▥▥▥ 159 rms ☒ 159 ⇌ ➤
⇌ ▣ ᴄᴮ ◉ ▨

Location: Next to the cathedral. If any hotel in Spain deserves the rare five-star *Gran Lujo* rating, this is it. It was built on the orders of Ferdinand and Isabella in the early 16thC to shelter pilgrims, and boasts an extravagant 1678 Plateresque entrance with exquisite detailing, and four cloistered courtyards of the 16th and 18thC, with fountains, Gothic gargoyles and topiary. In 1954, this Hospital Real de Peregrinos was converted to a hotel, and there was no stinting of facilities in the spacious, lavish rooms. Canopied beds, antique writing desks and carpets are typical, as is swift attendance to the slightest needs.

‡ ☐ ☑ ✁ ♨ ⚐ ♟ ⚑

✑ Until 1985 it seemed that the city's hoteliers had decided that there was no point in attempting to compete with **Los Reyes Católicos**. But that year, the five-star **Araguaney** (*Alfredo Brañas 5* ☎(981) 595 900 ▥▥▥) was inaugurated. While it can't compete in grandeur and historical evocation, it lays on every contemporary amenity and diversion, including a heated pool and *discoteca*. Somewhat older alternatives are Peregrino (*Rosalía de Castro s/n* ☎(981) 591 850 ▥▥), a high-rise slightly away from the city center, and **Santiago Apostol** (*Carretera del Aeropuerto s/n* ☎(981) 587 138 ☐), erected in anticipation of the recent World Cup held in Spain. Expect only functional accommodations at these two.

⇌ Anexo Vilas

Avenida de Villagarcia 21 ☎(981) 598 387 ▥▥ ▭ ▰ ♀ ▣ ◉ ᴄᴮ
▨ *Last orders 11pm. Closed Mon.*

With the demise of the lamented restaurant Chitón, this traditional old-timer rises by default to the top of the Santiago dining scene, surpassing its older family-run sibling, **Vilas**. It endeavors to compile an edible library of Galician cuisine, including the classic *crema de nécoras, xarrete* and *lenguado a la marina.* Service is brisk.

⇌ **Alameda** (*Av. de Figueroa 15* ☎(981) 584 796 ▥▥▥) is a sidewalk café, where the cuisine is usually good; the popular **Vilas** (*Rosalía de Castro 88* ☎(981) 591 000 ▥▥) offers tempting Galician specialties; **Don Gaiferos** (*Rúa Nueva 23* ☎(981) 583 894 ▥▥) carries the regional theme of its decoration through in stalwart Galician dishes. Other possibilities include: **El Caserío** (*Bautizados 13* ☎(981) 585 980 ☐ to ▥▥); **La Tacita de Oro** (*Av. General Franco 31* ☎(981) 563 255 ▥▥); **La Trinidad** (*San Clemente 6* ☎(981) 583 392 ▥▥).

Places nearby

Rías Bajas ★   Although Santiago is about 35km (22 miles) inland, the lovely Rías Bajas are close enough for a day-trip. Leave the city by the Pontevedra road, a dual highway leading through rolling countryside dotted with walled farms, which brings you, after 20km (12 miles), to **Padrón**, where St James' disciples are said to have landed from Judea with his coffin.

≋ There is an excellent roadside restaurant, **Fogar de Breogan** (☎*(981) 811 134* ▮▮▯), 14km (9 miles) s of Santiago. Its chicken dishes, highly seasoned with garlic, are first-rate.

From Padrón a narrow bridge with Roman foundations crosses the river Ulla into the tidy fishing village of **Puentecesures**. Take the road leading to Villagarcía de Arosa, and after 11km (7 miles) you'll come to **Catoira**, where towers remain from a fortress built as protection against the Barbary pirates. Find the bridge that crosses the widening Ulla, and on the other side, bear right (N) and then left (SW) on the road to Santa Eugenia de Riveira. This road skirts the Sierra de Barbanza and, for much of its length, hugs the Ría de Arosa. When you arrive in La Puebla del Caramiñal, take the narrow road to Curota. About 6km (4 miles) up into the mountains is the **Mirador del Curota**, which has outstanding views of the Rías Bajas.

Take the road back to La Puebla, turn right (SW) and continue to the substantial fishing community of **Riveira**. Follow the main road N toward Noya, which now traces the lower bank of the **Ría de Muros y Noya**. There are several good swimming beaches along this stretch, which has almost escaped modern development. At **Noya**, a sleepy village typical of this area, you can choose whether to return directly to Santiago on the C543 or to make a detour along the peacefully scenic N shore of the *ría* to the charming port of **Muros**.

An overnight stop. For an interesting extension of the previous tour requiring an extra day, continue along the coastal road toward **Carnota**, a village that claims to possess the longest *hórreo* in Galicia. The road carries on to **Corcubión**, which enjoys an attractive location on the *ría* of the same name.

➷ The comfortable **Motel El Hórreo** (*Santa Isabel* ☎*(981) 745 500* ▮▮▯), near the beach, is a possible place to stop for the night.

Whether or not you decide to stay, carry on through the village of Finisterre to Cabo Finisterre, which translates as "land's end." The sometimes alarmingly narrow road ends at a lighthouse with dramatic views of the sea and mountains.

Return to Corcubión, now heading N on the La Coruña road. At Berdoyas, turn left (W) toward **Mugía**, a fishing village with another lighthouse and the pretty **Nuestra Señora de la Barca** church. Take the same road back, turning N to **Cereijo**, where you might pause for a look at the *palacio*.

Another detour just beyond Cereijo takes you to Camariñas, on the edge of its own *ría*, with a road leading to the stunning panoramas of **Cabo Villano**. Follow the route back to **Vimianzo**, where you will find a restored *castillo*. Continue NE to Bayo, picking up the C545 for the 55km (34 miles) return to Santiago along a lightly traveled road.

Santillana del Mar

*Map **12**B6. Santander. 30km (19 miles) SW of Santander; 171km (107 miles) E of Oviedo. Population: 4,000* **i** *Plaza Mayor* ☎*(942) 818 251.*

So far this enchanting medieval farming village has weathered the swarms of tourists, at the cost of only a few souvenir stores, bars and restaurants. The cobbled street from the main road leads past stone manor houses, some half-timbered, many with balconies and metal or wood balustrades, most with heraldic shields.

Sights and places of interest

On one side of the *plaza mayor* stands the 16thC mansion of Barreda-Brachos, now a *parador*, named after the titular hero of an 18thC French novel. Opposite is the 15thC **Torre de los Borjas**, distinguished by its pointed arch. The **collegiate church** (*open June-Sept 9am-1pm, 4-8pm; Oct-May 10am-1pm, 3-7pm* 🔳 *for cloister*) is currently being renovated. The coarseness of some of the details on the portal and the capitals betray its 12thC origins, illustrating the raw power of the Spanish Romanesque style. Composed of paintings, small polychrome statues and finely worked silver border pieces, the main altar seems almost gaudy in this austere setting.

Sight nearby

Altamira Caves

2km (1¼ miles) s of Santillana del Mar. Admission limited.
The celebrated prehistoric paintings of bison, deer and hunters, delicately applied to the walls and ceilings of the Altamira Caves at least 14,000yrs ago, have astonished viewers with their artistry ever since their discovery in 1879. Unfortunately, the crowds of eager visitors and consequent changes in atmosphere threatened the stability of the pigments, and the caves were closed to the public for some years. They were recently opened again, but on a restricted basis, while scholars continue to explore the means by which the paintings can be preserved. To visit the cave and what has been described as the "Sistine Chapel of Quaternary Art," write three months in advance to the **Centro de Investigación y Museo de Altamira** (*39330 Santillana del Mar, Spain*). State the number of visitors involved and two or three preferred dates. Groups are limited to five persons, with a maximum total of 40 per day. Chances of entrance are better during the week in the off-season. The nearby museum and another cavern called the Cave of the Stalactites can be entered without reservations.

Los Infantes

Av. L'Dorat 1 🕿 *(942) 818 100* ❚❚❏ *to* ❚❚❚❏ *30 rms* 🛏 *30* 🍴 ⇌
Location: On the main road leading into the village. This charming hotel is perfect for languid romantic weekends, with polished wood shutters, ancient ceiling timbers, pots of flowers and a dining room fireplace. The basement disco is muffled. Cock crows substitute for early morning alarm clocks.
📼 🏄 ⚓ ⛳ 🍸 ⭕

🍷 Parador Nacional Gil Blas

Plaza Ramón Pelayo 8 🕿 *(942) 878 000* ❚❚❚❏ *to* ❚❚❚❚❏ *45 rms* 🛏 *45* 🍴 ⇌
AE ⬧ 🟦 VISA
Location: In the main village square. Castilian nobility chose to gather in this village from the 13th to the 17thC, but none of their palatial homes surpasses this one, with its spacious patio and salons. A visit to Santillana del Mar is incomplete without staying at this excellent inn; as a result it is very popular, and advance reservations are necessary at all times of the year, except the depths of winter.

🍷 The **Altamira** (*Cantón 1* 🕿 *(942) 818 025* ❚❏) is an acceptable alternative to the **Parador** or **Los Infantes**. If it, too, is *completo*, clean lodgings are available in the unnamed houses on the side streets which simply declare they have *habitaciones*. It is wise to inspect them first, however.

⇌ Substantial meals are on hand in the three hotel dining rooms and at **Los Blasones** (*Plaza de Gándara* 🕿 *(942) 818 070* ❚❏). There is also a *tapas* bar in the *plaza mayor.*

Santo Domingo de la Calzada

Map 12C6. Logroño. 67km (42 miles) ε of Burgos; 47km (30 miles) w of Logroño. Population: 6,000.
The name of the town translates as "St Dominick of the Causeway," and is based on an intriguing medieval tale. Observing the streams of pilgrims trudging to and from Santiago de

Compostela at the height of the 11thC religious fervor, a recluse living by the river Oja constructed a bridge singlehanded to ease their passage. He then built a road and a hospital, and converted his home into a hostel. The former hermit, Domingo, was canonized, and his remains were buried in the cathedral. His bridge is still in use, and parts of the walls survive around the town he founded.

Cathedral †
Plaza del Santo. Open 9am-7pm.

Begun in the 12thC in the Romanesque mode, it was completed during the 13thC in Gothic style, which dominates. The separate Baroque tower was added in the 18thC. In the s transept is the 16thC tomb of St Dominick. Visitors may be startled by the presence of a live rooster and hen in a cage opposite the shrine. They symbolize a legend of a cock returning to life after its roasting to protest about the unjust execution of a pilgrim, ending happily with the wrongly accused victim being resurrected and freed.

☜ The hostel created by St Dominick is the basis of the **Parador Nacional Santo Domingo de la Calzada** (*Plaza del Santo 3* ☎*(941) 340 300* ▥ *to* ▥). Its most impressive feature is a reception room of rounded and pointed stone arches with a colored glass skylight.

☲ Vegetables, lamb and game are especially good at the **Parador** (*address and* ☎*as hotel* ▥); at **El Rincón de Emilio** (*Plaza de Bonifacio Gil 7* ☎*(941) 340 990* ▥), try the typical Castilian mixed vegetable dish, called *menestra*, either with pork or fish. The town is at the edge of the Rioja district, so wines in all restaurants are at least satisfactory and often memorable.

Segovia
*Map **12D5**. Segovia. 88km (55 miles) NW of Madrid; 111km (68 miles) SE of Valladolid. Population: 53,500 ℹ Plaza Mayor 10 ☎(911) 430 328.*

At the core of Segovia is an ancient walled village founded by the Celts and brought to prominence by the Romans, who arrived in 80BC. They erected an aqueduct that is still in use. The medieval quality of the old city is embodied in several Romanesque churches and a 14th-15thC castle. Isabella was recognized as Queen of Castile in Segovia, which was also a center of the failed Comuneros rebellion.

Events In June, festivals associated with the days of San Juan and San Pedro.

Sights and places of interest
Acueducto Romano
The double-tiered aqueduct cuts across the city, leading from the old town toward the mountains to the E. Constructed of granite blocks without mortar, the existing length is nearly 6,552m (21,500ft), the maximum height over 27m (90ft).

Alcázar
Plaza del Alcázar ▨ *Open Mon-Fri 10am-2pm, 4-6pm, Sat and holidays 10am-6pm.*

With its pointed conical turrets of gray slate, this medieval castle has a vaguely Bavarian aspect, commanding the high ground above the confluence of the Eresma and Clamores rivers at the w end of the town. Fire damaged most of the fortress in the 19thC, so while the towers are authentic, the rest is a re-creation barely a century old. Exhibition rooms show some original fixtures, and paintings, armor and weaponry. Among the buildings that can be seen from the Alcázar's roof and windows is the **Monasterio del Parral**.

Cathedral †
Plaza Mayor. Open May-Sept 9am-7pm, Oct-Apr 9am-1pm, 3-7pm.

The last major Gothic cathedral built in Spain dominates the skyline with its tall square bell tower topped by a cupola. It was built in the 16thC, and Renaissance elements can be seen in both the main tower and the dome above the transept crossing. However, the cloister (▨) remains from an earlier church destroyed during the Comuneros revolt and in style is purely Gothic. A **museum** exhibits ecclesiastical artifacts and illuminated manuscripts. More intriguing is the **Sala Capitular**, which has 17thC Flemish tapestries based upon designs by Rubens.

Other sights

Frequently too much is made of the several 10th-13thC Romanesque churches of Segovia, most of which are decayed, unused or marred by thoughtless "improvements" and modern additions. Those most often mentioned are the **Iglesia de San Martín** (*Juan Bravo*), **Iglesia de San Millán** (*Av. Fernández Ladreda*) and **Iglesia de San Estéban** (*Plaza San Estéban*). Simply strolling through the winding streets of the old town is more rewarding, using the Plaza del General Franco, behind the **cathedral**, as an orientation point.

Sights nearby

Coca Castle
50km (31 miles) NE of Segovia 🚗 *Open 10am-1pm, 4-6pm.*
Built in the 15thC for Fonseca, the Archbishop of Sevilla, this massive fortress marks the Moors' greatest achievement in military architecture.

La Granja de San Ildefonso
11km (6 miles) SE of Segovia 🚗 *X compulsory. Open 10am-1pm, 3-5.30pm. Closed some holidays.*
The patron was Philip V, grandson of Louis XIV, the gardens are lovely, with statuary, fountains, cascades, rows of chestnut trees and flower beds, but this certainly isn't a duplicate of Versailles. Unfortunately, the 26 fountains are turned on only for a few days in summer. The interior of the palace is grandly Rococo, with gilt and white overlays, ceiling murals, grand chandeliers, mirrors, tapestries, and silk and velvet wall coverings.

Monasterio del Parral
1km (½ mile) N of the town center 🚗 *Open May-Sept 10am-1pm, 3-7pm; Oct-Apr 10am-1pm, 3-6pm.*
The 15thC Transitional Gothic-Renaissance monastery is just across the Eresma river from the **Alcázar**. There is a remarkable retable by Juan Rodríguez (1528).

Riofrio
11km (6 miles) S of Segovia 🚗
The entrance is off the N603 that connects the A6 *autopista* with Segovia. Two signs remind you to close gates to keep the grazing cattle and almost tame deer from straying. The **palace** (🚗 *opening hours same as La Granja de San Ildefonso*) in the grounds was built by Isabel Farnese, wife of Philip V. It contains a hunting **museum** (🚗) — the primary use of the small palace was as a hunting lodge — and a number of carefully preserved living quarters.

🛏 **Parador Nacional de Segovia** 🏨
Carretera de Valladolid s/n ☎*(911) 430 462* ▮▮▮ *80 rms* ▭ *80* ▤ ⟶
⟶ ⇌ 🅰🅴 ⓒ ⓓ 🆅🅸🆂🅰
Location: On a hill 2km (1¼ miles) S of the city. Opened only in 1978, this *parador*, instantly recognizable by its stepped-back levels and bristling with balconies, proves that modern hotel architecture needn't be dull. Massive angled concrete beams give cathedral dimensions to the public areas, the other principal materials being brick and black slate. Potential severity is softened by much greenery and many accomplished contemporary prints and paintings. It has excellent facilities and superb views, of which the restaurant takes full advantage. Among its unusual specialties, try salmon in orange sauce.
▱ ⇅ 🖼 🏊 ⚓ ⛷ ≪ ≋ 🎯 ⛳ ☂

🛏 Before the **Parador** was built, **Los Linajes** (*Dr. Velasco 9* ☎*(911) 431 712* ▮▮▮) ruled the roost, for it is quiet, traditional and located at the edge of the old quarter; **Acueducto** (*Av. del Padre Claret 10* ☎*(911) 424 800* ▮▮▮) is dated but comfortable.

🍴 **Mesón de Cándido** 🍽
Plaza del Azoguejo 5 ☎*(911) 428 102* ▮▮▮ *to* ▮▮▮▮ ▭ 🍷 ▤ ⟶ 🍷 🅰🅴
ⓒ ⓓ 🆅🅸🆂🅰 *Last orders 11pm.*
Parts of this famous, traditional restaurant date back to 1760. Wall paintings, framed foreign currency, antlers, flintlocks, copper pots, letters of commendation, braids of garlic, handpainted plates, powder horns and

memorabilia that have accumulated over the years cover the walls of the ground-floor tavern and five upstairs dining rooms. Photos show that past clients included Salvador Dalí, Princess Grace of Monaco, the present King, Juan Carlos, and José Ortega y Gasset, among many. They came, no doubt, for the peerless *cochinillo asado* or *truchas frescas*.

⇌ Mesón Duque

Cervantes 12 ☎ *(911) 430 537* **|||** ⌷ ■ ▤ ⏀ ʏ *AE* ⑨ *VISA* Last orders 11pm.

A mere stripling compared to **Mesón de Cándido**, this restaurant has only been around since 1895. It is nearly as atmospheric, however, on several levels, with a similar menu, and not one but two bars. The more rustic, two floors below, has a wider selection of *tapas* and an antique oven from which the roast suckling pigs emerge.

La Seu d'Urgell (Seo de Urgel)

Map 15C10. Lleida. 133km (83 miles) NE of Lleida; 20km (12 miles) s of Andorra la Vella. Population: 10,000.

An arresting location in the mountain-backed valley of the river Segre overwhelms the man-made attractions of La Seu. Dairy farming is important to the local economy and cheese made in this area is distributed throughout the country. A 12thC Romanesque **cathedral** dominates the town. It has a fine 13thC **cloister** and a **museum** containing religious relics and an illuminated 11thC manuscript.

≈≈ An agreeable overnight stop before entering or after leaving Andorra, 9km (5½ miles) N, can be made at either of two good inns. In town, **Parador Nacional de Seo de Urgel** (*Santo Domingo s/n* ☎ *(973) 352 000* **|||**) is a charmless modern entry in the chain, with sufficient facilities; 1km (½ mile) s on the road to Lleida is **El Castell** (☎ *(973) 350 704* **|||**), which enjoys magnificent views. Both hotel dining rooms are superior to any others in the area.

Sevilla (Seville)

Map 6H4. Sevilla. 123km (76 miles) N of Cádiz; 138km (86 miles) SW of Córdoba. Population: 680,000 ℹ Av. Constitución 9 ☎ (954) 221 404.

The Iberians or possibly Phoenicians founded the riverside settlement that Julius Caesar encountered on an excursion up the Guadalquivir in 45BC. Despite nearly six centuries of occupation, transition of authority to the Vandals and then the Visigoths proceeded with little apparent turmoil in the 5thCAD. The Moors easily absorbed the city in 712, and various Arab factions ruled until the triumph of Ferdinand III of Castile in 1248. In the 14thC Pedro the Cruel made a lasting impact, manifest in the **Alcázar**, a palace incorporating portions of a pre-existing Moorish castle. Still greater prosperity came with the discovery of the New World, as Sevilla was the principal port for the returning treasure galleons. Commerce and the arts flourished during the resultant Golden Age, which nurtured the native artists Velázquez, Zurbarán and Murillo, but this flame flared and died with the endless wars of Philip IV and the erosion of control over the colonies.

Today Sevilla is the principal city of *Andalucía* and the fourth largest in Spain. Its canning and textile industries are still served in part by the Guadalquivir. The city straddles the river, with its major monuments, business offices and **Barrio de Santa Cruz** on the E bank, the fairgrounds and factories on the W bank.

Events In Holy Week, processions by ancient brotherhoods (*cofradías*) associated with 52 local churches. These solemn parades are led by *pasos* — massive "floats" with images depicting saints or stages of the Passion in meticulous detail. In front and behind troop penitents in conical hoods, masks and robes in designated colors. Most of the men carry large candles, but some drag heavy chains or timber crosses along the entire route. It is an acutely moving spectacle.

In Apr, Feria de Sevilla. The annual fair that follows Holy Week began as a livestock auction. Now, behind a great illuminated gateway at the edge of a field, 1,000 canvas *casetas* (little houses), some humble, others grand, are erected by families, unions, clubs and political parties. From dusk, occupants of the *casetas* dance a type of choreographed flamenco called the *sevillana*. Most of the tents are open to passersby.

Men, boys and some women don traditional riding habits with flat-brimmed hats, short snug jackets and tooled leather chaps. Other women and girls dress in brightly colored dresses with tiered ruffled skirts, fringed shawls around their shoulders, carnations or roses in their hair. In the late afternoon, the wealthy and titled circulate in carriages drawn by matched pairs of horses with cockades and braided tails. Or a gentleman goes on horseback, sometimes with a lady riding pillion behind him, with one arm around his waist.

In June, folk-dancing competitions.

Sights and places of interest

Alcázar ⅢⅢ ★
Plaza del Triunfo s/n 🖼 ✗ *Open 9am-12.45pm, 3-5.30pm.*
Only minor fragments of the Almohad palace survive; most of what is now standing was commissioned by Pedro the Cruel in the 14thC. Evidently he admired the Alhambra in *Granada*, for his Mudejar architects clearly emulated that grand complex of gardens and residences. The entrance is on the s side of the Plaza del Triunfo. Immediately inside is a Moorish patio, but continue through an arched wall into the **Montería court**. Directly ahead is the facade of the Alcázar itself, and on the right the **Cuarto del Almirante** (Admiral's Apartment), commissioned by Isabella to house the officers in charge of activities in the New World.

Inside, on the first floor, the **royal apartments** are notable for their tile murals, Mudejar details and *artesonado* ceilings. Return to the courtyard and enter the main building through the Puerta Principal, which leads into the **Patio de las Doncellas** (Courtyard of the Maidens), decorated with tiles, paired columns and arabesques. Most impressive is the **Salón de Embajadores** (Hall of Ambassadors), dominated by an intricately detailed dome. It is amusing to speculate whether the Christian kings knew that the scrollwork on the walls celebrates the glories of Allah. A banqueting hall and Philip II's apartment follow, leading on to the tiny **Patio de las Muñecas** (Courtyard of the Dolls). Descend to the vaulted Arab baths and then follow passageways through the Montería courtyard to the **apartments of Charles V**, where there are superb 16thC Flemish tapestries. This tour also affords glimpses of the soothing gardens created for Charles V.

Ayuntamiento
Plaza Nueva s/n.
The joyful Plateresque style of the 16thC is exemplified by the facades of this town hall. Step into the lobby for a glimpse of the impressive interior.

Barrio de Santa Cruz ★
Just E of the **cathedral**, whitewashed houses of the former Jewish quarter crowd narrow lanes that dip and twist beneath cascades of flowers and widen into squares with fountains ringed by orange trees. Peep through doors to inner patios, thick with greenery and tiled with colorful *azulejos*. Spontaneous ambling along these narrow streets can be infinitely rewarding.

Casa Lonja and Archivo General de Indias ☆
Plaza del Triunfo 🖼 *Open 10am-2pm. Closed Mon. Enter from Av. Queipo de Llano.*
Originally an exchange designed by Juan de Herrera in the 16thC, this building has a somber exterior but a memorable grand staircase inside. On the first floor are the Indies Archives, a large collection of maps and documents relating to the American colonies, including letters signed by Columbus and Magellan.

Casa de Pilatos
Plaza de Pilatos 🖼 *Open summer 9am-1pm, 3-7pm; winter 9am-1pm, 3-6pm.*
Reputed to be modeled on the house of Pontius Pilate in Jerusalem, this Mudéjar mansion took about 60yrs to complete during the 15th-16thC which partly accounts for the imposition of Gothic and Renaissance elements. It boasts many fine tiles.

Cathedral 🏛 ✝ ★
Av. de la Constitución. Open 10.30am-1pm, 4.30-6.30pm. Enter through the main door in the w facade.
Only St Peter's in Rome and St Paul's in London are larger than this impressive cathedral. The mosque that originally stood here was used as a church from the Christian Reconquest in 1248 until it was razed to make way for the present building in 1401. Only the **Giralda** and **Patio de los Naranjos** (Courtyard of the Orange Trees), on the N side, remain from the mosque.

The architecture blends Gothic and Renaissance, except for the principal portal, on the w side, which is modern but fortunately consistent in design. The interior is vast — almost 40 columns virtually disappear into darkness at the ceiling. They form the central nave with double aisles on either side, which are in turn bordered by chapels. There are 75 stained-glass windows, some of which have been dated back to the early 16thC.

Turn left from the main entrance, then right along the N wall, and the second chapel contains two Murillo canvases, *San Antonio de Padua* and *Christ's Baptism*. Continue (E) to see the magnificent choirstalls in the nave, with a 16thC grille (*reja*). At the door from the Patio de los Naranjos, turn right (S) along the transept for a glimpse of the **capilla mayor**, its sumptuous Gothic retable and a 16thC *reja*. Behind the *capilla mayor* is the domed Renaissance **capilla real** (royal chapel), where Alfonso X is buried. The highlight is a costumed wooden statue of the *Virgen de los Reyes*, allegedly given to Ferdinand III by Louis IX of France in the 13thC. King Ferdinand is entombed in the silver shrine below the altar, and stairs lead down to the tombs of Pedro the Cruel, who was largely responsible for the Alcázar, and his mistress María de Padilla, who lived there.

Returning to the main floor, turn left (S) from the *capilla real* into the vestibule of the Puerta de las Campanillas and carry on into the **Sala Capitular** (chapterhouse). An elliptical room echoed by its dome, it contains a number of Murillos, including a large canvas of the *Conception* above the throne. Retrace your steps into the main part of the cathedral, then turn left immediately into the **Sacristía Mayor**, which houses the **treasury** and a lavish display of religious artifacts and paintings including two representations of the *Virgin* by Zurbarán. The next chapel leads to the Gothic **Sacristía de los Cálices**, where there are two more Murillos and a Goya.

At the end of the S transept there is a monument to Columbus, and in the floor by the main door is the tomb of his son, Fernando.

Giralda 🏛 ★
Plaza del Triunfo 🖼 *Open summer 10.30am-1pm, 4-6.30pm; winter 10.30am-1pm, 4-5.30pm.*
This pinkish square tower functions as an adjunct to the **cathedral**, but began as a Muslim minaret. Climb to the top for a superb view of the city. The lower third of the structure is of austere stonework typical of the Almohads; the 12thC central portion is of brick, employed in a decorative lattice scheme embracing Moorish horseshoe windows and pointed arches; the comparatively florid 16thC upper stories include a large bell chamber, balconies and sculptures, surmounted by an angel weathervane representing *Faith*. Yet the effect of the whole is total harmony.

Hospital de la Caridad ☆
Temprano s/n 🖼
The 17thC hospital for the indigent has a pleasing facade at the end of a small park that extends to the riverside Paseo de Cristóbal Colón. Inside are paintings by Valdés Leal and Murillo; the latter was also responsible for the lovely tile murals on the front of the church.

Museo Arqueológico Provincial
Plaza de América s/n 🖼 *Open 10am-2pm, 5-8pm. Closed Mon.*
Archeological finds from the region, notably Itálica, the Roman city NW of Sevilla, and objects of the Paleolithic, Phoenician, Carthaginian, Greek and Moorish eras.

Museo de Arte Contemporáneo
Santo Tomás 5 🖼 *Open 10am-2pm, 4-7pm. Closed Mon.*

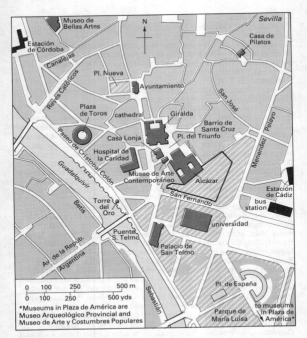

Near the entrance to the **Alcázar** is an 18thC chapterhouse displaying the works of Spanish artists of the last 100yrs.

Museo de Arte y Costumbres Populares
Plaza de América s/n *Open 10am-2pm, 4-7pm. Closed Mon, Aug.*

The popular arts are represented by displays of costumes, farm implements, musical instruments, housewares, saddles, weapons, clothing and accessories. Some of the costumes are typical of those worn during festivals.

Museo de Bellas Artes
Plaza del Museo 9 *Open 10am-2pm, 4-7pm. Closed Mon, Sun afternoon.*

The pride of this former 17thC convent is a collection of paintings by El Greco, Zurbarán, Murillo and Velázquez. They are supplemented by works of lesser artists of the Sevilla school. The building is being extensively restored.

Palacio de San Telmo
Av. de Roma.

On the E bank, just s of the San Telmo bridge, the former ducal palace has served educational purposes since its completion in 1796. Originally a naval college, now a seminary, its best feature is the Baroque main entrance.

Parque de María Luisa

The park runs s along the river from the **Palacio de San Telmo** and was once part of the estate. During the 1929 Ibero-American Exposition, it was the principal site for exposition buildings. The largest of these is the massive semicircular government house on the E side of the park, in front of which is the Plaza de España, partially enclosed by moats. Boat rides are available, and the paths are bordered by flowers and orange trees.

Plaza de Toros
Paseo de Cristóbal Colón s/n *Open for bullfights.*

This plaza, **La Maestranza**, is a showcase of the bullfighting art that equals or surpasses any such arena in the world. The 18thC structure esthetically enhances the events, with a perfect oval enclosed by a series of graceful arches.

Torre del Oro ☆
Paseo de Cristóbal Colón 🖾 *Open 10am-1pm. Closed Mon.*
The tower of gold, so called because of the color of the tiles that once covered it, formed part of the 13thC Moorish fortifications and is now a maritime museum. Standing alone beside the river, at the E end of the San Telmo bridge, it provides splendid views. In the past it has been used as a prison; now it is a maritime museum.

Universidad
San Fernando.
Sevilla is the city of Carmen, the fiery heroine of the novel and opera. Her prototype toiled in the mid-18thC *fábrica de tabacos* (cigar factory) that is now the university.

Hotels

Alfonso XIII 🏨 🏛
San Fernando 2 🕿 *(954) 222 850*
🕾 *72725* ▥ *148 rms* 🖾 *148* ☷
▬ ▬ ☷ AE ⊕ ⊙ VISA
Location: Facing the Jardines del Alcázar. Built to house guests at the 1929 Exposition, the stately Alfonso XIII rather ponderously simulates a *palacio*, but renovation has lightened its sobriety and new management has restored its solid reputation. The lobby fountain surrounded by tables is the cocktail hour rallying point for Sevilla's establishment. Every major attraction is within walking distance.
🖾 ‡ ☐ 🖻 🦢 ⇌ 🎯 ⍦

Colón
Canalejas 1, Sevilla 1 🕿 *(954) 222 900* 🕾 *72726* ▥ *to* ▥ *261 rms*
🖾 *261* ☷ ▬ AE CB ⊕ ⊙ VISA
Location: A short walk N of the bullring. Long the choice of the bullfighting crowd, both for its proximity to the Plaza de Toros and the decorative motifs of some of its public rooms, it was closed for extensive renovation. Scheduled to reopen in summer 1987, it can be assumed that it will resume its place among the city's most smoothly run contemporary hotels. Some rooms have balconies, and all are air conditioned. See *Restaurants*.
‡ 🖻 🎯 ⍦

Doña María
Don Remondo 19 🕿 *(954) 224 990* ▥ *to* ▥ *61 rms* 🖾 *61* ☷ AE
⊕ VISA
Location: Near the central Plaza del Trunfo. This small enchantress is tucked into a side street only steps from the **cathedral**, **Giralda** and **Alcázar**. Antiques and paintings crowd its public rooms. The bedrooms, however, are rather cramped and need sprucing up. The staff at Döna María is professional and alert. There is a lobby bar and a top-floor pool.
‡ ☐ 🖻 ⍦ ⇜ ⇌ ⍦

Inglaterra
Plaza Nueva 7, Sevilla 1 🕿 *(954) 224 970* 🕾 *72244* ▥ *to* ▥ *120 rms* 🖾 *120* ☷ ▬ ▬ ▬ AE ⊕
⊙ VISA
Location: Bordering the Plaza Nueva. It droops here and there from heavy use, but that can be counted as testimony to its desirability, especially in location, for it is near everything of importance. The public and private rooms are functional if rather low-key.
‡ ☐ 🖻 🦢 ⍦

Los Lebreros
Luis de Morales 2 🕿 *(954) 579 400* 🕾 *72772* ▥ *to* ▥ *439 rms*
🖾 *439* ☷ ▬ ▬ AE ⊕ ⊙ VISA
Location: Near the soccer stadium. Los Lebreros (the rabbit hunters) presents a brisk contemporary face to as many as 832 guests a night. Echoing marble lobbies and somewhat constricted bedrooms are characteristic.
‡ ☐ 🖻 🦢 ⇜ ⇌ 🎯 ⍦

Macarena Sol
Juan de Rivera 2 🕿 *(954) 375 700*
🕾 *72815* ▥ *285 rms* 🖾 *285* ☷
▬ ⇌ AE CB ⊕ ⊙ VISA
Location: In the northern sector, next to the Arab walls. This is among the stylish entries of the ubiquitous Sol chain, with a lively lobby emulating a Moorish patio, a pleasant staff at the front desks, and rooms equipped not only with color TV but with satellite video. An "English" bar and the snack-bar beside the pool provide respite from touring. The "executive floor" promises special services and extra touches of comfort, such as a reservation service. The only major liability is its distance from the center.
‡ 🖻 🎯 ⍦

Nuevo Lar
Plaza de Carmen Benitez 3 🕿 *(954) 410 361* 🕾 *72816* ▥ *139 rms*
🖾 *139* ☷ ▬ ▬ ▬ ⊕ ⊙ VISA

Sevilla

Location: Five streets N of the Barrio de Santa Cruz. Convenience is the Nuevo Lar's principal asset, an appeal sometimes marred by offhanded service and uneven facilities. It might not be exciting, but it is soothing.
🍴 ⬛ 🖂 👪 ⅄

🏷 A selection of alternative hotels include the following: **Alcázar** *(Menéndez Pelayo 10* ☎*(954) 231 991* ▥); **América** *(Jesús del Gran Poder* ☎*(954) 220 951* ▯ *to* ▥); **Bécquer** *(Reyes Católicos 4* ☎*(954) 228 900* ▥ *to* ▥▥); **Fernando III** *(San José 21* ☎*(954) 217 307* ▥); **María Luisa Park** *(Carrero Blanco 26* ☎*(954) 456 011* ▥ *to* ▥▥); **Monte Carmelo** *(Tura 9* ☎*(954) 279 000* ▯ *to* ▥); **Murillo** *(Lope de Rueda 7* ☎*(954) 216 095* ▯); **Pasarela** *(Av. de la Borbolla 11* ☎*(954) 231 980* ▥▥); **Porta Coeli** *(Av. Eduardo Dato 49* ☎*(954) 570 040* ▥▥ *to* ▥▥).

Restaurants

El Burladero
Canalejas 1 ☎*(954) 222 900* ▥ ☐ 🍽 ▦ ⅄ AE ⑥ VISA *Last orders midnight.*
Long one of Sevilla's favorite dining spots, El Burladero was closed along with the Colón hotel in which it was housed. Both were scheduled to reopen in the summer of 1987. The intent, obviously, was to upgrade facilities. Whether the kitchen measures up to former standards is another question, but the odds favor an acceptable experience.

La Dorada
Virgen de Aguas Santas 6 ☎*(954) 455 100* ▥ ☐ 🍽 ▦ ⅄ VISA *Last orders 11.30pm. Closed Sun.*
Every recipe containing seafood, familiar and exotic, is explored at La Dorada. Fish are fried in the incredibly airy style of Málaga. Among other dishes, both *dorada* or *lubina* baked to moist tenderness in a shell of salt are delicious; also look on the menu for *sopa de mariscos*, *chanquetes* (whitebait), *salmonetes*, *boquerones* and *rodaballo*.

Figon del Cabildo
Plaza del Cabildo s/n ☎*220 117* ▥ ☐ 🍽 ▦
Culinary wonderment is infrequently purveyed in Sevilla, so settle for the warmth and competence you will find here. To get there, locate the pedestrian passage opposite the main door of the cathedral. It leads to an enclosed plaza dominated by the restaurant. Beyond the busy bar in front are two floors of dining rooms, including an open-air terrace. Ingredients are market fresh, prepared in traditional or mildly inventive ways: garlic soup, artichoke hearts with baby eels and tournedos with shrimp are good, but there are a few disappointments in the balance of the card. It is the best of a local chain that includes **El Rincon de Curro** (below), **Bodegón El Riojano** and **José Luis La Cabaña del Pastor.**

Hostería del Laurel
Plaza de Los Venerables 5 ☎*(954) 220 295* ▥ ☐ 🍽 ▦ ⅄ ⑥ VISA *Last orders 11.30pm.*
The atmospheric bar is hung with *serrano* hams and bundles of herbs, befitting the surrounding **Barrio de Santa Cruz.** Stop in for a *fino* (sherry) or beer with a slab of cheese, or pick your way through the low tables and up to the more formal dining room on the first floor, where the specialties include *jamón*, *merluza* and *fritura mixta.*

Mesón del Moro
Mesón del Moro 6 ☎*(954) 218 796* ▥ ☐ 🍽 ▦ AE ⑥ ⑥ VISA *Last orders 11.30pm.*
Accept this *mesón* for what it is: a sophisticated restaurant for tourists. The light brick walls and arches are alleged to be Moorish. Whether they are or not, these underground rooms breathe the romance of ages. Seafood dishes include *corvina a la marinera* (sea bass in a spicy sauce), and *róbalo al hinojo* (sea perch with fennel).

Modesto
Cano y Cueto 5 ▥ ☐ 🍽 ▦ ⅄ ⑥ VISA *Last orders midnight. Closed Mon.*
Proclaimed by many as the best tavern in town, eating, drinking and talking are of equal importance. At the busy, friendly bar make your way toward the *tapas* spread along the marble top. Choose from *angulas*, *coquinas* or the mysterious *pescado frito*. Upstairs is a dining room.

El Rincón de Curro
Virgen de Luján 45 ☎*(954) 450 238* ▥ ☐ 🍽 ▦ AE ⑥ VISA *Last*

orders 11.30pm. Closed Sun.
Formal dinners of regional dishes —
frito Sevillano, *cordero asado*, *almejas con langosta* — with occasional
Franco-Italian specialties are offered
in a gracious setting. Little is likely
to disappoint in this restaurant,
which is believed by some to
challenge the best in the city, and
from May-Sept the air conditioning
is a blessing.

Río Grande
Betis 70 ☎(954) 273 956 ▮▮▮▮ ▭
🖳 🍴 🎴 AE ⑥ VISA *Last
orders midnight.*
The dining terrace sprawls above the
river, opposite the Torre del Oro and
next to the w end of San Telmo
bridge, affording a magnificent view.
This location and the relatively
elaborate interior trappings at Río

Grande mean high but generally
justifiable prices. The performance
of the kitchen can be uneven, the
odds favoring good if not superlative
selections. *Perdiz a la salsa castellana*,
sopa de ajo and *paella* are among the
house specialties.

▭ Other useful restaurants are:
Casa Senra (*Bécquer 41* ☎(954) 370
338 ▮▮); **Enrique Becerra** (*Gamazo
2* ☎(954) 213 049 ▮▮); **La Isla** (*Arfe
25* ☎(954) 215 376 ▮▮); **El Mero**
(*Betis 1* ☎(954) 334 252 ▮▮); **Mesón
Don Raimundo** (*Argota de Molina 26*
☎(954) 223 355 ▮▮); **Or-Iza** (*Betis
61* ☎(954) 279 585 ▮▮); **Paco
Ramos** (*Reyes Católicos 21* ☎(954)
217 574 ▮▮); **San Marco** (*Cuna 6*
☎(954) 212 440 ▮▮); **La Taberna
Dorada** (*José Luis de Casso 18*
☎(954) 654 150 ▮▮);

Nightlife
Flamenco long ago slid into audience participation and choreographed
prancing that has denied its improvisational vitality and innate eroticism.
Able performers persist, however, and in Sevilla they congregate at **Los
Gallos** (*Plaza de Santa Cruz 10* ☎(954) 212 154) and **Curro Velez** (*Rodó 7*).
Don't arrive before midnight; the early show is for tourists, and the dancers
and guitarists barely work up a sweat. Otherwise, prowl the alleys of the
Barrio de Santa Cruz, along which are a number of friendly bars and clubs.

Shopping
Calle de las Sierpes (Street of the Snakes), running N from Plaza San
Francisco to Plaza Campana, is a narrow pedestrian precinct which is good
for shopping. **Barrio de Santa Cruz** also has a number of attractive stores,
discounting the tackier souvenir emporia. Look in at **Cerámicas Sevilla**
(*Pimienta 9* ☎(954) 215 749), where prices are fair for pottery and tiles in
local style. They will ship purchases abroad.

Places nearby
Carmona (*33km/21 miles E of Sevilla*).   There are substantial
remains of both the Arab and Roman civilizations here, notably a
Roman **necropolis**, just W of the town, an Arab **Alcázar**, a
Mudejar **convent** and a ruined Moorish **fortress**, now a *parador*.

🏨 **Parador Nacional Alcázar del Rey Don Pedro** (☎(954) 141 010 ▮▮)
touches the rim of a *mesa* (plateau) and is bracketed on the other sides by
crumbling 16thC fortifications. Rooms are immaculate but routine. There is
a swimming pool.

Itálica (*9km/5½ miles NW of Sevilla*).   Archeology buffs will find
this 3rdCBC ghost town engaging for its remains of mosaic floors
and an amphitheater.

Sigüenza
*Map **13**D7. Guadalajara. 129km (80 miles) NE of Madrid;
96km (60 miles) S of Soria. Population: 6,000.*
The town climbs in steps up the side of a hill from the river
Henares to a Moorish castle at the summit. Although battered in
the Civil War, Sigüenza retains much of its charm and a number of
its historic buildings, including a buttressed **fortress-cathedral**
cited as one of the most beautiful in Iberia. Around the *plaza mayor*
are arcades, balconied mansions and a 16thC **Ayuntamiento**. As
the 12thC **Castillo de los Obispos** is now a four-star *parador*,

Sigüenza makes a delightful overnight destination on the Madrid-Zaragoza route.

Sights and places of interest

Cathedral †
Open 11.30am-2.30pm, 4-6pm. If the doors are locked during opening hours inquire at the sacristy.

The building of this cathedral spanned two centuries and two architectural styles: it was begun in 12thC Romanesque and completed in 14thC Gothic. The two styles are blended with exceptional harmony, and even the later Mudejar, Renaissance and Plateresque additions are gracefully incorporated. The nave is spatially divided into three aisles by mammoth pillars sheathed in slender columns. On the left (N) is a chapel portal that combines Gothic, Renaissance and Mudejar motifs. Farther along the same wall, the chapel of St Librada contains the vault of the local patron saint. To the right (S) along the transept is the sanctuary, with its twin pulpits in alabaster, and the **Doncel Chapel**, where a superb sculpture of a boy, who died in Isabella's service, reposes. The late Gothic **cloister** is off the N side of the nave. One of its chapels has 17thC Flemish tapestries.

Museo Diocenso
Open May-Sept 11.30am-2.30pm, 5-7pm; Oct-Apr 11.30am-2.30pm, 4-6.30pm.

An *Annunciation* by El Greco and an *Immaculate Conception* by Zurbarán, as well as a number of crucifixes and religious sculptures are exhibited.

☞During the Middle Ages the castle that is now **Parador Nacional Castillo de Sigüenza** (☎(911) 390 100 **▥** to **▥▥▥▥**) was also a bishop's residence, and that flavor has been scrupulously re-created in its restoration.

≡Within the strictures laid down by the central authority, the chefs at the **Parador** (☎*as hotel* **▥▥**) demonstrate admirable flair. In Calle General Mola there are two neighboring inns, both simple and competent: try partridge at **El Moderno** (☎(911) 390 001 **▥**), or roast kid at **El Doncel** (☎(911) 391 090 **▥** to **▥▥▥**).

   El Doncel also has 16 rooms (**▥**).

Sitges

Map 15D10. Barcelona. 53km (33 miles) NE of Tarragona; 43km (27 miles) SW of Barcelona. Population: 12,000.

For many years a suburban seashore retreat for the well-to-do of Barcelona, Sitges is now a destination for thousands of Northern Europeans who arrive every week in summer. Most of the fishermen have fled to less crowded ports, leaving the broad arc of beach to sunbathers. The streets by the beach are crammed with souvenir stores and snack-bars. Beyond them are the palatial homes of the turn-of-the-century rich. The best time to visit Sitges is early June or Sept.

Events   In late May, fiesta. Streets are completely covered by a carpet of flowers.

   In Sept, harvest festival.

Sights and places of interest

Museo del Cau Ferrat
Fonollar s/n ▩ *Open 10am-1pm, 4-6pm. Closed Mon afternoon.*

Two paintings by El Greco are the highlights although they seem out of context in a collection that concentrates on the arts and crafts of Catalunya. This building was the home of the writer-artist Santiago Rusiñol, who was clearly a man of catholic interests; there are photos, autographs and archeological relics as well as drawings and ceramics.

Museo Maricel de Mar
Fonollar s/n. See Museo del Cau Ferrat for entry details.

This handsome building next to the Museo del Cau Ferrat serves essentially as an annex, but focuses on drawings and art objects of the Middle Ages and Renaissance-Baroque period.

Museo Romántico Casa Llopis
San Gaudencio 1 🔊 *Open 10am-2pm, 4-6pm. Closed Mon.*
The late 18thC building complements the collection within, which is of the Romantic period. Clocks, furnishings, musical instruments, dioramas, music boxes, porcelain and clothes are second in popularity to a delightful assembly of antique dolls and mannequins.

🏨 Calípolis
Passeig Maritimo s/n 🕿 *(93) 894 1500* 📞 *57599* 🎞 *to* 🎞 *179 rms* 📺 *179* 🎛 🍽 = 🚗 AE CB 🅿 ⓓ 🆚 *Closed Nov-Mar.*
Location: On the road facing the beach. Ask for a room at the front for a fine view, or at the back for peace and quiet. Although there is no swimming pool, the sea is just across the street and there is a public pool nearby. Clients are granted a discount at the local golf club. The dining room is adequate. Rooms should be reserved well in advance.
‡ ✉ 🚿 ⚞ 🦃 ☀ ⅄

🏨 Terramar
Passeig Maritimo s/n 🕿 *(93) 894 0050* 🎞 *to* 🎞 *209 rms* 📺 *209* ← = ⓟ ⓓ 🆚 *Closed Nov-May.*
Location: On the beach road, next to the golf club. Shambling service and indifferent decor aside, this is the choice for the determinedly active visitor who wants tennis courts, golf courses, stables and water. It is at the w end of the central beach and therefore a bit of a hike from the town center.
‡ ✉ 🚿 ⚓ ⚒ ☇ 🏇 ♫ ✓ 🐎 ☀ ⅄

🏨
Leading the rest of the pack is **Antemare** (*Nuestra Señora de Montserrat 48-50* 🕿 *(93) 894 0600* 🎞 *to* 🎞), a small, quiet, relatively modern building only a couple of streets from the sea; **Los Pinos** (*Passeig Maritimo s/n* 🕿 *(93) 894 1550* 🎞 *to* 🎞) is even smaller, but has similar attractions.

🍴 La Masia ✿
Paseo Vilanova 164 🕿 *(93) 894 1076* 🎞 🖵 🍽 ⚞ 🚗 ⌁ ⅄ ⓟ ⓓ 🆚
Do try and make the short trek to this rustic roadside inn at the edge of town. Catalan culinary wizardry combines with reasonable prices and an excellent wine cellar to elevate it above most of the other contenders. Such original specialties as *cazuela de conejo con caracoles* and *cabrito* make a happy contrast to the conventional dishes.

🍴 Mare Nostrum
Passeig de la Ribera 60-62 🕿 *(93) 894 3393* 🎞 🖵 🍽 🚗 ⅄ ⓟ ⓓ 🆚
Closed mid-Dec to mid-Jan and Wed.
Directly on the seafront, this popular old favorite has tables set outside in warm months and delivers seafood that is often subtle and refined. Since the fish and crustaceans excel, meat dishes are secondary. The specialties include *sopa de mariscos*, *lenguado* and *higos frescos* (fresh figs).

🍴
Fish in several guises and the steak with peppers are undeniably good at **Fragata** (*Passeig de la Ribera 1* 🕿 *(93) 894 1086* 🎞); **El Greco** (*Passeig de la Ribera 72* 🕿 *(93) 894 2906* 🎞) strives for an English ambience. The outdoor tables take advantage of the promenade.

Soria
Map **13**D7. *Soria. 106km (66 miles)* s *of Logroño; 226km (140 miles)* NE *of Madrid. Population: 32,000* ℹ *Plaza Ramón y Cajal* 🕿 *(975) 212 052.*
Capital of a province with the unfriendly reputation of having the coldest weather in the land, Soria is surrounded by wild, windswept countryside. Its early history remains unfathomed; it is known only that the Romans and the Moors occupied the city, and that it was reconquered by Alfonso VII in the 10thC. It suffered less than most cities in succeeding centuries, and as a result, many Romanesque structures have survived.

Sights and places of interest
A Romanesque cloister is joined to Soria's light-filled Gothic **cathedral** (*Plaza de San Pedro s/n* 🔊 *open summer 8.30am-2pm, 4.30-7pm; winter*

8.30-10.30am, 6-8pm), which is named for San Pedro and has an intriguing altarpiece in the *capilla mayor*. On the opposite bank of the Duero from the main part of the city, the 13thC Romanesque **Claustro de San Juan de Duero** (*Carretera de Almajano*) is the most interesting part of a complex of buildings erected by the Knights Hospitalers. Only the arcaded gallery of an unusual Moorish-Romanesque pattern remains. A **museum** in the adjoining church contains Roman mosaics, jeweled ceremonial objects and archeological relics.

Soria's two finest Romanesque churches are **Iglesia de San Juan de Rabanera** (*Caballeros s/n*), with a beautiful portal, a largely unaltered exterior, altarpieces of various styles and an interesting Byzantine cupola, and **Iglesia de Santo Domingo** (*Plaza Condes de Lérida s/n*), which was commissioned by Alfonso VIII and Eleanor of England and was inspired by a church in Poitiers.

Finds from the site of the ancient town of Numancia (see *Sight nearby*, below) are on view in **Museo Numantino** (*Paseo del General Yagüe s/n* 🚾 *Closed for renovation*); they include Celtiberian and Roman artifacts.

Sight nearby
Numancia
7km (4 miles) NE of Soria 🚾 Open summer 10am-1.30pm;
3.30-8pm; winter 10am-1.30pm, 3.30-sunset; Sun and holidays
10am-1pm, 3-5pm. Closed Mon.
Little remains apart from street plans, the lines of vanished fortifications and a few columns of the ancient Roman city and of the Celtiberian settlement upon which it was built.

🏨 **Parador Nacional Antonio Machado** (*Parque del Castillo s/n* 🕿(975) 213 445 ▥) is a small, quiet, modern inn next to the ruined castle, overlooking the city and river. Although Soria's other hotels do not match the *Parador*, **Alfonso VIII** (*Alfonso VIII 10* 🕿(975) 226 211 ▥) is central; **Caballero** (*Eduardo Saavedra 4* 🕿(975) 220 100 ▯) is comparable but not as central.

🍽 Eat at the **Parador** (*address and* 🕿 *as hotel* ▥) for the best meals in town. The specialties at **Casa Garrido** (*Manuel Vicente Tutor 8* 🕿(975) 222 068 ▯) and **Mesón Castellano** (*Plaza Mayor 2* 🕿(975) 213 045 ▥) are the roast meats typical of Castile.

Places nearby
Almazán (*35km/22 miles s of Soria*).   Remains of Moorish fortifications guard the old town. In the *plaza mayor* is the 12thC Romanesque church of **San Miguel**, with Mudejar elements, and nearby the Renaissance **Palacio de Altamira**.
El Burgo de Osma (*56km/35 miles sw of Soria*).   One of Spain's under-publicized small treasures, this is an almost intact Renaissance town frozen in time, complete with fortifications, arcaded streets, Plateresque facades and a delicate 13thC cathedral with its Baroque tower rearing above the whole town.
Tarazona (*68km/42 miles NE of Soria*).   This picturesque home of the kings of Aragón invites a visit. It rises from the banks of the river Queiles in clusters of earth-toned houses dominated by the 13thC Gothic **cathedral**. There are a number of charming streets on the opposite side of the river.

🏨 The best of three modest hotels is **Brujas de Bécquer** (*Carretera N-122 km 41* 🕿(976) 640 404 ▯).

Talavera de la Reina
Map 12E5. Toledo. 117km (73 miles) sw of Madrid; 78km (49 miles) NW of Toledo. Population: 66,000.
Manufacture of fine hand-painted *azulejos* (tiles) and household objects has made this town famous and sustained its workers from

the 13thC. There are a few moderately interesting old structures dotted throughout the town, and *aficionados* of the *arte taurino* might care to know that the renowned matador Joselito was slain in the local bullring in 1920.

Sights and places of interest

For an overview of the chief industry of the community of Talavera de la Reina, pay a visit to the **Museo Ruiz de Luna** (*Plaza Primo de Rivera 5*). A similar lesson is offered by the **Ermita Nuestra Señora del Prado** (*1km/¹/₂ mile E on the Madrid road*) and the nearby church ablaze with tiles, which dates from the 14thC.

🕭 On the road sw to Portugal is **León** (*Carretera de Extremadura, km 119* ☎(*925) 802 900* ▥), small and unprepossessing, but with a swimming pool that is a welcome surprise in the blazing Castilian summer. In the town, **Talavera** (*Av. Gregorio Ruiz 1* ☎(*925) 800 200* ▯) is a comparable alternative.

Hotel nearby
Oropesa (*32km/20 miles w of Talavera de la Reina*).

Fashioned from a grand medieval *castillo* with vaulted halls and corridors leading past inglenooks and crannies, **Parador Nacional Virrey Toledo** (*Plaza del Palacio 1* ☎(*925) 430 000* ▥) is one of the earliest and most admirable *paradores*. It has magnificent views of the Sierra de Gredos and the Tajo valley.

▤ **Príncipe** (*Av. Príncipe 1* ☎(*925) 803 447* ▥) and **El Arcipreste** (*Bandera de Castilla 14* ☎(*925) 804 092* ▯) feature regional dishes, with a sprinkling of foreign specialties.

Shopping

Stop first at **Artesanía Talaverana** (*Av. de Portugal 32*) where, despite its pronounced air of commercialism, two floors of exhibits and workshops convey the craftsmanship of the artisans at work on a great variety of ceramics. Before buying, browse through **Cerámica Nuestra Señora del Prado** (*15 Reyes Católicos*), **Cooperativa de la Purísima** (*Plaza de las Descalzas 2*) and any of the other studios that might catch your eye. Vases, pitchers, bowls, candlesticks, jugs and complete dinner services are available.

Tarragona

*Map **15**D10. Tarragona. 258km (160 miles) NE of Valencia; 105km (65 miles) SW of Barcelona. Population: 117,000*
i *Fortuny 4* ☎(*977) 233 415.*

The earliest settlement of Tarragona is thought to date back to the 3rd millenium BC, preceding even the Iberians. Imperial Rome won the city from Carthage in 218BC, and in time chose it as capital of the entire province of Spain. Assaulted and razed by Visigoths and Moors, it never regained that stature. Substantial Roman remains, an authentic medieval *barrio* and a good beach are reasons for at least a brief stay.

Events In Aug, fiesta of St Magín; in Sept, fiesta of St Tecla. Parades, fireworks and dancing in the plazas.

Sights and places of interest

Cathedral † ☆

Llano de Catedral s/n ▨ *Open 10am-1pm, 4-7pm.*

The w side bristles with additions tacked on at whim but visually pleasing. Entry is through the **cloister**, which is nearly as engaging as the cathedral itself. Most of the capitals are carved in floral or mythical themes. Inside the dimly lit cathedral, the prominent feature is the exuberant **retable of St Tecla**, placed in the central apse. It was created by the artist Pere Johan *c.*1430. A small **museum** displays medieval retables and statues.

Museo Arqueológico
Plaça del Rei s/n ☎ (977) 201 101 ▨ *Open Tues-Sat 10am-1.30pm, 4-7pm, Sun and holidays 10am-1.30pm, closed Mon.*

This new municipal museum houses, in carefully conceived displays, archeological finds from several digs in Tarragona. Most are Roman, and they include superb mosaics, fragments of capitals, cornices, friezes, statues, household implements and coins.

Paseo Arqueológico ☆
▨ *Open summer 10am-8pm; winter Mon-Sat 10am-1.30pm, 4.30-6.30pm, Sun and holidays 10am-2pm.*

In few places are the many cultures which have battled over Spain so profoundly evident as here at the Paseo Arqueológico. Much of the wall around the old city still exists. At its base are the huge boulders laid by unknown pre-Iberian builders, some about 10m (33ft) high. On top of the boulders, skillfully hewn and in sharp contrast, are the Roman improvements. Higher still are the subtler additions of the Augustinian era and, here and there, remnants of the Moors and Visigoths in guard towers and sections of wall. Windows, balconies and whole buildings were then cut through or superimposed during the Middle Ages and, during the War of the Spanish Succession, the English built outer fortifications along the N and W edges of the original wall. The *paseo* is between these structures, past cannons and ancient gateways.

Other sights

Also in Tarragona are the **Museo Paleo-Cristiano y Necropolis** (*Av. de Ramón y Cajal, opening hours same as Museo Arqueológico*) and, next to the Museo Arqueológico, the ruins of the **Palacio de Augusto**. If you venture just outside Tarragona you will find a fine section of Roman **aqueduct** can be seen.

☞ There is nothing memorable about **Imperial Tarraco** (*Rambla Vella 2 ☎ (977) 233 040* ▥ *to* ▥), but it is the best in town, with spacious rooms and a site high above the harbor; **Lauria** (*Rambla Nova 20 ☎ (977) 236 712* ▥) makes fewer pretensions, but is as well located, equally comfortable, and cheaper; a notch below is **París** (*Maragell 4 ☎ (977) 236 012* ▥), in a pleasant square.

La Rambla
Rambla Nova 10 ☎ (977) 238 729 ▥ ⬜ ▰ ▦ ☵ AE CB ◉ ⊙ VISA *Last orders 11pm.*

Cool gray and white, semi-formal, and blissfully air conditioned in hot months, La Rambla has a reliable and conservative kitchen, specializing in *sopa bullabesa*, *brocheta de pescados* and *tortillas*. It is easy to find your way there as it is near the end of the main commercial street which culminates in a view of the sea.

Sol Ric
Via Augusta 227 ☎ (977) 236 829 ▥ ⬜ ▰ ⊜ ⊸ ☵ *Last orders 11pm. Closed Dec 15-Jan 15.*

About 1km (½ mile) out of town, this consciously picturesque fish restaurant is crowded with Catalan farming and kitchen implements. Doors are wide open in summer, a central fireplace warms in winter. The food is good, not remarkable, but the waiters are cheery and try to be helpful. Be warned that the house wine is served in a long-spouted *porrón*, a Catalan wine pitcher that is tipped to direct a thin stream into the mouth from several inches away. Specialties at Sol Ric include such delicacies as *bacalao al horno*, *almejas a la marinera* (clams in a sauce of onions, tomatoes, garlic and white wine) and *langostinos*.

Terrassa *(Tarrasa)*
Map **15D10**. *Barcelona. 27km (17 miles)* NW *of Barcelona; 145km (80 miles)* SE *of Lleida. Population: 160,000* ℹ *Plaza Eduardo Maristany ☎ 894 1230.*

Textile industries are responsible for the growth of contemporary Terrassa. It was founded as Egara in the late Roman period, but the most interesting of its ancient structures date to the subsequent Visigothic occupation.

Sights and places of interest
Iglesias Prerománicas de Egara †
Parque de Vallparadis.

In a park NW of the town center are three Pre-Romanesque churches built between the 9th and 12thC. They are, in their most ancient parts, among the oldest Christian houses of worship in Spain, all the more impressive for decorative elements that reach as far back as the 4thC. Particularly engaging is the church of **San Miguel**, once a 5thC baptistry. The pillars supporting the domed ceiling are Roman, and Byzantine arches frame the crypt, which has a variety of 7th-12thC paintings. **Santa María** shows French Romanesque influence, although the apse is 9thC, and there is also a portion of 4thC mosaic panel, probably Roman. The church contains a polychrome 10thC retable and 12thC paintings depicting the *Martyrdom of St Thomas Becket*. **San Pedro**, the third church, is the least remarkable.

Museo Castillo Cartuja Vallparadis
Salmerón 17 ▨ Open 10am-2pm, 4-7pm. Closed Mon.

This museum has a miscellany of ceramics, paintings, sculptures and architectural fragments belonging to the 10th-19thC.

Museo Textil
Salmerón 19-21 ▨ Open 10.30am-1.30pm, 5-8pm.

Displays are not confined to local textiles, but include Japanese, Moorish, Indian and Turkish fabrics. Priestly garments and antique looms and tools can also be seen.

❧ **Egara** (*Onésimo Redondo 1 ☎(93) 780 1533 ▯*) is acceptable.

Teruel
*Map **14E8**. Teruel. 150km (83 miles) NW of Valencia; 145km (80 miles) NE of Cuenca. Population: 27,000 **i** Tomás Nogués 1 ☎(974) 602 279.*

The Romans sacked the village of Teruel out of pique in the 3rdCBC, the Moors battered it into submission, the Catholic Monarchs chose to slaughter Jews reluctant to leave the country, and, in the Civil War, both the Falangists and Loyalists laid siege to the city during the fierce winter of 1937.

Sights and places of interest
Cathedral †
Begun in the 13thC, but enlarged later, this cathedral has a Mudejar tower and an especially fine, painted *artesonado* ceiling. The 16thC dark wood main retable is by Gabriel Jolí.

Iglesia de San Pedro †
Hartzenbusch s/n. Open 10am-1pm, 5-7pm.

The "Lovers of Teruel" — a tragic story reminiscent of *Romeo and Juliet* — are entombed here, and the street outside is named after the 19thC dramatist who wrote about them. The church is Gothic, but has a Mudejar tower and 18thC Churrigueresque overlays.

Torres Mudéjares
Five towers of Mudejar design that miraculously survived Teruel's disasters are positioned around the city. They belong to the 13th and 16thC, and are associated with churches, the earliest and most notable of which are **El Salvador** and **San Martín**. They are 13thC, arched at the base, with tiles and narrow bricks in typical decorative patterns.

❧ **Parador Nacional de Teruel** (*Carretera Zaragoza s/n ☎(974) 601 800 ▯▯*), away from the town center, is a modern building in Mudejar style with spacious rooms and surrounded by attractive gardens; efficiency and good facilities characterize **Reina Cristina** (*Paseo Generalísimo 1 ☎(974) 606 860 ▯▯*).

⇌ The **Parador** (*address and ☎ as hotel ▯▯*) is better but **El Milagro** (*Carretera Teruel-Zaragoza s/n ☎(974) 603 095 ▯*) is cheaper and certainly competent.

Place nearby
Albarracín (*36km/23 miles W of Teruel*). This pretty village,

where rose-tinted houses perch on a ridge encircled by the
Guadalaviar river, has been declared a national monument.
Architecturally it is frozen in the moment of its highest glory, two
centuries before Columbus. It has Mudejar buildings, Islamic
galleries with carved wooden balustrades, a cathedral and a lovely
plaza mayor.

Toledo

*Map 7F5. Toledo. 69km (43 miles) s of Madrid; 116km (72
miles) N of Ciudad Real. Population: 58,000 i Puerta de la
Bisagra ☎ (925) 220 843.*

Toledo does not disappoint. Its history embodies all that has gone
into the fashioning of modern Spain and when you come upon the
city in the vastness of the Castilian plateau, it stands bold and
tawny on its granite hill moated by the green Tajo, a medieval
huddle of roofs, domes and towers.

The site was built up by the Romans under the name of Toletum
and was later occupied by the Visigoths, who made it their capital
in 554. After the conversion of King Reccared to Catholicism in
587 it also became the religious capital, and the archbishops of
Toledo have since been the primates of Spain. The city fell to the
Moors in 711 and later became an independent Moorish kingdom.
Alfonso VI captured it in 1085, moved there with his court, and
Toledo remained the capital of Spain until the transfer to Madrid
in 1561 by Philip II.

Under the tolerant rules of Ferdinand III and Alfonso X, Toledo
became the most important Jewish town in Spain and the home of
a famous school of translators and scholars. The city's synagogues
date from this period.

Toledo is famous as the adopted home of Domenikos
Theotokópoulos, who, under the name of El Greco, became one of
the most celebrated of Spanish painters.

Events In Holy Week and Corpus Christi, balconies are hung
with damask and tapestry, and brightly colored religious statues
are paraded through the streets.

Sights and places of interest

Alcázar 🏛
Capuchinos ▨ Open summer 9.30am-7.30pm; winter 9.30am-6pm.
Standing at the highest point of the city, the Alcázar was built on a Roman
site by Alfonso VI, and its first governor was El Cid. Charles V decided to
convert the fortress into a royal residence, entrusting the work to Alonso de
Covarrubias. The imposing s facade was added by Philip II and designed by
Herrera. During its long history, the building has been much damaged and
restored and was reduced to ruins during the Civil War. You can still see the
underground galleries in which some 600 women and children took refuge
during the eight-week siege. It has now been restored to its condition at the
time of Charles V.

Casa y Museo del Greco
*Paseo del Tránsito ▨ Open Tues-Sat 10am-2pm, 4-7pm, Sun
10am-2pm. Closed Mon.*
In the workroom there is a signed *St Francis and Brother León* and in the
first-floor studio another version of the *St Peter Repentant* in the cathedral.
The museum on the first floor contains a series of portraits of Christ and the
Apostles, one of the artist's son and a view of Toledo. The private chapel
with its polychrome Mudejar ceiling contains an altarpiece with a picture by
El Greco of *San Bernardino de Siena*. There are views from the garden of the
cigarrales (country houses) along the banks of the Tajo.

Cathedral 🏛 † ★
*Plaza Mayor. Open summer 10.30am-1.30pm, 3.30-7pm; winter
10.30am-1.30pm, 3.30-6pm.*
Among the largest and most magnificent in Spain, the cathedral with its eight
great doors is flanked by flying buttresses and surmounted by a tower 91m

(300ft) high. It was begun in French Gothic style during the reign of Ferdinand III in 1227 and, with Spanish variations, finished in 1493. The interior, dark, vast and gloomy in the Spanish style, has five naves and many chapels.

The main feature of the **sanctuary**, entered by a richly decorated grille, is the huge, flamboyantly carved gilded altarpiece. The **choir** ★ possesses a magnificent series of 15th and 16thC walnut stalls with carvings by Rodrígo Alemán (*c*.1495), depicting the conquest of Granada by the Catholic Monarchs in 1492. The upper parts are by Berruguete and Juan de Borgoña. In the **Mozarabic chapel** beneath the dome, mass is still celebrated according to the Mozarabic ritual. In a little room behind the sanctuary, the cupola has been opened up with a rose window, so that light streams down on the *Transparente*, a vast group of swirling religious forms by the Baroque artist Narciso Tomé.

The **chapterhouse** and its antechamber both contain remarkable multicoloured Mudejar ceilings and murals by Juan de Borgoña (*c*.1533), and there are two portraits by Goya. Most of the cathedral's paintings, some of them outstanding, are hung in the galleries of the **sacristy**. They include El Greco's portraits of the Apostles and his remarkable *El Expolio* (Christ stripped of his robes); Titian's fine portrait of *Pope Paul III*; *The Holy Family* by Van Dyck; the *Taking of Christ* by Goya; the strikingly coloured *Burial of Christ* by Bellini; and two canvases by Rubens. The **belfry** affords a panorama of the city.

Church of San Juan de los Reyes †

Reyes Católicos. Open summer 10am-2pm, 3.30-7pm; winter 10am-1pm, 3-6pm.

The church forms part of the monastery built by the Catholic Monarchs and was originally destined as their burial place. The delicate stone tracery is by the Flemish architect, Juan Gas, and the **cloisters**, Flamboyant in style with Mudejar *artesonado* vaulting, are superb.

Museo de Santa Cruz ☆

Cervantes 🖼 *Open summer 10am-7pm; winter 10am-6pm. Closed Mon, Sun afternoon, Christmas week.*

The building was begun by Cardinal Pedro González de Mendoza as a hospital and finished by Isabella. Its striking Plateresque facade was designed by Covarrubias. The museum contains a large and well-arranged collection of 16th and 17thC paintings, including 22 by El Greco, of which the most famous is his *Altarpiece of the Assumption* (1613). There are also primitive paintings, Flemish tapestries and pictures by such artists as Juan de Borgoña, Morales and Ribera.

Puente de Alcántara

This picturesque bridge was first built by the Romans, restored by the Moors in 997 and reconstructed by Alfonso X in 1258. The tower at the w end is Mudejar dating from 1484, and the Baroque arch at the other end was added in 1721. It is a place to pause, with the rocky gorge of the Tajo on either side, and ahead, the walls, towers and houses climbing steeply up the hill.

Puerta del Sol

Of 14thC construction with circumscribed horseshoe arches, this is perhaps the finest of the city gates. In the brickwork above is an extraordinary sculpture of two girls bearing on a charger the head of an *alguacil* (officer of the law) condemned for raping them. Just to the side of the gate is the little hermitage of **Cristo de la Luz**, built as a mosque in the 10thC and converted to a church in the 12thC.

Sinagoga de Santa María la Blanca

Reyes Católicos 🖼 *For opening times see Church of San Juan de los Reyes.*

The main synagogue of Toledo in the 12thC, in 1405 this was converted into a church by the Knights of Calatrava. The interior, in Almohad style, has five tiered aisles divided by horseshoe-shaped arches supported by octagonal pillars. The capitals, carved with pine cones and strapwork, and other decorative work are exceptional.

Sinagoga del Tránsito ☆

Paseo del Tránsito. For opening times see Church of San Juan de los Reyes.

Built in the 14thC, this synagogue was also converted into a church in 1492. Small and unpretentious from the outside, it contains magnificent Mudejar work including an *artesonado* ceiling of cedarwood and 54 windows with lace-like stone tracery. Adjoining is a **Sephardic museum** with manuscripts, robes, books, two beautiful silver caskets and other Jewish relics.

Other sights

In the public gardens to the N are the remains of a **Roman circus**. The old and new **Bisagra Gates** are in the former Moorish ramparts: Alfonso VI made his entry into the city in 1085 through the old gate; the new gate, with its massive round crenellated towers, was rebuilt by Covarrubias in 1550. Corresponding to the Alcántara bridge (see above) to the E is the 14thC **St Martin's bridge** to the W. In the **Plaza del Zocodover**, at the center, the **Posada de la Sangre**, where Cervantes is said to have stayed, was rebuilt after its destruction during the Civil War.

Among Toledo's many churches, **Santo Tomé** has a fine 14thC Mudejar tower and contains El Greco's masterpiece *The Burial of the Count of Orgaz*; **San Román** also has a distinctive Mudejar tower and has been converted into a **Visigothic museum** with carved stonework and bronze jewelry of the period; and **Cristo de la Vega**, on the site of a 7thC Visigothic temple, possesses a memorable Mudejar apse. Also of interest is the **Hospital de Tavera** (▨ *open 10am-1.30pm, 3.30-6pm*), now a school; the large dining saloon contains Titian's portrait of *Charles V* and a number of important paintings by El Greco.

❧ Parador Nacional Conde de Orgaz
Paseo de los Cigarrales ☎ *(925) 221 850* ▨▨▨ *57 rms* ▭ *57* ▦ ☚ ☚
🅰🅴 ⊕ ⊙ 🆅🅸🆂🅰

Location: Just S of Toledo across the Tajo. Situated on the hill of El Emperador with fine views of the city, this modern *parador*, built in traditional Toledan style, is the best hotel in the area.
⌂ ♣ ◪ ◁≪ ☀ ♈

❧ **Alfonso VI** (*General Moscardó 2*) ☎ *(925) 222 600* ▨▯) is a large step down from the *parador* but looks directly across the street to the Alcázar; **Alamarza** (*Carretera Piedrabuena 47* ☎ *(925) 223 866* ▯) is quiet with lovely views, about 3km (2 miles) outside the city; **Carlos V** (*Plaza Horno Magdalena 1* ☎ *(925) 222 600* ▨▯) fronts on to a picturesque twisting lane between the cathedral and Alcázar.

❧ ☴ Hostel del Cardenal
Paseo de Recaredo 24 ☎ *(925) 220 862* ▨▯ ▦ ☚ 🅰🅴 ⊕ ⊙ 🆅🅸🆂🅰 *Last orders 11pm.*

Housed in a beautiful 18thC baronial mansion, and set in a shaded garden. Specialties include suckling pig and lamb, roasted in a wood-fired oven, and, in spring and summer, fresh asparagus and strawberries from Aranjuez. Known primarily as a restaurant, the Hostal also has 27 comfortable rooms.

☴ Venta de Aires
Circo Romano 25 ☎ *(925) 220 545* ▨▯ ▦ ☚ 🅰🅴 ⊕ ⊙ 🆅🅸🆂🅰 *Last orders 11pm.*

This is an old and famous restaurant. In winter it is warm and intimate, and in summer you may eat in the large garden. The former proprietress, Señora Modesta, catered for King Alfonso XIII's hunting parties, reflected in such dishes as the celebrated stewed partridge, *tortilla de patatas a la magra* (potato omelet with fillet of pork), garlic soup and the regional Manchego cheese.

☴ **Casa Aurelio** (*Sinagoga 6* ☎ *(925) 222 097* ▨▯) serves a variety of well-cooked local dishes, including garlic soup, *menestra de verduras*, roast lamb, partridge and quail. The wines are from its own vineyard and from Méntrida. Appetizing *plats du jour*, including typical regional dishes, are featured at the atmospheric **Chiron** (*Paseo de Recaredo 1* ☎ *(925) 220 150* ▨▯). **La Botica** (*Plaza Zocodover 13*) is a stylish new spot on the main square with a *tapas* bar in front from which to view activities outside, and a handsome dining room upstairs. **Emperador** (*Carretera del Valle 1* ☎ *(925) 224 691* ▨▯) is a pleasant restaurant located outside the city center. Try the *tapas* at **Hosteria Aurelio** (*Santo Tomé 21* ☎ *(925) 222 036* ▯).

Shopping

Like other tourist centers, Toledo is jammed with souvenir stores selling gimcrack religious figures and pictures. It has been famous for centuries for its sword blades; but genuine Toledo knives and the intricately worked *orfevrerie* are not cheap and should be bought in a good store. The same is true for the traditional damask.

Toro

Map 11D4. Zamora. 33km (21 miles) E of Zamora; 63km (39 miles) w of Valladolid. Population: 10,000.

The ancient town spreads over a long mound above the river Duero. Hannibal apparently founded a settlement here in the 3rdCBC, and he was followed by the Romans. Despite its rather bedraggled air, Toro has been declared a national monument for its wealth of 12thC Romanesque churches and buildings.

Sights and places of interest

Colegiata de Santa María la Mayor 🏛 ✝ ☆
Plaza del Espolón 🖼 *Open June-Sept 10.30am-1.30pm, 5-8pm; at other times inquire at the town hall.*

A superb and relatively unaltered example of the Romanesque style, this collegiate church was built between the 12th and 13thC. This chronology led to the construction of a magnificent w portal in the emerging Gothic mode. The **sacristy** contains a painting entitled *Virgen de la Mosca* (Virgin and the Fly), which includes a representation of Queen Isabella.

Other sights

Among Toro's other important buildings are the 13thC Romanesque-Mudejar **Iglesia de San Lorenzo**, with a retable by the regional artist Fernando Gallego, and the 14thC **Convento del Sancti Spiritus**, which houses the tomb of Beatriz of Portugal, wife of Juan I of Castile. The town is also well known for its **Plaza de Toros**, built in 1828, which is one of the oldest in Spain, and for the **Palacio de las Leyes** where the Cortes met in 1506 to confirm Ferdinand's right to the throne after Isabella died.

🛏 **Juan II** (*Paseo del Espolón 1* ☎*(988) 690 300* 🔳) has fair amenities, fine views of the countryside and a location near **Colegiata de Santa María la Mayor** (see above).

🍽 **Juan II** (*address and* ☎ *as hotel* 🔲) features wines and recipes of the area and is the local choice for family celebrations.

Torremolinos

Map 7I5. Málaga. 45km (28 miles) NE of Marbella; 14km (9 miles) sw of Málaga. Population: 40,000 i Bajos de la Nogalera ☎*(952) 381 578.*

Torremolinos has borne the brunt of the successive tidal waves of Northern Europeans that have overwhelmed this coast since the late 1950s. Uncontrolled development has brought cheap jack vacation housing and trashy nightclub strips, but there is another side to Torremolinos. The long beachfront, broken only by a mass of rock that separates the newer part of the town from the former fishing village of **La Carihuela**, is ideal for a few days' hedonistic respite from the solemn rounds of churches and Moorish castles.

Hotels, hostels and guest houses are on every corner, interspersed with restaurants, bars, cafés and shellfish stands. The following suggestions can only hint at their number and diversity.

Hotels

Cervantes
Las Mercedes s/n ☎*(952) 384 033*
🅰 *77174* 🔳 *to* 🔳 *400 rms* 🛏 *400*
▦ 🛎 🍽 🍷 *AE CB* ⊙ ⊙ *VISA*
Location: In the town center. Operated and fitted out with greater dash and efficiency than is usual in this sun-baked venue, the Cervantes might be the choice for those intent on mixing a touch of work with their pleasure. Not that the sensual self is neglected,

with two pools (one with an underwater viewing window), a music bar and a convenient location near the largest concentration of stores and nightclubs.
⬦ 🖽 🏊 ≋ 🏌 ⛵ ♈ ◉

Don Pablo
Paseo Maritimo ☎*(952) 383 888*
🅰 *77252* 🔳 *429 rms* 🛏 *429* ▦
🛎 🍽 *AE CB* ⊙ ⊙ *VISA*

Torremolinos

Location: Beside the beach, slightly E of the town center. Hints of Mudejar brickwork and coffered ceilings touch the vast reception rooms. Few vacation needs are neglected, with two heated pools, a sauna, gymnasium, hairdresser, masseuse, billiard room, four bars and nightly dancing. Bathrooms have heated towel rails, and the single rooms have double beds, which is unusual in Spain.

♨ ⚐ 🖼 🐾 ⚓ ⇌ 🐟 ♒ ✓ 🛶 🛎
🔵 ⊙

Miami
Aladino 14 ☎ (952) 385 255 ⅢⰔ 27 *rms* 🛏 27 🚗
Location: Three streets from La Carihuela beach. As quiet as Torremolinos will permit it to be, this delightful inn stands behind giant cacti and banana palms in a residential district that was once a fishing village. A cousin of Picasso built the villa that was the core of the present building, filling it with old and charmingly quirky objects.

🏠 ⚐ ⚓ ⇌ ⚓ 🐟 ♒ ♈

Montemar
Av. Montemar ☎ (952) 381 577 ⅢⰔ 42 *rms* 🛏 42 ☷ 🚗 🚗 AE ⊙ ⓒ VISA
Location: Residential area W of the town center. A sign at the door suggests that tourism began on the Costa del Sol with the construction of this 1934 tavern. The inner courtyard is typically Andalucian, with a ground-floor loggia supporting the balconies above. Although situated at a distance from the beach, the Montemar can boast a fair-sized pool and good amenities.

🏠 ⚐ 🐾 ⚓ ⇌ 🐟 ♒ ♈

Parador Nacional del Golf
Apartado 324 de Málaga ☎ (952) 381 255 ⅢⰔ 40 *rms* 🛏 40 ☷ 🚗
🚗 AE ⊙ ⓒ VISA
Location: 7km (4¹/₂ miles) E of the town, on the Málaga road. As a rule, *paradores* don't have many recreational facilities, apart from the odd swimming pool. This one is an exception, with a vast circular pool on the way to the beach, tennis courts a step from the entrance, and the first green of an 18-hole golf course not far beyond.

🏠 ♨ ⚐ 🐾 ⚓ ⇌ 🐟 ♒ ✓ ♈

🗝 Other hotels with a range of good facilities include: **Al-Andalus** (*Av. de Montemar s/n* ☎ (952) 381 200 ⅢⰔ *to* ⅢⰔ); **Don Pedro** (*Av. del Lido s/n* ☎ (952) 386 844 ⅢⰔ); **Meliá Costa del Sol** (*Paseo Marítimo* ☎ (952) 386 677 ⅢⰔ); **Meliá Torremolinos** (*Av. Carlotta Alessandri 109* ☎ (952) 380 500 ⅢⰔ); **Las Palomas** (*Carmen Montes 1* ☎ (952) 385 000 ⅢⰔ); **Pontinental** (*Apartado 75* ☎ (952) 381 400 ⅢⰔ); **Príncipe Sol** (*Paseo Colorado 26* ☎ (952) 384 100 ⅢⰔ).

Restaurants

El León de Castilla
Casablanca s/n, Pueblo Blanco ☎ (952) 386 959 ⅢⰔ ⬛ 🍴 🚗 🏠 ♈ AE ⊙ ⓒ VISA *Last orders 11pm.*
In a hidden square of white houses draped with flowers this restaurant has friendly, helpful staff who are willing to behead, betail, bone and skin fish before serving them. The specialties are *sopa de cebolla*, *angulas de Aguinaga* and *cordero asado*.

El Roqueo
Carmen 35, La Carihuela ☎ (952) 384 946 ⅢⰔ ⬛ 🍴 ♈ *Last orders 11pm. Closed Nov and Tues.*
If you are immobilized by too vast a choice, this family-run fish restaurant is better than most. An intriguing dish is *lubina* or *dorada a la sal*, where the whole fish is baked in a casing of salt, removed before serving. Other specialties include such dishes as *boquerones* and *fritura malagueña*.

🍽 **El León de Castilla** and **El Roqueo** lead into districts where there are dozens of other alternative eating places. Among those to look out for are the self-explanatory **Pizzeria El Paseo** (*Paseo Marítimo* ⅢⰔ) and **Marrakech** (*Carretera de Benalmádena* ☎ (952) 382 169 ⅢⰔ); more inexpensive restaurants include **Casa Juan** (*Humilladero 16, La Carihuela* ☎ (952) 384 100 ⅢⰔ) for seafood, **Cacerola** (*María Barrabino s/n* ☎ (952) 383 943 ⅢⰔ) for facsimiles of English favorites, and **Marsalo** (*María Barrabino s/n* ⅢⰔ) for standard Spanish dishes; in the area around the Pueblo Blanco complex, look for the vegetarian restaurant, **Salud** (*Casablanca s/n, La Nogalera* ⅢⰔ), **El Caballo Vasco** (*Casablanca s/n, La Nogalera* ☎ (952) 382 336 ⅢⰔ), and **Estocolmo** (*Paraje de la Fuente 9* ☎ (952) 385 929 ⅢⰔ), all are worth a visit. Also worth a look is **Frutos** (☎ (952) 381 450 ⅢⰔ) is situated on the road to Málaga.

Nightlife

Bars, discos and flamenco clubs, many of which have ephemeral lives, are too numerous to count. Avenida Carlotta Alessandri, w of the town center, is one of the main nightclub districts. **Piper's** attracts multitudes of youngsters, while **Numero Uno** and **Joy** draw a mixture of people and seem to have staying power. Bars are numerous around Pueblo Blanco.

Tortosa
Map 14E9. Tarragona. 85km (53 miles) sw of Tarragona; 195km (121 miles) ne of Valencia. Population: 32,000.
Although its origins are Roman and Moorish, there is little to recall that past in this dusty agricultural center. The most powerful monument is a rusted towering oddity planted in the middle of the Ebro river to mark the last great battle of the Civil War, fought here in 1938. The Gothic **cathedral** was begun in the 14thC, and later embellished with Baroque overlays. Until the 14thC, Moors, Jews and Christians are said to have lived peacefully here for nearly 100yrs; the Jewish quarter lies beneath the Moorish fortifications which still bristle across the crest of the higher hills.

🛏 Enclosed by Moorish ramparts, **Parador Nacional Castillo de la Zuda** (☎(977) *444 450* ▮▮ *to* ▮▮▮) was built in 1976 to take advantage of the panoramas of river and sierra to the w and the old town to the s; it makes Tortosa a logical stop en route from France to Valencia.

🍴**San Carlos** ♣(*Av. Felipe Pedrell 46* ☎(977) *441 048* ▮▮) is a happy discovery, concentrating on rather pricey shellfish and exotica of the sea; portions are daunting, sauces splendid and the setting is unpretentious.

Trujillo
Map 6F4. Cáceres. 47km (30 miles) e of Cáceres; 86km (54 miles) ne of Mérida. Population: 9,500 i Plaza Mayor ☎(927) 320 653.
If its *plaza mayor* had been in a larger town, Trujillo might have gained the attention it really deserves. From the Madrid-Lisbon road, the curtain walls of a Moorish castle on the summit of a solitary hill catch the eye. Extremely narrow streets wind up through clustered houses to the *plaza mayor*, which was not planned but could hardly be more handsome. High above is the deserted *castillo*, and in the center an equestrian statue of the conquistador *Pizarro*, born here in 1476. Little has changed in three centuries, except for the addition of a parking lot and Coca-cola in the bars.

Sights and places of interest
Ayuntamiento Viejo
Plaza Mayor. Unpredictable opening hours.
The old town hall is distinguished by three tiers of arches, each tier more squat than the one below. Mildly interesting murals inside illustrate the building's present function as a law court.
Casa de las Cadenas
Plaza Mayor.
Draped across the front of the 12thC house is a heavy chain, the symbol of immunity from taxes granted to the Orellana family by Philip II.
Iglesia de San Martín †
Plaza Mayor.
Behind the *Pizarro* statue is a 15thC granite church rebuilt in the 16thC in Renaissance style but with surviving Gothic traces. Inside there is an imposing nave and several interesting vaults.
Palacio Duques de San Carlos
Plaza Mayor 🕐 *Open 9am-1pm, 3-6pm. Ring the bell to gain entry.*
The 16thC ducal residence is now a convent. The exterior shows early Renaissance detailing and sculptured figures, but the inner courtyard on two levels is especially handsome. Resident nuns act as guides.

Tudela

Palacio Marqués de la Conquista
Plaza Mayor.
On the plaza side of this building is a loggia, along the roof line are statues at 2m (6½ft) intervals, and four stories of windows have iron grilles with curlicued tops. The prominent feature, however, is a corner pointed-arch window with a balcony and surmounted by a Plateresque family shield in high stone-relief.

🦐 Parador Nacional de Trujillo
Plaza de Santa Clara s/n ☎ *(927) 321 350* ▐▐▐▐ *46 rms* 🛏 *46* 🍽 ➡ ≋
Ⓐ Ⓒ ⑩ ⑩ ⑩
Location: One block off the main road. Vaulted ceilings, tile dados and low doorways reveal the origins of this new addition to the *parador* chain as a 16thC convent, once named Santa Clara. The bedrooms are hardly monastic, commodious as they are, with four-poster twin beds and bleached wood furniture. The dining room surpasses any other in town. Just remember to duck your head when returning to bed.
🏠 ‡ 🖂 👰 🏛 ♈

Tudela
Map 13C7. Navarra. 83km (52 miles) s of Pamplona; 81 km (51 miles) nw of Zaragoza. Population: 26,000 ℹ *Plaza Fueros* ☎ *(948) 821 539.*

At the heart of the principal Navarra farm district known as the Ribera, Tudela is concerned with producing, canning and distributing crops, such as lettuce, asparagus, artichokes, peas, peppers and beans. Its agricultural history reaches back before the Moors, who assumed control of the settlement in the 8thC and held it until their defeat by the forces of Alfonso I in 1114. Much of their architectural legacy still remains. The 13thC Gothic **cathedral** *(open 8.30am-1pm, 4.30-8pm)* was built on the ruins of a mosque, but has a significant representation of styles from the Romanesque to the Baroque. Fragments of the old *mezquita* can be seen in the **cloister**.

There are a number of Renaissance mansions nearby, and in the old Moorish quarter the 12thC **Iglesia de San Nicolás** was renovated in the 18thC, but has a fine Romanesque portal.

🦐 **Morase** *(Paseo de Vadillo 13* ☎ *(948) 821 700* ▐ *)* is good value and has the most capable restaurant in town; at a pinch, **Tudela** *(Carretera de Zaragoza s/n* ☎ *(948) 820 558* ▐ *)* is clean but dull.

Túy *(Tui)*
Map 10C2. Pontevedra. At the principal border crossing between n Portugal and Galicia; 124km (77 miles) n of Porto; 29km (18 miles) s of Vigo. Population: 15,000 ℹ *Edificio de la Aduana Ave. Portugal* ☎ *(986) 600 757.*

Its strategic position on the river Miño made Túy desirable to ancient traders, although its origins are uncertain. A Spanish stronghold through repeated conflicts with Portugal during the Middle Ages, the town has been bypassed by more recent wars. The two-tiered road and railroad bridge connecting Túy to Valença do Minho was designed by Gustave Eiffel, famous for a certain engineering feat farther north. The **fortress-cathedral**, begun at the end of the 12thC, is remarkable because the original Romanesque Gothic style was respected through the 300yrs required to complete its central parts. Conversely, the interior adornments incorporating sturdy supports against occasional earthquakes belong largely to the Renaissance.

🦐 Parador Nacional San Telmo
☎ *(986) 600 300* ▐▐▐▐ *16 rms* 🛏 *16* 🍽 ➡ Ⓐ Ⓒ ⑩ ⑩ ⑩
Location: Four streets n of the river Miño crossing. Its small size and proximity

to the frontier make advance reservations or at least early arrival essential. It
is modern, but emulates a Galician manor house.

⌂ ⧖ ⚓ ⭍ ⇌ ⚲

Ubeda

*Map 8H6. Jaén. 57km (36 miles) NE of Jaén; 204km (127
miles) SE of Albacete. Population: 32,000 i Plaza de los
Caídos 2 ☎(853) 750 897.*

For its multitude of Renaissance palaces, mansions and churches,
Ubeda has been dubbed the "Salamanca of Andalucía." It was one
of the first towns in this region to be recaptured, in the 13thC,
from the Moors. The Christians then eradicated most traces of the
former rulers, so the Moorish influence is less pronounced here
than it is farther S. Instead, the dominant architectural themes
belong to the Italian Renaissance, with surfaces of the lacy
scrollwork and heraldry of the Isabeline and Plateresque styles.

Sights and places of interest

The road from Jaén and Baeza passes the enormous 16thC **Hospital de
Santiago**, which is often compared with *El Escorial*. The arcaded inner
court has a dramatic staircase beneath polychromed vaulting. The major
church in Ubeda itself, **Iglesia de San Pablo**, is a blend of basic Gothic
construction and Renaissance additions. The W door is 13thC Gothic, the S
portal 16thC Isabeline, the bell tower Plateresque.

The triangular main square, **Plaza del General Saro**, has arcaded
sidewalks where café tables stand, and a clock tower dating from the Middle
Ages with a 17thC cupola. The monumental core of the old town, **Plaza
Vázquez de Molina**, is a large rectangular plaza with a garden, statues and
broad paved areas. Among the several mansions and municipal buildings that
enclose it is the 16thC **Palacio del Deán Ortega**, its subdued facade in
marked contrast to the adjacent **Capilla del Salvador**, a splendid 16thC
Renaissance church; the 16thC **Palacio de las Cadenas**, which takes its
name from the chains delineating the forecourt; and, opposite, **Santa María
de los Reales Alcázares** with Gothic elements inside and Renaissance
overlays outside.

Given its isolation, Ubeda is a lively town which has markets and a street of
crafts studios (Calle Valencia) including a prolific pottery.

⚮ **Parador Nacional Condestable Dávalos**
Plaza Vázquez de Molina 1 ☎(953) 750 345 ⫴ *25 rms* ▭ *25* ⇔ ☰
☰ AE ⓪ ⑩ VISA
Location: In the center of the old town. Transformed in 1931 from 16thC palace
to *parador*, this building is preserved, not restored, almost exactly as it was.
Floors undulate, lintels tilt, moldings waver. The entrance is up a broad
staircase leading onto a courtyard that is open to a glass roof. This is
surrounded by 16 slender columns and a dado of blue and white tiles, the
space filled with ferns and ivy. Necessary renovation was recently completed.
The restaurant is the best for miles.
⌂ ⧖ ⫽ ⚓ ⚲

Place nearby

Baeza *(9km/5½ miles SW of Ubeda).* A minor gem of the early to
high Renaissance, Baeza has a shaded **paseo**, a plaza with a
fountain of Roman sculptures in the center, a 13thC Gothic
cathedral, an **Ayuntamiento** with a fine Plateresque exterior, and
the **Palacio de Jabalquinto** with an Isabeline facade.

Valdepeñas

*Map 7G6. Ciudad Real. 200km (124 miles) S of Madrid;
198km (123 miles) NE of Córdoba. Population: 26,000.*
Valdepeñas is a tidy agricultural town serving the vineyards of the
SW district of the huge grape-growing region of La Mancha; its
name is synonymous with the wines produced in its *bodegas*. The
town is well located for an overnight stop on the drive from Madrid

to the Costa del Sol, and its principal sight is a **Gothic church** with Plateresque details. Unlike in *Jerez de la Frontera*, there are no regular tours of *bodegas* ending up in jolly tasting rooms, although visitors are welcome at the vintners' cooperative called **La Invencible**, on Calle Caro Patón, three streets w of the town center.

Meliá El Hidalgo ♣
Carretera Madrid-Cádiz, km 194 ☎ *(926) 323 254* ▥ *54 rms* ▭ *54* ▦
◁━ ▱ AE ① ⓒ VISA
Location: 6km (4 miles) N of Valdepeñas. The vineyards come right up to the parking lot of this comfortable hotel, which offers a good range of facilities.
🏊 ⚓ ≈ ▾ ⛾

▤ **Gala** *(Arpa 3* ☎ *(926) 323 339* ▥▯*)* is located in a building which provides entertainment for the whole evening; downstairs is a large pub with music and a separate *discoteca*. The restaurant, however, qualifies as a "find," so new at the time of initial inspection that the light switches had still not all been wired. Specialties include *judías con perdiz* and *solomillo pimienta* (thick steak grilled to perfection and coated in a piquant pepper sauce, with a hint of orange). There is a short but select list of local wines at very fair prices.
Mesón del Vino *(Seis de Junio 26* ▥▯*)* is usually reliable.

Valencia
Map 9F8. Valencia. 177km (111 miles) N of Alicante; 360km (223 miles) S of Barcelona. Population: 745,000 **i** *Paz 46* ☎ *(96) 332 4096.*
Spain's third largest city, a major port, an agricultural and manufacturing hub, Valencia has been a focus of political and historical ferment since the Greeks initiated its mercantile tradition in the 2ndCBc. Carthaginians, Romans, Visigoths, Moors, assorted feudal lords and monarchs have fought over it ever since. In the Civil War, it was the last major city to hold out against the victorious rebel armies. Its devastation then accounts for the relative paucity of extant architectural landmarks. It remains a vibrant metropolis well worth exploration, especially during *Las Fallas*.

They have wine, grapes, and melon, ices, songs, dances and the guitar … their great joys and relaxations are religious shows.
Richard Ford, *Handbook for Travellers in Spain*, 1845

Events   In mid-Mar, *Las Fallas*. One of the most exuberant and consuming fiestas in all Spain: towering tableaux (*ninots*) constructed of papier mâché, rags and wood fill every main square. The scenes they illustrate are often fanciful or risqué and always satirical. At midnight on Mar 19, St Joseph's Day, the vast figures are set on fire. The festival was originated by carpenters' guilds burning their wood shavings. Today, massive firework displays light the sky for hours.
    In May, fiestas of the Virgen de los Desamparados and of Corpus Christi. Religious and secular processions.
    In late July and late Dec to mid-Jan, important *ferias* (fairs).

Sights and places of interest
Cathedral † ☆
Plaza de la Virgen ▩ *Open 10am-1.30pm, 4-7pm.*
The campanile on the left of the Baroque facade called the **Miguelete** (▩) was built in the 14th-15thC. Octagonal in shape and Gothic in style, it has 207 interior steps to the roof.
    The cathedral, known as La Seo, was begun in 1262 and completed in 1480, and reflects the Flamboyant Gothic style. An ill-advised Neoclassical

Mesón La Fragua
Paseode Zorrilla 10 ☎(983) 337 102 ▮▮▮▯ ▭ ■ ▤ Y AE ◉ ◉ VISA
Last orders 11.30pm. Closed Sun dinner.

Valladolid's restaurants rarely improvise, but within the limits of the Castilian kitchen they leave few recipes unturned. Of the trio of *mesones* mentioned here, La Fragua is the best. There is a hall leading past cases of trophies awarded to the management, an active *tapas* bar, an open grill heaped with glowing coals adjacent to the large kitchen, and finally four dining rooms. The decoration is typical brick and beams. The vast menu includes *rape frío con langostinos*, *chuletón a la brasa* and *lubina encebollada* (lightly fried sea bass), and also has daily specialties.

Mesón Panero
Marina Escobar 1 ☎(983) 301 673 ▮▮▮▯ to ▮▮▮▮▯ ▭ ■ ▤ ♫ AE ◉ ◉
VISA Last orders 11.30pm. Closed Sun dinner in winter.

At once formal and festive, this *mesón* takes greater care with its Castilian specialties than most. Stuffed partridges and cod in several guises are prominent on the menu. Wines are reasonably priced.

The reason for the name **Mesón Cervantes** (*El Rastro 6 ☎(983) 306 138* ▮▮▮▯) is the nearby house in which the author allegedly lived; traditional Castilian dishes are served in three small, muted rooms. Other traditionally Castilian restaurants in this conservative city include **La Goya** (*Puente Colgante 79 ☎(983) 231 259* ▮▮▮▯) and **El Figon de Recoletos** (*Acera Recoletos 3 ☎(983) 396 043* ▮▮▮▯), which concentrates on succulent roasts slow-baked in Madrid style.

Nightlife

Sheraton (*Vega 3*) is the disco currently in vogue. **Stilton Pub** (*Colmenares 1 ☎(983) 225 131*) aspires to British elegance, with paintings of 19thC Englishmen hanging on green walls. In the pinkish, columned, high-ceilinged **Recoletos** (*Recoletos 11 ☎(983) 229 415*), a disc jockey mans a booth in a corner, but there is only talk, no dancing. **El Moscardón** (*San José 7 ☎(983) 279 163*) has live jazz or folk music on most nights.

Place nearby

Tordesillas (*30km/19 miles SW of Valladolid*). On the bank of the Duero and at an important junction of the Madrid-Galicia and Burgos-Salamanca roads lies this small market town, which was the headquarters of the 16thC Comuneros revolt. Its major sight, **Monasterio de las Claras**, originally built as a palace by Alfonso XI and enlarged for use as a convent by his son, Pedro the Cruel, has some excellent examples of Mudejar craftsmanship, including a magnificent patio.

Parador Nacional de Tordesillas (*Carretera Salamanca, km 152 ☎(983) 770 051* ▮▮▮▯) was built in 1958; service, food and housekeeping all meet the high standards typical of the state chain.

Vascongadas y Navarra (*Basque Provinces and Navarre*)

Map ***13-14****C7&8. Adjoining the Cantabrian Sea and the W end of the Pyrenees bordering France. Airports: Bilbao, Vitoria.*

Las Vascongadas comprise the three Basque provinces of Alava, Vizcaya and Guipúzcoa that flank the corner of the Cantabrian Sea (Bay of Biscay) adjoining France. Its inhabitants prefer the phrase País Vasco (Basque Country), or better still, Euskadi, the name in the ancient Basque language. Although Navarra to the SE is a distinct region, its western half is populated by Basques and its capital, *Pamplona*, has a clear Basque identity. The Basques feel themselves to be a captive nation along with their fellows on the French side of the Pyrenees.

Vic

The origins of the Basques' language, Euskara, have never been
identified and the issue is confused by eight spoken dialects. Their
ancestors probably preceded the Indo-European races that now
populate the continent. For most of their written history, they
have successfully resisted the intrusions of such would-be
conquerors, as the Romans, Moors, Vandals, and Charlemagne.
Only the Catholic Monarchs and their successors have been able to
impose their will over the Basques. In spite of the recent granting
of an unprecedented measure of autonomy, separatist feeling still
runs high in the Basque country. Extremists of the ETA (Euzkadi
Ta Azkatasuna) organization have claimed responsibility for scores
of bombings and murders over recent decades. But support for the
terrorists from the larger Basque community appears to be
waning.

Vic (*Vich*)
*Map 15D10. Barcelona. 66km (41 miles) N of Barcelona;
79km (50 miles) SW of Girona. Population: 30,000.*
This prosperous, industrial town girdled by hills is famous
throughout *Catalunya* for its sausages and *charcuterie*. Other
industry centers on leather, food processing and textiles. The site
has been occupied since ancient times.

Sights and places of interest
Cathedral †
Open 10am-2pm, 4-7pm.
Construction first began on this site in the 11thC, and the extant
Romanesque tower and cloister belong to that period. Most of the rest of the
cathedral was completed at the start of the 19thC. Various renovations that
took place over the eight centuries include the 15thC alabaster retable in the
ambulatory, which, together with the Gothic tomb opposite, is attributed to
the sculptor Pedro Oller. Murals by José María Sert depict scenes from the
life of Christ and his Apostles. The cloister was finished in two stages; the
12thC lower tier is surmounted by a more richly chiselled 14thC upper story.
The ungainly tomb in the center is of the 19thC Catalan philosopher Jaime
Balmes. José María Sert is buried in a side gallery.
Museo Episcopal
Plaza del Obispo Oliva 🖼 *Open summer 10am-1pm, 4-7pm; winter
10am-1pm, Sun and holidays 10am-2pm.*
The museum is in a mansion built in 1809. Most impressive of its varied
collection are Catalan Romanesque paintings on wood and polychrome
ecclesiastical sculptures dating from the 10thC. Other exhibits include
illuminated manuscripts, furniture, jewelry, coins, vestments and a 14thC
alabaster retable by Bernat Saulat.

Other sights
In and near the *plaza mayor* are three more 17thC Gothic churches, a portion
of a 2ndC Roman temple containing a small lapidary collection, and a 15thC
Ayuntamiento. Sections of 14thC fortifications and circular towers
surrounding the town can still be seen.

🛏 **Parador Nacional de Vic**
☎ *(93) 888 7211* ▥ *to* ▥ *31 rms* 🖼 *31* ▦ ━ ☰ ☱ 🅰🅴 ⊙ 🔾
ⓋⒾⓈⒶ
Location: 14km (9 miles) E of Vic. Cool modernity characterizes the interior
and fixtures here, but this 1972 *parador* offsets that impression with
gratifying mountain panoramas that can be viewed from most of its public
and private rooms, and recreational facilities that exceed those of most other
paradores.
▱ ✤ ⏚ 🐾 ⚲ ⛷ ⛸ ⇶ ℘ ♈

━ **Mamma Mia** (*Passeg 61* ☎ *886 3998* ▥) purveys, not unexpectedly,
competent versions of Italian recipes; **La Taula** (*Plaza Don Miguel de
Clariana 4* ☎ *(93) 886 3229* ▥) picks and chooses among the various
regional kitchens of Spain.

Vigo

*Map 10C2. Pontevedra. 28km (18 miles) NW of Túy; 156km
(97 miles) SE of La Coruña. Population: 271,000* **i** *Avenidas
s/n* ☎*(986) 213 057.*

A vigorous Atlantic port city, Vigo is involved in shipping and
seafood processing. Its newer districts are pleasant but its
attraction lies in the small old town and fishermen's quarter, both a
stone's throw from the waterfront. Sir Francis Drake is no hero in
these parts. The most noteworthy of the many marauders to
descend upon this coast over the centuries, he bedevilled with
particular zest the port cities of Galicia, from whence the
"Invincible Armada" was launched. He sacked Vigo in 1585 and
1589, and in 1702 a combined English and Dutch force attacked a
Spanish treasure fleet, which was returning from the Americas,
sending many gold-laden galleons to the bottom of the Ría de
Vigo. They have yet to be recovered.

Sights and places of interest

For splendid panoramas of bay, city and the offshore **Islas Cíes**, go up to the
park that surrounds the **Castillo del Castro** or drive 1km (½ mile) N to the
Ermita de la Guía. Ancient houses with glazed balconies and numerous
shellfish taverns line the few colorful streets of the **old town**. Pause at the
tables outside where women industriously shuck oysters. Make your choice,
then take the plate into the nearest bar to eat with a glass of wine.

☞ The central, modern **Bahía de Vigo** (*Cánovas del Castillo 5* ☎*(986) 226
700* **IIII** *to* **IIII**) succeeds in avoiding sterility and its rooms and restaurants
have magnificent views; **Ciudad de Vigo** (*Concepción Arenal 4-6* ☎*(986) 227
820* **IIII** *to* **IIII**) is a standard commercial hotel typical of the upper-middle
category; the modest but well-appointed **Samil Playa** (*Av. de Samil s/n*
☎*(986) 232 530* **IIII** *to* **IIII**) is across the street from the popular Samil beach.

⇛ **El Castillo**
Monte del Castro ☎*(986) 421 111* **IIII** ⌷ ■■ ▦ ➳ ⌄ ⊙ ⊙ ⓋⒾⓈⒶ *Last
orders 11.30pm. Closed Mon.*
Take advantage of the view from the El Castro castle at this mildly ambitious
bistro tucked up against the N wall. Galician specialties, such as *vieiras
especiales*, *ternera* and *merluza a la brasa*, bear a hint of Francophile subtlety.

⇛ **El Mosquito** ♣
Plaza de J. Villavicencio 4 ☎*(986) 433 570* **IIꞈ** ⌷ ■■ ▦ ⌄ ⓋⒾⓈⒶ *Last
orders 11pm. Closed Sun.*
The dining room is at the back, past the bar and the crowded kitchen where
clouds or steam issue from black pots. Although it certainly isn't plush and the
waitresses can be disorganized at peak times, the *frutas del mar* are
plump, succulent and prepared with greater grace than is customary. Roast
leg of kid is the only meat that deserves to be mentioned, and it is excellent.

⇛ **Puesto Piloto Alcabre**
Av. Atlántica 194 ☎*(986) 297 975* **IIII** ⌷ ■■ ➳ ⌄ ⓋⒾⓈⒶ *Last orders
11.30pm. Closed Sun dinner.*
This animated local restaurant draws inspiration from the French and Italian
cuisines as well as the Spanish, and has, as its specialties, *arroz con vieiras*,
empanadas and *bonito*. Stylish surroundings, alert attendance and pleasant
views of the city are added attractions.

Place nearby

Bayona (*21km/13 miles SW of Vigo*).　Romans, Goths and Moors
battled over this strategic peninsula, constantly razing and
rebuilding its fortifications. The existing ramparts date from the
17thC with sections from the 16thC.

☞ Spain's second largest *parador*, **Parador Nacional Conde de Gondomar**
(*Carretera de Bayona, km 1.6* ☎*(986) 355 000* **IIꞈ** *to* **IIII**) was built in 1966 in

the Galician *pazo* style. It is enclosed within extensive 17thC battlements and enjoys fine views.

Vilanova i la Geltrú (*Villanueva y Geltrú*)

Map 15D10. Barcelona. 50km (31 miles) SW of Barcelona; 46km (29 miles) NE of Tarragona. Population: 45,000.

The bay occupied by this small city serves industrial and touristic needs not altogether successfully. There is a good beach and a mildly interesting fishermen's quarter.

Sights and places of interest

Biblioteca-Museo Balaguer
Av. Victor Balaguer s/n ☒ *Open Tues-Sat 10am-1pm, 4-7pm, Sun 10am-2pm. Closed Mon.*
This museum is named after the 19thC Catalan writer and holds an eclectic collection of rare books, archeological objects, Oriental artworks and El Greco paintings.

Castillo de la Geltrú
De la Torre s/n. Entry details as for Biblioteca-Museo Balaguer.
Although it has been repeatedly restored, this 13thC castle-mansion has a pleasing aspect and now houses a small museum of paintings and ancient Catalan and Moorish artifacts.

Museo Romántico Provincial
Mayor 32 ☒ *Open Easter-Sept 10am-1.30pm, 4-7pm; Oct-Easter 10am-1.30pm, 4-6pm. Closed Mon, or Tues when Mon is holiday.*
This grand mansion of the early 19thC is a time capsule of that period. If everything is not as it was then, no modern visitor can tell. Furniture, crystal, clocks, billiard tables, kitchen implements, crockery, silverware and bed linen are all laid out, as if awaiting the imminent return of the owners.

☞ **César** (*Isaac Peral 4-8* ☎ *(93) 815 1125* ▮▮) is quiet and has a tree-shaded patio.

☲ Seafood is paramount at **Peixerot** (*Passeig Maritim 56* ☎ *(93) 815 0625* ▮▮) and **Chez Bernard et Marguerite** (*Ramón Llull 4* ☎ *(93) 815 5604* ▮▮). Both restaurants are above average.

Vitoria (*Gasteiz*)

Map 13C7. Alava. 64km (40 miles) SW of Bilbao; 112km (69 miles) NE of Burgos. Population: 189,000 ℹ (Alava) Parque de la Florida ☎ *(945) 249 564.*

Capital of the Basque province of Alava, Vitoria was founded as a walled hilltop city by Sancho the Wise, King of Navarra, in 1181; the most famous episode in its history was Wellington's defeat of Joseph Bonaparte in 1813, a victory which virtually decided the Peninsular War. Centered on the cathedral, the old town, with its narrow concentric streets and escutcheoned baronial houses, still remains, but modern Vitoria is an expanding industrial and commercial city.

The sprawling wasteland of concrete apartment blocks and arterial roads on Vitoria's northern approaches may well deter all but the visitor wishing to stop over for the night on the long road south.

The city lies a little to the w of the wine-growing district of La Rioja, and some excellent wines can be sampled in Vitoria's restaurants.

Event In Aug, Fiesta de la Virgen Blanca.

Sights and places of interest

Catedral de Santa María ✝
Santa María.
Built in the 14thC, the cathedral preserves a fortified appearance. The most interesting external feature is the ornate doorway with its Gothic vaulting and

statues. Inside, there are paintings by Rubens and Caravaggio and an impressive *Descent from the Cross* after the school of Van Dyck. An intriguing detail is the bullfighting scene carved on the capital of a pillar between the nave and s aisle.

Other sights

The streets of the old town around the cathedral are linked by steps named after the different trades. The **Plaza de la Virgen Blanca** is lined by old houses with grilles and shields, and at the center is a large monument commemorating the Battle of Vitoria. In the porch of **Iglesia de San Miguel** there is a late Gothic polychrome statue of the *Virgen Blanca*, the city's patron. A niche at the back used to contain the *machete* (or cutlass) over which the procurator-general was sworn into office, on pain of being beheaded if he failed to uphold the city's *fueros* (rights). This is now in the town hall. The **Casa del Cordón** in the Cuchillería, the former street of the cutlers, has a room with a beautiful 13thC Gothic ceiling. In the Correría, the **Portalón**, restored to its 15thC state, houses old utensils, as well as having a stable and cellars with an old wine press. The **archeological museum** (*open Mon-Fri 10am-2pm, 5-7pm; closed Mon*) contains some interesting Celtiberian and Roman finds.

Two museums in the modern part of the city are of interest. The **fine arts museum** (*open Tues-Fri 11am-2pm, 5-7pm, Sat, Sun 11am-2pm*) is devoted mainly to the Flemish school, but also has paintings by Ribera and Carreño. The collection of the **museum of arms and armor** (*open Mon-Fri, Sun 11am-2pm, 5-7pm, Sat and holidays 11am-2pm*) ranges from prehistoric axes to Japanese armor in lacquered steel.

≈ The large, spacious and modern **Canciller Ayala** (*Ramón y Cajal 5* ☎*(945) 220 800* ▐▐▐▌) has comfortable air-conditioned rooms and is the best hotel in Vitoria. A smaller establishment, **Desiderio** (*Colegio San Prudencio 2* ☎*(945) 251 700* ▐▌▔) has no restaurant, but is handy for sightseeing in the old quarter. **General Alava** (*Av. Gasteiz 79* ☎*(945) 222 200* ▐▐▌), a large, modern hotel set in a garden, also lacks a restaurant. **Parador Nacional de Argómaniz** (*Argómaniz, 12km/7 miles outside Vitoria* ☎*(945) 282 200* ▐▐▌) is located on a height within the old Palace of Los Larrea, with splendid views over beautiful countryside. The restaurant specializes in Basque and Navarra dishes and Rioja wines.

≡ Dickens

San Prudencio 17 ☎*(945) 231 882* ▐▐▌ ▤▤ ▥▥ ▨▨ *Last orders 11pm. Closed Aug and Sun.*

With a bar in English style, this is one of the most fashionable places in Vitoria. The cuisine is both *nouvelle* and Basque. Among the best dishes are the pasties of red sea scorpion and of mushrooms with crayfish tails, and the fillets of duck with pears in puff pastry. Traditional fare includes heads of hake, frog's legs, angler fish with Chacolí, baked fish and roast beef. There is a good four-year-old Rioja house wine.

≡ Dos Hermanas

Madre Vedruna ☎*(945) 243 696* ▐▐▌ ▤▤ ▥▥ ▨▨ *Last orders 11pm. Closed mid-Aug to mid-Sept and Sun.*

This dignified and spacious restaurant has been run by the Aguirianos family for almost a century. Game, particularly hare in red wine and partridge *a la cazadora*, is a speciality. The menu lists many regional dishes — stewed oxtail, trout with ham, lamb in *chilindrón* sauce, pig's mouth and *pisto* (*ratatouille*).

≡ Elguea

Cruz Blanca 8 ☎*(945) 225 040* ▐▔ ▤▤ ▥▥ ▨▨ *Last orders 11pm. Closed mid-Aug to mid-Sept, Tues, Sun dinner.*

One of the most popular restaurants in Vitoria, serving simple but well-cooked local dishes. It has its own Rioja from the Alavesa.

Zamora

Map 11D4. Zamora. 65km (40 miles) N of Salamanca; 96km (60 miles) W of Valladolid. Population: 55,000 **i** *Pio XII s/n* ☎*(988) 230 027.*

The old section of this busy provincial capital gives little sense of history or even of architectural uniformity. The exception is its fine collection of Romanesque churches, which have either survived in a relatively pure state, or have unobtrusive additions in later styles.

Event In Holy Week, processions. Visitors are drawn from the entire region. There is even a museum devoted exclusively to a collection of the floats used in the processions year after year.

Sights and places of interest
Cathedral †
Plaza del Castillo s/n.
Its most impressive feature is the great dome, decorated in a scallop pattern borrowed from the Byzantines, and the massive square tower. Most of the building dates from the 12thC, with few later additions. There is a **museum** (*open 11am-1pm, but these times are unpredictable*) which contains a number of 15thC Flemish tapestries.

Other sights
Churches to seek out, all within walking distance of the **Parador**, are **Iglesia de Santa María la Nueva** in the Plaza de Santa María, **Iglesia de Santiago el Burgo** (*currently closed for renovation*) on Calle Santa Clara, and the two 12thC Romanesque churches on Calle Ramos Carrión, **Iglesia de la Magdalena** and **Iglesia de San Ildefonso**. In the Plaza de Zorilla is the 16thC **Palacio de los Momos**, with its Flamboyant Gothic facade. (*All opening hours are unpredictable.*)

⚙ Parador Condes de Alba y Aliste 🏨 🏛
Plaza Viriato 🕿 *(988) 514 497* 🏨🏨 *19 rms* 🛏 *19* 🍴 ☰ ⚞ AE ⦿ ⦿ VISA

Location: *On the edge of the old quarter.* This *parador* is a destination in itself. The 15thC palace has been restored, rather than reconstructed, several times. Damaged during the 16thC Comuneros revolt, it was restored by the Count of Alba. In the 18thC it was converted into a hospice, and in 1968 into a *parador*. Glazed corridors overlook the large interior court. A horse and knight in armor stand by the staircase, tapestries fill the walls and plants creep up corners. The rooms at the back have views of the river.
⌂ ≋ 🅿 🕶 ☇ ⚓ ⇌ 🏊

⚙ II Infantas (*Cortinas de San Miguel 3* 🕿 *(988) 512 875* ❚☐ *to* ❚❚☐) is centrally located, but **Rey Don Sancho** (🕿 *(988) 523 400* ❚❚☐), 3km (2 miles) N on the N630, is preferable and has a good restaurant.

☰ Parîs (*Av. de Portugal 14* 🕿 *(988) 514 325* ❚❚☐) has a Gallic ambience but a regional menu; the fish dishes excel.

Zaragoza (*Saragossa*)
Map 14D8. Zaragoza. 150km (93 miles) W of Lleida; 71km (45 miles) SW of Huesca. Population: 675,000 ℹ Glorieta Pío XII s/n 🕿 *(976) 230 027.*
The Romans called this thriving industrial provincial capital Caesaraugusta, the Moors Sarakusta, which finally led to the present name. Spain's fifth largest city lies along the S bank of the river Ebro in an agricultural region made fertile long ago through irrigation. After the expulsion of the Moors in 1118, Alfonso I made this capital of the Kingdom of Aragón, a position of influence which it held until the marriage of Ferdinand of Aragón and Isabella resulted in the move to Castile.

During the 19thC War of Independence, the French brutally killed half of the civilian populace in two long sieges in 1808-9. The rebuilt city is essentially modern, with broad avenues and much Neoclassical architecture.

While Zaragoza is not a major destination on most visitors' itineraries, it is a logical stop on a trip between Barcelona and

Madrid or the Pyrenees and the south.
Event   In Oct, Fiesta de la Virgen del Pilar.

Sights and places of interest

Aljafería
Castillo s/n **▨** *✗ compulsory. Open 10am-1pm. Closed holidays.*
Surprisingly this 11thC Moorish *alcázar* survived the Christian fervor, albeit with most of its interior fixtures removed. *Artesonado* ceilings and the recessed altar known as a *mihrab* are original, as are many decorative panels employing Arabic script and floral motifs. In the past it has been headquarters of the Inquisition, a barracks, a hospital and a prison. It is currently being renovated.

Basílica de Nuestra Señora del Pilar †
Plaza Catedrales.
Zaragoza's new cathedral was completed during the 16th-17thC using elements of previous churches that once stood on the same site. The rectangular cathedral has a tall belfry at each of its four corners and ten cupolas sheathed in colored tiles. Goya painted one of the frescoes for the interior **Capilla de Nuestra Señora del Pilar**. Beneath it are three altars, one holding a cloaked wooden image of the Virgin with a halo of gemstones, representing a vision by St James on his way to Galicia. Some of the cupola paintings are also by Goya.

La Lonja
Plaza Catedrales. Open 9am-2pm.
Splendid Plateresque detailings characterize both the exterior and interior of the fine Gothic-Renaissance exchange. The great hall is supported by two dozen columns and Gothic vaulting.

Museo Provincial de Bellas Artes
Plaza Sitios 6 **▨** *Open Tues-Sat 10am-2pm. Closed Mon.*
Roman artifacts dominate the ground-floor galleries; the first floor is devoted to Spanish paintings by Goya, Bayeu and Ribera.

La Seo † ☆
Plaza de la Seo.
In 1120, after Alfonso I defeated the Moors, the mosque was razed and construction of the cathedral began. It was not completed until 1520, and although essentially Gothic it incorporates every architectural mode from Mudejar to Renaissance to Baroque. The dome over the crossing is 16thC, the bell tower 17thC, the main portal 18thC. Inside, double aisles and chapels surround the 15thC choirstalls, bordered by a 16thC grille. The *capilla mayor* has an alabaster altarpiece and lantern, both of the 15thC. The **tapestry museum** (**▨** *open 9am-2pm, 4-6pm*) displays Gothic and Renaissance tapestries, and the **treasury** (*entry details same as tapestry museum*) has a collection of ecclesiastical relics, sculptures, chalices and intricately embroidered robes.

Hotels

Gran Hotel
Costa 5, Zaragoza 1 ☎ *(976) 221 901* **◉** *58010* **▥** *169 rms* **▭** *169* **▦**
▬ ⇶ *AE* **◉** **◉** *VISA*
Location: Three streets E of the Paseo de la Independencia. This stately old hotel was completely overhauled in a 1983 reconstruction intended to approach the elegance of the Ritz hotels in *Barcelona* and *Madrid*.
↕ ⌂ ⛵ ♈

Rey Alfonso I
Coso 17, Zaragoza 3 ☎ *(976) 218 290* **◉** *58226* **▥** *to* **▥** *117 rms*
▭ *117* **▦ ⇶** *AE* **◉** **◉** *VISA*
Location: Just w of the Plaza de España. This hotel is beginning to show its age. The ground-floor cafeteria is a constant buzz of activity, the first-floor bar-restaurant is always full and — perhaps as a result — parking is a serious problem.
↕ ⌂ ⚓ ♈

≈ Other recommended hotels are: **Corona de Aragon** (*César Augusto 13* ☎(976) 430 100 **▥**); **Palafox** (*Casa Jiménez s/n* ☎(976) 237 700 **▥**); **Ramiro I** (*Coso 123, Zaragoza 1* ☎(976) 298 200 **▥**); **La Romareda** (*Asín y Palacios 11, Zaragoza 9* ☎(976) 351 100 **▥**).

SPECIAL INFORMATION

Restaurants

Los Borrachos ♣
Paseo de Sagasta 64 ☎ *(976) 275 036* ▥ ⊡ ▦ ▤ ╼ ⅄ 𝐴𝐸 ⊕ ⊙
𝑉𝐼𝑆𝐴 *Last orders 11.30pm. Closed Aug and Sun.*
Caza, hígado con uvas, mero a la piña, pâté de la casa and *lenguado* are frequent specialties in this quirkily homespun restaurant. There is a good relationship between price and quality of food.

Costa Vasca
Coronel Valenzuela 13 ☎ *(976) 277 339* ▥ ⊡ ▤ ⅄ ⊕ ⊙ 𝑉𝐼𝑆𝐴 *Last orders 11pm. Closed Sun, Christmas.*
Diners at Costa Vasca are greeted by the host dressed in his chef's apron and then ushered to the crisply decorated first-floor dining room. A champagne cocktail and a *tapa* of sausages are brought, unbidden, by the attentive staff. Helpings of carefully prepared dishes, including *solomillo* and *merluza*, are abundant.

Mesón del Carmen
Hernán Cortés 4 ☎ *(976) 211 151* ▥ ⊡ ▦ ▤ ⅄ ⊕ ⊙ 𝑉𝐼𝑆𝐴 *Last orders 11.30pm.*
This local landmark is a totally authentic Aragonese restaurant. Regional specialties include *menestra de verduras*, *magras con tomate* and *ternasco al horno*.

⇶ Other useful restaurants include: **Horno Asador Goyesco** (*Manuel Lasala 44* ☎*(976) 356 871* ▥); **Savoy** (*Coso 42* ☎*(976) 224 916* ▥); **Txingudi** (*Agustin de Quinto 4* ☎*(976) 457 475* ▥).

Restaurant nearby
Villanueva de Gallego (*14km/9 miles N of Zaragoza*).

La Casa del Ventero (*Paseo del 18 de Julio 24* ☎*(976) 115 187* ▥) is run by a couple — Tonio from Aragón and Mireille from Lyon in France. He is in charge of the dining room; she is responsible for the kitchen. The menu concentrates on regional dishes, but also features imaginative specialties, particularly from France. Examples include bass cooked with fennel, salmon *en croûte* and stuffed shoulder of lamb. There is a good wine list, and it is advisable to reserve a table.

Biographies

The following selection of notable figures associated with Spain pays particular attention to those mentioned in this book.
'Abd-al-Rahman III, al-Nasir li-din-Allah (792-852)
First Caliph of Córdoba and perhaps the greatest of the Moorish rulers of al-Andalus, under whom it became one of the most powerful states in Europe.
Azaña y Díaz, Manuel (1880-1940)
Prime minister 1931-33 and 1936 until elected President of the Second Republic. He was titular head of the Republican Government during the Spanish Civil War, resigning in 1939.
Balboa, Vasco Núñez de (c.1475-1519)
Balboa discovered the Pacific Ocean by crossing the isthmus of Panama. Soon afterward he was executed by a vengeful former superior.
Benítez, Manuel (1936-)
"El Cordobés" emerged as a matador in the late 1950s and electrified millions of bullfighting *aficionados* by his flamboyant, swaggering style. He performed in provincial *corridas* well into his late forties.

Boabdil "el Rey Chico" (died c.1538)
Last Moorish ruler in Spain who, having dethroned his father in 1482, was forced to surrender Granada to the Catholic Monarchs 10yrs later.

Cano, Alonso (1601-67)
Known as the Spanish Michelangelo because of his creative versatility as architect, sculptor and court painter, he is most famous for his *Life of the Virgin* in Granada Cathedral.

Cervantes, Miguel de (1547-1616)
The reigning figure of Spanish letters, certainly in terms of the universality of his work, Cervantes lived more fully than any of his fictional characters. Armed with little formal education but a wide-ranging curiosity, he left Castile for Italy in 1569, becoming in turn aide to a cardinal and a soldier. He returned to Spain and wrote *Don Quixote de la Mancha* which was published in 1605 to great critical acclaim.

Charles I of Spain (1500-58)
As Emperor Charles V, he was for nearly 40yrs both King of Spain and Holy Roman Emperor. Almost constant warfare marked his tenure, and this resulted in the depletion of much of his European Empire.

Churriguera, José (1665-1725)
His name was given to the ornate and sumptuous Churrigueresque style of architecture, developed by members of his family and the Quiñones family.

Cid, Rodrigo Díaz de Vivar (c.1043-99)
A knight who served both Moorish and Castilian kings, "El Cid" is immortalized in the ballad *El Cantar de Mío Cid*, which proclaims his heroic role in the wars against the Moors.

Columbus, Christopher (1451-1506)
Genoese explorer sponsored by Ferdinand and Isabella to discover a western route to China. (See **Ferdinand II of Aragón** and **Isabella I of Castile**.) He actually landed in the Bahamas and was the first European to reach the Americas, thus opening up the New World to Spain.

Cortés, Hernán (1485-1547)
Commissioned by Diego de Velázquez to head an expedition to Mexico, he seized the capital in 1521, earning for himself the title "Conqueror of Mexico."

Covarrubias, Alonso de (1488-1570)
One of the great Plateresque architects, who achieved early recognition as a consultant for *Salamanca* cathedral, and later became master of the works at *Toledo* cathedral.

Dalí, Salvador (1904-   )
A Surrealist of enormous public stature, famous for his eccentricity. His work combines exquisite draftsmanship with an often macabre vision.

Falla, Manuel de (1876-1946)
Although influenced by such international composers as Ravel and Debussy, Falla's music was largely dominated by Spanish flamenco and folk music.

Ferdinand III of Castile (1199-1252)
He united the two kingdoms of Castile and León and made successful advances in the war to reconquer Spain from the Moors. He was canonized in 1671.

Ferdinand II of Aragón (1452-1516)
All of Spain except Granada became united for the first time on his marriage to **Isabella I of Castile** in 1469. The Moors were finally defeated at Granada in 1492 and he became Ferdinand V of Spain. Ferdinand and Isabella, usually referred to as *Los Reyes Católicos*,

the Catholic Monarchs, ended feudal anarchy and supported great building and educational programs.

Franco, Francisco (1892-1975)
A general at 32, Franco associated himself with the political right and, at the start of the Civil War, assumed command of the Nationalist forces. By the end of the war he had consolidated the splintered rightist parties under the Falangist rubric. In 1947 he declared Spain a monarchy with himself as regent, later nominating the present king as his successor.

García Lorca, Federico (1898-1936)
Playwright, poet and musician inspired by every aspect of Spanish life. His liberal political views led to his death at the hands of Nationalist soldiers during the Civil War.

Gaudí i Cornet, Antonio (1852-1926)
Catalan architect of unique and audacious designs, employing sinuous and fantastical forms and eccentric materials. Most famous of his buildings is the Templo de la Sagrada Familia in *Barcelona*.

Godoy, Manuel (1767-1851)
Adviser to Charles IV and lover to his queen, Godoy became prime minister at 25. His intrigues with Napoleon led to his downfall in 1808 followed by the abdication of the king and the placing of Napoleon's brother Joseph on the throne.

Goya y Lucientes, Francisco José de (1746-1828)
His early works combine elements of Neoclassicism with Rococo gaiety and vivid color, and contrast strongly with the dramatic and sinister paintings of his later years, most notably the so-called Black Paintings. Goya was court painter for many years and his savagely satiric style was apparently viewed merely as Realism.

Greco, El (1541-1614)
Domenikos Theotokópoulos, a Cretan who studied painting in Rome and under Titian in Venice before settling in Toledo in 1577. He developed an expressionistic style characterized by elongated features and a preference for dark colors.

Ignatius of Loyola, St (1491-1556)
A soldier turned missionary, he founded the Society of Jesus in Rome in 1540. Under his guidance, the Jesuits became a major influence in the Counter-Reformation.

Isabella I of Castile (1451-1504)
She succeeded her brother Henry IV in 1474 but had to battle for five years with her niece "La Beltraneja" in order to retain her position. With her husband Ferdinand V (see **Ferdinand II of Aragón**) she was a dominant force in the final stages of the Reconquest of Spain from the Moors. She sponsored the expeditions of **Columbus** and established the Inquisition against Jews, Moors and Protestants.

Joselito (1895-1920)
This was the professional name of José Gómez, who was acknowledged as a matador of skills rivaled only by the nearly legendary **Manolete**. The inevitable comparisons may be unfair to both, for Joselito was killed by a bull at 25.

Juan Carlos de Borbón y Battenburg (1938-   )
Grandson of Alfonso XIII, last King of Spain before the Civil War. He was chosen and groomed as a successor to **Franco**. Since the beginning of his reign he has done much to guide the tender democracy toward increasing stability.

Lope de Vega Carpio, Félix (1562-1635)
Prolific poet, novelist and dramatist, he is regarded as the founder of the Spanish theater.

Manolete, Manuel Rodríguez y Sánchez (1883-1923)
Most famous of all Spanish bullfighters, renowned for skill and

grace, he was tragically killed in a *corrida* at Linares.
Medina Sidonia, Duke of (1550-1619)
Commander-in-chief of the ill-fated Armada in 1588. Despite this disaster he was retained by **Philip II**, and suffered further defeats at Cádiz and Gibraltar.
Miró, Joan (1893-1983)
His abstract and lyrical brand of Surrealism, influenced by Paul Klee, has enjoyed huge success around the world.
Murillo, Bartolomé Estéban (1617-82)
Sevilla's most honored painter focused on religious themes and portraits, their piety underscored by his characteristically dramatic use of light. He died of injuries sustained in a fall from a scaffold while at work on a church mural in Cádiz.
Ortega y Gasset, José (1883-1955)
Philosopher and humanist, who received international acclaim on the publication of *The Revolt of the Masses*. He also founded the Institute of Humanities in Madrid.
Philip II (1527-98)
Also King of Portugal from 1580. Married first to Mary Tudor of England. His desire to retain the Spanish Empire intact was frustrated by wars with Italy, the Low Countries and England, which resulted in the loss of the Northern Provinces and the defeat of the Armada. He supervised personally the building of the *Escorial*.
Philip V (1683-1746)
The first of the Bourbons to assume the Spanish throne. This act precipitated the War of the Spanish Succession, which lasted until 1714 when, after the Treaty of Utrecht, Philip was recognized as King of Spain. During this time Gibraltar was ceded to the British.
Picasso, Pablo (1881-1973)
The most renowned artist of the 20thC, whose versatile career encompassed several major modern movements. His feelings about the Spanish Civil War were represented in *Guernica* (in the Prado Museum, *Madrid*).
Pizarro, Francisco (c.1476-1541)
With his partner and rival, Diego de Almagro, he conquered Peru in 1533 with a tiny force, largely by treachery and cunning. He was later murdered by Almagro's son.
Primo de Rivera, José Antonio (1903-36)
Son of the dictator, Miguel Primo de Rivera, the supreme ruler of Spain from 1923-30, José Antonio founded the Falangist party and was killed by Loyalists in the Civil War. Both he and his father were heroes of the victorious Nationalists.
Ribera, José (1591-1652)
A Baroque artist who worked for much of his life in Naples, at that time a Spanish possession. His somber early work, inspired by Caravaggio, later gave way to brighter colors.
Segovia, Andrés (1893-1986)
Through his adaptations of early Spanish music and his virtuosity, he established the guitar as a serious classical instrument. **De Falla** and Villa-Lobos both wrote works especially for him.
Siloé, Diego de (c.1495-1563)
Sculptor and architect whose works are characteristic of the Spanish High Renaissance. He succeeded Enrique de Engas as master of the works at *Granada* cathedral, which is generally considered his finest work.
Tapies, Antonio (1923-)
Catalan leader of the Spanish Abstractionist painters who emerged in the 1960s. His concern with surface texture has led him to experiment with a variety of mixed media.

Teresa of Avila, St (1515-82)
A pragmatic mystic whose writings are still admired for their lively wit and good humor. She was an important reforming influence on the Carmelite order, founding no less than 17 religious communities around the country.

Torquemada, Tomás de (1420-98)
Confessor and inquisitor-general to the Catholic Monarchs, he became head of the Inquisition in 1483 and was noted for his ruthless punishment of offenders. He was largely responsible for the expulsion of Jews from Spain in 1492.

Trajan (c.AD52-117)
A Spaniard who became the first Roman emperor from the provinces. He was succeeded by another Spaniard, Hadrian, who was born in the Roman city of Itálica near Sevilla.

Velázquez, Diego Rodríguez de Silva (1599-1660)
Master of atmospheric portraiture, he was hailed as the greatest painter of his century. At 25 he was appointed court painter to Philip IV and subsequently painted many members of the royal family. His sharply delineated chiaroscuro evolved in his later works into a subtler yet richer use of light.

Vespucci, Amerigo (1454-1512)
In the service of Spain, he made several expeditions along the coast of South and Central America, proving that the discoveries of **Columbus** were not the Indies but a separate continent — to which his name was given.

Wellington, Arthur Wellesley, Duke of (1767-1852)
As commander of the allied forces during the Peninsular War, he forced Napoleon's army back into France in 1814 and as a result was created both Duke of Wellington and Duke of Ciudad Rodrigo — titles still held by the present duke.

Zurbarán, Francisco (1598-1664)
One of Spain's finest religious painters. He traveled around monasteries depicting episodes from the lives of the saints, often using monks as his models. In 1628 he was appointed official painter to Sevilla.

Spanish wines

Spain has for too long been tagged with producing inexpensive wine in branded bottles; in fact the country makes wines in perhaps a greater variety of styles than any other in the world. They include the famous apéritif and dessert wines of Jerez and Málaga, the table wines of the Rioja, now challenging those of France, the *pétillant* young growths of Galicia in the wet northwest, together with a whole gamut of still and sparkling wines from Catalunya, a host of very drinkable *ordinaires* from the great central plateau, and numerous brandies, vermouths and liqueurs.

In general, Andalucía in the hot south makes fortified wines for drinking before or after a meal; the temperate north produces the best table wines; while the sturdy wines from the prolific central area are for everyday drinking. There is hardly a region of Spain, apart from the wet north coast and the more mountainous districts, which does not make wine of some kind.

It is not difficult to visit the larger *bodegas* (wineries) but for the smaller ones a knowledge of Spanish is helpful, as well as a letter from a wine shipper or an introduction from a local contact such as the manager of your hotel.

Jerez and Andalucía

Sherry, the most famous of Spanish wines, was well known as "sack" in medieval times and even earlier, and has been shipped from Spain in increasing quantities since Sir Francis Drake's raid on Cádiz and "rape of the butts" in 1587. It comes in various styles, of which the most important are the light, dry *finos*, such as "Tío Pepe" or "La Ina", drunk chilled as an apéritif; the amber-colored and fuller-bodied *amontillados* with their nutty flavor; the *olorosos*, dark, fragrant, full in body and higher in alcohol, but still, in their natural state, as in "Rio Viejo," completely dry and drunk as apéritifs; and the dessert wines, such as "Bristol Cream," made, according to type, by sweetening either *olorosos* or *finos*.

Together with Puerto de Santa María to its s and Sanlúcar de Barrameda, the home of *manzanilla*, to the NW, *Jerez de la Frontera* is the main center for sherry production. The vineyards lie in rolling, hilly country, mainly to the N and W of Jerez, and the best of the grapes are grown in the *albariza* soil, dazzlingly white in the strong summer sun, giving the landscape an unreal, almost lunar aspect. The most pleasant times to visit Jerez are in the late spring or early fall when the vines are changing color, and it is at its liveliest during the colorful Fiesta de la Vendimia, or harvest festival, held in early September.

Of all wine establishments, the great arched sherry *bodegas*, so often likened to cathedrals, are perhaps the grandest in scale. Here the wine is matured in long tiers of oak butts known collectively as *soleras* by a process of continuous blending or "refreshment," so that the young wine slowly takes on the characteristics of the older, making it possible to maintain the style of a particular sherry year in, year out.

You may visit the largest *bodegas*, such as those of González Byass, Pedro Domecq and Williams & Humbert, simply by turning up at visiting hours, which are normally 9.30am-1pm and you will be shown around by an English-speaking guide. In other cases it is advisable to telephone beforehand or to enlist the help of the Exportadores de Sherry SA (☎*(956) 341 046*), where they speak English. All the visits end with a generous tasting and there is often a small shop where the wines and the traditional sherry glasses or *copitas* may be bought.

All the *bodegas* have points of special interest apart from their wines. At Pedro Domecq, they will show you butts laid down for Pitt, Nelson, Wellington and others; González Byass cherishes some small sherry-fed mice; in the beautiful gardens at Harvey's there is a pool containing a 65-year-old Mississippi alligator; Williams & Humbert maintain large stables and a magnificent collection of coaches and harness-work, used each year at the harvest festival; Caballero in Puerto de Santa María has restored the old Castle of San Marcos; while the *bodegas* of Lustau are built into the old city wall of Jerez. Apart from such *pièces de resistance*, most of the old *bodegas*, notably those of Osborne, Duff Gordon and Terry in Puerto de Santa María, and Garvey and Valdespino in Jerez, are built around charming, hidden patios, hung with bougainvillea or lined with olives or palms. More functional in style, some of the new *bodegas* are outstanding examples of modern architecture, particularly that of the enormous Bodegas Internacionales, the largest single building in Jerez.

Andalucía produces two other well-known wines. Those from Montilla-Moriles, whose production centers on the attractive hill town of Montilla, 35km (22 miles) s of Córdoba, are very similar to sherry (the styles are the same), but are traditionally fermented in earthenware jars before being matured in *solera*. The heyday of the sweet dessert wines of Málaga was in Victorian times, but Málaga produces others less sweet, such as the glorious bittersweet Scholtz "Solera 1885," also made in *solera*, but resembling a good tawny port.

Rioja

The Rioja, an upland district lying along the Ebro valley on the fringes of the Basque country, makes the best-known of Spanish table wines. Predominantly red, they are fairly light in body, resembling Bordeaux more than Burgundies, and are characterized by their oaky nose and flavor resulting from long maturation in cask. The region has been making wines since pre-Roman times, but in their present style they date from the phylloxera epidemic of the late 19thC in France, when *vignerons* from over the border settled in the region and introduced the wine-making methods current in Bordeaux, notably the destalking of the grapes and prolonged maturation in 225 liter (49.5 gallon) oak *barricas*.

Most of the large *bodegas* receive visitors (*a list is available from Wines of Spain, 22 Manchester Square, London W1M 5AP, UK, or, in Spain, contact Grupo de Exportadores in Logroño ☎ (941) 222 837*), but it is always advisable to telephone the *bodega* the day before to make arrangements. The largest group of *bodegas* is in Haro, capital of the sub-region of La Rioja Alta, which, with the adjacent Rioja Alavesa, produces the most delicate wine. Haro is the home of such famous firms as Bilbainas, CVNE, Federico Paternina, La Rioja Alta, Muga and López de Heredia, and also the government wine laboratory and the wine shop of Juan González Muga, specializing in old and rare vintages and "special offers" of Rioja from local *bodegas*. Another interesting port of call is the Casa del Vino in Laguardia, an information center for the wine from the Rioja Alavesa with extensive and extremely well-laid-out exhibits.

Production of the wines is strictly supervised by the Consejo Regulador, which authorizes the use of small labels on the back of the bottle to categorize different qualities. Of the select types, *vino de crianza* must be aged for not less than two calendar years, of which one at least must be in oak casks of 225 liters. The red *reservas* spend a year in cask and two in bottle, while the *gran reservas* are matured for two years in cask and three in bottle, and must be aged for a total of seven years before leaving the *bodega*. The Rioja also makes attractively fresh and fruity white wines, "cold fermented" and without age in oak.

Vintage chart of Rioja wines

1964	excellent	1978	very good
1968	good	1979	poor
1970	excellent	1980	good
1971	poor	1981	very good
1972	very poor	1982	excellent
1973	good	1983	good
1974	average	1984	average
1975	average	1985	good
1976	good	1986	good
1977	very poor		

Navarra

Navarra is noted for its red and rosé wines, made from the same grape varieties as those from the Rioja, which it borders in the E. Some of the most select come from the Señorío de Sarría and the Vinícola Navarra, both near Pamplona. Those from the Riberia

Baja in the Ebro valley to the s, whose largest *bodega* is that of Julian Chivite, are fuller-bodied and more alcoholic.

Catalunya

The best of the still wines from Catalunya rival those of the Rioja; it also produces the great bulk of Spanish sparkling wine and excellent brandies made by the Charentais method. The Penedès, centering on the wine towns of Vilafranca del Penedès and San Sadurní de Noya, lies just sw of Barcelona. *Bodegas* such as Masia Bach, Marqués de Monistrol, René Barbier and Jean León make good wines, both white and red, but the best-known Catalunyan still wines are from Bodegas Torres in Vilafranca, which exports world-wide. This family-owned concern has displayed great initiative, both in acclimatizing noble vines from abroad, such as the Chardonnay and Cabernet Sauvignon, and in its technical methods (it was a pioneer in Spain of "cold fermentation" for wines like its "Viña Sol" and "Esmeralda"), and the red "Gran Coronas Black Label" was in 1980 judged even better in its 1970 vintage than Château Latour by an international jury in Paris. The *bodegas* of Torres in Vilafranca (☎*(93) 890 0100*) may be visited without a prior appointment.

The sparkling wines from the Penedès are made strictly by the Champagne method, albeit from local grapes, and have become increasingly popular in world markets because of their very reasonable price and good quality. The industry centers on San Sadurní de Noya, a place hollow with cellars, where the largest concerns are those of Codorníu and Freixenet; both welcome visitors without appointment. The visit to Codorníu, which entertains some 160,000 visitors each year, is especially interesting. Said to be the largest maker of sparkling wines in the world, it is set in decorative gardens, and the old buildings have been declared a national monument. There are some 14km (9 miles) of underground cellars, and the old press house has been converted into an extensive wine museum. The other museum in this area which you should certainly visit is the Museo del Vino in Vilafranca del Penedès, which contains Greek, Roman and Phoenician amphorae, old wine-making equipment, tableaux of wine-making through the ages, and collections of drinking vessels and paintings. The visit ends in a small bar, where local wines may be sampled.

There are various other demarcated regions in Catalunya making worthwhile wines, notably those of Tarragona and Priorato in the s of the province, and of Alella and Ampurdán-Costa Brava n of Barcelona. Pereleda might well be your first stop after crossing the Pyrenees from France. The winery, near Figueras, centers on a 14thC monastery and castle and also embraces an interesting wine museum open to visitors.

Castilla la Vieja

This heartland of Old Spain, extending northward and westward from Madrid, makes a variety of very drinkable wines. Some 40km (25 miles) e of Valladolid, the small domain of Vega Sicilia makes some of the most sought-after red wines of Spain, intensely fruity in bouquet and flavor, and obtainable only at the best hotels and restaurants. Visits are strictly by appointment, and here you will need an introduction from an established wine merchant or shipper.

A little farther to the e along the Duero river, Peñafiel is making red wines of growing prestige, mainly in the local cooperative. Its cellars for maturing the wines lie beneath the fairytale castle; if paying a visit, do not fail to see the extraordinary medieval jousting ground below the castle. To the w of Valladolid, Rueda has long been famous for wines in the manner of sherry, but is now producing and shipping fresh and attractive young white wines, notably the Marqués de Riscal. In León, the crisp red and white wines, made by VILE (Vinos de León), a consortium of local growers, have achieved considerable success abroad.

Galicia

Galician wines are entirely individual; made with grapes from high-growing vines, they have a slight bubble on the tongue and much resemble the *vinhos verdes* or "green wines" of neighboring Portugal. Best are the fruity and fragrant Albariños from Cambados, near Pontevedra, which celebrates a festival in mid-Aug, where they may be sampled in variety.

Wine in bulk

The great bulk of wine for everyday drinking comes from the vast central plateau of La Mancha, stretching s from Madrid toward Andalucía. Best of the reds, fresh and clear, is Valdepeñas, often served in the *tabernas* of the old quarter of Madrid; the whites have been much improved by cold fermentation. The other great supplier of everyday wines is the Levante, the area on the Mediterranean coast stretching southward from Catalunya. Wines such as those from the demarcated zones of Valencia, Alicante, Yecla and Jumilla are full-bodied, spicy and high in alcohol in the Mediterranean manner, but less expensive than Riojas or Catalan wines and well worth trying. The wines of the Baleares — always excepting the well-made estate growths of José L. Ferrer from Binisalem in Mallorca — are generally similar, and the islands are, on balance, importers of wine from the mainland.

Spain for children

The Spanish notion of "family" means that children are involved in everything that the family does. This fact leads to a significant absence of specifically children-oriented entertainment, but a few exceptions to this are suggested below.

Zoos and game parks

Most large cities have at least a small zoo, usually within the confines of their major parks, but those that are best arranged and maintained are in Madrid and Barcelona. In *Madrid*, the zoo (*half-price for children*) is in **Casa del Campo**, w of the city, and has as its primary attraction a panda couple and one of the only panda cubs ever born in captivity. In *Barcelona*, the substantial zoo (*half-price for children*) is along the se border of **Parque de la Ciudadela**. Skillfully laid out and managed, it incorporates an aquarium with an arena for performing dolphins. Near **Porto Cristo**, on the island of *Mallorca*, is the **Auto Safari Mallorca**. An hour's drive through an imitation of the African veldt allows visitors glimpses of wild animals grazing. At the end is a small zoo of tame animals, some of which can be fed.

Amusement parks

Barcelona has two *parques de atracciones*, one on **Tibidabo**, the other on **Montjuic**, the two hills looming above the city. The first is an amusing relic of the 1930s, with tame airplane rides and a

Ferris wheel; the other strives for 1960s modernity, but lacks joyfully terrifying roller coaster thrills (*opening times for both are erratic, so ask the conserje at your hotel to check before setting out*). There is another rather tame amusement park in **Casa del Campo** in *Madrid*. On the Costa del Sol, near Benalmádena, is **Tivoli World** (*Arroyo de la Miel* ☎*(952) 441 896/9 for information* ✉), an ambitious amusement park which tries hard to give good value with over 30 rides, and free live attractions such as performances of the cancan and flamenco.

Museums and monuments

Since little effort is made by most museums to cater to the curiosity of youngsters, the majority will predictably bore them within minutes. However, the more bloodthirsty exhibits, for example in wax museums, tend to draw their attention. There is **Museo de Cera** (see *Other museums* in *Madrid*) and the heavily advertised version on Las Ramblas in Barcelona.

The armory of **Palacio Real** in *Madrid* has not only knights on horseback but also child-size suits of armor designed for the royal progeny. Comparable attractions include **Museo Naval** (see *Other museums* in *Madrid*) and **Museo Marítimo** in *Barcelona*, with a replica of Columbus' *Santa María* moored nearby.

Castles

No other country gratifies children's fantasies of daring knights and fierce dragons as Spain does. The city of *Avila* is surrounded by medieval walls, and many others retain their fortifications. Children will particularly enjoy staying in castles, many of which have been converted into *paradores*. Especially evocative are those at *Alarcón*, *Sigüenza* and Oropesa (see *Hotel nearby* in *Talavera de la Reina*).

Sports and activities

Bullfighting

Although long ago eclipsed in the numbers of its *aficionados* by soccer, bullfighting remains popular. As an activity, it falls into an unclassifiable area between sport and ritual. The season is from early March to mid-October, although fights are occasionally scheduled at fiesta times in winter. Weekly fights are held in the arenas during the season, usually on Sunday, often on one or two other nights, and on feast days. They begin promptly at the scheduled hour, usually 5 or 6pm, and last about two and a half hours. Six bulls, all specially bred and weighing approximately 450kg (992lbs), compose a standard card, with three *matadores* taking on two each, in rotation.

Once the opening parade of participants is over, the *corrida* has three distinct acts, or *tercios*. In the first, after the bull's release, the *matador* and his *peones* (assistants) attract his attention with capes, quickly taking refuge behind the stockade that encircles the arena. After observing the bull's movements, the *matador* approaches the animal carrying a large flowing cape, magenta on one side, yellow on the other. The colors are traditional but have no effect on the bull, which is color-blind. When the bull charges, the *matador* moves the cape in an often complicated series of maneuvers, intended both to test the bull and to display his artistry. Two men on horseback, the *picadores*, now enter the ring, wearing flat-brimmed hats with rounded crowns and armored leggings and carrying long lances with steel points. The bull is goaded into charging the right side of the heavily padded horse, while the *picador* thrusts a pike into his shoulders. The bull is encouraged to repeat the act once or twice. Should the *picador* jab or pump the pike into the bull or take too long in making the animal back off, a crescendo of derisive whistles comes from the enthusiastic audience.

In the second *tercio*, the bull is incited into a charge and men called *banderilleros* run toward him, dancing out of the way of the horns while simultaneously thrusting three pairs of *banderillas* (ribboned darts) into the beast's withers, where they are meant to stay. Some *matadores* place their own darts to please the crowd.

The final *tercio*, the *faena*, begins with the *matador* ceremoniously saluting the *presidente* (the presiding official of the proceedings). He then dedicates the bull to a friend or to the crowd. Then, accepting a *muleta* (a small red cape sewn to a stick) from an assistant, he carries this and a sword toward his still very dangerous opponent. Again and again, the animal is made to charge. The *matador* is judged by the artistry of his capework and his daring in placing himself in ever greater jeopardy. After some minutes, he goes to the stockade, exchanges swords, and returns to the bull. With the *muleta* in his left hand, pointing down and to the side, he looks along the blade of the sword toward the hump of the bull's back. Catching the drama of the moment, the *matador* finally lunges forward, attempting to thrust the blade into the narrow space between the animal's shoulders and down into its heart. Rarely is the thrust true, and further attempts must be made until the bull goes down. Once in the sand, the bull is dispatched with a stab into his brain, either with a dagger or a special sword called a *verduguillo*.

A good performance by a *matador* is acknowledged by one of several degrees of symbolic award, signalled by the crowd waving white handkerchiefs in the direction of the *presidente*. If he responds with a similar signal, one of the bull's ears is presented to the *matador*. If the *aficionados* persist, the other ear is bestowed, and on very rare occasions when it has been a spectacular performance, the tail as well. The *matador* then makes a triumphal circuit of the arena, brandishing his trophies, and dodging a barrage of flowers, hats and the wineskins called *botas*. A team of horses then drags the bull from the ring, and the sand is raked ready for the next fight.

There are also variations of the *corrida*; a *rejoneo* features a *toreador* in Andalucian riding costume who conducts the entire *corrida* singlehandedly, from horseback, often an additional attraction to the usual card. At a *goyesca*, called after the painter, Goya, the *matadores* are dressed in 18thC costume; and a *novillada* is for apprentice *matadores* against younger, smaller bulls.

Tickets are purchased at the bullring on the day of the fight, at kiosks and offices around town a day or two before or, for an extra commission, the hotel hall porter can obtain them. Seats are in several categories and price ranges, varying from the "*sol*" section, in the sun, the least expensive, to "*sombra*," in the shade throughout, the most costly; their relative proximity to the ring will make a difference too. Seats are normally uncomfortable, so rent a pillow from the vendors inside the arena. Ticket prices also vary according to the importance of the bullring, the box-office appeal of the *matadores*, and whether the *corrida* is part of a larger celebration. It is important to arrive on time, or you may find the gates closed.

Casino gambling

Although casinos have only recently been introduced to Spain, there are now 18, mainly in resort areas outside large cities. Customers must be 21yrs old or over and must show their passports before paying the admission charge. All casinos have adequate restaurants and discos, or nightclubs, or both. Games usually included are chemin de fer, blackjack, American craps, French roulette, and *punto y banco*. Slot machines are usually available. Casinos are presently in operation at the following locations: Alfajarín (near Zaragoza), Benalmádena, Ibiza, Lloret de Mar (near Girona), Palma Nova (Mallorca), Marbella, Perelada (near Girona), Puzol (near Valencia), San Javier (near Murcia), San Pedro de Ribas (near Barcelona), San Sebastián, Santander, La Toja (near Pontevedra), Torrelodones (near Madrid) and Villajoyosa (near Alicante).

Fishing and hunting

Opportunities for these activities are equally widespread, but obtaining the proper permissions and licenses is a chore. For information on that subject, write well in advance to Instituto Nacional para la Conservación de la Naturaleza, Gran Via 35, Madrid, or contact the nearest branch of the Spanish National Tourist Office. Spain is well supplied with game, from ibex (unique to Spain) to wild boar, deer, duck, partridge and chamois. There are over 800 hunting preserves, largely in the mountains, which also provide good trout and salmon fishing. The best locations are the Gredos mountains near Madrid, the Picos de Europa near Santander, and several places throughout the Pyrenees. Deep-sea fishing trips can be arranged at the majority of large ports along the Cantabrian coast, the Costa Brava and Costa del Sol.

Football (soccer)

This is the sport that comes first in the affections of Spanish sports fans. Stadiums in the larger cities accommodate 100,000 or more people. The season is Sept-June and games are usually played on Sunday, starting in the late afternoon.

Golf

Enthusiasts are fond of the numerous courses along the Costa del Sol, some of them private resort communities, others owned by hotels (see hotels in *A-Z*). Madrid has at least ten golf clubs, including La Herrería, Las Lomas-El Bosque and Club de Campo. There are exchange arrangements with clubs in other countries, but it is best to ask your hotel hall porter to check details. In Catalunya there are courses at El Prat and Sitges, sw of Barcelona. In the Alicante region there are courses at Peñas Rojas and Almaina Park, and in the NW there are courses near San Sebastián, La Coruña and Santander. Clubs and caddies are available to rent at all courses; in the private clubs, expect to pay both a visitor's fee and green fees.

Jai-alai

A Basque game that enjoys favor throughout the country and in the Americas, *jai-alai*, also called *pelota*, is played in an enclosed court called a *frontón*, high-ceilinged and usually about 60m (197ft) long. The players have long, curved baskets attached to their throwing arms, in which they catch the solid ball and propel it against the back wall at incredible speeds. Fast, unrelenting and dangerous, the game is easy to grasp (apart perhaps from the scoring system), and most major cities in the N have at least one *frontón*.

Sailing

Sailing is popular in the Islas Baleares and in the resort areas of the Costa Brava and Costa del Sol. Sportfishing boats and crewed or bare-boat charter yachts can be rented at every city with a nautical club, as, for example, at Alicante, La Coruña, Estepona, Marbella, Palma de Mallorca, San Sebastián and Torremolinos. The nearest branch of the Spanish National Tourist Office will have the relevant lists.

Skiing

Few resorts have the cachet of those in the Alps, but the pistes are just as challenging and often less crowded, while costs are lower. Best-developed and organized are those three or four hours' drive N of Barcelona, for example Baqueira-Beret, El Formigal, Núria, Masella and especially La Molina, which has hosted international competitions. About an hour's drive W and N of Madrid, there are sites with less difficult runs including the resorts of Navacerrada, Valdesqui and Valcotos. In the Sierra Nevada near Granada, with a season that sometimes extends from late October to early May, the Solynieve resort is paramount. The mountains inland of the Cantabrian coast have ski centers at Alto Campo and Braña Vieja, both about an hour's journey from Santander. To the N of Zaragoza is Sallent de Gállego, which is now rapidly gaining in popularity.

Tennis

Facilities are available in every resort area as well as in individual hotels (see hotels in *A-Z*), and the majority of courts are hard-surface.

Excursion to the Islas Canarias (Canary Islands)

Area: 7,273sq.km (2,808sq. miles). Population: 1,394,288. Divided into eastern and western administrative provinces, Gran Canaria and Tenerife, they are 1,150km (713 miles) SW of Spain and 115km (71 miles) W of the African coast in the Atlantic Ocean. Getting there by air: Iberia operates a regular service from New York to Las Palmas and Lanzarote, as well as daily flights (except Sun) from New York to Tenerife. All flights go via Madrid. Getting there by ship: Sea Air Holidays (733 Summer St., Stamford, Connecticut 06901 ☎(203) 356 9033) runs winter cruises to the islands; Cunard (555 5th Ave., New York, NY 10017 ☎(212) 880 7500) offers a QE2 cruise May 28-June 5; Melia Travel (12 Dover St., London W1X 4NS, UK ☎(01) 409 1884) has car ferry services from Spain. Getting around the islands: there are regular inter-island air and boat services — inquire locally for details.

Although Spanish is, of course, the language spoken here, similarities between the archipelago and mainland Spain go no further than this. Until the 15thC, the isolated native population was still living in the Stone Age. During the 1400s, however,

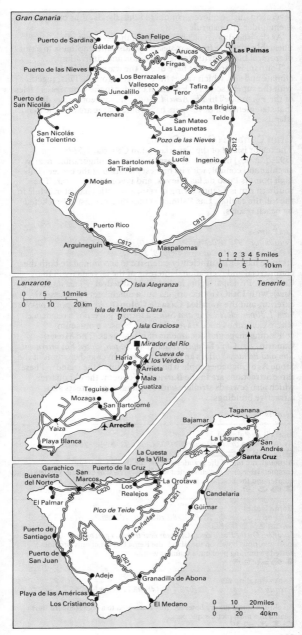

213

several Spanish explorers conquered the islands, thus bringing them under Spanish rule.

As the islands are volcanic in origin, the terrain is often unearthly, veering from a majestic, windswept emptiness to a riot of tropical blooms with dense vegetation and cultivation.

Tourism is paramount here due to the warmth of both climate and sea, which varies little all year around. This, together with the superb scenery, led Virgil to refer to the Canaries as "Isles of the Fortunate" in *The Aeneid*. Today many people may dispute that statement, for developers have ruined large areas of the major islands.

Gran Canaria (*Grand Canary*)

The major island of the Canarias, Gran Canaria, 1,532sq.km (592sq. miles) in area, is of classic volcanic configuration, nearly circular and conical, with its highest elevation at the center. This high point is **Pozo de las Nieves**, and is accessible by car. The southern rim is a sandy string of resorts of little character, while in the NE, the capital, **Las Palmas**, stands on a peninsula bracketed by beach resorts.

Las Palmas

Population: 375,000. Airport: 30km (19 miles) s ☎ (928) 254 140
i Parque de Santa Catalina ☎ (928) 264 623.

Its wide harbor is sufficiently extensive to accommodate both the commercial and recreational interests of the largest city in the Canarias. Principal sights include the **cathedral** (*Plaza de Santa Ana*), with 15thC Gothic origins but a much later Neoclassical exterior, and the so-called **Casa de Colón** (*Colón* ☎ *open Mon-Sat 9am-1.30pm, closed Aug and Sun*), a former governor's residence where Columbus once stayed that now houses a **museum** containing maps and documents of his voyages. The **Museo Canario** (*Dr. Chill* ☎ *open 10am-1pm, 3-5pm, closed Sat afternoon, Sun and holidays*) offers an insight into the lives and customs of the Stone Age Guanche people who once inhabited the islands. These three attractions are in the **Barrio de Vegueta**, the old quarter, which also rewards strollers with its picturesque streets and attractive buildings.

Hotels

Iberia (Las Palmas)
Av. Marítima del Norte s/n ☎ (928) 361 133 ☎ 95413 |||| *300 rms*
▭ *300* ▦ ⟷ ⟷ ⟷ AE ⊙ ⊙ VISA
Although not one of the grandest hotels, the Iberia is certainly commendable, and is well-located within easy reach of both the Vegueta quarter and the beaches.
✿ ✿ ⚓ ⇌

Reina Isabel
Alfredo L. Jones 40 ☎ (928) 260 100 ☎ 95103 |||| *240 rms* ▭ *240* ▦
⟷ ⟷ AE ⊙ ⊙ VISA
Location: On the Paseo de las Canteras near the main part of town. One of the most luxurious hotels on the island, the Reina Isabel not only provides a heated swimming pool but a sauna as well.
✿ ✿ ⇌ ⚐ ⇌

Santa Catalina 🏛
Parque Doramus s/n ☎ (928) 243 140 |||| *209 rms* ▭ *209* ▦ ⟷ ⟷ AE
⊙ VISA
An old-fashioned luxury hotel recently renovated to a high standard, it is located in a most picturesque park.
▱ ✿ ⚓ ⇌ ⚲

Restaurants

El Acuario ⌂
Plaza de la Victoria 3 ☎ *(928) 273 432* ▮▮ ▤ Ⓐ Ⓔ ⑩ ⑩ ⑩ ⑨⑤⑨ *Closed Sun.*
The inspiration here is French, especially in the seafood dishes. The shellfish assortments are well worth trying.

Le Francaise
Sargento Llagas 16 ☎ *(928)268 762* ▮▮▮ *to* ▮▮▮▮ *Closed Sun.*
This family-run restaurant is comparable in achievement and culinary bias to **El Acuario**, but specializes in beef dishes.

Mesón de La Paella
José Maria Durán 47 ☎ *(928)273 432* ▮▮▮ ⑨⑤⑨ *Closed Sun.*
This is the place for good classical Spanish cuisine, featuring the Valencian *paella*, and traditional Catalan and Basque dishes.

≡ Other restaurants include: **Hamburgo** (*General Orgaz 54* ☎*(928)222 745* ▮▮▮); **House of Ming** (*Paseo de las Canteras* ☎*(928)274 573* ▮▮▮); **Tenderette** (*León y Castillo 91* ☎*(928)246 957* ▮▮▮).

Lanzarote
Comprising an area of 818sq.km (313sq. miles), Lanzarote is the most easterly of the Islas Canarias and consequently the closest to Africa. As on the other islands, the north is lush and fertile while the south is bare and dry. Its volcanic origins are clearly evident in the lava fields, numerous craters and fields strewn with volcanic pebbles.

Arrecife
Population: 30,000. Airport: 6km (4 miles) sw ☎*(928) 811 450*
i *Parque Municipal* ☎*(928) 811 860.*
The capital is located on the E coast, and takes its name from the offshore reefs which outline it. The main sights are the **Castillo de San Gabriel** (*open 9am-1pm, 3-7pm*), a 16thC fortress which now houses a **museum of archeology and anthropology**, and the **Puerto de las Naos,** the main harbor to the N of the town.

≈ **Arrecife Gran Hotel** (*Av. Mancomunidad s/n* ☎*(928) 811 254* ▮▮▮) has all the usual facilities, including tennis courts, a swimming pool, a restaurant, air conditioning and a pleasant garden terrace.

≡ One of the newest and most able eateries is **La Tabaiba** (*Playa de las cucharas s/n* ▮▮▮).

Tenerife
Dramatic topography is the essence of Tenerife, the largest island of the Canarias. No mainland peak equals the height of **Teide**, which is over 3,660m (12,000ft) and usually dusted with snow even in this tropical climate. A ridge of mountains bisects the island, and the north is green, the south arid.

Santa Cruz
Population: 200,000. Airport: 13km (8 miles) w ☎*(922) 257 940* **i** *La Marina 57* ☎*(922) 242 227.*
The port is nearly as busy as **Las Palmas**, but the largest city on Tenerife has less to offer in the way of sights and places of interest. The **Museo Arqueológico y Antropológico** (*Bravo Murillo s/n* ☒ *open 9am-1pm, 4-6pm, closed Sat afternoons and Sun*) displays Guanche artifacts and features mummies preserved by a sophisticated process carried out by these simple people. In 1797,

Nelson lost his arm in the attack on the **Castillo del Paso Alto** (*Av. Anaga s/n*), on the shore NE of the center of town.

From Santa Cruz, tours of the island are enjoyable and nearly always include the resort town of **Puerto de la Cruz**, the pretty village of **La Orotava** on the route up to the Pico de Teide, and the collapsed crater of **Las Cañadas**.

🔊 In Santa Cruz, the **Mencey** (*José Naveiras 38* ☎(922) 276 700 ▮▮▮▮) enjoys an enchanting tropical garden, the perfect antidote for northern mid-winter malaise. Facilities include tennis courts and a swimming pool.

🔊 **Las Chozas** (*Carretera El Jardín* ☎(922) 342 054 ▮▮▯) features mixed fried fish in the delicate Andalucian style and manages a wisp of chic. **El Rinconcito** (*Carretera del Botánico 22* ☎(922) 382 035 ▮▮▯) is the place for a special treat, but reserve ahead. Flamboyant preparations of a variety of international dishes include curries, lobster flambé, and fillet of pork in a Calvados sauce, but these only hint at the chef's prolific repertoire. Catalan seafood is the emphasis of **Magnolia** (*Carretera del Botánico 5* ☎(922) 342 054 ▮▮▯). The owner comes up with intriguing variations, such as traditional Catalan bread soaked in tomato pulp, but served with succulent snails.

Place nearby
Puerto de la Cruz (*36km/23 miles SW of Santa Cruz*). The growth of the N shore town is entirely due to tourism which has led to a proliferation of hotels and restaurants.

🔊 **Botánico** (*Av. Richard Yeoward s/n* ☎(922) 381 400 ▮▮▮▮) has good facilities, displayed with panache. Comparable alternatives include **Ybarra Semiramis** (*Urbanización La Paz* ☎(922) 385 551 ▮▮▮▮), **Meliá Puerto de la Cruz** (*Av. Marqués Villanueva del Prado s/n* ☎(922) 384 011 ▮▮▮▮) and **El Tope** (*Calzada de Martiánez 2* ☎(922) 385 052 ▮▮▯). Each has a heated swimming pool.

🔊 Consensus points to **Andrea's** (*Urbanización La Paz* ☎(922) 385 209 ▮▮▯), which serves *nouvelle* Basque food with appropriate trappings, and **Gordo Otto** (*Generalísimo 3* ☎(922)382 696 ▮▮▯), which provides Germanic food and ambiance.

A guide to Spanish

This glossary covers the basic language needs of the traveler: for pronunciation, essential vocabulary and simple conversation, finding accommodations, visiting the bank, shopping, using public transportation or a car, and for eating out.

Pronunciation
Spanish is a phonetic language in which the spelling matches the pronunciation. Letters whose pronunciation is not obvious are the *r*, which is trilled as in Scots; *c*, before *e* or *i* and *z*, which are lisped; *g*, before *e* or *i* and *j*, which are pronounced like the *ch* in lo*ch*; *h*, which is always silent; *v*, which is pronounced like *b*; *ll*, pronounced as in mi*ll*ion.

Stress is on the penultimate syllable in words ending in a vowel, *n* or *s*. Other words are stressed on the last syllable. Exceptions are indicated by a written accent, e.g. inglés.

There is considerable regional variation in pronunciation, for example in southern Spain *ci*, *ce* and *z* are usually pronounced as *s*; *s* may be silent; *ll* may be pronounced as *y*. The rules given here follow standard Castilian pronunciation.

Vowels

a	as the *a* in f*a*ther; e.g. p*a*t*a*ta
e	as the *e* in l*e*t; e.g. p*e*seta
i	as the *i* in pol*i*ce; e.g. l*i*tro
o	as the *o* in p*o*t; e.g. p*o*llo
u	as the *oo* in f*oo*d; e.g. m*u*cho
	before another vowel as the *w* in *w*ell; e.g. c*u*ando
y	as the Spanish *i*; e.g. *y*o

Consonants

b	soft, with the lips slightly apart; e.g. sá*b*ado
c	hard, as in *c*at; e.g. *c*ator*c*e
	before e or i, lisped as the th in *th*in; e.g. do*c*e
d	between vowels and at end of word, as the *th* in *th*an; e.g. come*d*or
g	hard, as in *g*et; e.g. *g*racias
	before e or i, guttural, as the *ch* in lo*ch*; e.g. *g*ente
h	never sounded; e.g. *h*otel
j	as the *ch* in lo*ch*; e.g. aba*j*o
ñ	as the *ni* in o*ni*on; e.g. maña*n*a
r	trilled; e.g. ta*r*de
v	like the Spanish *b*; e.g. *v*ino
x	like the *x* in bo*x*; e.g. pró*x*imo
	between e and a consonant, as an *s*; e.g. e*x*portación
z	as the *th* in *th*in; e.g. die*z*

Letter groups

cc	*kth*; e.g. dire*cc*ión
ch	as the *ch* in *ch*urch; e.g. dere*ch*o
ll	as the *lli* in mi*lli*on; e.g. a*ll*í
qu	as the *c* in *c*at; e.g. *qu*eso
rr	strongly trilled; e.g. ce*rr*ado

Gender

Gender has been indicated where appropriate. Adjectives are given in the masculine form, with the alternative ending used when it accompanies a feminine noun.

Reference words

Monday	lunes	Friday	viernes
Tuesday	martes	Saturday	sábado
Wednesday	miércoles	Sunday	domingo
Thursday	jueves		

January	enero	July	julio
February	febrero	August	agosto
March	marzo	September	septiembre
April	abril	October	octubre
May	mayo	November	noviembre
June	junio	December	diciembre

1	uno	13	trece	32	treinta y dos
2	dos	14	catorce	40	cuarenta
3	tres	15	quince	50	cincuenta
4	cuatro	16	dieciséis	60	sesenta
5	cinco	17	diecisiete	70	setenta
6	seis	18	dieciocho	80	ochenta
7	siete	19	diecinueve	90	noventa
8	ocho	20	veinte	100	cien
9	nueve	21	veintiuno	200	doscientos
10	diez	22	veintidós	500	quinientos
11	once	30	treinta	1,000	mil
12	doce	31	treinta y uno		

Words and phrases

First primero, -a
Second segundo, -a
... o'clock las ... (la una)
Quarter-past ... ... y cuarto
Half-past ... ... y media

Third tercero, -a
Fourth cuarto, -a
Quarter to ... ... menos cuarto
Quarter to six las seis menos cuarto

Mr señor/Sr
Mrs señora/Sra
Miss señorita/Srta

Ladies señoras
Gents caballeros

Basic communication

Yes sí
No no
Please por favor
Thank you gracias
I'm very sorry lo siento mucho/perdón/perdone
Excuse me perdone/perdóneme
Not at all/you're welcome de nada
Hello hola (informal); oiga (telephoning), dígame (answering telephone)
Good morning buenos días
Good afternoon buenas tardes
Good night buenas noches
Goodbye adiós
Morning mañana (f)
Afternoon tarde (f)
Evening tarde (early), noche (after dark)
Night noche (f)
Yesterday ayer
Today hoy
Tomorrow mañana
Next week La semana próxima
Last week la semana pasada
... days ago hace ... días
Month es (m)
Year año (m)
Here aquí
There ahí, allí
Over there allá
Big grande
Small pequeño, -a
Hot caliente
Cold frío, -a
Good buen(o), -a
Bad mal(o), -a
Beautiful bello, -a
Well bien
Badly mal
With con
And y
But pero
Very mucho
All todo(s), toda(s)
Open abierto, -a
Closed cerrado, -a
Entrance entrada (f)
Exit salida (f)
Free (unoccupied or free of charge) libre
Left izquierda

Right derecha
Straight ahead todo seguido
Near cerca (de)
Far lejos (de)
Above encima
Below abajo
Front delante (de)
Behind detrás (de)
Early temprano
Late tarde
Quickly rápido
Pleased to meet you. Encantado, -a; mucho/tanto gusto.
How are you? ¿Cómo está usted?(formal); ¿Cómo estás?/ ¿Qué tal?(familiar)
Very well, thank you. Muy bien, gracias.
Do you speak English? ¿Habla usted inglés?
I don't understand. No comprendo/no entiendo.
I don't know. No sé.
Please explain. ¿Puede usted explicarme, por favor?
Please speak more slowly. ¿Puede usted hablar más despacio, por favor?
My name is ... Me llamo ...
I am American/English. Soy norteamericano, -a/inglés, -esa
Where is/are ... ? ¿Dónde está/ están ... ?
Is there a ... ? ¿Hay un/una ... ?
What? ¿Qué?
How much? ¿Cuanto?
That's too expensive. Eso es demasiado ...
Expensive caro, -a
Cheap barato, -a
I would like ... quisiera/querría ...
Do you have ... ? ¿Tiene usted ... ?
Where is the rest room? ¿Dónde está el aseo?
Where is the telephone? ¿Dónde está el teléfono?
Just a minute. Un momento. (On telephone: no cuelgue.)
That's fine/OK. Está bien.
What time is it? ¿Qué hora es?
I don't feel well. Me siento mal/no me encuentro bien.

218

Accommodations

Making a reservation by letter

> *Dear Sir, Madam,*
> *Muy señor mío, muy señora mía:*
> *I would like to reserve one double room (with bathroom), one twin-bedded room*
> *Quisiera reservar una habitación doble (con cuarto de baño), una habitación con dos camas*
> *and one single room (with shower) for 7 nights from*
> *y una habitación sencilla (con ducha) por 7 noches desde*
> *12 August. We would like bed and breakfast/half board/full board,*
> *el 12 de agosto. Quisiéramos desayuno/media pensión/pensión completa,*
> *and would prefer rooms with a sea view.*
> *y preferiríamos habitaciones con vista al mar.*
> *Please send me details of your terms with the confirmation.*
> *Por favor envíeme sus condiciones y precios con la confirmación.*
> *Yours faithfully,*
> *Le saluda atentamente*

Arriving at the hotel

I have a reservation. My name is …
Tengo una reserva. Me llamo …
A quiet room with bath/shower/WC/wash basin …
Una habitación tranquila con baño/ducha/wáter/palangana …
    overlooking the sea/park/street/back.
… con vista al mar/al parque/a la calle/atrás.
Does the price include breakfast/service/tax?
¿El precio comprende desayuno/servicio/impuestos?
This room is too large/small/cold/hot/noisy.
Esta habitación es demasiado grande/pequeña/fría/caliente/ruidosa.
That's too expensive. Have you anything cheaper?
Eso es demasiado caro. ¿Tiente usted algo más barato?
Where can I park my car?
¿Dónde puedo aparcar?
Is it safe to leave the car on the street?
¿Se puede dejar el coche en la calle?
Have you got a room?
¿Tiene usted una habitación?
Floor/story   piso (m)/planta (f)
Dining room/restaurant   comedor (m)/restaurante (m)
Lounge   salón (m)
Porter   mozo (m)/maletero (m)
Manager   director (m)
What time is breakfast/dinner?   ¿A qué hora se sirve el desayuno/la cena?
Can I drink the tap water?   ¿Se puede beber el agua del grifo?
Is there a laundry service?   ¿Hay servicio de lavado?
What time does the hotel close?   ¿A qué hora cierra el hotel?
Will I need a key?   ¿Me hará falta una llave?
Is there a night porter?   ¿Hay un portero de noche?
I'll be leaving tomorrow morning.   Me marcharé mañana por la mañana.
Please give me a call at …   ¿Puede usted despertarme a … por favor?
Come in!   ¡Adelante!/¡Pase usted!

Sights

Ayuntamiento   town hall   Lonja   exchange
Casa   house   Plaza mayor   main square

Shopping

Where is the nearest?   ¿Dónde está … más cercano, -a?
Can you help me/show me … ?   ¿Puede usted ayudarme/enseñarme … ?
I'm just looking.   Sólo estoy mirando.
Do you accept credit cards/travelers cheques?   ¿Acepta usted tarjetas de crédito/cheques de viaje?
Can you deliver to … ?   ¿Puede usted enviar a … ?

Words and phrases

I'll take it.   Me lo llevo.
I'll leave it.   No me lo llevo.
Can I have it tax-free for export?   ¿Puedo comprarlo libre de impuestos para
  exportación?
This is faulty. Can I have a replacement/refund?   Este tiene una
  falta.   ¿Puede cambiármelo/devolverme el dinero?
I don't want to spend more than …   No quiero gastar más
  de …
Can I have a stamp for … ?   Quiero un sello para …

Shops

Antique store   tienda de
  antigüedades
Art gallery   galeria de arte (f)
Baker   panaderia (f)
Bank   banco (m)
Beauty parlor   salón de belleza (m)
Bookstore   libreria (f)
Butcher   carniceria (f)
Cake shop   pasteleria (f)
Clothes store   tienda de moda (f)
Delicatessen   mantequeria (f)
Department store   grandes
  almacenes (m)
Fish store   pescaderia (f)
Florist   floreria (f)
Greengrocer   verdulería (f)
Grocer   tienda (f) de
  ultramarinos
Hairdresser   barbería (men's),
  peluquería (women's)
Hardware store   ferretería (f)

Jeweler   joyería (f)
Market   mercado (m)
Newsstand   quiosco de periódicos
  (m)
Optician   óptico (m)
Perfumery   perfumería (f)
Pharmacy/chemist   farmacia (f)
Photographic store   tienda de
  fotografía (f)
Post office   oficina de correos (f)
Shoe store   zapatería (f)
Souvenir store   tienda de recuerdos
  (f)
Stationer   papelería (f)
Supermarket   supermercado (m)
Tailor   sastrería (f)
Tobacconist   estanco (m)
Tourist office   oficina de turismo
  (f)
Toy store   juguetería (f)
Travel agency   agencia de viajes (f)

At the bank

I would like to change some dollars/pounds/travelers cheques.
Quisiera cambiar unos dólares/unas libras esterlinas/unos cheques de
  viaje.
What is the exchange rate?
¿A cuánto está el cambio?
Can you cash a personal check?
¿Puede usted cobrarme un cheque personal?
Can I obtain cash with this credit card?
¿Puedo sacar dinero con esta tarjeta de crédito?
Do you need to see my passport?
¿Quiere usted ver mi pasaporte?

Some useful goods

Antiseptic cream   crema antiséptica
  (f)
Aspirin   aspririna (f)
Bandages   vendas (f)
Band-aid   esparadrapo (m)
Cotton   algodón (f)
Diarrhea/upset stomach
  pills   píldoras (f) para diarrea/el
  estómago trastornado
Indigestion tablets   tabletas (f) para
  indigestión
Insect repellant   repelente (m) para
  insectos
Laxative   laxante (m)
Sanitary napkins   compresas (f)
Shampoo   champú (m)

Shaving cream   crema de afeitar
  (f)
Soap   jabón (m)
String   cuerda (f)
Sunburn cream   crema (f) para
  quemaduras del sol
Sunglasses   gafas de sol (f)
Suntan cream/oil   crema (f)/
  aceite (m) bronceador
Tampons   tampones (m)
Tissues   pañuelos de papel (m)
Toothbrush   cepillo de dientes
  (m)
Toothpaste   oasta de dientes (f)
Travel sickness pills   píldoras (f)
  para mareo

Bra   sostén (m)
Coat   abrigo (m)
Dress   vestido (m)
Jacket   chaqueta (f)

Pants   pantalones (m)
Pullover   sueta (f)
Shirt   camisa (f)
Shoes   zapatos (m)

Skirt falda (f)
Socks calcetines (m)
Stockings/tights medias (f)/
  leotardos (m)

Swimsuit traje de baño (m)
Underpants for women bragas
  (f), for men calzoncillos (m)

Film película (f)
Letter carta (f)
Money order giro postal (m)

Postcard tarjeta postal (f)
Stamp sello (m)
Telegram telegrama (f)

Motoring

Service station estación de servicio
Fill it up. Lleno/llénelo por favor.
Give me ... pesetas worth. Déme ... pesetas por favor.
I'd like ... liters of gas. Quiero ... litros de gasolina.
Can you check the ... ? ¿Puede usted mirar el/la ... ?
There is something wrong with the ... Hay algo que no va bien en
  el/la ...

Battery batería (f)
Brakes frenos (m)
Exhaust tubo de escape (m)
Fan belt correa (f) de ventilador
Lights luces (f)
Oil aceite (m)
Tires neumaticos (m)
Water agua (m)
Windshield parabrisas (m)
My car won't start. Mi coche no arranca.
My car has broken down/had a flat tire. Tengo un coche averiado/un
  neumático pinchado.
The engine is overheating. El motor se calienta.
How long will it take to repair? ¿Cuánto tardará en repararlo?

Car rental

Where can I rent a car? ¿Dónde puedo alquilar un coche?
Is full/comprehensive insurance included? ¿Está incluido un seguro a todo
  riesgo?
Is it insured for another driver? ¿Es asegurado para otro conductor?
Unlimited mileage kilometraje ilimitado
Deposit depósito (m)
By what time must I return it? ¿Para qué hora debo devolverlo?
Can I return it to another depot? ¿Puedo devolverlo a otra agencia?
Is the gas tank full? ¿Está lleno el depósito de gasolina?

Road signs

Al paso drive slowly
¡Alto! stop
Aparcamiento permitido parking
  permitted
Calle bloqueada road blocked
Calzada deteriorada bad road
  surface
Ceda el paso yield
Centro ciudad town center
Cuidado caution
Deslizamientos ice on road
Despacio slow

Desviación detour
Dirección única one way
Obras road works
Otras direcciones other directions
Paso a nivel level crossing
Peaje toll
Peligro danger
Prohibido aparcar no parking
Salida de emergencia emergency
  exit
Todas direcciones all directions

Other methods of transportation

Aircraft avión (m)
Airport aeropuerto (m)
Bus autobús (m)
Bus stop parada de autobús (f)
Coach autocar (m)
Ferry/boat ferry/barco (m)
Ferry port puerto (m)
Hovercraft aerodeslizador (m)

Railroad station estación (f)
Train tren (m)
Ticket billete (m)
Ticket office taquilla (f)
One-way de ida
Round trip de ida y vuelta
Half fare medio billete

221

Words and phrases

First/second class   primera/segunda clase
Sleeper/couchette   coche-cama (m)/litera (f)
When is the next ... for ... ?   ¿A qué hora sale el próximo ... para ... ?
What time does it arrive?   ¿A qué hora llega?
What time does the last ... for ... leave?   ¿A qué hora sale el último ... para ... ?
Which platform/quay/gate?   ¿Qué andén/muelle/barrera?
Is this the ... for ...?   ¿Es éste el ... para ...?
Is it direct? Where does it stop?   ¿Es directo? ¿Dónde para?
Do I need to change anywhere?   ¿Tengo que hacer transbordo?
Please tell me where to get off.   ¿Me diría usted cuando tengo que apearme?
Take me to ...   Lléveme a ...
Is there a dining car?   ¿Hay un coche-comedor?

Food and drink

Have you a table for ...?   ¿Tiene usted una mesa para ...?
I want to reserve a table.   Quiero reservar una mesa.
A quiet table.   Una mesa tranquila.
A table near the window.   Una mesa al lado de la ventana.
Could we have another table?   ¿Nos puede dar otra mesa?
Set menu   menú fijo
The menu, please.   ¿Puedo ver el menú?
I'll have ...   Tomaré ...
Can I see the wine list?   ¿Puedo ver la lista de vinos?
I would like ...   Quisiera ...
What do you recommend?   ¿Qué recomienda usted?
I did not order this.   No he pedido esto.
Bring me another ...   Tráigame otro/otra ...
The bill please.   La cuenta, por favor.
Is service included?   ¿Está incluído el servicio?

Breakfast	desayuno (m)	Vintage	vendimia (f)
Lunch	almuerzo (m)	Dry	seco
Dinner	cena (f)	Sweet	dulce
Hot	caliente	Salt	sal (f)
Cold	frío, -a	Pepper	pimienta (f)
Glass	vaso (m)	Mustard	mostaza (f)
Bottle	botella (f)	Oil	aceite (m)
Half-bottle	media botella (f)	Vinegar	vinagre (m)
Beer/lager	cerveza (f)	Bread	pan (m)
Draft beer	cerveza de barril	Butter	mantequilla (f)
Orangeade/lemonade	naranjada/limonada (f)	Cheese	queso (m)
		Milk	leche (f)
Mineral water	agua mineral (m)	Coffee	café (m)
Iced	fría/ ... con hielo	Tea	té (m)
Carbonated	gaseoso, -a	Chocolate	chocolate (m)
Still	sin carbonato	Sugar	azúcar (m)
Fruit juice	zumo de fruta (m)	Steak	filete (m)
Flask/carafe	jarra (f)	well done	muy hecho
Red wine	vino tinto (m)	medium	regular
White wine	vino blanco	rare	poco hecho
Rosé wine	vino rosado	very rare	muy poco hecho

Menu decoder

Abadejo	fresh cod	Al(l)ioli	garlic mayonnaise
Aceite (de oliva)	(olive) oil	Almejas	clams
Aceitunas	olives	Almendras	almonds
Acelgas	Swiss chard	(en) Almíbar	(in) syrup
Achicoria	chicory	Anchoas	anchovies
(en) Adobo, adobado	marinated, pickled	Anguila	eel
		Angulàs	baby eels
Aguacate	avocado	Apio	celery
Ahumado, -a	smoked	Arroz	rice
Ajillo, ajo	garlic	Asado	roast
Albaricoques	apricots	Avellanas	hazelnuts
Albóndigas	spiced meat balls	Aves	poultry
Alcachofa	artichoke	Azafrán	saffron
Alcaparras	capers	Bacalao	dried salt codfish

Berenjena aubergine, eggplant
Besugo sea bream
Biftec, bistec steak, beefsteak
Bocadillos sandwiches
Bonito tuna
Boquerones a kind of anchovy
(a la) Brasa charcoal broiled
Braseado, -a braised
(en) Brochetas skewered
Buey beef
Bullab(v)esa Mediterranean fish soup
Buñuelitos, buñuelos fritters with a wide variety of fillings
Butifarra seasoned pork sausage
Caballa mackerel
Cabrito kid
Calabacín baby marrow, zucchini
Calamares (en su tinta) squid (in their own ink)
Caldereta lamb or fish stew
Caldeirada poached fish in garlic and paprika sauce/fish and seafood stew
Caldo broth or soup-stew of meat and vegetables
Callos tripe
Camarones shrimps
Cangrejo de mar, de río crab, crayfish
Caracoles snails
Carne meat
Carnero mutton
(de la) Casa of the restaurant
Caza game
Cazuela, cazuelita casserole
Cebolla onion
Cebón steer/fattened beef
Centolla (large) crab
Cerdo pork
Cerezas cherries
Champiñones mushrooms
Chile chili red pepper
Chilindrón thick tomato sauce made with ham and red peppers
Chipirones squid
Chorizo spiced pork sausage
Chuleta chop, usually veal
Chuletón large beef or veal rib steak
Cigalas crayfish
Ciruela plum
Cochinillo suckling pig
Cocido stew of meat and vegetables with many regional variations
Cocido, -a cooked, boiled
Col cabbage
Coliflor cauliflower
Conejo rabbit
Coquinas small clams
Corazón heart
Corb(v)ina sea bass or perch
Cordero lamb
Corzo roebuck
Costra crust
Crema cream
Criadillas sweetbreads
Crudo, -a raw
Cuajada de leche similar to yogurt

Dorada gilthead bream
Dulces sweets, desserts
Duro hard (-boiled)
Empanada meat, fish or seafood pie
Empanado, -a fried in breadcrumbs
Ensalada salad
Entremeses appetizers
(en) Escabeche, escabechado pickled, marinated
Escalfado poached
Escarola endive
Escudella catalana thick soup with meats and vegetables
Espárragos asparagus
Espinacas spinach
Estofado stew(ed)
Esturión sturgeon
Fabada asturiana butter beans stewed with ham, sausage, etc.
Faisán pheasant
Fiambres cold cuts
Fideos pasta, noodles
Filete fillet, usually steak
Flan caramel pudding
Frambuesas raspberries
Fresas, fresones strawberries
Fresco, -a fresh
Frío, -a cold
Frito, -a fried
Fritura fried dish/fritter
Fruta fruit
Galletas biscuits
Gambas, gambones large prawns
Ganso goose
Gazpacho chilled vegetable soup
Gratinado, -a browned, with cheese or breadcrumbs
Guindillas hot red peppers
Guisado stew/stewed
Guisantes peas
Habas broad beans
Helado ice cream
Hervido, -a boiled, poached
Hígado liver
Hinojo fennel
Hoja leaf
(al) Horno baked
Huevas fish roe
Huevos eggs
  al plato fried or baked
  revueltos scrambled
Jabalí wild boar
Jamón ham
Judías beans
(en su) Jugo (in its own) juice
(sopa) Juliana soup of thin-sliced vegetables
Lacón pork shoulder
Lamprea lamprey
Langosta spiny lobster
Langostino large prawn
Lechazo young lamb
Lechón suckling pig
Lechuga lettuce
Lengua tongue
Lenguado sole
Lentejas lentils
Liebre hare

Words and phrases

Limón   lemon
Lombarda   red cabbage
Lomo   loin (usually of pork)
Lubina   sea bass
Magras   lean, air-cured ham
Mantecado   enriched ice cream
Mantequilla   butter
Manzana   apple
Mariscada   mixed grill of seafoods
Mariscos   seafood
Mejillones   mussels
Melocotón   peach
Menestra de legumbres/verduras
   mixed sautéed vegetables flavored
   with ham
Merluza   hake
Migas   fried bread croutons
Mollejas   sweetbreads (usually veal)
Moluscos   mussels
Morcilla   blood sausage, black
   pudding
Morcillo   shank
Mújol   mullet
Naranja   orange
Nécoras   small crabs
Nueces   nuts, walnuts
Ostras   oysters
Paella   saffron rice dish with meat,
   fish or seafood
(a la) Parrilla   grilled, broiled
Parrillada (de mariscos, de
   pescados)   grilled or broiled
   seafoods or fish
Pasas   raisins
Pastel   pâté/pie, pastry, cake
Patatas   potatoes
Pato   duck
Pavo   turkey
Pechuga   breast (usually chicken)
Pepinillos   gherkins
Pepinos   cucumber
Pera   pear
Perca   perch
Perdiz   partridge
Perejil   parsley
Pescadillas   whiting/small hake
Pescado   fish
Pez espada   swordfish
Pichón   pigeon
Pierna   leg
Pimientos   sweet peppers
Piña   pineapple
Pinchitos   de carne kebab
Pisto   stew of mixed vegatables
   often with egg
(a la) Plancha   grilled
Plátano   banana
Platija   plaice

Pollo   chicken
Pomelo   grapefruit
Potaje   soup
Puerros   leeks
Pulpitos   tiny octopuses
Pulpo   octopus
Queso   cheese
Quisquillas   small shrimps
Rábanos   radishes
Rabo de toro/buey   oxtail
Rape   monkfish
Rebozado, -a   fried in batter or
   breadcrumbs
Relleno, -a   stuffed
Remolacha   beetroot
Repollo   cabbage
Riñones   kidneys
(de) Rúo   freshwater
Róbalo   sea perch
Rodaballo   turbot
(a la) Romana   deep-fried
Salado,-a   salted
(en) Salazón   cured
Salchicha   sausage
Salchichón   salami
Salmonete   red mullet
Salsa   sauce
Salteado, -a   sautéed
Sandía   watermelon
Sesos   brains
Setas   wild mushrooms
Solomillo   tenderloin
Sopa   soup
Surtido   assortment
Tartaleta   savory or sweet tart
Ternasco   baby lamb
Ternera   veal
Tocino   bacon
Toro (de lidia)   beef (from the
   bullring)
Tortilla   omelet
Tortitas   waffles
Tortuga   turtle
Tostado,-a   toasted
Tronco   slice
Trucha   trout
Trufas   truffles
Turrón   nougat
Uvas   grapes
(al) Vapor   steamed
Venado   venison
Venera   scallops
Verduras   vegetables
Vieiras   scallops
Zanahorias   carrots
Zarzuela   stew of fish or
   shellfish
Zumo   juice

Index and gazetteer

Within this index and gazetteer are listed towns, villages and places of interest covered in this book; major entries, important sights and general categories such as hotels, restaurants and places nearby form sub-entries. Map references refer to the maps at the end of the book. Important sights and places of interest are also listed separately, both under their most common names and in general categories such as Archeological sites or Caves. Important artists, novelists etc. are also listed. Specific hotels and restaurants are not indexed individually but are easily located within *A-Z* entries. *Paradores* have been listed separately.

Page numbers in **bold** indicate the main entry; page numbers in *italic* refer to illustrations and two-color maps.

Index

227

Index

Index

229

Index

Index

Index

Index

Index

238

Index

SPAIN

LEGEND

Area Maps

0   25   50   75 km

=O= Superhighway (with access point)
— Main Road
— Secondary Road
— Other Road
— Scenic Route
N431 Road Number
– – – Ferry
⌐⌐⌐ Canal
━━ Railway
✈ Airport
✦ Airfield
— International Boundary
– – – National Park Boundary
⛪ Monastery, church
∴ Ancient site, ruin
♜ Castle
⚓ Good Beach
■ Other Place of Interest
14▶ Adjoining Page No.

City Maps

▇ Major Place of Interest
▢ Other Important Building
▢ Built-up Area
▢ Park
†　† Named church, church
✚ Hospital
ℓ Information Office
✉ Post Office
✋ Police Station
☎ Parking Lot
P Railway Station
M Metro (Subway) Stations
++++ Funicular Railway
→ One Way Street
▨▨▨ Stepped Street

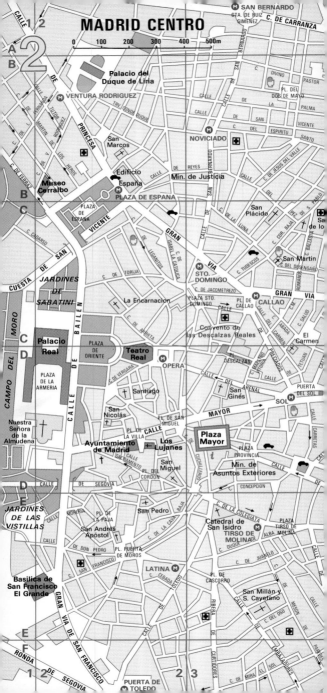

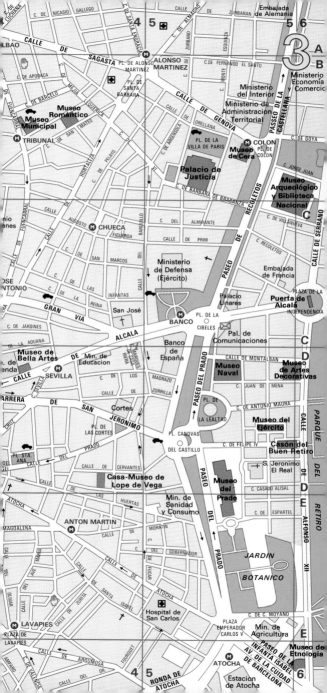

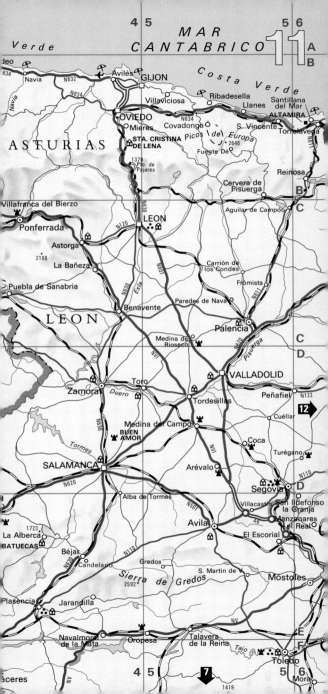